THE AMERICAN
COMMUNITY COLLEGE

Arthur M. Cohen
Florence B. Brawer

THE AMERICAN COMMUNITY COLLEGE

SECOND EDITION

Jossey-Bass Publishers

San Francisco • London • 1989

THE AMERICAN COMMUNITY COLLEGE
by Arthur M. Cohen and Florence B. Brawer

Copyright © 1989 by: Jossey-Bass Inc., Publishers
350 Sansome Street
San Francisco, California 94104
&
Jossey-Bass Limited
28 Banner Street
London EC1Y 8QE

Library of Congress Cataloging-in-Publication Data

Cohen, Arthur M.
    The American community college / Arthur M. Cohen, Florence B.
Brawer.—2nd ed.
        p.   cm.—(Jossey-Bass higher education series)
    Bibliography: p.
    Includes index.
    ISBN 1-55542-178-4 (alk. paper)
    1. Community colleges—United States.   I. Brawer, Florence B., date.
II. Title.   III. Series.
LB2328.C55   1989
378'.052—dc20   89-45588
                                                                              CIP

Manufactured in the United States of America

The paper in this book meets the guidelines for
permanence and durability of the Committee on
Production Guidelines for Book Longevity of the
Council on Library Resources.

JACKET DESIGN BY WILLI BAUM

SECOND EDITION

Code 8951

The Jossey-Bass
Higher Education Series

EDUCATIONAL RESOURCES INFORMATION CENTER

ERIC ▸ **Clearinghouse For Junior Colleges**

UNIVERSITY OF CALIFORNIA, LOS ANGELES

The material in this publication is based on work sponsored in part by the Office of Educational Research and Improvement, U.S. Department of Education, under contract number [RI 88062002]. Its contents do not necessarily reflect the views of the Department or any other agency of the U.S. Government.

Contents

Foreword to the First Edition

This book appears at a time of great significance to the community college. The decade of the 1980s will mark a turning point in its history. It is already evident that the community college is experiencing the effects of lean years following an unusually long succession of fat years when a new college appeared each week and double-digit enrollment increases were announced annually. Especially threatening are the public's efforts to curtail spending by propositions such as 13 (California) and 2½ (Massachusetts) and by caps on enrollment. Significant for the future may be the end of the campaign to transmute the community college into a new kind of institution, neither college nor high school—an idea espoused by Edmund J. Gleazer, who recently retired as president of the American Association of Community and Junior Colleges. These developments and many others mentioned by Cohen and Brawer may denote for the community college maturity, as well as the end of the Golden Age.

Cohen and Brawer's book will take its place alongside books by such community college giants as Koos, Eells, Bogue, and Medsker. Their comprehensive, incisive, interpretive analysis of the community colleges covers nearly all facets of the college. They start with a historical analysis of the origins and development of the college and end with a critique of the college's critics. In between, chapters are devoted to administrators, students, and faculty. Four chapters, almost one-third of the book, are devoted to the curriculum functions. Chapter One offers the rationale used throughout most of the book. The authors state that their function is to present information and examine the many viewpoints that have been advanced. From this approach, they do not expect to find ultimate answers but hope that better questions will result.

Those acquainted with the authors will not be surprised that they undertook this formidable task. They know that Cohen and Brawer have been immersed in community college research for more than two decades. During that time they have visited hundreds of community colleges, associated with nearly all those who have written on the college, reviewed thousands of documents sent for inclusion in the collection of the ERIC Clearinghouse for Junior Colleges since it was organized in 1966, edited the quarterly New Directions for Community Colleges series from its origin in 1973, and conducted major research in the humanities and sciences through the Center for the Study of Community Colleges. There is hardly a subject or topic on community college education that does not appear in one or more publications that have been written by them or produced under their guidance. Their book is a distillation of this vast experience and knowledge and is a capstone to the many articles and books they have written individually and as coauthors.

The [original] thirteen chapters describe, probe, and dissect every facet of the institution, sometimes sympathetically, at other times critically, although seldom superficially. Despite the kaleidoscopic nature of the community college, the authors' comprehensive, incisive treatment brings into focus the changes it has undergone since its modest beginnings as a liberal arts junior college to the multifaceted giant community college of the 1960s and 1970s. Now, the incipient reform movement calls into question the sacrosanct principles of the open door and equal opportunity. Instead of the new institution, neither high school nor college, the authors see a return to an expanded version of the college of the postwar era of the 1940s and 1950s.

In chapter after chapter the authors make clear that research as often as not raises more questions than answers. In the areas of teaching and especially learning, the profession has made very little progress in evaluating its efforts. A historical survey of the research in these two areas would, if presented graphically, look much like graphs depicting the course of the economy, with cyclical changes representing the rise and fall of particular theories. One would like to see the trend line in community college learning slope upward;

but, as Cohen and Brawer intimate, the trend line here, as in nearly all segments of education, would have a downward slope. Despite all the labors, the results, except as reported by those in charge of the experiments, are of minor significance unless one gains some comfort that the educators have learned which ideas and theories do not produce results.

Although the authors modestly assert that answers to current problems will not be found, one wonders whether it is possible for two of the most prominent students of the community college, with strong convictions expressed in many publications, to submerge these convictions in questions in such a comprehensive, wide-ranging book. Their strategy of wondering, offering information, and examining many viewpoints has enabled them to range further afield speculatively, seemingly without committing themselves. Yet questions, no matter how carefully worded, often suggest the answers the authors would have given if they had been taking the test instead of administering it. It is noteworthy that in the four curriculum chapters the authors dispense with questions; they substitute their convictions. How could it be otherwise with authors who have been immersed in the study of the community college for two decades?

The reader will be confronted with the many paradoxes surrounding the community college. The most nettlesome is, as the authors point out, that it is called a college, but elementary-grade subjects—arithmetic, reading, writing—rank high in terms of courses offered and students enrolled. Another: Although it has been the fastest-growing segment of education, it seems to be the least known. After seventy-five years it has yet to adopt a name that describes its functions. "Identity" or "image" remains one of the most serious concerns of community college educators—a concern that has been with them almost from the beginning. It will, the authors imply, remain with them as long as the community college remains for students a second or lower choice rather than an equal choice with other higher education institutions and as long as educators and leaders of their professional organizations continue to emulate chameleons in adopting and dropping one educational fad after another, all in the name of innovation.

One of the most intriguing chapters is "The Social Role."

The reader will find here the arguments of the leading critics that the community college has failed to provide upward mobility or access to higher education. Briefly, the authors describe the criticisms and, at times, raise questions about their validity. They resist the temptation to be apologists, pointing out that the persistence of doubts concerning the community college's role in furthering upward mobility derives "from a gap in perception" of the educators.

In their chapters "Collegiate Function" and "General Education," the authors make a strong plea for "liberal education for the informed citizen." The community colleges, they maintain, must "provide some portions of the education for the masses that tends toward encouraging exercise of the intellect." They offer a "model for effecting general education for a free people in a free society."

Because this book records the many changes that affect the community college and, more important, the way educational leaders react to them, it will appeal to those who seek only the "facts." How many? What courses and curricula? Where from? At the other extreme it will help those seeking to understand the philosophy—philosophies perhaps—that has propelled this institution to its present status. The critics—the community college personnel and the authors' colleagues who are involved in research on the institution—will find much to applaud and probably more to contend with. Although the authors will welcome the plaudits, they will not be disappointed if they elicit disagreement. They have strong beliefs and they are critics. So they will welcome the opportunity to be on the receiving end for the sake of starting a dialogue that they believe is urgently needed as educational leaders struggle to find solutions in the new, unfamiliar environment of zero growth and fiscal retrenchment.

September 1981   John Lombardi
                                             Former President
                                             Los Angeles City College

Preface

This is the second edition of a book published originally in 1982. It is about the American community colleges, institutions that offer associate degrees and occupational certificates to their students and a variety of other services to the communities in which they are located. These 1,250 colleges range in size from fewer than 100 to more than 30,000 students. Around one-fifth of them, mostly the smaller institutions, are privately supported. The others, the larger comprehensive structures, are found in every state.

Audience

In this edition, as with the first, our purpose is to present a comprehensive, one-volume text useful for everyone concerned with higher education: college staff members, graduate students, trustees, and state-level officials. The descriptions and analyses of each of the institution's functions can be used by administrators who want to learn about practices that have proved effective in other colleges, by curriculum planners involved in program revision, by faculty members seeking ideas for modifying their courses, and by trustees and officials concerned with college policies regarding curriculum and student flow.

The book focuses mainly on the past quarter century, when the community colleges underwent several major changes. During that time the number of public two-year institutions nearly doubled, and their enrollments increased tenfold. The relations between administrators and faculty changed as multicampus districts were formed and as contracts negotiated through collective bargaining became common. Institutional financing was affected both by tax limitations and by a continuing trend toward state-level funding. The proportion of students transferring to universities fell, and those transferring from universities rose. The collegiate function was shaken as career and community education made tremendous strides and as the colleges grappled with problems of teaching the functionally illiterate.

The book is written in the style of an interpretive analysis. It includes data summaries on students, faculty, curriculum, and many other quantifiable dimensions of the institutions. It explores the inversion of institutional purpose that resulted in the career programs serving as the basis for transfer and the transfer programs becoming areas of terminal study. It explains how students' pattern of college attendance forced a conversion from a linear to a lateral curriculum pattern, from students taking courses in sequence to students dropping into and out of classes almost at will. It shows how general education can be reconciled with the career, compensatory, community, and collegiate education functions and how counseling and other auxiliary services can be integrated into the instructional program. And it examines some of the criticism that has been leveled at the community college by those who feel it is doing a disservice to most of its matriculants, especially the ethnic minorities.

A revised edition of our work is warranted now because several changes have occurred since the first edition appeared. In the colleges faculty power has consolidated, only to be met by countervailing power concentrated at the state level. Mandatory and recommended testing and placing of students has spread. Compensatory education has become more prominent, taking its place as a curriculum function second only to career and collegiate education. And administrators and governing boards must attend ever more to state-level directives regarding institutional functioning and funding.

Yet many things have remained the same. College organization, instruction, and institutional purpose are not different. The colleges are still concerned with providing relevant educational services to their clients, who attend for various reasons. Most of the issues that we noted at the end of each chapter in the first edition are repeated herein; the most intractable problems are never solved. As I. F. Stone noted in his book *The Trial of Socrates,* "Change is a constant but so is identity. The whole truth can only be achieved by taking both into consideration" (1987, p. 69).

We have made several major changes in the book. The chapter organization remains the same, but we have added a chapter on the future of the community colleges (Chapter Fourteen). Within each chapter we have updated the tables and graphs to depict the most recent data, and we have incorporated new examples of the services that the colleges provide. We have expanded our discussions of student flow, institutional finance, instruction, student services, and curricular functions by providing recent information in these areas. We have simplified definitions and reanalyzed the relationships among the various college purposes and functions. We have added commentary on assessing students and institutional outcomes but deleted the annotated bibliography because a more comprehensive bibliography is available in the volume *Key Resources on Community Colleges: A Guide to the Field and Its Literature* (Cohen, Palmer, and Zwemer, 1986).

Overview of the Contents

Chapter One recounts the social forces that contributed to the expansion and contemporary development of the community colleges. It examines the ever-changing institutional purposes, showing how their changes come in conflict with funding patterns and structures. It traces the reasons that local funding and control have given way to state-level management, and it questions what the shape of American higher education would be if there had been no community colleges.

Chapter Two displays the changing patterns of students from the point of view of their age, ethnicity, and goals. The reasons for part-time attendance patterns are explored. There is a particular emphasis on minority students. The chapter also examines attrition, showing that the concept is an institutional artifact masking students' true achievements; and it reviews the recent moves toward student assessment.

Chapter Three draws on national data to show how the full-time and part-time faculty differ. It examines tenure, salary, work load, modes of faculty evaluation, professional associations, and faculty preparation. It discusses the relations between moonlighting and burnout and the conflict between instructors' desires for better students and the realities of the institutions in which they work.

Chapter Four reviews the changes that have taken place in college management as a result of changes in institutional size, the advent of collective bargaining, reductions in available funds, and changes in the locus of control. Examples of varying modes of college organization and the role of each administrator within them are presented, along with an assessment of the status of institutional research.

Chapter Five describes the various funding patterns, showing how they have followed shifts in mode of organization. Relations between the level of tuition and equity and efficiency in institutional operations are explored. The chapter details the effects of fiscal limitation measures and shows how various cost-saving practices have been installed. It also considers the effects of state-level funding changes.

Chapter Six discusses the rise of learning resource centers and the stability in instructional forms that has been maintained despite the introduction of mastery learning, computer-assisted instruction, and a host of reproducible media. Data are presented from several surveys of instructors regarding their teaching practices, their goals, and the types of support services they use. And responses to the recent calls for assessing instructional effects are analyzed.

Chapter Seven traces the student personnel functions, including counseling and guidance, recruitment and retention, orientation, and extracurricular activities. It also considers financial aid and the shifting patterns of articulation, detailing the efforts to enhance student flow from community colleges to senior institutions.

Chapter Eight considers the rise of occupational education as it has moved from a peripheral to a central position in the institutions. No longer a terminal function for a few students, career education now serves people seeking new jobs and upgrading in jobs they already have, students gaining the first two years of a career-oriented bachelor's degree program, relicensure candidates, and hobbyists. The chapter also discusses career education's contributions to the community.

Chapter Nine traces the decline in student literacy at all levels of education and shows how community colleges are bearing the brunt of ill-prepared students. It reviews specific college programs to enhance students' basic skills, examines the controversies surrounding student mainstreaming and restrictive programming, and explores the options of screening students at entry on a course-by-course basis or, instead, allowing students to enter any course of their choice but requiring simultaneous remedial assistance. The rise of compensatory education to a level of importance second only to that of collegiate and career studies is detailed.

Chapter Ten considers adult and continuing education, lifelong learning, and community services as they now operate. It recounts numerous examples of cooperative arrangements between colleges and community agencies, asks how funding can be maintained for this function, and explores how the major institutional associations continue to promote community education. The chapter also indicates how the definitions of community education can be strengthened by a reclassification on the basis of students' intent.

Chapter Eleven considers the rise and fall of the liberal arts. It reports national survey data on enrollment trends in all subject fields and shows that the decline of the liberal arts has resulted not only from students' intent to use the two-year college as an entry to the workplace but also from the failure of the lower schools to prepare students to read, write, and think. The effects of this decline on instructors, degrees awarded, and percentage of students transferring to senior institutions are also noted.

Chapter Twelve traces the ebb and flow of general education through interdisciplinary courses and shows how the concept has suffered from failure of consistent definition. An upswing in general education is predicted because of the recent renewed emphasis on transfer studies and core curriculum. The chapter offers a plan for reviving general education in each of the colleges' dominant curricula.

Chapter Thirteen examines the philosophical and practical questions that have been raised about the community college's role in leveling the social-class structure in America in general and in enhancing student progress toward higher degrees in particular. It shows how the same data can be used to reach different conclusions when the critics do not properly consider the differences between social equalization and equal access for individuals. The chapter poses alternative organizational forms within existing community colleges so that both equity and access and an avenue for individuals to attain higher degrees can be maintained.

Chapter Fourteen projects the trends in student and faculty demographics and indicates the areas where change will occur in college organization, curriculum, instruction, and student services. It also comments on the ascendant role of compensatory education and projects the future of moves toward assessing college outcomes.

Sources

The information included in this book derives from many sources but predominantly from published observations and findings. The major books and journals and the Educational Resources Information Center files have been searched for documents pertaining to each topic. We have also relied on our own surveys conducted since 1974 through the Center for the Study of Community Colleges.

This attention to the extant literature has both positive and negative features. On the plus side, it enables us to plot trends in curriculum, faculty functioning, patterns of student attendance, and college organization. On the other side, it limits our sources of information to surveys and written material. Surveys necessarily condense unique activities into percentages, thereby muting some of the vibrancy that colleges and their offerings manifest. Researching just the available literature limits our awareness of college practices to a view of institutions where the staff have written descriptions for general distribution.

Although we have relied primarily on printed sources and on our own research studies, we have also sought counsel from the many community college staff members around the country whom we meet during their visits to the ERIC Clearinghouse for Junior Colleges at UCLA, at conferences, and during our visits to their own institutions. However, even though we have drawn on all these sources and tried to present an evenhanded treatment, we must admit that we have our prejudices. We are advocates for the community colleges, believing that they have an essential role to play in the fabric of American education. We are advocates for their educative dimension, the aspect of their effort that affects human learning. And we favor especially the collegiate and general education functions, feeling that they must be maintained if community colleges are to continue as comprehensive institutions.

Above all, we are critical analysts, concerned more with examining the ideas undergirding the community colleges' functions than with describing the operations themselves. We wonder about the interrelations of funding, management, curriculum, and teaching. And we are concerned about the shape that the institutions have taken as increasing percentages of their students attend part-time and as their curriculum has taken more a lateral than a linear form.

This latter point deserves elaboration. Which college serves best? One with 10,000 students, each taking one class? One with 5,000 students, each taking two classes? Or one with 2,500 students, each taking four classes? In all cases the cost is about the same, but the institutions are quite different. In the first example, the college has a broad base of clients, and its curriculum has a lateral form composed of disparate courses, such as those offered through university extension or adult education centers. In the second, the curriculum has taken a more linear shape, and the implication is that students are expected to progress toward a certificate or degree. The third type of college has apparently restricted admission to those who can attend full-time, and its courses are arrayed in sequential fashion, each of them demanding prerequisites.

The shape that an institution takes is not derived accidentally. Deliberate measures can be effected to bring about an emphasis in one or another direction. The policymakers who would serve the broadest base of clients would offer courses at night and in off-campus locations, allow students to enter and withdraw from classes without penalty at any time, and engage in vigorous marketing campaigns to attract people who might not otherwise consider attending college. Those who see their college as serving best if it enrolls full-time students would offer courses on campus only, install strict academic probation and suspension standards, demand advance registration, and enforce course prerequisites. The point is that either extreme, or any position between, could be taken by officials operating colleges within the same state, under the same sets of regulations. We believe that the function of the analyst is to bring these types of options to the attention of people within the colleges so that they become aware that their institutions can be changed and that these changes need not be undertaken haphazardly. At the same time, we recognize that, in an institution whose budget depends on student enrollments and whose mission is to serve as many people as possible, most college managers see no need to standardize the disparate attendance patterns.

Numerous changes in American society and in public outlook have occurred in recent years, but the colleges have been affected hardly at all. The national debt has skyrocketed, along with interest payments that must be borne for decades to come. The number of homeless people and immigrants, documented and undocumented, has grown substantially. Drug abuse, white-collar crime, gangs armed with automatic weapons, and the number of unwed teenage mothers have become national scandals. The threats of nuclear war, nuclear plant explosions, and toxic waste seem unabating. Yet the colleges continue as always, adjusting somewhat to the students' tendencies to take fewer courses per term but not at all to the cosmic issues noted above. What can they do? They are schools, able only to minister to their clients. They cannot directly resolve any of the major issues confronting society. Broad-scale social forces swirl about them, but the colleges are propelled mainly by their internal dynamics—a point that can be readily recognized by viewing the differences between institutions in the same types of communities.

Acknowledgments

No long-sustained project of this kind ever operates in isolation, nor is it the work of its authors alone. For this book and the research on which it is based, many people provided assistance. For the first edition, we were especially grateful to Stanley Turesky of the Office of Planning and Analysis, National Endowment for the Humanities, which sponsored the research dealing with the humanities, and to Raymond Hannapel of the National Science Foundation, who oversaw the science projects conducted by the Center for the Study of Community Colleges. More recent information-gathering projects were supported by the Andrew W. Mellon Foundation, Claire List, project officer; and by the Ford Foundation, Alison Bernstein, project officer.

We have included the late John Lombardi's foreword to the first edition in this volume because we continue to value his insights. He dedicated his professional life to the community colleges. His writings, several of which are cited in this book, reveal the analytical approach he took to every issue concerning the institutions.

Several staff members of the ERIC Clearinghouse for Junior Colleges at UCLA helped put the second edition together. Anita Colby and Mary Hardy used their expert knowledge of the ERIC data base to find documents regarding all aspects of institutional functioning. Shirley Coll did much of the typing, under the direction of Glenda Childress, who put the manuscript together in its final form. UCLA graduate students Debra Banks and Gary Railsback helped find data and update tables. UCLA adjunct professor Leslie Koltai offered helpful comments on the governance chapter. The university provided a sabbatical leave so that Arthur Cohen could draft the text. Florence Brawer was supported throughout by the Center for the Study of Community Colleges.

Los Angeles, California　　　　　　　Arthur M. Cohen
July 1989　　　　　　　　　　　　　Florence B. Brawer

The Authors

Arthur M. Cohen has been a professor of higher education at the University of California, Los Angeles (UCLA), since 1964. His teaching emphasizes curriculum and instruction in higher education and the community college as an institution. He received his bachelor's and master's degrees in history from the University of Miami. His doctorate was taken in higher education at Florida State University.

As director of the ERIC Clearinghouse for Junior Colleges since 1966, Cohen has been involved with the literature about community colleges, stimulating writing in the field and disseminating information analysis papers to all practitioners. As president of the Center for the Study of Community Colleges since 1974, he has conducted several national research studies of faculty, curriculum, and instruction.

Cohen has served on the editorial boards of numerous journals and on the advisory boards or boards of directors of several professional associations. His extensive writings include *Dateline '79: Heretical Concepts for the Community College* (1969), *Objectives for College Courses* (1970), and *Key Resources on Community Colleges: A Guide to the Field and Its Literature* (1986, with J. C. Palmer and K. D. Zwemer).

Florence B. Brawer is research director of the Center for the Study of Community Colleges. A former research educationist at UCLA, psychometrist, and counselor, she received her bachelor's degree in psychology from the University of Michigan and her master's and doctoral degrees in educational psychology from UCLA. She is the author of *New Perspectives on Personality Development in College Students* (1973) and the coeditor of *Developments in the Rorschach Technique,* volume 3 (1970).

Cohen and Brawer together wrote *Confronting Identity: The Community College Instructor* (1972), *The Two-Year College Instructor Today* (1977), and *The Collegiate Function of Community Colleges* (1987). Together with other ERIC staff members, they wrote *A Constant Variable: New Perspectives on the Community College* (1971) and *College Responses to Community Demands* (1975). Cohen and Brawer have also edited several series of monographs published by the Center for the Study of Community Colleges and the ERIC Clearinghouse for Junior Colleges. Since 1973 they have been editor-in-chief and associate editor, respectively, of the Jossey-Bass quarterly series New Directions for Community Colleges.

THE AMERICAN
COMMUNITY COLLEGE

One

Background:
Evolving Priorities and Expectations of the Community College

The American community college dates from the early years of the twentieth century. Several social forces contributed to its rise. Most prominent were the need for workers trained to operate the nation's expanding industries; the lengthened period of adolescence, which mandated custodial care of the young for a longer time; and the drive for social equality, which supposedly would be enhanced if more people had access to higher education. Community colleges seemed also to reflect the growing power of external authority over everyone's life, the peculiarly American belief that people cannot be legitimately educated, employed, religiously observant, ill or healthy unless some institution sanctions that aspect of their being.

Across the country the ideas permeating higher education early in the century fostered the development of these new colleges. Science was seen as enhancing progress; the more people who would learn its principles, the more rapid the development of the society. The new technologies demanded skilled operators. Individual mobility was held in the highest esteem, and the notion was widespread that people who applied themselves most diligently would advance most rapidly. Social institutions of practical value to society were being formed. This was the era of the Chautauqua, the settlement house, the Populists. And in the colleges the question

1

"What knowledge is of most worth?" was rarely asked; the more likely question was "What knowledge yields the greatest tangible benefit to individuals or to society?" The public perceived schooling as an avenue of upward mobility and as a contributor to the community's wealth. Veblen's (1918) and Sinclair's ([1923] 1976) diatribes against domination of the universities by industrialists were ineffectual outcries against what had become a reality.

Publicly supported universities, given impetus by the Morrill Acts of 1862 and 1890, had been established in every state. Although many of them were agricultural institutes or teacher-training colleges little resembling modern universities, they did provide a lower-cost alternative to private colleges. The universities were also pioneering the idea of service to the broader community through their agricultural and general extension divisions. Access for a wider range of the population was increasing as programs to teach an ever-increasing number of subjects and occupations were introduced. Schools of business, forestry, journalism, and social work became widespread. People with more diverse goals led to more diverse programs; the newer programs attracted greater varieties of people.

Probably the simplest overarching reason for the growth of community colleges is that an increasing number of demands were being placed on the schools at every level. Whatever the social or personal problem, schools were supposed to solve it. As a society we have looked to the schools for racial integration. The courts and legislatures have insisted that the schools mitigate discrimination by merging students across ethnic lines in their various programs. The schools are expected to solve problems of unemployment by preparing students for jobs. Subsidies awarded to businesses that train their own workers might be a more direct approach, but we have preferred paying public funds to support career education in the schools. The list could be extended to show that the responsibility for doing something about drug abuse, alcoholism, teenage pregnancy, inequitable incomes, and other individual and societal ills has been assigned to the schools soon after the problems were identified. The schools were even supposed to ameliorate the long-standing problem of highway deaths. Instead of reducing speed limits and requiring seat belts, many states enacted laws requiring the schools to provide driver education courses.

Despite periodic disillusionment with the schools, the pervasive belief has been that education, defined as more years of schooling, is beneficial. It was not always that way. Earlier centuries, other societies, did not ascribe such power to or make such demands of their schools. Illich (1971, p. 8) has said, "We often forget that the word *education* is of recent coinage. . . . Education of children is first mentioned in French in a document of 1498. . . . In the English language the word *education* first appeared in 1530. . . . In Spanish lands another century passed before the word and idea of education acquired some currency." But the easily accessible, publicly supported school became an article of American faith, first in the nineteenth century, when responsibility for educating the individual shifted from the family to the school, then in the twentieth, when the schools were unwarrantedly expected to relieve society's ills. The community colleges thrived on the new responsibilities, grown large because the colleges had no traditions to defend, no alumni to question their role, no autonomous professional staff to be moved aside, no statements of philosophy that would militate against their taking on responsibility for everything.

Definitions of the Two-Year College

Two generic names have been applied to two-year colleges. From their beginnings until the 1940s, they were known most commonly as junior colleges. Eells's (1931) definition of the junior college included the university branch campuses offering lower-division work either on the parent campus or in separate facilities; state junior colleges supported by state funds and controlled by state boards; district junior colleges, usually organized by a secondary school district; and local colleges formed by a group acting without legal authority. At the second annual meeting of the American Association of Junior Colleges, in 1922, a junior college was defined as "an institution offering two years of instruction of strictly collegiate grade" (Bogue, 1950, p. xvii). In 1925 this definition was modified slightly to include the statement "The junior college may, and is likely to, develop a different type of curriculum suited to the larger and ever-changing civic, social, religious, and vocational needs of the entire community in which the college is located. It is understood that in this case, also, the work offered shall be on a level appropriate for high-school graduates" (p. xvii). But the instruction was still expected to be "of strictly collegiate grade"; that is, if such a college offered courses usually offered in the first two years by a senior institution, "these courses must be identical, in scope and thoroughness, with corresponding courses of the standard four-year college" (p. xvii). Skill training alone was not considered sufficient to qualify an institution for the appellation *community college;* a general education component must be included in the occupational programs: "General-education and vocation training make the soundest and most stable progress toward personal competence when they are thoroughly integrated" (p. 22).

During the 1950s and 1960s, the term *junior college* was applied more often to the lower-division branches of private universities and to two-year colleges supported by churches or organized independently, while *community college* came gradually to be used for the comprehensive, publicly supported institutions. By the 1970s the term *community college* was usually applied to both types.

Several names in addition to *community* and *junior* have been advanced, but none has taken hold. The institutions have been called "Two-Year College," "City College," and "County College," and nicknamed "People's College," "Democracy's College," and "Anti-University College"—the last by Jencks and Riesman (1968), who saw them as negating the principles of scholarship on which the universities had been founded.

Sometimes, deliberate attempts have been made to blur the definition. For example, during the 1970s the American Association of Community and Junior Colleges (AACJC) sought to identify the institutions as community education centers standing entirely outside the mainstream of graded education. In 1980 the AACJC began listing "regionally accredited proprietary institutions" in addition to the nonprofit colleges in its annual *Community, Junior, and Technical College Directory.*

We define the community college as *any institution accredited to award the Associate in Arts or the Associate in Science as its highest degree.* That definition includes the comprehensive two-year colleges as well as many of the technical institutes, both public and private. It eliminates most of the publicly supported area vocational schools and adult education centers and most of the proprietary business and trades colleges. However, numerous institutions in the latter group, the fastest-growing sector of postsecondary education in the 1980s, are being accredited to award associate degrees; hence, they will tend to be included in the two-year-college category. In fact, by 1985 "half of the private 2-year institutions were organized as profit-making entities," according to the U.S. Education Department's National Center for Education Statistics, which had begun counting them as part of the group (Adelman, 1987, p. 5).

Development of Community Colleges

The development of community colleges should be placed in the context of the growth of all higher education in the twentieth century. As secondary school enrollments expanded rapidly in the early 1900s, the demand for access to college grew apace. The 30 percent of the age group graduating from high school in 1924 grew to 75 percent by 1960. And 60 percent of the high school graduates entered college in the latter year. Put another way, 45 percent of the eighteen-year-olds entered college in 1960, up from 5 percent in 1910. As Green (1980) aptly put it, one of the major benefits of a year of schooling is a ticket to advance to the next level. (Notably, as high school graduation rates stabilized at 72–75 percent in the 1970s and 1980s, the rate of college going leveled off as well.)

However, the states could have accommodated most of the people seeking college attendance simply by expanding their universities' capacity, as indeed was the practice in a few states. Why community colleges? A major reason is that several prominent nineteenth- and early-twentieth-century educators wanted the universities to abandon their freshman and sophomore classes and relegate the function of teaching adolescents to a new set of institutions, to be called junior colleges. Proposals that the junior college should relieve the university of the burden of providing general education for young people were made in 1851 by Henry

Tappan, president of the University of Michigan; in 1859 by William Mitchell, a University of Georgia trustee; and in 1869 by William Folwell, president of the University of Minnesota. All insisted that the universities would not become true research and professional development centers until they relinquished their lower-division preparatory work. Other educators—such as William Rainey Harper, of the University of Chicago; Edmund J. James, of the University of Illinois; and Stanford's president, David Starr Jordan—suggested that the system followed in European universities and secondary schools might be emulated. That is, the universities would be responsible for the higher-order scholarship, while the lower schools would provide general and vocational education to students through age nineteen or twenty. Harper also contended that the weaker four-year colleges, instead of wasting money by doing superficial work, might better become junior colleges. And, in fact, by 1940, of 203 colleges with enrollments in 1900 of 150 or fewer students, 40 percent had perished, but 15 percent had become junior colleges (Eells, 1941a).

In California it probably would have been feasible to limit Stanford and the University of California to upper-division and graduate and professional studies because of the early, widespread development of junior colleges in that state. Such proposals were made several times but were never successfully implemented. But grades 13 and 14 were not given over exclusively to community colleges in any state. Instead, those schools developed outside the channel of graded education that reaches from kindergarten to graduate school. The organization of formal education in America had been undertaken originally from both ends of the continuum. Dating from the eighteenth century, the four-year colleges and the elementary schools were established; then, during the nineteenth century, the middle years were accommodated as the colleges organized their own preparatory schools and as public secondary schools were built. By the turn of the twentieth century, the gap had been filled. If the universities had shut down their lower divisions and surrendered their freshmen and sophomores to the two-year colleges, these newly formed institutions would have been part of the mainstream. But they did not, and the community colleges remained adjunctive.

Their standing outside the tradition of higher education—first with its exclusivity of students, then with its scholarship and academic freedom for professors—was both good and bad for the community colleges. Initially, it gained them support from influential university leaders who sought a buffer institution that would cull the poorly prepared students and send only the best on to the upper division. Later, it enabled them to capitalize on the sizable amounts of money available for programs in occupational education, to accept the less well-prepared students who nonetheless sought further education, and to organize continuing education activities for people of all ages. But it also doomed them to the status of alternative institutions. In some states—notably, Florida and Illinois—upper-division universities were built so that the community colleges could feed students through at the junior level. But even there the older publicly supported universities clung to their freshman and sophomore classes, and the community colleges remained on the periphery. As a result, many community college leaders sought four-year-college status for their institutions. Successful in some instances, this movement had virtually subsided by the late 1960s.

Community colleges developed also as upward extensions of secondary schools. Diener (1986) has compiled several nineteenth- and early-twentieth-century papers promoting that idea. Included are statements by Henry Barnard, the first United States commissioner of education; John W. Burgess, a professor at Columbia College; William Rainey Harper; and Alexis Lange, of the University of California. In 1871 Barnard proposed that the schools in the District of Columbia be divided into five sectors, one of which would be *"Superior and Special Schools,* embracing a continuation of the studies of the Secondary School, and while giving the facilities of general literacy and scientific culture as far as is now reached in the second year of our best colleges" (Diener, 1986, p. 37). In 1884 Burgess recommended that the high schools add two or three years to their curriculum to prepare students for the work of the university. Harper also proposed that high schools extend their programs into the collegiate level: "Today only 10 percent of those who finish high school continue the work in college. If the high schools were to provide work for two additional years, at least 40 percent of those finishing the first four years would continue until the end of the sophomore year" (pp. 57–58). (His figures on the ratio of college attendance were remarkably prescient.) Lange regarded the junior college as the culmination of schooling for most students, with the high school and junior college together forming the domain of secondary education. But in his view the junior college would do more than prepare young people for college; it would also train for "the vocations occupying the middle ground between those of the artisan type and the professions" (p. 71).

In 1919 McDowell submitted the first doctoral dissertation describing the junior college movement. He found the roots of the junior college in the works previously cited and acknowledged that the universities had supported the junior college because of their need to divert the many freshmen and sophomores whom they could not accommodate. He also traced the expansion of secondary schools into grades 13 and 14 and the conversion of many church colleges and normal schools into junior colleges.

Much of the discussion about junior colleges in the 1920s and 1930s had to do with whether they were expanded secondary schools or truncated colleges. The school district with three types of institutions (elementary schools with grades 1–6, junior highs with grades 7–10, and combined high schools and junior colleges with grades 11–14) was set forth as one model. This 6–4–4 plan had much appeal: curriculum articulation between grades 12 and 13 would be smoothed; the need for a separate physical plant would be mitigated; instructors could teach in both high school and junior college under the same contract; superior students could go through the program rapidly; occupational education could be extended from secondary school into the higher grades; and small communities that could not support self-standing junior colleges would be helped by appending the college to their secondary schools. The 6–4–4 plan also allowed students to change schools or leave the system just when they reached the age limit of compulsory school attendance. Most students did (and do) complete the tenth grade at age sixteen. A high school that continues through grade 12 suggests that students would stay beyond the compulsory age, whereas a system that stops at grade 10 coincides with the age when students can leave.

Would a four-year junior college beginning at grade 11 enhance schooling for most students? Those who completed the tenth grade and chose to go beyond the compulsory age would enter a school in their home area that could take them through the sophomore year or through an occupational program. But hardly any public school districts organized themselves into a 6-4-4 system—possibly because, as Eells (1931) suggested, this system did not seem to lead to a true undergraduate college, complete with school spirit. He mentioned also the ambition of junior college organizers to have their institutions elevated to the status of senior institutions. However, the idea did not die; the notion of a Middle College High School, a secondary school built within a community college (described by Cullen and Moed, 1988), has gained some interest recently and may presage a new move toward a 6-4-4 or a 6-3-5 plan.

Arguments in favor of a new institution to accommodate students through their freshman and sophomore years were fueled by the belief that the transition from adolescence to adulthood typically occurred at the end of a person's teens. William Folwell contended that youths should be permitted to reside in their homes until they had "reached a point, say, somewhere near the end of the sophomore year" (quoted in Koos, 1924, p. 343). Eells (1931) posited that the junior colleges allowed students who were not fit to take the higher work to stop "naturally and honorably at the end of the sophomore year" (p. 91). "As a matter of record, the end of the second year of college marks the completion of formal education for the majority of students who continue post–high school studies" (p. 84). They would be better off remaining in their home communities until greater maturity enabled a few of them to go to the university in a distant region; the pretense of the higher learning for all could be set aside. Harvard president James Bryant Conant viewed the community college as a terminal education institution: "By and large, the educational road should fork at the end of the high school, though an occasional transfer of a student from a two-year college to a university should not be barred" (quoted in Bogue, 1950, p. 32).

The 1947 President's Commission on Higher Education articulated the value to be derived from a populace with free access to two years more of study than the secondary schools could provide. Because, as the commission put it, around half of the young people can benefit from formal studies through grade 14, the community colleges have an important role to play. The commission also suggested changing the institutional name from junior college to community college because of the expanded functions.

Expansion of Two-Year Colleges

Junior colleges were widespread in their early years. Koos (1924) reported 20 in 1909 and 170 ten years later. By 1922 thirty-seven of the forty-eight states contained junior colleges, this within two decades of their founding. Of the 207 institutions operating in that year, 137 were privately supported. Private colleges were most likely to be in the southern states, publicly supported institutions in the West and Midwest. Most of the colleges were quite small, although even in that era the public colleges tended to be larger than the private colleges. In 1922 the total enrollment for all institutions was around 20,000; the average was around 150 students in the public colleges and 60 in the private.

By 1930 there were 450 junior colleges, found in all but five states. Total enrollment was around 70,000, an average of about 160 students per institution. California had 20 percent of the public institutions and one-third of the students; and, although the percentages have dropped, California never relinquished this early lead. Other states with a large number of public junior colleges were Illinois, Texas, and Missouri; Texas and Missouri also had sizable numbers of private junior colleges. By 1940 there were 610 colleges, still small, averaging about 400 students each.

The high point for the private junior colleges came in 1949, when there were 322 privately controlled two-year colleges, 180 of them affiliated with churches, 108 independent nonprofit, and 34 proprietary. As Table 1 shows, they then began a steady decline. By 1986 the median-sized private nonprofit college had fewer than 500 students; 79 percent had fewer than 1,000. By contrast, the median public college enrolled nearly 3,000 students, and 20 percent had more than 7,000.

Table 1. Numbers of Public and Private Two-Year Colleges, 1900–1987.

Year	Total	Public		Private	
		Number	Percentage	Number	Percentage
1900–01	8	0	0	8	100
1915–16	74	19	26	55	74
1921–22	207	70	34	137	66
1925–26	325	136	42	189	58
1929–30	436	178	41	258	59
1933–34	521	219	42	302	58
1938–39	575	258	45	317	55
1947–48	650	328	50	322	50
1952–53	594	327	55	267	45
1954–55	596	336	56	260	44
1956–57	652	377	58	275	42
1958–59	677	400	59	277	41
1960–61	678	405	60	273	40
1962–63	704	426	61	278	39
1964–65	719	452	63	267	37
1966–67	837	565	68	272	32
1968–69	993	739	74	254	26
1970–71	1,091	847	78	244	22
1972–73	1,141	910	80	231	20
1974–75	1,203	981	82	222	18
1976–77	1,233	1,030	84	203	16
1978–79	1,234	1,047	85	187	15
1980–81	1,231	1,049	85	182	15
1982–83	1,219	1,064	87	155	13
1984–85	1,222	1,067	87	155	13
1986–87	1,224	1,062	87	162	13

Source: American Association of Community and Junior Colleges, Community, Junior, and Technical College Directory, 1960, 1976, 1979, 1980; Palmer, 1987b.

More than any other single factor, access depends on proximity. Even the highly selective University of California's urban campuses draw at least three-quarters of their entering freshmen from within a fifty-mile radius. Hence, the advent of the community college as a neighborhood institution did more to open higher education to broader segments of the population than did its policy of accepting even those students who had not done well in high school. Throughout the nation, in city after city, as community colleges opened their doors, the percentage of students beginning college expanded dramatically. During the 1950s and 1960s, whenever a community college was established in a locale where there had been no publicly supported college, the proportion of high school graduates in that area who began college immediately increased, sometimes by as much as 50 percent. The pattern has not changed. According to a survey by the College Entrance Examination Board (1986), 94 percent of the two-year-college matriculants nationwide are residents of the state in which the college is located; 96 percent commute. (The figures for four-year colleges are 76 and 41 percent, respectively.)

Fueled by the high birthrates of the 1940s, this rapid expansion of community colleges led their advocates to take an obsessive view of growth. Growth in budgets, staff, and students was considered good; stasis or decline was bad. It is a peculiar, but readily understandable, view. When budgets, enrollments, and staff are on an upswing, anything is possible; new programs can be launched, and new staff members can be found to operate them. It is much easier to hire a new composition teacher than to assign remedial English classes to a history instructor whose course enrollments have declined. Small wonder that the college leaders made growth their touchstone. The philosophy is that new programs serve new clients; the conclusion is that the institution that grows fastest serves its district best.

Obviously, though, expansion cannot continue forever. In 1972 M. J. Cohen studied the relationship between the number of community colleges in a state, the state's population density, and its area. He found that community colleges tended to be built so that 90–95 percent of the state's population lived within reasonable commuting distance, about 25 miles. When the colleges reached this ratio, the state had a mature community college system, and few additional colleges were built. As that state's population grew larger, the colleges expanded in enrollments, but it was no longer necessary to add new campuses. In the early 1970s seven states had mature systems: California, Florida, Illinois, New York, Ohio, Michigan, and Washington. In these states the denser the population, the smaller the area served by each college, and the higher the per-campus enrollment. Applying his formula of the relationship between number of colleges, state population, and population density, Cohen showed that 1,074 public community colleges would effectively serve the nation. In 1986, 1,062 such colleges were in operation, and the number had hardly changed in the prior ten years; thus, the formula seems valid.

Diversity marked the organization, control, and financing of colleges in the various states. Like the original four-year colleges and universities, the junior colleges grew without being coordinated at the state level. "Without doubt, the weakest link in the chain of cooperation for junior colleges is in the lack of authority for leadership and supervision at the state level. . . . By and large, the junior college in the United States has been growing without plan, general support, or supervision, and in some states almost as an extralegal institution" (Bogue, 1950, pp. 137–138). According to Blocker, Plummer, and Richardson (1965, p. 76), the colleges were "a direct outgrowth of customs, tradition, and legislation," and their "confused image . . . [was] related to state and regional differences and legislation and to the historical development of the institution."

Various organizing principles dictated construction of the junior colleges. The Educational Commission of the Baptist Church coordinated the Baptist junior college development in Texas. Elsewhere, four-year private colleges struggling to maintain their accreditation, student body, and fiscal support might abandon their upper-division specialized classes to concentrate on freshman and sophomore work and thus become junior colleges. The University of Missouri helped several struggling four-year colleges in that state to decapitate themselves and become private junior colleges. In other southern states where weak four-year colleges were prevalent, this dropping of the upper division also took place, accounting for the sizable number of private junior colleges in that region. Originally, over half of the private colleges were single-sex institutions, with colleges for women found most widely in New England, the Middle West, and the South.

Junior colleges were organized also by public universities wanting to expand their feeder institutions. The first two-year colleges in Pennsylvania were established as branch campuses of the Pennsylvania State College. The state universities of Kentucky, Alaska, and Hawaii also organized community colleges under their egis. Some public universities established two-year colleges on their own campuses. A University Center System gave rise to several two-year institutions in Wisconsin, and the University of South Carolina founded several regional campuses.

Many community colleges in California, Texas, and elsewhere grew out of secondary schools. In Mississippi they were spawned by the county agricultural high schools. But many were founded without legal sanction. Eells (1931) found that public colleges operating in eleven states were not authorized by general legislation or special legislation; most had been organized as extensions of public school systems "on the theory that since they were not expressly forbidden by law, they were allowed" (p. 40).

Although community colleges now operate in every state and enroll half of the students who begin college in America, they found their most compatible climate early on in the West, most notably in California. One reason may have been that many of the ideals of democracy first took form in the western states, where women's suffrage and other major reforms in the electoral process were first seen. But the western expansion of the community college must also be attributed to the fact that during the eighteenth century and the first half of the nineteenth, while colleges sponsored by religious institutions and private philanthropists grew strong elsewhere, the West had not yet been settled. In the twentieth century it was much easier for publicly supported institutions to advance where there was little competition from the private sector. California became the leader in community college development because of support from the University of California and Stanford University, a paucity of small denominational colleges, and strong support for public education at all levels. Even now, more than half of the college students in Arizona, Washington, and Wyoming, as well as California, are in community colleges.

The 1907 California law authorizing secondary school boards to offer postgraduate courses "which shall approximate the studies prescribed in the first two years of university courses," together with several subsequent amendments, served as a model for enabling legislation in numerous states. Anthony Caminetti, the senator who introduced the legislation, had been responsible twenty years earlier for the act authorizing the establishment of high schools as upward extensions of grammar schools. The extent of the influence, if any, of Alexis Lange, a University of California advocate of community colleges, or President Jordan of Stanford on Senator Caminetti is not certain. Lange had been a student at the University of Michigan and was aware of attempts there to truncate the university. By chance he moved to California in 1890 and brought the idea with him, writing about it extensively.

Actually, the law of 1907 only sanctioned a practice in which many of the high schools in California were already engaged. Those located at some distance from the state university had been offering lower-division studies to assist their students who could not readily leave their home towns at the completion of high school. When Fresno took advantage of the law to establish a junior college in 1910, one of its presenting arguments was that there was no institution of higher education within nearly 200 miles of the city. (Such justifications for two-year colleges have been used throughout the history of the development of those institutions.) Subsequent laws in California authorized junior colleges to open as districts entirely independent of the secondary schools, and this form of parallel development continued for decades. By 1980 nearly all the junior college districts had been separated from the lower-school districts.

The beginnings of the two-year college in other states that have well-developed systems followed similar patterns, but with some variations. Arizona in 1927 authorized local school districts to organize junior colleges. In 1917 a Kansas law allowed local elections to establish junior colleges and to create special taxing districts to support them. Michigan's authorizing legislation was passed the same year. Public junior colleges had already begun in Minnesota before a law was passed in 1925 providing for local elections to organize districts. Missouri's legislation permitting secondary schools to offer junior college courses dates from 1927, although junior colleges were established there earlier. Most of the community colleges in New York followed a 1949 state appropriation to establish a system of colleges to "provide two-year programs of post-high-school nature combining general education with technical education, special courses in extension work, and general education that would enable students to transfer" (Bogue, 1950, p. 34). Each state's laws were amended numerous times, usually to accommodate changed funding formulas and patterns of governance.

Tillery and Deegan (1985), in their study of community colleges in the United States, describe four stages of development. In the early period, 1910–1930, the colleges were organized primarily as extensions of the secondary school districts. (Dougherty, 1988, has also emphasized the importance of the local school boards in the early years of community college development.) In the second era, 1930–1950, the colleges were more likely to be formed within separate, local districts. State-level coordination marked the third stage of development, 1950–1970. Since 1970 institutional consolidation, with a shift toward increased state control and funding, has been dominant.

But these patterns are not uniform. Many aspects of college operations continue as they were when the institutions were under the local control of school boards; faculty evaluation procedures and funds awarded on the basis of student attendance are prime examples. And sometimes, just as one characteristic of the college changes in the direction of higher education, another moves toward the lower schools. In 1988 the California legislature passed a comprehensive reform bill that made many community college management practices correspond with those in the state's universities; but in the same year a proposition that was passed under public initiative placed college funding under guarantees similar to those enjoyed by the K–12 system.

Curricular Functions

The various curricular functions noted in each state's legislation usually include academic transfer preparation, vocational-technical education, continuing education, remedial education, and community service. All have been present in the public colleges from the start. In 1936 Hollinshead wrote that "the junior college should be a community college meeting community needs" (p.111), providing adult education and educational, recreational, and vocational activities and placing its cultural facilities at the disposal of the community. Every book written about the institution since has also articulated these elements.

The academic transfer, or collegiate, studies were meant to fulfill several institutional purposes: a popularizing function, a democratizing pursuit, and a function of conducting the lower division for the universities. The popularizing activity was to have the effect of advertising higher education, showing what it could do for the individual, encouraging people to attend. The democratizing function was realized as the community colleges became the point of first access for people entering higher education; by the late 1970s, 40 percent of all first-time-in-college, full-time freshmen and around two-thirds of all ethnic minority students were in the two-year institutions. The function of relieving the universities from having to deal with freshmen and sophomores was less pronounced, although colleges beginning at the junior year were opened in the 1960s in Florida and Illinois to take the flow from the two-year colleges of those states. Instead, community colleges made it possible for universities everywhere to maintain selective admissions requirements and thus to take only those freshmen and sophomores that they wanted.

In 1930 Eells surveyed 279 junior colleges to determine, among other things, the types of curricula offered (Eells, 1931). He found that 69 percent of the semester hours were presented in academic subjects, with modern foreign languages, social sciences, and natural sciences predominating. The 31 percent left for nonacademic subjects included sizable offerings in music, education, and home economics, and courses similar to those offered in extension divisions. At that time there was little difference between the curricula presented in public colleges, whether state controlled or locally controlled, and in private denominational or independent institutions; but the older the institution, the more likely it was to be engaged in building a set of nonacademic studies. The universities accepted the collegiate function and readily admitted the transferring students to advanced standing, most universities granting credit on an hour-for-hour basis for freshman and sophomore courses. Bogue (1950, p. 73) reported that "60 percent of the students in the upper division of the University of California at Berkeley, according to the registrar, are graduates of other institutions, largely junior colleges."

Vocational-technical education was written into the plans in most states from the earliest days. In the 1970s the U.S. Office of Education popularized *career education,* which is used throughout this book as a collective term for all occupational, vocational, and technical studies. Originally conceived as an essential component of "terminal study," education for students who would not go on to further studies, career education in the two-year colleges was designed to teach skills more complicated than those taught in high schools. Whereas secondary schools in the 1930s were teaching agriculture, bookkeeping, automobile repair, and printing, for example, junior colleges taught radio repair, secretarial services, and laboratory technical work. Teacher preparation, a function of the junior college in the 1920s, had died out as the baccalaureate became the requirement for teaching, but a sizable proportion of the occupational curriculum in the 1930s was still preprofessional training: prelaw, premedicine, pre-engineering. According to Eells (1931), in 1929 the proportional enrollment in California public junior colleges was 80 to 20 in favor of the collegiate; in Texas municipal junior colleges, it was 77 to 23. By the 1970s the percentage of students in career education had reached parity with that in the collegiate programs.

The continuing education function arose early, and the percentage of adults enrolled increased dramatically in the 1940s. The 1947 President's Commission on Higher Education emphasized the importance of this function, and Bogue (1950, p. 215) noted with approval a Texas college's slogan, "We will teach anyone, anywhere, anything, at any time whenever there are enough people interested in the program to justify its offering." He reported also that "out of the 500,536 students reported in the 1949 [AACJC] *Directory,* nearly 185,000 are specials or adults" (p. 35).

Remedial education—also known as developmental, preparatory, or compensatory studies—grew as the percentage of students poorly prepared in secondary schools swelled community college rolls. Although some compensatory work had been offered early on, the disparity in ability between students entering community colleges and those in the senior institutions was not nearly as great in the 1920s as in the 1980s. Koos (1924) reported only slightly higher entering test scores by the senior college matriculants. The apparent breakdown of basic academic education in secondary schools in the 1960s, coupled with the expanded percentage of people entering college, brought compensatory education to the fore.

The community service function was pioneered by private junior colleges and by rural colleges, which often served as the cultural centers for their communities. Early books on two-year colleges display a wide range of cultural and recreational events that institutions of the time were presenting for the enlightenment of their communities. Public two-year colleges adopted the idea as a useful aspect of their relations with the public, and in some states special funds were set aside for this function. By 1980 the AACJC *Directory* listed nearly 4 million community education participants, predominantly people enrolled in short courses, workshops, and noncredit courses. The community service function also included spectator events sponsored by the colleges but open to the public as well as to students.

This book presents separate chapters on each curricular function: collegiate (academic transfer), career (vocational-technical), and compensatory (remedial) education. Community service and continuing education are merged, and general education is accorded treatment on its own. Student guidance, often mentioned as a major function, is covered in the chapter on student services. Yet all the functions overlap, because education is rarely discrete. Community college programs do not stay in neat categories when the concepts underlying them and the purposes for which students enroll in them are scrutinized. Although courses in the humanities are almost always listed as part of the collegiate program, they are career education for students who will work in museums. A course in auto mechanics is for the general education of students who learn to repair their own cars, even though it is part of the offerings in a career program. Collegiate, career, continuing education—all are intertwined. Who can say when one or another is occurring?

The definitions are pertinent primarily for funding agents and accreditation associations and for those who need categories and classification systems as a way of understanding events. "Career" education is that which is supported by Vocational Education Act monies and/or is supposed to lead to direct employment. When a course or program is approved for transfer credit to a senior institution, it becomes part of the "collegiate" function. When it cannot be used for associate degree credit, it is "compensatory" or "community" education. That is why community college presidents may say honestly that their institutions perform all tasks with great facility. When confronted with the charge that their school is not doing enough in one or another curriculum area, they can counter that it is, if the courses and students were only examined more closely. All education is general education. All is potentially career enhancing. All is for the sake of the broader community.

Changing Emphases

Community colleges have effected notable changes in American education, especially by expanding access. Well into the middle of the twentieth century, higher education had elements of mystery within it. Only one young person in seven went to college, and most students were from the middle and upper classes. To the public at large, which really had little idea of what went on behind the walls, higher education was a clandestine process, steeped in ritual. The demystification of higher education, occasioned by the democratization of access, has taken place steadily. Given marked impetus after World War II by the GI Bill, when the first large-scale financial aid packages were made available and people could be reimbursed not only for their tuition but also for their living expenses while attending college, college going increased rapidly, so that by the time enrollments leveled off in the 1970s, three in every eight persons attended.

The increase in enrollments was accompanied by a major change in the composition of the student body. No longer sequestered enclaves operated apparently for the sons of the wealthy and educated, who were on their way to positions in the professions, and for the daughters of the same groups, who would be marked with the manners of a cultured class, the colleges were opened to ethnic minorities, to lower-income groups, and to those whose prior academic performance had been marginal. Of all the higher education institutions, the community colleges contributed most to opening the system. Established in every metropolitan area, they were available to all comers, attracting the "new students": the

minorities, the women, the people who had done poorly in high
school, those who would otherwise never have considered further
education.

During this same era community colleges contributed also to
certain shifts in institutional emphasis. They had always been an
avenue of individual mobility; that purpose became highlighted as
greater percentages of the populace began using colleges as a step
up in class. The emphasis in higher education on providing trained
personnel for the professions, business, and industry also became
more distinct. Admittedly, it is difficult to identify the students who
sought learning for its own sake or who went to college to acquire
the manners that would mark them as ladies or gentlemen; perhaps
students whose purposes were purely nonvocational were rare even
before 1900. But by the last third of the twentieth century, few
commentators on higher education were even articulating those
purposes. Vocationalism had gained the day. College going was for
job getting, job certifying, job training. The old values of a liberal
education became supplemental—adjuncts to be picked up incidentally, if at all, along the way to higher-paying employment.

Other shifts in institutional emphasis have been dictated not
by the pronouncements of educational philosophers but by the
exigencies of financing, the state-level coordinating bodies, the
availability of new media, and the new student groups. There has
been a steady increase in the public funds available to all types of
educational institutions, but the community colleges have been
most profoundly affected by the sizable increases in federal appropriations for occupational education. Beginning with the Smith-
Hughes Act in 1917 and continuing through the Vocational
Education Acts of the 1960s and later, federal dollars have poured
into the education sector. Community colleges have not been remiss
in obtaining their share. Their national lobbyists have worked
diligently to have the community college named in set-asides, and
the colleges have obtained funds for special occupational programs.
The career education cast of contemporary colleges is due in no
small measure to the availability of these funds.

State-level coordinating agencies have affected institutional
role. Coordinating councils and postsecondary education commissions, along with boards of regents for all higher education in some

states, have attempted to assign programs to the different types of institutions. These bodies may restrict lower-division offerings in community colleges. In some states continuing education has been assigned; in others it has been taken away from the colleges.

The new media have had their own effect. Electronic gadgetry has been adopted, and elaborate learning resource centers have been opened on campus. Because learning laboratories can be made available at any time, it becomes less necessary for students to attend courses in sequence or at fixed times of day. The new media, particularly television, have made it possible for institutions to present sizable proportions of their offerings over open circuit. The colleges have burst their campus bounds.

But the new students have had the most pronounced effect. The community colleges reached out to attract those who were not being served by traditional higher education: those who could not afford the tuition; who could not take the time to attend a college on a full-time basis; whose ethnic background had constrained them from participating; who had inadequate preparation in the lower schools; whose educational progress had been interrupted by some temporary condition; who had become obsolete in their jobs or had never been trained to work at any job; who needed a connection to obtain a job; who were confined in prisons, physically handicapped, or otherwise unable to attend classes on a campus; or who were faced with increased leisure time. The colleges' success in enrolling these new students has affected what they can offer. Students who are unable to read, write, and compute at a level that would enable them to pursue a collegiate program satisfactorily must be provided with different curricula. As these students become a sizable minority—or, indeed, a majority—the college's philosophy is affected. Gradually, the institution's spokespersons stop talking about its collegiate character and speak more of the compensatory work in which it engages. Gradually, the faculty stop demanding the same standards of student achievement. Part-time students similarly affect the colleges as new grading policies are adopted to accommodate students who drop in and out, and new types of support systems and learning laboratories are installed for those who do not respond to traditional classroom-centered instruction.

Overall, the community colleges have suffered less from goal displacement than have most other higher education institutions. They had less to displace; their goals were to serve the people with whatever the people wanted. Standing outside the tradition, they offered access. They had to instruct; they could not offer the excuse that they were advancing the frontiers of scholarship. Because they had expanded rapidly, their permanent staffs had not been in place so long that they had become fixed. As an example, they could quite easily convert their libraries to learning resource centers because the libraries did not have a heritage of the elaborate routines accompanying maintenance and preservation of large collections. They could be adapted to the instructional programs.

In 1924 Koos was sanguine about the role of the junior college in clarifying and differentiating the aims of both the universities and the secondary schools. He anticipated an allocation of function "that would be certain to bring order out of the current educational chaos. . . . By extending the acknowledged period of secondary education to include two more years . . . allocation of purpose to each unit and differentiation among them should take care of themselves" (p. 374). Koos believed that most of the aims and functions of the secondary school would rise to the new level, so that the first two years of college work would take on a new significance. These aims included occupational efficiency, civic and social responsibility, and the recreational and esthetic aspects of life. The universities would be freed for research and professional training. Further, the college entrance controversy would be reduced, and preprofessional training could be better defined. Duplication of offerings between secondary schools and universities would also be reduced by the expansion of a system of junior colleges.

Clearly, not many of Koos's expectations were borne out. He could not have anticipated the massive increase in enrollments; the growth of universities and colleges and the competition among them; or the breakdown in curriculum fostered, on the one hand, by part-time students who dropped in and out of college and, on the other, by the institutions' eagerness to offer short courses, workshops, and spectator events. His scheme did not allow for the students who demanded higher degrees as a right, crying that the colleges had discriminated against them when the degrees were not awarded as a matter of form. And he was unaware of the importance that students and educators alike would place on programs related to job attainment.

Current Issues

The revolution in American education, in which the two-year college played a leading role, is almost over. Two years of postsecondary education are within the reach—financially, geographically, practically—of virtually every American. Two generations have passed since President Truman's Commission on Higher Education recommended that the door to higher education be swung open. Now community colleges are everywhere. There are systems with branches in inner cities and rural districts and with programs in prisons and on military bases. Classes are offered on open-circuit television, on Saturdays, and at all hours of the night. Open-admissions policies and programs for everyone ensure that no member of the community need miss the chance to attend.

But the question remains, "Access to what?" Should community colleges educate for further studies, or should they be the capstone for graded education? Can they be both? Those who would make the community college the elementary school for further learning have been in headlong retreat. Capstone, or terminal, education currently takes the form of so-called compensatory studies, in which students are given one last chance to learn minimal language and computational competencies. Occupational education stands like a colossus on its own.

To Bogue in 1950, the critical problems of the community colleges were these: devising a consistent type of organization, maintaining local or state control, developing an adequate general education program integrated with the occupational, finding the right kinds of teachers, maintaining adequate student guidance services, and getting the states to appropriate sufficient funds. These problems have never been satisfactorily resolved.

Fifteen years later, Blocker, Plummer, and Richardson (1965) identified nine issues: maintaining comprehensive programs, serving equally well the wide variety of unselected students, adapting to changes in society or becoming static, giving the community anything that anyone wants while continuing to maintain educational integrity, maintaining fiscal support, finding sufficient educational leaders to staff the institutions, adopting the best patterns of administration and organization, avoiding division into vocational schools and college-transfer institutions, and getting society to accept the notion that all individuals have a right to education as far as they want to go. Most of these problems have also persisted.

Recent changes in both intra- and extramural perceptions of community colleges have led to further issues. Some of these shifts are due to educational leadership at the state and the institutional level, but more are due to changing demographic patterns and public perceptions of institutional purposes. First, there has been an inversion in the uses of career and collegiate education. Career education was formerly considered terminal. Students were expected to complete their formal schooling by learning a trade and going to work. Students who entered career programs and failed to complete them and then failed to work in the field for which they were trained were considered to have been misguided. Collegiate programs were designed to serve as a bridge between secondary school and baccalaureate studies. Students who entered the programs and failed to progress to the level of the baccalaureate were considered dropouts.

Since the 1970s, however, high proportions of students who complete career programs have been transferring to universities. Career programs typically maintain curricula in which the courses are sequential. Many of these programs, especially those in the technologies and the health fields, articulate well with baccalaureate programs. Most have selective admissions policies. Students are forced to make an early commitment, satisfy admissions requirements, maintain continual attendance, and make satisfactory progress. This pattern of schooling reinforces the serious students, leading them to enroll in further studies at a university. The collegiate courses, in contrast, are more likely to be taken by students who have not made a commitment to a definite line of study, who already have degrees and are taking courses for personal interest, or who are trying to build up their prerequisites or grade point averages so that they can enter a selective admissions program at the community college or another institution. Thus, for many students enrolled in them, the collegiate courses have become the catchall, the "terminal education" program.

A second issue is that by the 1970s the linear aspect of community colleges—the idea that the institution assists students in bridging the freshman and sophomore years—had been severely reduced as a proportion of the community colleges' total effort. The number of students transferring was reasonably constant, but most of the expansion in community college enrollments was in the areas of career and continuing education. The collegiate programs remained in the catalogues, but students used them for completely different purposes. They dropped in and out, taking the courses at will. Among California community college students, Hunter and Sheldon (1979) found that the mean number of credit hours completed per term was between seven and eight, but the mode was three—in other words, one course. The course array in the collegiate programs was more accurately viewed as lateral than as linear. Not more than one in ten course sections enforced course prerequisites; not more than one course in ten was a sophomore-level course. What had happened was that the students were using the institution in one way whereas the institution's modes of functioning suggested another. Catalogues displayed recommended courses, semester by semester, for students planning to major in one or another of a hundred fields. But the students took those courses that were offered at a preferred time of day or those that seemed potentially useful. In the 1980s many colleges took deliberate steps to quell that pattern of course attendance, but nationwide it was still the norm.

Third, a trend toward less-than-college-level instruction has accelerated. In addition to the increased number of compensatory courses as a proportion of the curriculum, expectations in collegiate courses have changed. To take one example, students in community college English literature courses in 1977 were expected to read 560 pages per term, on average, whereas, according to Koos (1924), the average was three times that in *high school* literature courses of 1922. These figures are offered not to derogate community colleges but only to point out that the institutions cannot be understood in traditional terms. They are struggling to find ways of educating students whose prior learning has been dominated by nonprint images. The belief that a person unschooled in the classics was not sufficiently educated died hard in the nineteenth century; the ability to read *anything* as a criterion of adequate education has been questioned in an era when most messages are carried by wires and waves.

But all questions of curriculum, students, and institutional mission pale in the light of funding issues. Are the community colleges—or any schools—worth what they cost? Have the colleges overextended themselves? Do their outcomes justify the public resources they consume? Can they, should they, be called to account for their outcomes? Those questions have appeared with increasing frequency as public disaffection with the schools has grown. Whether the community colleges stand alone or whether they are cast with the higher or lower schools, their advocates will be forced to respond.

Several other current issues may also be phrased as questions. How much more than access and illusory benefits of credits and degrees without concomitant learning do the colleges provide? Are they in or out of higher education? How much of their effort is dedicated to the higher learning, to developing rationality and advancing knowledge through the disciplines? How much leads students to form habits of reflection? How much tends toward public and private virtue?

Is it moral to sort and grade students, sending the more capable to the university while encouraging the rest to follow other pursuits? Commenting on the terminal programs—the commercial and general education courses that did not transfer to the universities—Eells (1931, p. 310) noted: "Students cannot be forced to take them, it is true, but perhaps they can be led, enticed, attracted." And in his chapter on the guidance function, he stressed: "It is essential that many students be guided into terminal curricula" (p. 330). The "cooling-out" function (so named by Clark in 1960), convincing the students that they should not aspire to the higher learning, yielded an unending stream of commentary—for example, an issue of New Directions for Community Colleges entitled *Questioning the Community College Role* (Vaughan, 1980). But the question is still unanswered.

What would the shape of American education have been if the community colleges had never been established? Where would people be learning the trades and occupations? Apprenticeships were the mode in earlier times. Would they still dominate? Would the less-than-college-level regional occupational centers and area vocational schools be larger and more handsomely funded? Would different configurations have developed?

What would have happened to the collegiate function? How many fewer students would be attending college? Would the universities have expanded to accommodate all who sought entry? Community colleges certainly performed an essential service in the 1960s, when a mass of people demanded access. By offering an inexpensive, accessible alternative, these colleges allowed the universities to maintain at least a semblance of their own integrity. How many universities would have been shattered if community colleges to which the petitioners could be shunted had not been available?

If there had been no community colleges, what agencies would be performing their community services? How many of the services they have provided would be missed? Would secondary schools have better maintained their own curricular and instructional integrity if community colleges had not been there to grant students absolution for all past educational sins? Would other institutions have assumed the compensatory function?

Although such questions have been asked from time to time, they have rarely been examined, mainly because during most of its history the community college has been unnoticed, ignored by writers about higher education. The books on higher education published from the turn of the century, when the first community colleges appeared, through the 1960s rarely gave even a nod to the community college; one searches in vain for a reference to them in the index. In 1950 Bogue deplored the lack of attention paid to the junior colleges, saying that he had examined twenty-seven authoritative histories of American education and found only a superficial treatment of junior colleges or none at all. Rudolph's major history of the higher education curriculum, published in 1977, gave them a scant two pages. And seldom have the questions been answered or even considered by community college leaders and their counterparts in those four-year institutions that did not develop traditions of scholarship. Instead, the leaders have seized on a new term, *postsecondary education,* which supposedly allows the colleges engaged primarily in basic instruction to be placed in the same tent with the research universities.

Perhaps community colleges should merely be characterized as untraditional. They do not follow the tradition of higher education as it developed from the colonial colleges through the universities. They do not typically provide the students with new value structures, as residential liberal arts colleges aspire to do. Nor do they further the frontiers of knowledge through scholarship and research training, as in the finest traditions of the universities. Community colleges do not even follow their own traditions. They change frequently, seeking new programs and new clients. Community colleges are indeed untraditional, but they are truly American because, at their best, they represent the United States at its best. Never satisfied with resting on what has been done before, they try new approaches to old problems. They maintain open channels for individuals, enhancing the social mobility that has characterized America; and they accept the idea that society can be better, just as individuals can better their lot within it.

Two

Students:
Diverse Backgrounds, Purposes, and Outcomes

Two words sum up the students: *number* and *variety*. To college leaders the spectacular growth in student population, sometimes as much as 15 percent a year, has been the most impressive feature of community colleges. The numbers are notable: enrollment increased from just over 500,000 in 1960 to more than 2 million by 1970, more than 4 million by 1980, 5 million by 1987. During the 1960s much of the increase was due to the expanded proportion of eighteen- to twenty-four-year-olds in the population—the result of the World War II baby boom. There were more people in the college-age cohort, and more of them were going to college. Table 2 shows the percentage of the age group in all types of colleges. (The table actually overstates the rate of college going, because many undergraduates—half of the community college population currently—are older than age twenty-four.) Whereas in the early 1960s half of the high school graduates went to college, by the 1980s two-thirds of them were entering some postsecondary school—an increase occasioned in large measure by the community colleges' availability. By 1987, 45 percent of the American population aged twenty-five to thirty-four had attended college at least one year.

Reasons for the Increase in Numbers

The increase in community college enrollments may be attributed to several conditions in addition to general population expansion: older students' participation; physical accessibility; financial aid; part-time attendance; the reclassification of institutions; the redefinition of students and courses; and high attendance by low-ability, women, and minority students. Community colleges also recruited students aggressively; to an institution that tries to offer something for everyone in the community, everyone is potentially a student.

The colleges often sought out certain constituencies—older students in particular. Butcher (1980) found tuition waivers for seniors a typical practice nationwide. However, the recruitment of senior citizens did not alone account for the increase in the median age of students attending the colleges. The number of eighteen-year-olds in the American population peaked in 1979 and was 20 percent lower in 1986. In order to make up for the shortfall in potential younger students, the colleges expanded the programs attractive to older students. Numbers of working adults seeking skills that would enable them to change or upgrade their jobs or activities to satisfy

Table 2. Undergraduate Enrollment in U.S. Colleges and Universities as Compared to Eighteen- to Twenty-Four-Year-Old Population, 1900 to 1985.

Year	College-Age Population Eighteen to Twenty-Four Years (in Thousands)	Undergraduate Enrollment (in Thousands)	Percentage
1900	10,357	232	2.2
1910	12,300	346	2.8
1920	12,830	582	4.5
1930	15,280	1,054	6.9
1940	16,458	1,389	8.4
1950	16,120	2,421	15.0
1960	15,677	2,874	18.3
1970	24,712	6,274	25.4
1980	30,337	8,488	28.0
1985	28,492	9,114	32.0

Source: National Center for Education Statistics, Digest of Education Statistics, 1970, p. 67, and 1987, p. 18; Ottinger, 1987, table 4; and U.S. Department of Commerce, Bureau of the Census, Current Population Reports, Series P-20, Sept. 1986, table 5.

their personal interests were attracted because they could attend part-time.

Older students have swelled enrollments. According to the AACJC *Directory*, the mean age of students enrolled for credit in 1980 was twenty-seven, the median age was twenty-three, and the modal age was nineteen. A 1986 national survey conducted by the Center for the Study of Community Colleges found that the mean had gone up to twenty-nine, the median had increased to twenty-five, and the mode had remained at nineteen. Note the discrepancy among these three measures. The mean is the most sensitive to extremes; hence, a program for even a few senior citizens affects that measure dramatically. The median suggests that the students just out of high school and those in their early twenties who either delayed beginning college or entered community colleges after dropping out of other institutions accounted for half of the student population. This 50 percent of the student body that was composed of students aged eighteen to twenty-five was matched on the other side of the median by students ranging in age all the way out to their sixties and seventies. The mode reflects the greatest number; nine-teen-year-olds were still the dominant single age group in the institutions. Thus, a graph depicting the age of community college students would show a bulge at the low end of the scale and a long tail reaching out toward the high end.

Physical accessibility also enhanced enrollments. The effect of campus proximity on the rate of college going has been well documented. As an example, Tinto (1973) found that the presence of local colleges differentially affected the rate of attendance among high school graduates in Illinois and North Carolina. Most of the high-ability students would have attended college anyway, even if it meant leaving their hometown, but the rate of college going among lower-ability students increased dramatically when a public community college became readily available to them.

The availability of financial aid brought additional students as state and federal payments, loans, and work-study grants rose markedly. From the 1940s through the early 1970s, nearly all the types of aid were categorical, designed to assist particular groups of students. The largest group of beneficiaries was the war veterans; in California in 1973 veterans made up more than 13 percent of the total enrollment. Students from economically disadvantaged and minority groups were also large beneficiaries of financial aid; more than 30,000 such students in Illinois received state and local funds in 1974. Since the middle 1970s more of the funds have been unrestricted; by 1988 California community college students had borrowed over $500 million in guaranteed student loans (California Community Colleges, 1989).

As the age of the students went up, the number of credit hours each student attempted went down. In the early 1970s half of the students were full-timers; by the mid-1980s only one-third were (see Table 3). In 1986 just over one-fourth of the one million students in California were enrolled for more than twelve units, while nearly half were taking fewer than six units (California

Table 3. Part-Time Enrollments as a Percentage of Total Enrollments, 1963–1987.

Year	Opening Fall Enrollment	Part-Time Enrollment	Percentage
1963	914,494	488,976	53
1968	1,909,118	888,458	47
1969	2,234,669	1,064,187	48
1970	2,447,401	1,164,797	48
1971	2,678,171	1,290,964	48
1972	2,863,780	1,473,947	51
1973	3,100,951	1,702,886	55
1974	3,528,727	1,974,534	56
1975	4,069,279	2,222,269	55
1976	4,084,976	2,219,605	54
1977	4,309,984	2,501,789	58
1978	4,304,058	2,606,804	61
1979	4,487,872	2,788,880	62
1980	4,825,931	2,996,264	62
1981	4,887,675	3,059,768	63
1982	4,964,379	3,117,979	63
1983	4,947,975	2,998,648	61
1984	4,836,819	3,047,129	63
1985	4,751,903	2,873,466	60
1986	4,890,664	3,262,185	67
1987	5,057,453	3,389,524	67

Source: American Association of Community and Junior Colleges, *Community, Junior, and Technical College Directory*, 1965–1987.

Community Colleges, 1987a). And these figures do not include noncredit students enrolled in community continuing education, high school completion courses, and short-cycle occupational studies. The pattern was consistent throughout the country; in nearly all states with community college enrollments greater than 50,000, part-time students outnumbered full-timers. In some smaller states, such as Nevada, 90 percent of the community college students attended part-time (Fernandez, 1987).

The rise in the number of part-time students can be attributed to many factors: a decline in eighteen-year-olds as a percentage of the total population, an increase in the number of students combining work and study, and an increase in the number of women attending college, to name but a few. The colleges have made deliberate efforts to attract part-timers by making it easy for them to attend. Senior citizens' institutes; weekend colleges; courses offered at off-campus centers, in workplaces, and in rented and donated housing around the district; and countless other strategems have been employed. Few of the noncampus colleges count *any* full-timers among their enrollees. The Community College of the Air Force, headquartered in Alabama but with classes offered around the world, claimed 330,000 students in 1987, with only around 10 percent of them attending full-time.

The rise in part-time attendance has lowered the percentage of students attending community colleges past their first year. AACJC data for 1963–1973 showed a relatively constant ratio of about 2.4 freshmen to one sophomore; by the end of the decade, however, the proportion of students *completing* two years had dropped to less than one in five. Part of this decrease may be attributed to certificate programs that could be completed in one year, part to the massive increase in students without degree aspirations taking only a course or two for their own interest. The AACJC's dropping "freshman" and "sophomore" categories from its *Directory* after 1975 reflected the tendency of most colleges to avoid referring to their students' year of attendance. The preferred mode of classification was to designate those who wanted credits for transfer to a baccalaureate institution, those who sought occupational training, and "other." Not necessarily more accurate, at least this type of information differentiated students according to major funding sources: degree credit, occupational studies, and adult or continuing education.

The growth in total enrollments did not result alone from the colleges' attracting students who might not otherwise have participated in education beyond high school. Two other factors played a part: the different ways of classifying institutions and a redefinition of the term *student*. Changes in the classification of colleges are common. Private colleges become public; two-year colleges become four-year (and vice versa); adult education centers and proprietary trade schools enter the category, especially as they begin awarding degrees. The universe of community and junior colleges is especially fluid. From time to time, entire sets of institutions, such as trade and vocational schools and adult education centers, have been added to the list. As examples, in the mid-1960s four vocational-technical schools became the first colleges in the University of Hawaii community college system, and in the mid-1970s the community colleges in Iowa became area schools responsible for the adult education in their districts. Sometimes, institutional reclassification is made by an agency that gathers statistics; in 1980 the American Association of Community and Junior Colleges began adding proprietary trade schools to its *Directory* and more recently has expanded the number of technical institutes on its roster. (The National Center for Education Statistics, which takes a less expansive approach to classifying community colleges, reported 6.5 percent fewer students than the AACJC did in 1987.) All these changes add to the number of students tabulated each year.

Reclassification of students within colleges has had an even greater effect on enrollment figures. As an example, when the category "defined adult" was removed from the California system, students of all ages could be counted as equivalents for funding purposes. In most states the trend has been toward including college-sponsored events (whether or not such activities demand evidence of learning attained) as "courses" and hence the people attending them as "students." Further, the community colleges have taken under their egis numerous instructional programs formerly offered by public and private agencies, including police academies, hospitals, banks, and religious centers. These practices swell the enrollment figures and blur the definition of *student*, making it possible for community college leaders to point with pride to the enhanced enrollments and to gain augmented funding when enrollments are used as the basis for accounting. They also heighten imprecision in counting students and make it difficult to compare enrollments from one year to another.

Student Ability

Classification of students by academic ability revealed increasing numbers of lower-ability students. As Cross (1971) pointed out, three major philosophies about who should go to college have dominated the history of higher education in this country: the *aristocratic*, suggesting that white males from the upper socioeconomic classes would attend; the *meritocratic*, holding that college admission should be based on ability; and the *egalitarian*, which "means that everyone should have equality of access to educational opportunities, regardless of socioeconomic background, race, sex, *or ability*" (p. 6). By the time the community colleges were developed, most young people from the higher socioeconomic groups and most of the high-aptitude aspirants were going to college. Cross concluded: "The groups new to higher education in the decade of the 1970s will be those of low socioeconomic status and those with low measured ability. The movement is already underway; the majority of students entering open-door community colleges come from the lower half of the high school classes, academically and socioeconomically" (p. 7).

Survey data compiled annually by the Cooperative Institutional Research Program (CIRP) reveal the number of students with low prior school achievement in community colleges. Table 4 indicates the average high school grades of students enrolling in 1988 (Astin and others, 1988). Other data also reveal the lower academic skill level of entering freshmen. The American College Testing Program's entering test means for community colleges were considerably lower than the norm for all college students. In Illinois the mean for entering community college freshmen had dropped to 16.2 by 1979, down from 18.0 in 1973. This figure compares with a 1979 all-student national norm of 18.9 (Kohl and others, 1980).

Table 4. High School Grades of College Freshmen, 1988.

Average Grade in High School	Percentage of Enrollment	
	All Institutions	All Two-Year Colleges
A or A+	11	5
A-	13	7
B+	19	16
B	25	27
B-	14	17
C+	12	16
C	7	11
D	less than 1	1

Source: Astin and others, 1988.

(Nationwide, the community college norm was 16.0 in 1986.) And scores on the New Jersey College Basic Skills Placement Test consistently show that the four-year state colleges and universities enroll better-prepared students than the county (community) colleges (New Jersey State Department of Higher Education, 1986).

Although these data provide an overall view, they tend to obscure differences among sets of institutions. In states where public institutions of higher education are arrayed in hierarchical systems, most of the students begin in a community college, and the proportion of lower-ability students is greatest in such colleges. But where the publicly supported universities maintain open admissions, the prior school attainment of their entering freshmen differs little from that of two-year-college matriculants.

Community colleges have also matriculated a number of high-ability students. Like most other institutions of higher education, they have always sought out those students and made special benefits available to them. For example, beginning in 1979 Miami-Dade Community College gave full tuition waivers to all students graduating in the top 10 percent of their local high school classes (Morris and Losak, 1980). As many as 40 percent of that group were attracted to the college, and numerous colleges since have adopted such programs.

The prevalence of honors programs suggests also that the colleges have welcomed the better-prepared students. White (1975) surveyed 225 colleges in the North Central region and found that about 10 percent had formalized honors programs and that nearly half of the others made some provision for superior students. In that same year Olivas reported that more than 80 percent of the community colleges nationwide were making special arrangements, such as honors programs, honors classes, honor societies, provisions for independent study, and/or scholarships available for high-ability students. The Center for the Study of Community Colleges (1982) similarly found interdisciplinary courses, colloquia, and various extracurricular activities especially prepared for high-ability students in six large urban districts.

How do the high-ability students fare? A number of analysts believe that the community colleges have had a negative effect on such students. In 1977 Astin found that fewer students who had graduated in the top 20 percent of their high school classes were attending four-year colleges than fifteen years earlier; the decline was 16 percent for males, 9 percent for females. In contrast, the proportion of highly able males who were attending two-year colleges had increased by 10 percent, and the proportion of females had increased by 12 percent. He concluded that this shift away from four-year-college attendance, occasioned by the easily accessible two-year colleges, was proving detrimental to the higher-ability students, who, by virtue of attending community colleges, were reducing their chances for obtaining baccalaureate degrees. However, as detailed later in this chapter, the data on student attainment are not sufficiently precise to allow for such a sweeping conclusion.

Gender

Probably because it is easier to sort students by gender than by any other variable, differences between male and female college students have long been documented. Historically, among students of questionable ability, fewer women than men attended college. When funds were limited, more male than female high-ability students from low-income families entered college. Further, the women who went to college were more likely to be dependent on their families for support. College women in general have always had better high school records. Table 5, showing the distribution of

Table 5. High School Academic Performance of Entering
Community College Freshmen by Sex, 1988.

Average Grade in High School	Percentage of Enrollment	
	Men	Women
A or A+	4	6
A–	6	8
B+	14	18
B	25	29
B–	19	16
C+	18	14
C	14	8
D	1	1

Source: Astin and others, 1988.

high school grades among men and women entering community colleges, points up the difference. As measured by their high school grades, the full-time freshman women entering community colleges were more able than the men. They were more likely to be from lower-income families as well; 35 percent of the women and 26 percent of the men entering in 1988 were from families with less than $25,000 in annual income. Overall, as shown in Table 6, students entering two-year colleges were more likely to be from lower-income families than were those entering four-year institutions.

The percentage of women in community colleges, especially those enrolled as part-time students, had increased, so that by 1987 women accounted for 53 percent of all students—a proportion that had not changed for the prior four years (Palmer, 1988). However, these data concealed some important differences in the rate of college attendance among the states. Women represented 63 percent of the enrollment in Arkansas two-year colleges in 1984 (Byrd, 1985); 65 percent in the Kentucky community college system (Hauselman and Tudor, 1987); 59 percent in Illinois (Illinois Community College Board, 1988). The tendency was for women to far outnumber men among the part-timers; in California there were slightly more males among the full-time students, but the females

Table 6. Parental Income of Entering College Freshmen, 1988.

| | Percentage of Enrollment | |
Estimated Parental Income	All Institutions	All Two-Year Colleges
Less than $6,000	4	6
$6,000-9,999	3	4
$10,000-14,999	5	7
$15,000-19,999	5	7
$20,000-24,999	7	8
$25,000-29,999	7	8
$30,000-34,999	9	10
$35,000-39,999	9	10
$40,000-49,999	12	13
$50,000-59,999	12	11
$60,000-74,999	11	8
$75,000-99,999	7	5
$100,000-149,999	5	3
$150,000 or more	4	2

Source: Astin and others, 1988.

outnumbered them overall by 56 to 44 percent (California Community Colleges, 1987a).

There has been some change in the types of programs that community college students enter, although the traditionally female allied health and office fields still enroll high proportions of women, and the traditionally male fields of construction and transportation enroll high proportions of men. A study of California students found that only about 3 percent of matriculants in occupational programs were enrolled in nontraditional areas; that is, about 3 percent of students in welding and automotive programs were female, and 3 percent of students in the nursing and secretarial programs were male (Hunter and Sheldon, 1979). In Virginia 97 percent of the students in business and office skills programs and 94 percent of the students in nursing were women (Virginia State Department of Education, 1986). A review of the associate degrees awarded in 1983-84 in Pennsylvania showed some progress toward gender equity in business and management areas; but, except for computer programming and data processing, nearly all the students graduating from office skills programs were women. Men received

11 percent of the degrees in allied health and health science, and women received 8 percent of the degrees in engineering and engineering technologies (Pennsylvania State Department of Education, 1985).

Ethnic Minorities

The community colleges' diligence in recruiting students from segments of the population that had not previously attended college yielded sizable increases in college attendance by members of ethnic minorities. By 1986 community colleges, with 37 percent of the total enrollment in American higher education, were enrolling over 47 percent of the ethnic minority students: 43 percent of the blacks, 55 percent of the Hispanics, 56 percent of the Native Americans, and 42 percent of the Asians ("1986 Minority Enrollments . . . ," 1988). As shown in Table 7, in 1986 minority students constituted 24 percent of all community college enrollments nationwide. Naturally, the pattern differs from state to state depending on the minority population. California, Hawaii, Louisiana, Mississippi, New Mexico, and Texas had the highest percentages of minorities among their community college students. Minorities were also enrolled in significant numbers in other states that have well-developed community college systems; for example, in Illinois 60 percent of all blacks and 68 percent of all Hispanics in higher education were in community colleges (Illinois Community College Board, 1989).

These enrollments have nearly achieved parity with the student groups' proportion of the population. In Illinois, for example, 15.2 percent of the high school graduation class of 1985 were black, and 16.8 percent of the state's community college students were black (Illinois Community College Board, 1986b). Minorities comprised 9.1 percent of the population of Kansas and 9.3 percent of that state's community college students (Kansas State Department of Education, 1986); the figures in California were 32.4 and 34.3, respectively (Field Research Corporation, 1984). Single-college data often reflect this pattern; in 1986 Laredo Junior College (Texas), in a city where 93 percent of the population was Hispanic, counted 88 percent of the students as Hispanic, and Southwestern

Table 7. Percentages of Racial and Ethnic Composition of
Enrollments in Two-Year Colleges by State, 1986.

State	Alien	Black	Native American	Asian	Hispanic	White	Total Non-white
Alabama	0.5	20.1	0.2	0.3	1.6	77.4	22.6
Alaska	1.9	4.3	6.8	2.4	2.0	82.6	17.4
Arizona	0.8	3.2	4.6	1.6	11.7	78.1	21.9
Arkansas	0.3	19.6	0.7	0.7	0.6	78.1	21.9
California	2.4	7.8	1.4	9.3	13.4	65.7	34.3
Colorado	1.9	3.2	1.1	2.1	19.5	72.2	27.8
Connecticut	1.0	8.1	0.2	1.3	3.8	85.4	14.6
Delaware	0.7	12.1	0.4	1.2	1.4	84.3	15.7
Florida	2.0	9.1	0.3	1.4	11.4	75.7	24.3
Georgia	1.9	18.3	0.2	1.0	0.8	77.8	22.2
Hawaii	1.5	1.3	0.3	71.5	1.6	23.8	76.2
Idaho	2.2	0.4	0.8	0.4	1.7	94.5	5.5
Illinois	0.2	17.0	0.4	3.2	7.5	71.7	28.3
Indiana	0.1	10.2	0.4	0.5	1.0	87.9	12.1
Iowa	0.8	2.2	0.3	1.0	0.7	95.1	4.9
Kansas	0.6	6.1	2.4	0.8	2.0	88.1	11.9
Kentucky	0.2	8.2	0.4	0.4	0.2	90.6	9.4
Louisiana	1.6	28.7	0.3	1.8	3.5	64.1	35.6
Maine	0.3	0.2	0.6	0.3	0.1	98.5	1.5
Maryland	0.9	16.3	0.3	2.9	1.6	78.0	22.0
Massachusetts	1.0	6.3	0.3	2.0	4.0	86.5	13.5
Michigan	0.5	10.2	0.8	1.0	1.3	86.2	13.8
Minnesota	0.5	1.7	0.8	1.7	0.5	94.8	5.2
Mississippi	0.3	28.0	0.5	0.3	0.9	70.0	30.0
Missouri	0.5	12.1	0.3	0.7	0.7	85.6	14.4
Montana	0.1	0.2	20.8	0.1	0.2	78.6	21.4
Nebraska	0.3	4.9	2.1	0.8	1.4	90.6	9.4
Nevada	0.4	4.2	2.2	2.7	4.9	85.6	14.4
New Hamp.	0.3	0.7	0.1	0.2	0.3	98.3	1.7
New Jersey	1.1	10.6	0.3	2.8	7.3	77.9	22.1
New Mexico	0.4	1.8	13.7	0.5	22.2	61.4	38.6
New York	0.8	13.2	0.7	2.3	9.3	73.7	26.3
N. Carolina	0.5	17.9	0.9	0.9	0.6	79.2	20.8
N. Dakota	0.7	0.9	11.8	0.6	0.3	87.7	14.3
Ohio	0.4	8.9	0.3	0.6	0.8	89.1	10.9
Oklahoma	1.6	6.8	4.6	1.7	1.4	83.9	16.1
Oregon	0.7	1.3	1.0	3.3	1.8	91.9	8.1
Pennsylvania	0.2	9.4	0.2	1.4	1.5	87.4	12.6
Rhode Island	0.0	3.8	0.5	1.5	2.4	91.7	8.3
S. Carolina	0.5	25.0	0.3	0.6	1.2	72.5	27.5
S. Dakota	0.7	0.4	10.0	0.4	0.1	88.3	11.7
Tennessee	0.2	16.6	0.2	0.6	1.4	81.0	19.0
Texas	1.0	10.4	0.4	2.4	17.3	68.4	31.6
Utah	2.0	1.2	2.4	2.4	2.8	89.3	10.7
Vermont	0.8	0.4	0.4	0.2	0.2	98.1	1.9
Virginia	0.8	12.1	0.3	3.0	1.4	82.5	17.5
Washington	0.0	2.7	1.9	5.0	2.0	88.5	11.5

Table 7. Percentages of Racial and Ethnic Composition of
Enrollments in Two-Year Colleges by State, 1986, Cont'd.

State	Alien	Black	Native American	Asian	Hispanic	White	Total Non-white
W. Virginia	0.0	3.1	0.1	0.3	0.2	96.1	3.9
Wisconsin	0.1	5.4	0.8	1.5	1.2	91.1	8.9
Wyoming	0.4	1.2	1.6	0.4	2.7	93.7	6.3
Total U.S.	1.1	10.0	1.0	3.8	7.7	76.4	23.6

Source: National Center for Education Statistics, 1986a.

College had a 31 percent Hispanic student body in a California city
where 32 percent of the population was Hispanic (Rendon and
others, 1988). But there were shifts in participation rates, too;
Hispanic students in California community colleges increased by 44
percent between 1981 and 1986, while black student enrollments
were decreasing by 26 percent.

More so than in the universities, the community college
student population tends to reflect the ethnic composition of the
institution's locale. Community colleges in cities with high proportions of minorities—Chicago, Cleveland, El Paso, Los Angeles,
Miami, New York, Phoenix—enroll sizable numbers of minority
students. The evidence of neighborhood attendance is revealed
where the community college has several campuses in the same city.
At East Los Angeles College in the mid-1980s, 65 percent of the
students were Hispanic; at Los Angeles Southwest College, 87
percent were black; and at Los Angeles Pierce College, 75 percent
were white. This pattern was not confined to the cities; community
colleges in rural areas with high minority populations, as in many
areas of Mississippi, Texas, and California, similarly attracted large
numbers of minorities. Several community colleges were established
especially to serve Native Americans. Oglala Lakota College (North
Dakota), Haskell Indian Junior College (Kansas), Navajo Community College (Arizona), and Bacone Community College (Oklahoma)
are notable examples.

Because the issue of minority students' progress in college
has been so charged politically, the question whether the community colleges have enhanced or retarded progress for minority

students has been debated at length (see, for example, Astin, 1982; Richardson and Bender, 1987; Richardson and de los Santos, 1988). Those who say that the community colleges have assisted minority students point to their ease of access, low tuition, and minimal entrance requirements. They note the numerous programs that provide special services to minority students, and they applaud the efforts made to recruit them. Their most telling argument is that a sizable percentage of those students would not be in college at all were it not for the community colleges.

As detailed by Cohen (1988), several analysts have charged that minority students who begin their college education at a community college will do less well than those of equal ability who enroll at the senior institution and that this differential is greater for them than it is for the majority of students. These detractors have taken the position that because students who begin at a community college are less likely to obtain baccalaureate degrees, minorities are actually harmed by two-year institutions. What is the evidence? The best estimates suggest that white students, who comprise 75 percent of community college enrollment, obtain 85 percent of the associate degrees; black students, 13 percent of enrollment, obtain 8 percent of the associate degrees; Hispanic students, 6 percent of enrollment, obtain 4 percent of the degrees. (These figures suggest not only differential achievement but also the imprecision of the term *minority student*.)

It is difficult to disaggregate the effects of community colleges from the characteristics of the students who enter them. In general, students who enter community colleges instead of universities have lower academic ability and aspirations and are from a lower socioeconomic class. The various studies that have attempted to control for those variables frequently also attempt to control for the fact that minority students are more likely to attend school part-time, and the community colleges encourage part-time attendance. Minority students are also more likely to be from low-income families, and community colleges have low tuition.

The question whether community colleges are beneficial to minority students is thus unresolved. If sizable percentages of minority students would not attend any college unless there were a community college available, and if the act of attending college to take even a few classes is beneficial, then community colleges have certainly helped in the education of minority students. But if the presence of a convenient community college discourages minority students from attending senior institutions and reduces the probability of their completing the baccalaureate, then for those students who wanted degrees the college has been detrimental.

The question is not whether minority students tend to be concentrated in two-year colleges; they do. The question is not whether they tend to go through to the level of the associate degree and then transfer to the university; as a group they do not. The question is what effect the community colleges have on *all* their students. And the answer is that they have a similar effect on all their students, minority and majority. The colleges tend not to be designed primarily for the purpose of passing students through to the baccalaureate. The issue must be seen in its total context; it does not merely affect the minorities.

The program completion rate of minority groups in community colleges must also be viewed in association with their record in other levels and types of institutions. During the 1960s around 3 million pupils began the first grade each year; in the 1980s around 35,000 doctoral degrees were awarded annually. Obviously, most of the students left the school system somewhere along the way, but where? The progress made by these 3 million students in graded education was different for minority and majority students. As a group, minority students began at a point of lower academic achievement, and the difference between them and the majority students increased through the grades toward graduate school. Similarly, the number of minorities dropping out of graded education was greater at each year along the way.

Those who would understand the effect of community colleges should visualize two lines representing continuance in school. If one line shows majority students' persistence and the other minorities', the two will not be parallel; the line representing the majorities will show the lesser attrition. The lines will be farther apart (the difference between minority and majority students will be greater) at grade 14 than at grade 12; fewer of the minorities are in college. Figure 1 depicts the trends graphically. Those who argue that the community college does a disservice to minorities will

Figure 1. Progress in the Educational System. Percentage of
Cohort Entering Fifth Grade.

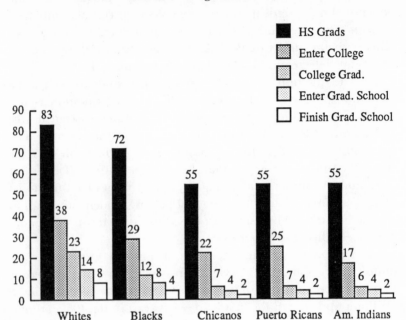

Source: Astin, 1982, p. 175.

point to the gap between minority and majority students' persistence in college. But they usually fail to note that a comparison between the groups for *any* two years of graded education, from kindergarten through the doctorate, would show a similar difference. Thus, because minority students tend to be clustered more in community colleges, the charge is made that they do less well in those institutions.

If the purpose of the collegiate enterprise is to pass most students through to the baccalaureate degree, then the community college is a failure by design. Its place in the total scheme of higher education ensures that a small percentage of its matriculants, minority or majority, will transfer to universities and obtain the baccalaureate. It draws poorly prepared students and encourages part-time and commuter status. Its students perceive the institution as being readily accessible for dropping in and out without penalty. They know they need not complete a program soon after leaving secondary school; the institution will be there to accept them later.

Whom do the community colleges best serve? Egalitarians would say that the institutions should maintain parity in the percentage of each ethnic group attaining each of the following goals: entering college, enrolling in transfer-credit courses, persisting in any courses, gaining the associate degree, gaining admittance to a high-level technological program, graduating from such a program, transferring to the university at any point, and transferring to the university at the junior level. In practice, however, this level of equivalence is impossible to attain, short of imposing strict quotas at every step. For the minorities as for any other identifiable student group, the question should be put more broadly: "The community college or what?" For most students in two-year institutions, *the choice is not between the community college and a senior residential institution; it is between the community college and nothing.*

Classifying the Students

The classification of students into special groups is more politically inspired than educationally pertinent. Women, ethnic minorities, and the handicapped were able to have their concerns translated into special programs only after they became politically astute. In the later 1960s and early 1970s, ethnic and women's studies courses were widely adopted, and programs for the handicapped, complete with their own funds, were established. By 1984 more than 800 ethnic studies courses were being offered in California community colleges, and one college in five included such a course in its general education graduation requirements (California State Postsecondary Education Commission, 1985b). However, the educative dimension of these programs—the desired learning outcomes—still rested on traditional academic forms. Where it did not, the students, however classified, were not well served.

Similarly, the program classifications—transfer, credit, evening, and so on—were hardly justifiable from the standpoint of education. They related to funding channels, not to teaching forms.

The temptation to place a course or a student in a category for which special additional funds were available was always present. The mature woman with a bachelor's degree, taking an art class for credit because it was taught by someone she admired and was scheduled at a time of day that was convenient for her, was not deserving of the special treatment accorded to "returning women," "the aged," or "students intending to transfer." She was there for her personal interest. Yet, because of the politically and institutionally inspired definitions, she would be counted each time the institution reported its numbers of women, aged, and transfer students.

The temptation to classify students has always been present. Assessments of community college students have been made from perspectives that span the social sciences: psychological, sociological, economic, and political. To the psychologist, community college students are pragmatic, little concerned with learning for its own sake. They are not self-directed or self-motivated; they need to be instructed. To the sociologist, the students are struggling to escape from their lower-class backgrounds; some do, but many are inhibited by a bias against leaving family and friends that a move in class would engender. To the economist, students from low-income families pay more in the form of forgone earnings as a percentage of total family income than their counterparts from higher-income groups, a differential that more than offsets the savings gained by attending a low-tuition institution. To the political scientist, students attending community colleges are given short shrift because the institutions are funded at a lower per capita level than the universities, and hence the students do not have equivalent libraries, laboratories, or faculty-student ratios available to them.

For decades community college students have been categorized as more practical, pragmatic, and short-term-goal oriented than students who begin at universities. On the Omnibus Personality Inventory (a multiphasic test standardized on students in two-year and four-year colleges and universities in the early 1960s), the one scale on which two-year-college students typically exceeded the others was Practical Orientation. Drawing on his lengthy experience as a community college administrator, Monroe (1972, pp. 199–200) asserted that "community college students tend to place more emphasis on receiving immediate goals and rewards than on postponing the possibility of winning greater rewards at some future date. . . . A relevant education means practical, occupationally oriented education."

But determining the reasons that students attend college is not an exact exercise. They come for a variety of reasons, and the same person may have a half-dozen reasons for attending. Much depends on the way the questions are asked and the interpretations that the respondents make. There can be little doubt that, although most students attend community colleges to better themselves financially, a sizable percentage are there for reasons of personal interest having nothing to do with direct fiscal benefit. The Center for the Study of Community Colleges' 1986 national survey found 36 percent seeking transfer; 34 percent, job entry skills; 16 percent, job upgrading; 15 percent, personal interest.

The conventional belief is that community college students—in contrast to students in four-year colleges—are less interested in academic studies and in learning for its own sake; instead, they are interested primarily in the practical, which to them means earning more money. Although some research evidence supports that belief, the perception that higher education is particularly to be used for occupational training seems to be pervasive among students in all types of institutions. According to CIRP data (Astin and others, 1988), 86 percent of the entering freshmen in two-year colleges noted "get a better job" as a very important reason in deciding to go to college; but 81 percent of matriculants in four-year colleges and universities gave the same reason. Similarly, although 77 percent of the freshmen entering two-year colleges gave as an important reason "make more money," 70 percent of freshmen at four-year colleges and universities said the same thing. All these figures were up from previous years.

Whether or not these characterizations are correct, they mean little to institutional planners. Certainly, community college students are realistic, in the sense that they use the institutions for their own purposes. But what students do not, in schools where attendance is not mandated? Certainly, many are from lower social classes than those attending the universities, but their class base is higher than that represented by the majority of Americans who do not attend college at all. Certainly, many are from the lower-income groups, but their attendance usually leads to higher earnings. Certainly, they welcome an instantly responsive institution; whether they are harmed by the college's failure to maintain standards in curriculum and a consistent philosophical base is less certain. And they do respond favorably to the variety of instructional media available to them, although the effects of nonpunitive grading and forgiveness for past educational sins on their proclivities for learning have not yet been traced.

Unaware of all these analyses, the students continue attending the community colleges for their own purposes. Those just out of high school may matriculate merely because they have been conditioned to go to school every time September appears on the calendar. Students of any age wanting a better job may attend because the career programs are connected to the employers. Those who have jobs but want additional skills may hope to find a short-term program that will teach them to use the new equipment that has been introduced in their industry. Many begin at the introductory level and learn complete sets of job skills enabling them to qualify for trades that they might have known nothing about before entering the programs. Some students seek out special-interest courses ranging from "The Great Books" to "Poodle Grooming," taking a course or two whenever one that strikes their fancy appears in the class schedule. Some use the community colleges as stepping stones to other schools, finding them convenient and economical entry points to higher education and the professions.

The community college certainly serves a broader sector of the population than does any other higher education institution. Flaherty (1988) compared the student body of an Illinois college with the population of the district it served. He found that 6.5 percent of the district's population aged seventeen and older was enrolled. Male enrollment in degree-credit courses was 2 to 1 over that in non-degree-credit areas, but female degree-credit enrollment was at a ratio of only 7 to 6. Nearly half of the continuing education students had a bachelor's degree, whereas only one-fourth of the general population of the district had a bachelor's degree. The family income for community college students was somewhat lower than the average family income in the district. A similar study conducted at a Maryland college found 5.2 percent of the adult residents of the district taking credit courses at the college (Nespoli and Radcliffe, 1983). In a study conducted by the Eagleton Institute of Politics (1987), the family income of students in New Jersey community colleges was much like the income level for the state as a whole. In general, the community colleges draw a wide variety of students—from those with low income to a sizable number of college-degree holders.

Transfer Rates

Reliable data on students intending to transfer are difficult to obtain. Many colleges have maintained policies of counting as a transfer student anyone who is taking a credit course but is not enrolled in an occupational program—a procedure that throughout the history of the community college has undoubtedly contributed to inflated figures on the number of students intending to transfer. Another procedure is to ask students about their intentions. However—except for those who already have higher degrees and those who are enrolled in occupational programs with a license to practice available at the end of their community college work—few students are willing to forgo their options for a higher degree; hence, few will say that they never intend to transfer to a senior institution. The community colleges have fostered the idea that periodic college attendance is not only available but also desirable. Their matriculants cannot reasonably be expected to say that they plan no further education.

The transfer rates for community college students must be considered in the light of student aspirations; here, different data support different conclusions. Among first-time, full-time freshmen entering two-year institutions, more than 80 percent aspire to at least a bachelor's degree eventually (Astin and others, 1988). However, when *all* entering students are asked their primary reason for attending, as in studies done in Virginia (Adams and Roesler, 1977), Maryland (Maryland State Board for Community Colleges, 1983), Illinois (Illinois Community College Board, 1986a), California (Field Research Corporation, 1984), and Washington (Meier, 1980), the proportion of bachelor's degree aspirants drops to around one-third, a figure corroborated in the Center for the Study of Community Colleges' 1986 survey of students enrolled in credit courses nationwide.

Reliable data on the number of students actually transferring are not readily obtainable either. The data may or may not reflect transfers to state colleges only, to private institutions, or to universities out of state. They may include students who transfer after taking only a few courses at the community college, those who stay out of school for a time before transferring, and so on. Data from the same state in successive years may not even be comparable. No one knows what the transfer numbers for the nation truly are. However, several crude estimates of transfer rates have been made. In Maryland, one of the few states where reliable data are collected, three years after initial enrollment in a community college, 18 percent of the students had transferred to an in-state university, 10 percent had graduated but not transferred, 14 percent were still enrolled, and 57 percent were not participants in the state's higher education system (Clagett, 1986). McIntyre (1987) concluded that half of the students who received bachelor's degrees from the California State University and one-fifth from the University of California "did some of their work at a California community college" (p. 158). The Washington State Board for Community College Education (1989) noted that 36 percent of the students graduating from Washington's public institutions had received credit for some courses completed at one of the state's community colleges. Using data from the National Longitudinal Study of the High School Graduating Class of 1972, Adelman (1988, p. 40) reported that "1 out of 5 individuals who attend two-year colleges eventually attends a four-year college. . . . This is the true 'defacto' transfer rate."

Merging data from the few states and colleges that collect them with the numbers of associate degrees awarded yields another estimate of transfer rates. In 1986 around 350,000 associate in arts and associate in science degrees were awarded by community colleges. Since around three-fourths of the students receiving associate degrees matriculate at senior institutions, a figure of 275,000 transfers with associate degrees seems a good estimate. Probably another 300,000 to 400,000 transfer without having received the degree. These figures suggest a transfer rate of around 12 to 13 percent of the total community college student population of 5 million. However, if the roughly 625,000 transfers are divided by the number of students who say that transfer is their primary reason for attending (around 1.7 million), the transfer rate goes up to 36 percent. Which figure is more reflective of the colleges' contribution to student progress?

Undoubtedly, the percentage of students who transfer from community colleges to senior institutions has declined in recent years. The absolute number of transferring students has increased because of expanding populations; but—when compared with the much greater increases in students who enroll in courses that lead to immediate employment, courses that enhance job skills, and courses taken only for personal interest—the number of traditional bacca-laureate-bound transfer students has shrunk as a percentage of the whole.

Goal Attainment and Dropout

To transfer to a senior institution, enter the job market, get a better job, or merely learn for one's own purposes: these are students' chief reasons for attending community colleges. How do they fare?

Several studies have pointed out the difficulties experienced by students who transfer. Statewide data collected in Illinois (Illinois Community College Board, 1986a), Florida (Florida State Department of Education, 1983), and Georgia (Hand and Prather, 1984a, 1984b), as well as at numerous individual colleges, including Delta College (Montesi, 1986), College of the Sequoias (Webb, 1985), and Community College of Philadelphia (1984), have shown that students transferring typically suffer a slight drop in grade point average. However, this tendency is not as pronounced as it was formerly, and several single-college studies show no difference (Lucas, 1986a, 1986b; Al-Sunbul, 1987; Scott, 1986; Beavers, 1982). Many students lose credits, although that loss also has been attenuated in recent years as statewide and individual college articulation agreements become more pronounced.

According to statewide studies conducted in Maryland (Radcliffe, 1984) and Illinois (Illinois Community College Board, 1986a) as well as at individual colleges, such as Nassau Community College (Fernandez and others, 1984), students who transfer to universities with a large number of credits and/or with an associate degree tend to do better than those who transfer with only a few credits. Statewide studies in Florida (Florida State Department of Education, 1983), Illinois (Anderson and others, 1986), and Kansas (Doucette and Teeter, 1985) show that students who transfer take longer to obtain baccalaureate degrees and are somewhat more inclined to drop out than are those who entered the university as freshmen. Menke (1980) found that baccalaureate recipients at UCLA who had transferred from community college took 1.4 years longer than natives did to earn the degrees.

The reasons that students transferring to universities have had a difficult time there can only be surmised. Possibly the native students were tied into an informal network that advised them on which professors and courses were most likely to yield favorable results. Transfers may have satisfactorily completed their distribution requirements at the community colleges but could not do as well when they entered the specialized courses at the universities. Community colleges may have been passing students who would have failed or dropped out of the freshman and sophomore classes in the senior institutions. And, as a group, the community college students were undoubtedly less able at the beginning. All these variables probably operated to some degree and tend to confound the reasons for junior-level dropout and failure.

Astin (1977) has said that, for those who begin at a community college, "even after controlling for the student's social background [and] ability and motivation at college entrance, the chances of persisting to the baccalaureate degree are substantially reduced" (p. 234). He found that the following factors lead to the attainment of a degree: residence on campus, a high degree of interaction with the peer group, the presence of good students on the campus, and full-time-student status. But these factors are rarely found in community colleges. Few two-year institutions have residence halls; in most states, especially those with a hierarchical public higher education system, the community college students are of lesser ability; most are part-timers; and most have jobs off campus. Thus, the combination of individual and institutional factors at the community college level operates distinctly to reduce the probability that any student will complete the two years and transfer to a baccalaureate-granting institution.

Determining the intrainstitutional procedures that affect dropout tells only part of the story. The colleges' efforts to recruit and enroll sizable numbers of students must also be considered. Community colleges have made tremendous efforts to bring in a variety of students. They established off-campus recruitment centers and sent vans staffed with counselors into shopping centers and parks. They advertised in newspapers and conducted telephone solicitations. Some of the advertising campaigns were planned as carefully as sophisticated marketing plans used by private business enterprises. These efforts shifted in the 1980s as budget reductions made it more difficult to provide noncredit activities for special groups. But attracting students to degree-credit programs remained a high priority in institutions where fiscal survival was tied directly to the number of people in classrooms. These efforts certainly contributed to maintaining enrollments, but they also tended to attract sizable numbers of students with only a casual commitment to college-level studies.

The admissions procedures alone, which allowed students to enter classes almost at will, certainly contributed to the dropout rate. Studies of the reasons that students drop out of college rarely considered the strength of their initial commitment, but it seems likely that a student who petitions for admission, takes a battery of entrance tests, and signs up for classes six months in advance of the term is more genuinely committed to attending than one who appears on the first day of classes without any preliminary planning. Data on students' ethnicity, prior academic achievement, and degree aspirations pale in comparison with the essential component, the degree of their personal commitment. Tinto (1975, p. 93) has asserted that any valid study of dropout must consider the intensity of the student's "educational goal commitment . . . because it helps specify the psychological orientations the individual brings with him into the college setting."

Studies of student dropout may be only marginally relevant to an institution that regards accessibility as its greatest virtue. The community colleges have organized themselves around the theme of ease in entrance, exit, and reentry. Having made a considerable effort to recruit students and to offer them something useful, most faculty members and administrators do want to keep them enrolled, at least until degree or program objectives have been fulfilled. But it is difficult for an institution built on the theme of easy access to limit easy exit.

How many students achieve their goals in community colleges? The information given by students on matriculation is typically flawed, representing a forced choice not often congruent with the students' actual purposes. Students usually have more than one reason for attending college, and the importance of one or another may shift over time. Students may enter because there are few attractive alternative pursuits and because they think it would be nice to have a college degree and, along the way, to be prepared for some type of higher-level employment. Few information-gathering forms force students to search themselves for the dominant purposes; even if they did, few students could make those distinctions consistently. Student goals shift frequently.

Student retention is the most frequently studied topic in the community college research literature. College staff members continually seek to determine why students drop out and whether their reasons are related to college practices. Most studies analyzing persistence in college find that personal factors are considerably more important than institutional factors in determining whether students stay or leave. Students drop out because of job-hour conflict, change of residence, transfer to another college, and other such personal matters as the difficulty in sustaining study and employment simultaneously or in managing family finances and responsibilities. Many drop out because they have obtained the goal for which they matriculated; they may have needed only a course or two to satisfy their objectives. And many students who have dropped out intend to return. These students, frequently part-time attendees, withdraw when employment or some other activity seems more attractive, but later they return and attend intermittently. The colleges may count them as dropouts when they fail to maintain enrollments in successive terms, but they prove often to be those who seek only a few courses now and then to satisfy their personal interests or to learn the skills they need for job entry or promotion.

This pattern of ad hoc attendance seems to fit the desires expressed and demonstrated by students who are using the colleges for their own purposes. Follow-up studies that have tended to confirm the institution's value for students with short-term goals include numerous single-college studies—for instance, at Mesa Community College (Montemayor and others, 1985), San Diego Community College District (1986), Butler County Community College (Olszak-McClaine, 1986), and Mercer County Community College (McMaster, 1984). The rare statewide studies that are done— for example, studies in Maryland (Rajasekhara, 1986)—usually find the same variables related to nonpersistence. Some studies have found that dropout is related to the field in which the student is enrolled. Business and occupational students are most likely to drop out—findings confirmed at John Tyler Community College (Hollins and Smith, 1986) and at Peralta Community College District (1985). Students in those programs would be likely to have attained their short-term goals. Similarly, studies such as one done by Tichenor (1986) have found that part-time students are more likely not to return in successive semesters than are full-time students.

In their quest to differentiate between personal and institutional reasons for student persistence, researchers have analyzed gender, age, and ethnic differences, but with little success. Persistence is much more goal related than demographic. Some studies have revealed that students who register late or at the last moment are more likely to drop out. Sova (1986) and Gray and Hardy (1986), for example, have shown the relationship between commitment, as revealed by time of registration, and student persistence. Cotnam and Ison (1988) found that sizable proportions of the students who leave plan on returning to obtain new skills or to fulfill the objectives for which they enrolled originally. To summarize a sizable body of research on student persistence: Retention and dropout seem to be concerns for the institution, not the individual. Few of the reasons that students give for leaving are amenable to amelioration by the college.

These findings have not deterred college leaders, who constantly seek ways of maintaining institutional enrollments. Puyear

(1987) details the marketing and retention efforts under way in Virginia's community colleges—efforts ranging from vigorous recruitment in the high schools to various types of intervention in the colleges. Some colleges have approached the problem of retention by organizing sophisticated student flow records, so that certain types of students in certain programs can be identified early and worked with to assist in retention. Lee (1987) and Lucas (1986b) detail these efforts at Los Rios Community College District and William Rainey Harper College, respectively. Some of the colleges have adopted marketing efforts, using techniques and organizational characteristics familiar to business corporations with consumer products to sell; Atwood-Canter (1985) provides an example of such an effort.

During the 1970s and 1980s community colleges awarded associate degrees and occupational certificates to only about 9 percent of their students each year. Some commentators find these figures distressing, saying that an institution ostensibly dedicated to human development should not deliberately encourage students to attend part-time and to leave without completing a program. But the students who attend community colleges for only a short time and then transfer or go to work without receiving a degree or certificate of completion may be the pragmatic ones. The associate degree itself has had little value in the marketplace—a fact acknowledged by the AACJC, which organized an "Associate Degree Preferred" campaign (Parnell, 1985) to encourage students to obtain degrees and employers to give preference to those who have them. The proponents of program completion policies must continually battle not only the students' and employers' perceptions but also the universities that readily accept transfers without associate degrees and the educators whose goal is to maintain the community colleges as passive environments providing ad hoc studies for anyone at any time.

Tracking

Curriculum tracking within the colleges has risen and fallen with the times. Throughout their early years the community colleges typically administered achievement tests to matriculants and attempted to place students in courses presumed consonant with their abilities. Students were shunted from transfer to remedial or occupational programs, a practice that gave rise to the "cooling-out" thesis. A 1968 report concerning *A Developmental Program for Metropolitan Junior College, Kansas City,* is instructive. The report recommends that a profile for each student be put together before the counseling interview. Then—

1. Students whose total profile presents a picture of being at or above the mean for college freshmen (on national norms) may be encouraged to enter a college-parallel program. . . .
2. Students whose total profile places them in the middle 50 percent could be expected to succeed in an associate degree collegiate-technical-level occupational education program.
3. Students in the top half of the lower quartile could be encouraged to enroll for a vocational-level program where the emphasis would be on specialized manipulative skills, rather than on further academic and cognitive work. It is unlikely that students in the lower quartile of academic ability will succeed in collegiate-technical-level programs.
4. Finally, those students whose profiles indicate that they are at or below the 10th percentile should be required to enroll in one or more developmental courses or clinics [p. 55].

Most institutions of the time also maintained academic probation, *F* grades, one-term dismissal of students not making satisfactory progress, transcripts required for admission, entrance tests, midterm grades, penalties for dropping classes after the eighth week, mandatory exit interviews, required class attendance, and mandatory orientation courses. However, during the early 1970s these practices fell into disfavor as many students demanded the right to enter courses of their own choosing. Further, measuring students' abilities has never been an exact science; a student deficient in one area of knowledge may be well qualified in another, and stories of abuses in program tracking are common. Educators rationalized their inability to assess their students accurately by saying that anyone had the right to try anything, even if it meant failure. The 1970s saw an erosion of course prerequisites as surely as the dress codes had been abandoned in an earlier day.

By the end of the decade, the pendulum had swung back, propelled more by the students than by changes in institutional philosophy. The career programs were being reserved for the favored few, while the transfer curricula were entered by those unqualified for the technologies or uncertain of their direction. This use of the collegiate courses by the less able, by those waiting for billets in the more desirable programs to open, and by those trying to make up deficiencies in prior preparation may have contributed to the high dropout rates. Subtly but decisively, the collegiate programs were being transformed into catchalls for the unable and/or uncommitted students.

More recently, the community colleges have groped for a middle ground between linear, forced-choice, sequential curricula and the lateral laissez-faire approach of letting students drop in and take any course they wanted. Recognizing that neither of the extremes was feasible and that neither best served the clients, the staff in most institutions attempted to maintain some semblance of counseling, orientation, and testing to determine why the students had appeared and how they could best be helped. But students were using the college for purposes other than those anticipated by the program planners. Except for those enrolled in the selective-admissions high-technology and allied health fields, few students attended courses in the sequence envisaged by program planners. The drop-in and drop-out approach had gained the day.

Even though the planned programs were often out of phase with students' course-taking patterns, the students seemed remarkably well satisfied with their experiences at community colleges. In study after study, the students have reported that the colleges had provided them with what they were looking for. Most graduates, as high as 90 percent and more in many studies (Maryland State Board for Community Colleges, 1983; Leone, 1984), said they would recommend the community college to others as a useful place to begin. Even Astin (1977) found community college students more satisfied than their university counterparts with the quality of their programs. He also found it "somewhat surprising that students at community colleges are relatively satisfied with the social life" (p. 235).

Assessment

Moves toward encouraging students to matriculate in and complete programs gained momentum during the 1980s. One of the first requirements was to test the students at entry, place them in the programs commensurate with their aspirations and abilities, and demand that they make steady progress toward completing the program. For example, Miami-Dade Community College established a policy of assessing students, mandating certain courses, and placing on probation or suspending students who were not making satisfactory progress toward completing a program—in short, reinstating the policies under which most institutions had operated fifteen years earlier (Middleton, 1981). During the first two years that the policy was in effect, several thousand students were dropped from the rolls, but enrollments eventually stabilized and student attendance patterns increasingly reflected the changed policy.

The practice of requiring testing and program placement spread, often prodded by legislators who were appalled at the dropout rates. Florida, Georgia, New Jersey, Tennessee, and Texas rules mandated that all entering students or students seeking degrees or transfer take tests in the basic skills. Most of the California colleges were requiring tests as the state moved toward obligatory placement procedures. And numerous community colleges in states where testing had not been mandated were beginning to require testing on their own. At least half of the colleges in Arizona were requiring that students take an English placement examination prior to registration (Rivera, 1981a, 1981b). The Southern Regional Education Board (Abraham, 1987) found that twice as many two-year colleges as four-year colleges in its region had policies governing testing and placement; almost one hundred combinations of seventy different tests were being used, including thirty-one different reading tests and thirty-six different standardized mathematics tests (Abraham, 1986). A national survey found that, although the majority of the two-year colleges accepted all persons over eighteen who had earned a high-school diploma, almost 90 percent of them used tests to place first-time students (Woods, 1985).

Resnick (1987) has likened the testing movement in higher education in the 1980s to a similar development in the high schools of America in the decade prior to 1925. He believes that the same developments gave rise to both: a rapid expansion in the percentage of the age group attending school; a curriculum shift away from the liberal arts to the so-called practical subjects; a policy of open access leading to automatic promotion; a shift from private to public schooling. These trends led to demands for accountability from many quarters, especially from legislatures alarmed at the rapidly increasing costs and the questionable effects.

The move was not without its detractors. Some felt that state-mandated testing would lead to a reduction in institutional ability to serve various types of clients. In 1988 a group of Latino rights organizations sued one of the colleges on grounds of discrimination in access (*Los Angeles Times,* May 15, 1988). Others deplored the tests' effects on curriculum; students take the courses that teach them to pass the tests, and mandated exit tests invariably are built on generalized content. And, as noted by Losak (1987), few people within the institutions were sufficiently sophisticated to prepare, administer, and interpret tests and report on institutional effectiveness. For most faculty members, who had never been called on to report student learning in any way other than by normative grades, a period of training would be required.

Still, any institution needs to demonstrate its usefulness to society if it is to continue to be supported. When a school that people are not obliged to attend continues to enroll greater segments of the population, its administrators can argue that it must be offering something of value to those who are investing their own time and money. They can also argue that enrolling ever greater percentages of the population is a social good because the more people who are exposed to schooling, the more likely it is that intellectual leaders will emerge from among them. If intellectual ability in the population is distributed on a probability basis, intelligent people will come forth if more are given access to schooling. By that line of reasoning, any restricted educational system runs counter to social policy, whether the restriction is by wealth, sex, race, or scholastic test.

Questions of program completion pale in that light. The better question to ask is *"Of what value is the community college even to those people who do not graduate or transfer to a baccalaureate degree-granting institution?"* By their nature, by deliberate intent, the community colleges sought to become open-access institutions. They vigorously recruited the part-timers, the commuting students, the students who were working off campus. To attract these students, they abandoned most of the punitive grading, academic probation, class attendance requirements, and other policies designed for the more traditional students. Who can estimate the extent of the social need they were fulfilling?

Issues

Institutional planners will continue to face questions about the numbers and types of students properly enrolled in community colleges. For example: How can they separate the serious students from the people attending merely for the financial benefits? How can they prevent the nonserious students from abusing the system without jeopardizing open access?

Questions of finances will also impinge. Should the colleges continue marketing their programs and attempting to recruit students from every source? Faced with limited finances and enrollment caps, as in Washington, they may have to reduce those efforts. What do static enrollments mean to an institution that has prided itself on growth?

Which groups have first claim on the institution? If enrollment limitations mean that some students must be turned away, who shall they be? Those of lesser ability? Those with indistinct goals? Lists placing the categories of potential students in order from highest to lowest priority may have to be developed.

The designations "transfer," "remedial," and "occupational" are institutionally inspired. They do not accurately describe the students' intentions. What more realistic categories might be defined?

Colleges can control the types of students they attract by

expanding or contracting off-campus classes and by enforcing student probation and suspension procedures more or less stringently, to name but two obvious means. Who should decide on the policies and hence the student types?

Historically, the community college student has been defined as one who is enrolled in a course. Yet some colleges have taken steps to purge their rolls of those who were not making satisfactory progress toward completing a program. Must the definition of *student* rest on sequential attendance? Can colleges find some other way of classifying people who want only to use the campus for the social interaction it provides?

How will the recent moves toward assessing students at entry and demanding that they make continual progress toward completing a program affect enrollments of various groups? How will they affect retention and program completion?

And the broadest questions of all: Which people benefit most from, and which are harmed by, an institution that allows all to attend at their pleasure? For which students should society pay full fare? The personal and social implications of these questions give way rapidly to the political and fiscal as soon as they are put to the test.

Three

---·····（◇◇）ᐳ·ᐧᐧ---

Faculty:
Building a
Professional Identity

As arbiters of the curriculum, the faculty transmit concepts and ideas, decide on course content and level, select textbooks, prepare and evaluate examinations, and generally structure the conditions of learning for the students. In common with nearly all teachers, they are not independent practitioners. They work in institutions and are subject to the rules thereof; the workplace shapes their behavior. At the same time, they communicate with their colleagues and take on the mores of the profession.

The Workplace

Community college instructors rarely write for publication, but when they do, and when they speak at conferences or are polled in surveys, they often reveal persistent concerns about their workplace. In an issue of New Directions for Community Colleges on the theme *Responding to New Missions,* one instructor began an article, "Let's be candid about the major issue in the community college today: the low academic achievement of its students" (Slutsky, 1978, p. 9). This instructor noted the demoralization of faculty members who had expected to be teaching college-level students but who found few able students in their classes. She reported the concern felt by instructors who believed that the decline in student ability was encouraged by institutional policies over

65

which the instructors themselves had no control. And she deplored the colleges' practice of recruiting students with offers of financial aid, remediation, and inappropriate occupational programs—and especially their attempts to retain on the rolls even those students who would not show up for class, let alone keep up with their course work.

Similar attitudes about the peculiarities of the community college environment were reported by the instructors interviewed by Seidman (1985). Those in the traditional academic disciplines were most likely to feel out of place because of their institutions' commitment to students and to curricula with which they had little affinity. But many found the community college a personally satisfying environment. They welcomed their role and were highly involved with their teaching.

People willingly endure incredible levels of discomfort when they believe that they are striving for a higher cause. The history of saints and soldiers, monks and missionaries reveals that when superordinate goals are dominant, participants relinquish the tangible rewards that they might otherwise think are their due. But when faith or patriotism wanes, demands for more immediate benefits increase, and the group must provide extrinsic incentives to sustain its members' allegiance. Eventually, a formal organization evolves, with ever stricter rules of conduct guiding the lives of its people, who themselves have since been transformed from participants into workers.

Many two-year colleges began as small adjuncts to public secondary schools, and their organizational forms resembled the lower schools more than they did the universities. Their work rules and curricula stemmed from the state education codes. Mandated on-campus hours for faculty members, assigned teaching schedules, textbooks selected by committees, and obligatory attendance at college events were common. Institutional size fostered close contact among instructors and administrators. The administrators held the power, but at least they were accessible, and face-to-face bargains could be struck regarding teaching and committee assignments. And as long as the institution enrolled students fresh from high school, the faculty could maintain consistent expectations.

The major transformation in the community college as a

workplace came when it increased in size and scope. Size led to distance between staff members; rules begat rules; layers of bureaucracy insulated people between levels. Decision making shifted from the person to the collectivity, decisions made by committees defusing responsibility for the results. The staff became isolates— faculty members in their academic-freedom-protected classrooms, administrators behind their rulebook-adorned desks.

As the colleges broadened their scope, the transformation was furthered: first career education, then adult basic studies, compensatory programs, and—unkindest of all from the faculty viewpoint— the drive to recruit and retain apathetic students. Numerous instructors—who may have regarded themselves as members of a noble calling, contributing to society by assisting the development of its young—reacted first with dismay, then with apathy or antagonism to the new missions articulated by college spokespersons. Feeling betrayed by an organization that had shifted its priorities, they shrank from participation, choosing instead to form collectivities that would protect their right to maintain their own goals. The *Gemeinschaft* had become a *Gesellschaft*.

Whether or not collective bargaining in community colleges resulted from this transformation, it did enhance faculty well-being, although not nearly as much as its proponents had hoped or as much as its detractors had feared. The working conditions most obviously affected were class size, the number of hours instructors must spend on campus, the out-of-class responsibilities that may be assigned to them, the number of students they must teach per week, and the funds available for professional development opportunities. Because all these elements were associated with contractual requirements, informal agreements between instructors and administrators about switching classes, trading certain tasks for others, released time in one term in return for an additional class in another, were rendered more difficult to effect. Work rules often specified the time that could be spent on committee service, media development, and preparing new courses. In brief, the contracts solidified the activities associated with teaching, binding them by rules that had to be consulted each time a staff member considered any change; hence, they impinged on the instructors as though they had been mandated by an autocratic administration.

The People

Although it is possible to generalize in only the grossest way when one is describing 275,000 people, demographically the community college faculty differ from instructors in other types of schools. The proportion of men is lower than in universities, higher than in secondary schools. Most of the faculty members hold academic master's degrees or equivalent experience in the occupations they teach; they are less likely to hold advanced graduate degrees than university profressors are. Their primary responsibility is to teach. They rarely conduct research or scholarly inquiry. They are more concerned with subject matter than are their counterparts in the secondary schools, less so than university professors. On a full-time basis they conduct four or five classes per term, thirteen to fifteen hours a week. Sixty percent are part-time employees at their colleges. Many, both full- and part-timers, sustain other jobs in addition to their teaching.

Except for increases in age and teaching experience, the demographics of community college faculty have been consistent over recent years. Full-time instructors, who account for fewer than half of the faculty by head count, teach three-fourths of the classes. Two-thirds are men. Studies conducted in the 1970s and 1980s showed the faculty's aging. One-third of the humanities instructors nationwide were thirty-five years of age or younger in 1975, but since few new instructors were employed during the ensuing years, that age group had dropped to 15 percent by 1983 (see Table 8). Well over half the faculty in 1983 had been at their current institution for more than ten years, up from only 17 percent in 1975 (see Table 9). In some districts this change was quite notable. For example, in 1983, 20 percent of the faculty teaching the liberal arts in the Los Angeles Community College District were sixty-one years of age or older. During this same period the proportion of minorities in the academic areas increased from 6 to 10 percent.

When the size and number of community colleges were increasing rapidly, the question of the proper training and experience for instructors was frequently debated. Should instructors have prior experience in the lower schools? Should they hold the doctorate? What qualities were needed? The answers varied, but

Table 8. Age of Humanities Faculty at Community Colleges.

Age	1975 (N = 1,493)	1983 (N = 1,467)
25 and under	1%	1%
26-30	12	3
31-35	20	11
36-40	16	21
41-45	13	19
46-50	14	14
51-55	10	13
56-60	8	8
61 and older	6	11

Source: Cohen and Brawer, 1987, p. 64.

Table 9. Length of Time Humanities Faculty Have Taught at
Present Institution.

Years	1975 (N = 1,493)	1983 (N = 1,467)
Less than one year	10%	7%
1-2 years	14	6
3-4 years	17	8
5-10 years	42	25
11-20 years	15	48
Over 20 years	2	6

Source: Cohen and Brawer, 1987, p. 64.

the flow of instructors into the community colleges can be readily traced.

Beginning with the earliest two-year colleges and continuing well into the 1960s, instructors tended to have prior teaching experience in the secondary schools. Eells (1931) reported a study done in the 1920s showing that 80 percent of junior college instructors had previous high school experience. In the 1950s Medsker (1960) found 64 percent with previous secondary or elementary school experience. Around 44 percent of new teachers of academic subjects entering two-year colleges in California in 1963 moved in directly from secondary schools, and others had had prior experience with them (California State Department of Education,

1963–64). However, as the number of newly employed instructors declined in the 1970s, the proportion of instructors with prior secondary school experience declined with it. More were coming from graduate programs, from the trades, and from other community colleges.

Preparation

The master's degree obtained in a traditional academic department has been the typical preparation. The doctorate has never been considered the most desirable degree; arguments against it may be found from Eells in 1931 (pp. 403–404) to Cohen and Brawer in 1977 (pp. 119–120). During the 1920s fewer than 4 percent of the instructors at two-year colleges held the doctorate. By the 1950s the proportion had climbed to between 6 and 10 percent, and there it remained for two decades; Blocker (1965–66) reported 7 percent; Bayer (1973), 6.5 percent; Medsker and Tillery (1971), 9 percent. By the mid-1970s it had reached 14 percent as fewer new instructors without the degree were being employed, and many of those already on the job were concurrently receiving advanced degrees. In the early 1980s the proportion exceeded 20 percent— largely because of the relatively stable employment scene, coupled with the tendency for instructors to obtain doctoral degrees so that they would move higher on the salary schedule. Table 10 shows the proportions of instructors holding bachelor's, master's, and doctor's degrees from 1930 through 1984. Graduate degrees were rarely found among teachers in career programs, where experience in the occupations along with some pedagogical training was considered the best preparation, but among the liberal arts instructors in many colleges, the proportion with the doctorate had surpassed 25 percent (Cohen and Brawer, 1987, p. 67).

Preservice Training. Regardless of the degree titles and types of programs, an emphasis on breadth of preparation and on people sensitive to the goals of the community colleges and the concerns of their students has been a standard recommendation. Calls for these types of people have been made not only by community college administrators but also by major professional and disciplinary

Table 10. Highest Degree Held by Instructors at
Two-Year Colleges (Percentages).

Year and Source	Less Than Bachelor's	Bachelor's	Master's	Doctorate
1930 Wahlquist (cited in Eells)	7	29	54	9
1941 Koos (cited in Monroe)	3	27	64	6
1957 Medsker (cited in Monroe; includes administrators)	7	17	65	10
1969 National Center for Education Statistics		17 (includes both)	75	7
1972 National Center for Education Statistics	3	13	74	10
1979 Brawer and Friedlander	3	8	74	15
1984 Carnegie Faculty Study (cited in Ottinger)	5	10	63	22

Sources: Eells, 1941a, p. 103; Monroe, 1972, pp. 148, 248; National Center for Education Statistics, *Digest of Education Statistics*, 1970, 1980; Brawer and Friedlander, 1979; Ottinger, 1987, p. 118.

associations. But few community college instructors were prepared in programs especially designed for that level of teaching. Few had even taken a single course describing the institution before they assumed responsibilities in it; a 1949 survey found that fewer than one-tenth of practicing instructors had taken such a course (Koos, 1950). Eells (1931) had recommended that people entering two-year-college instruction after having secondary school experience take intervening work at the university, but not many took that route.

Several well-integrated graduate school–based programs for preparing community college instructors have been established, and especially tailored degrees have been introduced on numerous occasions. The Master of Arts in Teaching received some support during the late 1960s, when colleges were expanding rapidly and seeking well-qualified staff, and the Doctor of Arts was promoted by the Council of Graduate Schools and the Carnegie Commission on Higher Education. The programs usually include a base of subject matter preparation in an academic department, some pedagogical preparation, and a period of practice teaching or internship. These programs continue to be offered, some at the more prestigious universities, but they have not become widespread; well over half of the Doctor of Arts in Teaching degrees awarded in 1981 were granted at just four institutions, and even at these institutions program enrollments had declined by one-third over the prior four years (Dressel, 1982). None, including the especially sponsored programs for instructors in areas of short supply, has ever developed as a major source of community college instructors.

In-Service Training. Although formal in-service training had been a feature of the community colleges throughout their history, calls for expanding that activity reached a peak as institutional expansion subsided, and relatively few new staff members were employed. Who would teach the new students and handle the different technologies? Faculty members already there had their own priorities, based on their expectations when they entered the college and their subsequent experience within it. Administrators had found it much easier to employ new instructors to perform different functions than to retrain old instructors—a procedure that worked well as long as expansion was rapid. But when the rate of change exceeded the rate of expansion, when new priorities were enunciated more rapidly than new funds could be found, the residue of out-of-phase staff members increased—hence the calls for staff development.

Several types of in-service preparation programs have been established. The most common have been discipline-based institutes, released time, sabbatical leaves, and tuition reimbursements for instructors to spend time in a university-based program, as well as short courses or workshops on pedagogy sponsored by single institutions or by institutional consortia. Studies such as those conducted in Iowa (D. J. Miller, 1985), Illinois (Wallin, 1982), New York (Winter and Fadale, 1983), and Texas (Richardson and Moore,

1987) revealed these preferences. Instructors sought courses and programs in their teaching field, offered by universities close at hand, so that they could gain further knowledge in their sphere of interest; degrees and credits that would enable them to rise on the salary schedule; and time off from their teaching responsibilities. Administrators, in contrast, preferred workshops and seminars offered on campus for the instructors, with the content centering on pedagogy and community college-related concerns.

Paid leaves for professional development were written into many negotiated agreements between faculty associations and their institutions. And some states—for example, Florida in the 1970s and California in the 1980s—appropriated sizable funds to be used for staff development at the college's discretion.

Salary, Tenure, Work Load

Comparisons of faculty salary, tenure, and work load shed light on the profession and the workplace. Except for the part-timers paid at an hourly rate, salary ranges for community college instructors have tended to be higher than in secondary schools, lower than in universities. Eells (1931) reported that the median salary of the best-paid instructors in the 1920s was about the same as that of a starting professor in the universities. But most community college instructors were able to reach the top of the salary scale in twelve or fifteen years, whereas in the universities more steps intervened although a higher ceiling was available. The ratio shifted somewhat when collective bargaining made deep inroads, and the tops of the salary schedules were lifted, but the university ranges remained greater. In the 1980s, according to tables showing average salaries in public institutions, community college faculty consistently received lower salaries than faculty in four-year colleges and universities. The differential widened from less than 7 percent at the beginning of the decade to nearly 10 percent in 1985–86 (Snyder, 1987).

Tenure patterns in community colleges more closely resemble those in the lower schools than they do the procedures in universities. Tenure is awarded after a single year or, in many cases, after a probation of two to three years; the practice rarely approximates the seven-year standard common in universities. Although tenure rules vary from state to state, in some states tenure is awarded simultaneously with the award of a full-time teaching contract. That is, after a one-year contract has been tendered and the instructor has fulfilled his or her responsibilities, a contract for the succeeding year can be demanded unless the institution can show cause that the instructor is not deserving of it. Often, unless it is included in the state laws governing community colleges, tenure becomes a negotiable item in contract bargaining.

Faculty work load, usually defined as the number of hours an instructor spends in a classroom and/or the number of students met per week, varies somewhat among teaching fields, but it has been relatively consistent over time. Koos (1925) reported 13.5 hours taught weekly by the full-time faculty in the public colleges of the 1920s, 14.9 hours in the private institutions. Numerous studies conducted since the 1920s have found 13 to 15 lecture hours per week to be the norm. However, this figure does not account for overload. In California, for example, 34 percent of all the full-time instructors were teaching additional courses for supplemental compensation (California State Postsecondary Education Commission, 1985a).

Class size is more variable than teaching hours. Many negotiated contracts specify the maximum number of students that can be assigned to a class, but student dropout invariably reduces class size before the end of the term. Instructors of physical education, music, studio courses in the arts, and courses in laboratory sections usually have the highest number of teaching hours but the smaller class sizes. In Illinois, for example, in the fall of 1987, lecture classes averaged 19.2 students, and laboratory classes averaged 12.8 students (Illinois Community College Board, 1988).

Although the number of hours taught (13–15) seems high when placed against the university faculty's 5 to 9 hours, Clark (1987), who has analyzed the work of both groups, contends that both spend the same amount of time on the job: "If professors teach only introductory courses, and do so frequently, they soon know the materials thoroughly. Little or no class preparation is needed. . . . And time spent on grading need not be any greater than elsewhere, since introductory contents are relatively easy to assess and can be quickly done, particularly by those who turn to machine-scored objective tests" (p. 230). The time spent on the job is the same, but the nature of the work is certainly different. And Cohen and Brawer (1977, p. 142) found that many community college instructors would willingly spend more time in scholarly pursuits, as the university professors do, if they had fewer classes to meet.

Part-Time Instructors

Community colleges have always employed numerous part-time instructors. When most of the colleges were small, Eells (1931) said that they should employ secondary school instructors to teach individual courses in physics, chemistry, and biology instead of having a single instructor present all the college courses in the sciences. Eells's rationale was that part-time specialists have "more expert knowledge" than full-time generalists. Hiring such instructors "makes for closer coordination of the curriculum in high schools and college" (p. 396). He also suggested that junior colleges should make use of university professors as part-time employees, thereby attaining closer coordination of the curriculum between these two institutions. When the community colleges grew large, the argument favoring the part-timers continued to be that the institutions could offer specialized courses in areas that could not support full-time instructors. In the foreign languages, for example, few institutions could afford to employ a full-time teacher skilled in presenting esoteric languages, whereas a part-timer could usually be found for a single course in Norwegian or Gaelic. Part-time instructors also represented a high proportion of the faculty in art, religion, and the numerous career programs that had been established. Specialized business fields have relied on local experts who bring an up-to-the-moment perspective to their teaching.

Part-time faculty members presented college administrators with several additional advantages. They were willing to teach at odd times and locations. Most significant for cost-conscious administrators, their compensation per class might be as little as one-fourth as much as the institution would have to pay a full-timer. In Illinois, for example, the median nine-month base salary for contracted faculty in 1986 was $30,583, and part-time faculty's salary rates averaged $290 per course semester hour. If each full-time instructor taught five three-hour courses per semester, the average course would cost $3,058, whereas the three-hour course taught by a part-timer would cost $870. And these figures do not include fringe benefits, which for the full-timers average $2,405 per year (Illinois Community College Board, 1987a), thus adding another $240 to each course. Moreover, the part-timers' right to their job was weaker; hence, they could be dismissed more readily when enrollments fell. In the 1970s a slowly evolving tendency toward pro rata pay and continuing contracts for part-timers began, but most of the part-time faculty still receive pay at a lesser rate and face the threat of discontinuance at the end of each term.

The ratio of part-time to full-time instructors has changed during various stages of community college development. In the early years sizable percentages of the instructors were part-timers. As the colleges matured, they were more able to support a corps of full-time instructors; in the late 1960s almost two-thirds were so employed. But since then the ratio of part-timers has increased, so that by 1987 they had reached 58 percent of the total (see Table 11). A dramatic example of that shift is seen in the figures for instructors in the sciences; between 1973 and 1984 the number of full-timers increased by 22 percent but the part-timers by 168 percent (National Science Board, 1986).

The sources of part-time teachers have shifted, too. The early junior colleges sought secondary school instructors because they were qualified teachers, and they sought university professors because they lent an aura of prestige. However, by the mid-1970s, only two-thirds of the part-timers working in community college academic programs were employed elsewhere. Instead many retired people were teaching a course or two, and young people completing their graduate studies at nearby universities were teaching part-time for the compensation it afforded and because it provided potential access to full-time positions. Nearly half of the part-timers were age thirty-five or younger.

Are the part-time instructors qualified? Do they teach as well as full-timers? Numerous studies have attempted to answer those questions, but the findings are inconclusive. Cohen and Brawer (1977) reported studies showing that the part-timers are less experienced. They have spent fewer years in their current institu-

Table 11. Numbers of Full-Time and Part-Time Instructors
in Two-Year Colleges, 1953–1987.

Year	Total Instructors	Full-Time Instructors		Part-Time Instructors	
		Number	Percentage	Number	Percentage
1953	23,762	12,473	52	11,289	48
1958	33,396	20,003	60	13,394	40
1963	44,405	25,438	57	18,967	43
1968	97,443	63,864	66	33,579	34
1973	151,947	89,958	59	61,989	41
1978	213,712	95,461	45	118,251	55
1979	212,874	92,881	44	119,993	56
1980	238,841	104,777	44	134,064	56
1981	244,118	104,558	43	139,670	57
1982	236,655	99,701	42	137,060	58
1983	251,606	109,436	43	142,170	57
1984	252,269	109,064	43	143,205	57
1985	228,694	99,202	43	127,681	56
1986	274,989	110,909	40	164,080	60
1987	256,236	107,608	42	148,628	58

Source: American Association of Community and Junior Colleges, Community, Junior, and Technical College Directory, 1955–1988.

tions, they are less likely to hold memberships in professional associations, they read fewer scholarly and professional journals, and they are less concerned with the broader aspects of curriculum and instruction and of the disciplines they represent. However, when they are working in the field—for example, when the local minister teaches a course in religious studies or when a realtor teaches courses in real estate—they may be more directly connected to the practical aspects of their work, and they may have a greater fund of knowledge than most full-time instructors. As for the routine aspects of the job, part-timers certainly seem to present few problems; they are just as likely to turn in their grade sheets on time, and their students rate them as highly as they do the full-timers.

The part-timers are difficult to classify because they are only marginally connected with the profession. They may be highly professionalized in another field, graduate students marking time until they complete their studies, or loosely affiliated teachers who commute from job to job, working when they are called upon.

Although they hold the same credentials as full-timers, they occupy a different status. They are chosen less carefully, the rationale being that because the institution is making no long-term commitment to them, there is no need to spend a great deal of time and money in selection. They may be evaluated differently; a California study found that numerous colleges had no evaluation policy for part-timers, and most that did used different procedures for them. Only half as many of the California colleges conducted in-service faculty development programs for part-timers as for full-timers. Three-fourths of the colleges failed to provide part-timers with office space (Sewell and others, 1976). Marsh and Lamb (1975) found that part-timers rarely participated in campus activities and had little contact with students out of class and practically no contact with their peers, a finding corroborated by two other studies (California Community and Junior College Association, 1978; Friedlander, 1979). Fewer than half of the colleges provided part-timers with even limited reemployment rights (California Community Colleges, 1987c).

A broader issue is related to the part-timers' effect on community college teaching as a profession. Clark (1988) deplores the widespread use of part-timers, calling it a "disaster for the professoriate. . . . Nothing deprofessionalizes an occupation faster and more thoroughly than the transformation of full-time posts into part-time labor" (p. 9). In Clark's view part-time work is "the extreme point in the attenuation of both disciplinary and institutional connections, leaving the academic worker relatively rootless" (p. 8). He ranks it as one of the three most debilitating aspects of the community college faculty member's life, the other two being "a weakening of the intellectual core of academic work" (which occurs "where instructors only teach introductory materials . . . to poorly prepared students") and the relative reduction in salary levels (pp. 9-10). Nonetheless, college managers are caught in a dilemma, since full-time instructors cost more per class.

Evaluation

The how and why of faculty evaluation have been considered since the community colleges began. Because of the colleges' roots in the lower schools, early evaluations were often conducted by administrators who visited classrooms and recorded their perceptions of instructors' mannerisms, appearance, attitude, and performance. As the colleges broke away from the lower schools, and as the faculty gained more power, evaluation plans became more complex. Peers and students were brought into the process, and guidelines were established for every step. These procedures often gained labyrinthine complexity; rules specified how often evaluations would be made, how much time they would take, who was to be involved, at what point the instructors would be notified of the results, which people or committees would notify them, how long an instructor's file would be maintained, who would have access to the file, and what steps would be involved in the appeal process.

Superficially, the procedures gave the appearance of attempting to improve instruction. Practically, they had little effect. If an instructor was to be censured, dismissed, or rewarded for exceptional merit, the evaluation records provided essential documentation. But only a minuscule percentage of the staff was affected. Instructors who wanted to improve could act on the commentary of peers, administrators, and students. Those who chose instead to ignore the feedback could do so. Only the instructors who were far distant from any semblance of good teaching—for example, those who failed to meet their classes regularly—could be called to task. In general, the most minimal evidence of classroom performance or student achievement satisfied evaluators.

Faculty associations' intrusion into the evaluation process proved a mixed blessing. Frequently, the contracts mandated that the whole faculty be involved in evaluation at every step of the way. This involvement would be a step toward professionalization because, by definition, a profession should police its own ranks, set standards of conduct, and exercise sanctions. However, faculty bargaining units leaned considerably more in the direction of protecting their members from judgments made by administrators than toward enhancing professional performance. The types of faculty evaluation in vogue at the time the contracts were negotiated tended to be written into the rules. The forms, checklists, and observations remained the same.

Still, faculty evaluation persists because it suggests that the institution and the profession are concerned with improving and policing their ranks. Nearly all institutions engage in it on some basis—from pro forma procedures to satisfy a set of rules, to more genuine attempts to affect instruction. As several studies have shown (for instance, Renz, 1984; Collins, 1986), evaluations related to instructional practices can be useful in enhancing perceived effectiveness; however, evaluations conducted for the primary purpose of satisfying external agencies have little effect and the staff tend to be dissatisfied with them. Attempts to link faculty evaluation with merit pay have been tried numerous times, but with limited success. Seniority remains dominant as a determinant of salary level.

Burnout and Satisfaction

The term *teacher burnout* entered the literature in the 1970s, although by the mid-1980s it was seen less frequently. It referred to instructors who were weary of performing the same tasks with few apparent successes and a lack of appreciation for their efforts. The term supplanted *dissatisfaction,* which connoted a malcontent. *Burnout* suggested people whose fatigue was caused by environmental pressures beyond their control. A reduced rate of institutional expansion had led to an aging faculty and, because most colleges paid increments for years of service, their faculty crowded toward the top of the salary schedules. Many members of that group found few new challenges in their work and despaired of facing a succession of years doing the same tasks for the same pay. They turned to other jobs on their off hours. Always present in some measure, moonlighting became more prevalent.

Actually, faculty satisfaction and dissatisfaction have been traced for some time. For the first half century of community college history, when most faculty members were recruited from the secondary schools, positive attitudes among the faculty were the norm. Moving from a secondary school to a college faculty position offered both higher status and a reduced teaching load. Consequently, most studies of faculty satisfaction found that it was related to the conditions under which the person entered the institution. Older faculty members—those who were appointed from secondary school positions, who entered teaching after retiring from a different type of job, who had made a midlife career change, or who were teaching in career programs after being affiliated with an occupation—showed up as the more satisfied groups. The younger instructors—who may not have thought of themselves as career teachers but who found themselves performing the same tasks year after year with little opportunity for the revitalization that accompanies a new challenge—were the dissatisfied ones.

Teacher burnout may well be more related to age and stages of adult development than to the workplace. Cohen and Brawer (1977) surveyed 1,998 instructors in 156 two-year colleges in 1975 and applied their construct of satisfaction to the responses. They found a high positive correlation between faculty age and satisfaction (in Table 12 compare the percentage of instructors in each age group with their percentage in the high-, medium-, and low-satisfaction columns). Lee (1977) traced adult development in that same sample of instructors and found satisfaction related to distinct developmental stages. Faculty members in their twenties and thirties were less satisfied, while those in their early forties seemed to be experiencing stress as they encountered a middle-age transition. Instructors fifty-six and older had a high level of satisfaction. Women of all ages revealed a greater concern for students. Lee

Table 12. Satisfaction Among Community College Faculty
Members by Age, 1975.

Age	N	Percentage of Total Sample	Satisfaction (Percent)		
			High	Medium	Low
Under 26	19	1.3	0.8	1.5	1.1
26–30	181	12.1	6.7	12.4	15.3
31–35	303	20.3	11.4	20.4	26.4
36–40	242	16.2	18.1	15.6	16.4
41–45	195	13.1	11.0	13.0	14.7
46–50	206	13.8	18.1	14.3	9.4
51–55	142	9.5	11.0	9.9	7.5
56–60	113	7.6	14.2	6.1	6.4
Over 60	92	6.2	8.7	6.8	2.8

Source: Cohen and Brawer, 1977, p. 27.

recommended that colleges begin providing mentors (older adults working with younger staff members) and in-service programs that would work with instructors during their transition stages.

However, burnout may be a more complex phenomenon. Organizational or external demands have often been related to dissatisfaction, whereas intrinsic attitudes have been considered responsible for satisfaction. Herzberg, Mausner, and Snyderman (1959) postulated a "two-factor theory"; that is, the elements leading to personal satisfaction are related to the content of the work, whereas the environment surrounding the worker leads to dissatis-faction. Several studies of community college instructors have traced this duality. Cohen (1973b) found that feedback from students was most likely to lead to feelings of satisfaction, whereas characteristics of the workplace, such as lack of support from ad-ministrators and colleagues or institutional red tape, led to dissatis-faction. Wozniak (1973) also identified interpersonal relations with students and a sense of accomplishment in teaching as determinants of satisfaction among the instructors he studied, whereas dissatisfac-tion stemmed from institutional policies, administrative demands, and similar extrinsic characteristics. Statewide studies of faculty in Pennsylvania (Hill, 1983) and New Jersey (Ryder and Perabo, 1985) have confirmed the thesis.

In the 1984 Carnegie survey of faculty in all types of colleges and universities (cited in Ottinger, 1987), community college faculty indicated that they value teaching higher-order students and higher-level classes and being involved more with their academic disci-plines. But they know how unlikely it is that these values can be realized; hence, they rationalize their work and enjoy what they have; to fail to do so would be to doom them to constant frustration.

This attitude of satisfaction coming from personal interac-tion with students and privacy in the classroom also found its way into the contracts negotiated by faculty representatives and the community college districts. In fact, it may have been one of the bases of the drive toward unionization. If a faculty member's feeling of self-worth depends in great measure on being left alone to fuse content and style of teaching, it follows that faculty members as a group are uniquely qualified to make decisions concerning what and how they shall teach. Thus, one reason for the polarization between the faculty and the administrators and trustees that accompanied the rise in collective bargaining may have been that the faculty sensed that only people who were currently engaged in instruction could understand the way instructors feel. "Recommendations about a new teaching method coming from faculty members are more likely to be considered by teachers while information presented by administrators . . . can be ignored" (Purdy, 1973, p. 181). In the CSCC studies faculty members rated their colleagues highest as potential sources of advice on teaching (Cohen and Brawer, 1977).

Many of the changes that have occurred since most faculty members were employed might have been expected to lead to dissatisfaction. An increase in the number of ill-prepared students made it more difficult for instructors to find satisfaction in effecting student achievement. A reduction in the number of specialized courses made it less likely that an instructor would be able to teach in an area of special interest. More students tended to be part-timers, dropping in and out of school; as a result, faculty could not sustain relationships with these students beyond one term. The percentage of students completing courses fell sharply, so that instructor satisfaction in seeing individual students through even a single course was reduced. More formal requests for measures of productivity were installed, along with demands that instructors present evidence of student achievement. And the feasibility of moving from community college to university teaching, or even from one college to another, was reduced as the demand for full-time instructors fell.

London (1978) discussed the effects of one community college on its instructors, noting that faculty members did not have a voice in determining the policy of admitting marginal students; they questioned the open-door policies, and the teaching of poorly prepared students adversely affected their morale. Seidman's (1985) broader sample of instructors similarly expressed dismay with their institutions' policies, which seemed to put these institutions in league with the welfare, parole, and mental health services of the state. They resented all activities that make the colleges seem like those agencies, even though they acknowledged that someone has to educate the masses. Additional detailed information is reported in the nationwide studies conducted by the Center for the Study of

Community Colleges (1978a, 1984). Instructors seemed generally satisfied with their jobs, regarding community college teaching as a worthy career in its own right. Few of them aspired to teach in senior institutions; most of the respondents said that "doing what I'm doing now" in five years would be quite attractive. In fact, that statement was the most popular of nine choices, including "faculty position at a four-year college or university." Similarly, Clark (1987) reported a high degree of satisfaction among instructors who enjoyed their involvement with students. In all the reports, however, faculty members deplored their lack of time to keep up in their field, to develop new teaching approaches, to prepare adequately for their classes, to discuss educational matters with their colleagues, to give adequate attention to individual students, or to participate effectively on faculty committees.

Desires

Like members of any professional group, most instructors would like to improve their working conditions. They want more professional development opportunities, sabbatical leaves, grants for summer study, provisions for released time, and allowances for travel. They also want more secretarial services, laboratory assistance, readers and paraprofessional aides, and other support services. They would like better students, too, more highly motivated and with stronger academic backgrounds. They would like better instructional materials. Many of them are not satisfied with the textbooks, laboratory materials, or collections of readings that they are using in their classes. Many want more and better laboratory facilities. Brawer and Friedlander (1979) reported these findings, and Seidman (1985) corroborated them.

Thus, faculty desires seem to have stabilized. Despite the rhetoric surrounding collective bargaining and contract negotiations, instructors were generally satisfied. They wanted to better their working conditions, but they tended not to aspire to positions at other levels of schooling. Some of their desires were much like those articulated by employees in other enterprises: security and a living wage. Continuity of employment and periodic salary increases were the minimum. The faculty felt threatened when enrollment declines or declining budgets boded to strike at those essentials.

But beyond the basics, the instructors seem unrealistic. They want better working conditions, but that translates into shorter working hours, better-prepared students, and smaller classes. Desirable as these might be, they are difficult to obtain because they run counter to college policies and budgetary realities. As long as colleges are reimbursed on the basis of the number of students attending, instructors will have a difficult time achieving more pay for fewer student contact hours. As long as colleges are pledged to maintain a door open to all regardless of prior academic achievement or innate ability, instructors will be unable to satisfy their desire for students who are better prepared.

Even when the desired changes in the workplace are more realistic, one goal is often in conflict with another. To illustrate: Faculty members, in general, want more participation in institutional decision making, but they dislike administrative and committee work. Seidman's interviewees reported that they could gain power as individuals only by becoming administrators. However, they do not aspire to be administrators; they resent the time spent on committees; they see their classroom activities and their meeting with students outside class as the portion of their workday that brings the greatest satisfaction. But administrative decisions are made in the context of committees, memoranda, and persuasion—a context similar to a political arena. Instructors will not easily attain their goal of participation in decision making as long as they shun the mechanisms through which decisions are made.

The matter of support services offers a second illustration of conflict between instructors' desires. Relatively few instructors have paraprofessional aides or instructional assistants available to them. However, only about one in eight expresses a desire for more of these types of assistants. Apparently, the ideal of the instructor in close proximity to the students remains a paramount virtue. Instructors seem unable to perceive themselves as professional practitioners functioning with a corps of aides. They want to do it all: interact with students, dispense information, stimulate, inspire, tutor—all the elements of teaching—through personal interaction. They do not realize the magnification of influence that they might obtain through relinquishing some portions of their work to para-professionals or assistants.

Through negotiated contracts instructors have tried to mitigate the untoward conditions of the environment and attendant feelings of dissatisfaction. These contracts often make it possible for instructors to be relieved of routine responsibilities and to change their milieu. Provisions for released time to work on course revisions or other projects related to teaching are often written into the contracts. Tuition reimbursement plans that pay instructors to study at universities have been included. Some contracts allow the faculty-student ratio to be spread across the academic department, making it possible to compensate for low enrollments in specialized courses with high enrollments in the department's introductory classes. Funds for travel and for sabbatical leave have also been negotiated.

However, the contracts may not offer enough. No contract can substitute for the feelings of self-worth engendered by the knowledge that one can always escape the current workplace by moving to a different institution. During the 1980s new full-time positions were scarce, and faculty exchange programs were not widespread. Nor could the contracts ameliorate the faculty's feeling that students were poorly prepared and that traditional programs, in which the instructors taught when they entered the institutions, were on the decline. The contracts' provisions for job protection through tenure and elaborate procedures for due process proved of minimal value to people who found themselves forced to teach subjects not of their choosing. The attempts to recruit students to the institution rang like false coin on the ears of instructors, who suspected, with good reason, that these students would be even less interested in affairs of the mind than those with whom they were already confronted. Administrative pleas for retaining students were hardly welcomed by instructors, who felt that students had a responsibility either to pursue the course work satisfactorily or to leave. And few instructors took kindly to calls for grading practices that would not penalize students for failing to perform course work adequately, a policy that had its zenith in the late 1970s and has become less popular since.

Professionalism

The faculty are more nearly teachers than members of a teaching profession. Few of them have access to aides; fewer still rely on them for assistance. Teaching is generally acknowledged to be a solo performance; the door to the classroom is jealously guarded. Collective bargaining has brought greater faculty control over the conditions of the workplace but little change in the process of instruction. For most faculty members, the longer they are at the college, the weaker their affiliation with their academic discipline becomes.

Some commentators have reasoned that the community college is best served by a group of instructors with minimal allegiance to a profession. They contend that professionalism invariably leads to a form of cosmopolitanism that ill suits a community-centered institution, that once faculty members find common cause with their counterparts in other institutions, they lose their loyalty to their own colleges. This argument stems from a view of professionalism among university faculties that has proved detrimental to teaching at the senior institutions; that is, as faculty allegiance turned more to research, scholarship, and academic disciplinary concerns, interest in teaching waned.

However, that argument suggests that a professionalized community college faculty would necessarily take a form similar to that taken by the university faculty. It need not. It more likely would develop in a different direction entirely, tending neither toward the esoterica of the disciplines nor toward research and scholarship on disciplinary concerns. The disciplinary affiliation among community college faculty is too weak, the institutions' demands for scholarship are practically nonexistent, and the teaching loads are too heavy for that form of professionalism to occur.

A professionalized community college faculty organized around the discipline of instruction might well suit the community college. The faculty are already engaged in course modification, the production of reproducible teaching media, and a variety of related activities centered on translating knowledge into more understandable forms. A profession that supports its members in these activities would be ideal. Teaching has always been the hallmark of the colleges; a corps of professionalized instructors could do nothing but enhance it. This form of professionalism might also be applied to curriculum construction. Whereas instructional concerns have been left to the faculty, the propagation of curriculum has been more an administrative charge. A professionalized faculty might well direct much of its attention to designing a curriculum to fit an institution that shifts priorities rapidly.

A professional faculty in charge of the essential conditions of its work could also reconceptualize the academic disciplines themselves to fit the realities of the community colleges. As an example, many of the traditional liberal arts courses are ill suited to the students in the career and compensatory programs that constitute most of the community college effort. More apposite instructional sequences could be designed for those students. Whether a professionalized community college faculty could succeed in the necessary curriculum reformation is not certain; it is certain that a disparate set of instructors cannot do so and that university professors or community college administrators will not lead in this essential reconstruction. Such disciplinary reconceptualization takes stimulation from peers, the contribution of individuals acting as proselytizers, and the application of thought about the core principles in each discipline as they pertain to the variant teaching roles that must be adopted for the different clients. These activities require a professionalized faculty. The future of both the collegiate and the general education functions in community colleges may hang in the balance.

Several efforts have been made to assist faculty professionalization. National journals directed toward two-year-college instructors in mathematics, journalism, and English have been established, and the faculty in some states—including Hawaii, Connecticut, Utah, and New York—have published their own journals. Statewide Academic Senate groups have expressed interest and gained power in curricular affairs. Professional associations, such as the Community College Social Science Association and the Community College Humanities Association, have been formed. Some institutions have fostered professionalism by supporting individual instructors through internal grants for course revision and media preparation. In colleges that employ instructional aides and paraprofessionals, the faculty play a managerial role. The number of foundation and federal grants available to community college instructors has increased, thus offering those faculty members with considerable professional commitment the opportunity to magnify their influence by managing curriculum development projects. In a few colleges the faculty have developed their own projects to modify institutional practices in testing and placing new students. And in a few, as detailed by Parilla (1986) and Vaughan (1988), faculty scholarship and research have been encouraged.

However, the road to professionalization is a long one, and some might say it should not be traveled anyway. All professions have been attacked for their unresponsiveness to clients and their overspecialization. Among faculty members a loss of confidence to prescribe what people should learn reveals a loss of faith in their own vocation. Some of their own professional associations have cautioned them against specifying the outcomes toward which they are teaching, lest they be held accountable, although the calls for institutional and program accountability that have become prevalent have mitigated those cries.

As for burnout, a feasible short-term solution might be to keep the faculty engaged in fulfilling the responsibilities of teaching that reach beyond the classroom. For example, the colleges might provide funds and released time to those who would build better instructional materials or who would conduct research on their programs' effects. Such a provision might also reduce the widespread incidence of instructors' working on jobs unrelated to their teaching.

Other changes seem imminent as instructors realize the importance of program support. The liberal arts instructors at a few colleges have organized lay advisory committees to provide links between campus and community. Composed of influential citizens, such groups have functions far beyond advising on the curriculum in particular programs. Like career education advisory councils, these groups help recruit students to the programs, assist with extracurricular presentations, act as guests in the courses, and, most important, support the programs. They provide a new set of peers for instructors to relate to, and they offer the college a community connection.

Instructors may well expand their role beyond that of class-room teachers to become presenters of information through collo-quia, seminars, lectures, recitals, and exhibitions offered for both students and the lay public. Most faculty members in the academic areas feel there are too few such presentations at their own colleges and want to devote more time to them. The more sophisticated contracts make provision for instructors to act in such capacities and also to manage learning laboratories, prepare reproducible media, or coordinate the work of the part-time faculty.

Some instructors understand the value of presenting infor-mation in large lecture sections. Departments that can generate sizable ratios of student contact hours have often taken advantage of large lectures to support their more specialized courses. Similarly, to enhance flexibility in instruction, college administrators might consider paying instructors from one department to teach short portions of courses in another or using community service funds to augment instructional budgets. These types of funding arrange-ments have proved difficult to effect, but formulas that pay colleges for total programmatic emphases might make them more feasible.

Although instructors at two-year colleges may be moving toward the development of a profession, its lines are as yet indis-tinct. The teaching loads take their toll, but as long as instructors insist on moonlighting and on having close personal contact with students in classes—the smaller the better—the attendant high cost of instruction makes it difficult for colleges to fund the alternatives that could be pursued. The most positive note is that the commun-ity college has become a well-known, visible workplace, not only among its own staff but also among the legislators and agency officials who make decisions affecting its directions. And, as a group, faculty members no longer look to the universities for their ideas on curriculum and instruction, nor do they see the community colleges only as stations on their way to university careers. Com-munity college instruction has become a career in its own right. Its flowering but awaits a more fully developed professional conscious-ness on the part of its practitioners.

Issues

Many of the key issues affecting the faculty center on the continuing untoward separation of the occupational and the academic; the private world of instruction; the separation of the remedial instructors; and the uncomfortably slow development of a unique professional consciousness. Some of these issues can be feasibly managed; others will persevere because of the nature of the profession and the institution.

Will the adversarial relations between the faculty and boards and administrators subside? Are they related primarily to contract negotiations, or are they based in the essence of the institution?

Can teacher burnout be mitigated through deliberate modification of the working environment? Or are moonlighting and psychic early retirement to be permanent conditions?

Will faculties engage in the necessary reconceptualization of their academic disciplines to fit the realities of their colleges? Or will the collegiate programs survive primarily as intellectual colonies of the universities?

Will instructors realize that paraprofessional aides are important for their well-being over the long term? That funds for new media can enhance their satisfaction?

Will administrators continue employing part-timers for the short-term salary savings that accrue? Or will they allow the faculty to build its profession and help it by minimizing the annual influx of teachers?

All these questions relate to the history of the colleges, to the funds available, and, above all, to whether college leaders perceive their institutions as labile structures responding readily to the whims of all comers or as centers of teaching and learning with an ethos of their own.

Four

Governance and Administration:
Managing the
Contemporary College

More has been written about governance and administration than about any other aspect of the community college. Why? Perhaps institutional management is more important or more complex than curriculum, instruction, or student services. Perhaps it presents more options. Perhaps the writers think that they can more easily persuade administrators to change organizational charts than instructors to change teaching practices. Or they may be on a Sisyphean quest for the one best management form. Or it may be simply that people concerned with managing institutions write more than those whose prime interest is teaching students.

The terms *governance* and *administration* or *management* are not discrete. They overlap and are often used interchangeably. They do not clearly depict either institutional functions or precise activities. Peterson and Mets (1987) define them as encompassing both structure and process: governance relates to decision making, management to executing the decisions. Corson (1960, pp. 12–13) defined governance as though the college itself were a government: "the process or art with which scholars, students, teachers, administrators, and trustees associated together in a college or university establish and carry out the rules and regulations that minimize conflict, facilitate their collaboration, and preserve essential individual freedom." However, he also noted the difficulty of separating the established policies from the practices maintained on

92

their behalf; the act of administering a policy is as much a part of that policy as is the statement of rules or laws on which it is based.

Numerous attempts to categorize governance and management have been made, most stemming from observations of university systems. Linear, adaptive, and interpretive systems constitute one set of categories. The linear are directly linked, the adaptive are responsive, and the interpretive are more culturally based (Chaffee, 1986). Other models of governance have attempted to separate the collegial from the political, viewing both as different ways of sharing authority. A management science approach views governance as rational, focused on decision making. A different model for college operations uses the term *organized anarchy* as a way of describing an environment in which no individual or group has much influence (Cohen and March, 1986). Weick (1976) popularized the term *loosely coupled systems* to describe colleges as groups of subunits that interact with one another in unpredictable ways.

In general, it seems that most of the excessively analytical models that have been proposed to explain the workings of universities do not aptly cover the less complex community colleges. However, Richardson (1975) suggested that models must be constructed if the colleges are to be understood. He therefore offered three major models to explain why colleges appear as they do. The bureaucratic model presents the college as a formal structure with defined patterns of activity that are related to the functions spelled out in law and policy decisions. The positions are arranged in the shape of a pyramid, and each series of positions has specified responsibilities, competencies, and privileges. This organization is held together by authority delegated from the top down, with persons at the top receiving greater benefits than those at the bottom; the lowest levels of the triangle are occupied by faculty and students. The political model (following Baldridge's 1971 model) postulates a state of conflict among contending forces—students, faculty, administrators, and trustees—each with different interests. In a quixotic plea for the colleges to become shared learning communities, Richardson (1975, p. ix) postulated a collegial model: "Instead of being at the bottom of a pyramid, faculty and students are part of a community of equal partners.

Authority is not delegated downward as in the bureaucratic model; rather, trustees share their authority with students and faculty as well as with administrators. Students and faculty members communicate directly with the board rather than through the president." The model is based on group process, the concept of community, the sharing of authority, and the making of decisions within a framework of participation and consensus.

Deegan (1985) also described bureaucratic, collegial, and political models and argued that governance can best be analyzed by means of a structure involving periodic examination of goals, staff, and various aspects of the institution. Similarly, Gollattscheck (1985) classified governance systems as bureaucratic, participatory, and conflict models; but he concluded that the style or model of governance has less influence on results than "the quality of care and maintenance the system receives" (p. 86).

The bureaucratic and political models seem most applicable to community colleges. The institutions are organized hierarchically, and compromises among contending forces chart their directions. Colleges are social organizations with their own rules. Despite all the rhetoric about satisfying student and community needs, the procedures maintained in community colleges tend toward protecting the staff's rights, satisfaction, and welfare. The collegial or participatory model is a delusion; the notion that students have much voice in college administration has little basis in reality.

Not excessively concerned with theoretical models, community college managers conduct their affairs typically embroiled in the complexities of the moment, perhaps hearkening to a golden era when rules were few and administration was simple. In its early years, when the junior college was often an adjunct of the local secondary school, the institution was usually administered by the high school principal or by a designate responsible to the principal. The local school board took up junior college affairs as part of its regular responsibilities. As the colleges separated themselves from the local school districts, the newly established boards of trustees similarly concerned themselves with budgetary matters and the selection of presidents who would keep the staff content and the college running smoothly, or at least keep the problems from becoming apparent to the public. Yet as long ago as 1931, when Eells wrote his book on the junior college, he noted that the areas of governance and administration were too varied and comprehensive to be treated completely. Although boards of trustees and administrators may have been able to govern without apparent conflict, issues of financing, staff morale, and conformity with state laws have always been present.

Governing Units

Different forms of college control have been more or less popular at one or another time. In the past two decades, the number of private junior colleges has declined, multiunit college groupings have increased, and nearly all colleges affiliated with local public school districts have severed that connection. The public colleges are now arrayed in single independent districts; multiunit independent districts; state university systems and branch colleges; and state systems, some with innovative patterns, such as noncampus colleges. Individual comprehensive colleges may include specialized campuses or clusters organized around curricular themes.

Independent two-year colleges—a category that includes church-related institutions, private nonprofit colleges, and proprietary schools operated for profit—have varying patterns of control. The ultimate control of church-related colleges is vested in the governing board of the church itself. Boards of control for other independents may be associated with the occupations emphasized, or they may be self-perpetuating bodies composed of concerned philanthropists. Directors of development, also known as fund raisers, are also usually prominent in the college's organizational chart. Because many private colleges still maintain residence halls, there may also be a director in charge of campus life. The proprietary schools are organized quite like the business corporations that they are, with sales and marketing as central features of the enterprise.

Regardless of organizational form, size seems to be the most important variable. In study after study—whether the topic of concern is students, curriculum, library holdings, or unit costs—institutional size, more than any other characteristic, differentiates publicly supported institutions from one another. In addition, the significant differences between public institutions and private junior colleges (which are almost all quite small) appear to be related as much to size as to control.

The Local District. Most public colleges in the nation are organized within single districts. A board of trustees, either elected locally or appointed by a governmental agency, establishes policy for the institution and employs a chief executive officer. Vice-presidents or deans manage business affairs, student personnel, academic instruction, and technical education. In most colleges the department chairpersons report to the dean of instruction or vice-president for instruction. However, in larger institutions, as shown in Figure 2, assistant superintendents and division deans may be added to manage detailed operations under each of the main functions.

The multiunit independent district dates from the 1930s, with Chicago and Los Angeles as early examples. There were ten such districts in 1964, forty in 1968, sixty-six in 1980, and seventy-two in 1987. As shown in Figure 3, these multicollege districts operate with a central district organization headed by a president or chancellor and staffed with research coordinators, personnel administrators, business managers, and numerous others responsible for overall academic, fiscal, and student services.

The multiunit districts typically arose when a college opened a branch campus that eventually grew to a size that warranted an independent administration. However, the trend has not been solely in the direction of single-district, multicollege operation. Some districts, with St. Louis and Miami-Dade as notable examples, operate under a single-college, multicampus format.

Multiunit districts are far more complex, structured, and formalized than single-college districts. Those who advocate centralizing administration generally stress greater economy and uniformity of decisions. After examining forty-five colleges in multiunit districts, Kintzer, Jensen, and Hansen (1969) concluded that highly centralized colleges are characterized by maximum uniformity, impartiality, and efficiency; however, the risk of depersonalization and low morale is increased. Lander (1977) showed that when multiunit districts in Arizona were formed, another stratum of administrators was inserted between the first-line administrators at each college and the district's chief administrator. He concluded that increased size—the major factor contributing to structural differences—forced increases in complexity of function, formality in communication, delegation of responsibility, and centralization of ultimate authority.

Chang's 1978 summary of the differences between centralization and decentralization points to the merits of each. A centralized structure is supposed to eliminate duplication of purchasing, data processing, facilities planning, personnel research, finance, physical plant, and contracting; standardize recruiting, fringe benefits, and payroll and affirmative action procedures; provide specialized personnel for collective bargaining purposes; foster the equal treatment of support services, salaries, promotions, grievances, and resource allocation; minimize rivalry and competition between campuses at the same time that it enhances recruitment campaigns, publicity, grantsmanship, community service, and coordination; facilitate educational program coordination and staff development; and permit the formation of vocational advisory committees for each vocational field rather than one area on separate campuses. At its best, a decentralized structure encourages campus initiative and creativity, allows each campus to respond to the community and students more rapidly, fixes responsibility at a lower structural level, fosters the development of leadership among campus administrators, and enhances staff morale by a greater degree of local participation in decision making.

In their examination of twelve urban multicampus districts, Jenkins and Rossmeier (1974) found that, in the opinion of faculty members and administrators, the most effective organization was one in which participation in decision making was maximized for staff members at all levels, regardless of the nature of the hierarchy. Thus, although decision making occurred with increasing frequency at district headquarters, the characteristics of multicampus districts did not preclude participation by staff members in all the units. However, in multiunit districts decision-making power has tended to gravitate toward the central district administration. Although many chancellors have attempted to share authority with

Figure 2. Traditional Organization Chart for a Large Community College.

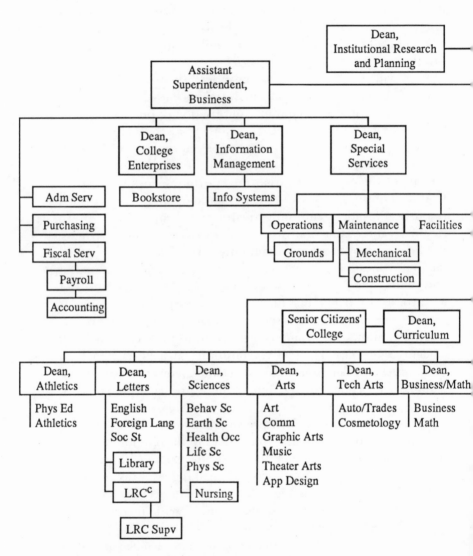

a Affirmative Action / Dean, Student Services
b Title IX / Dean, Arts
c Learning Resource Center

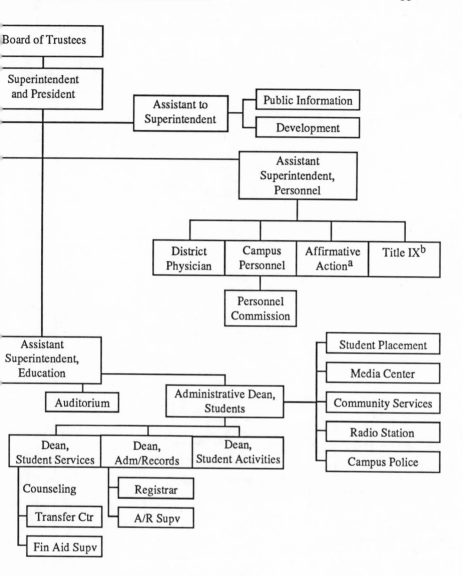

Figure 3. Organization Chart for a Multicollege District.

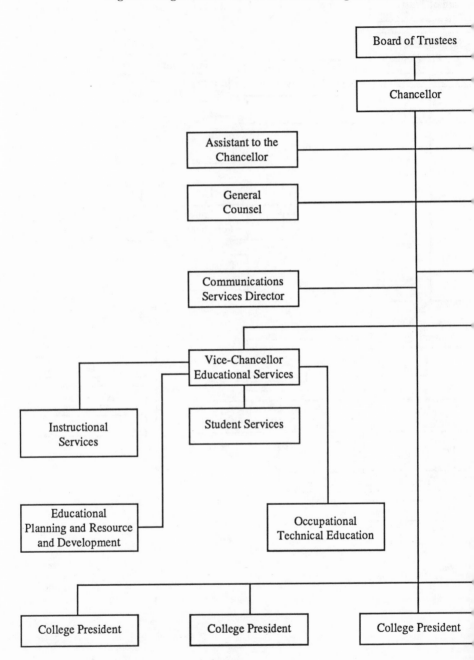

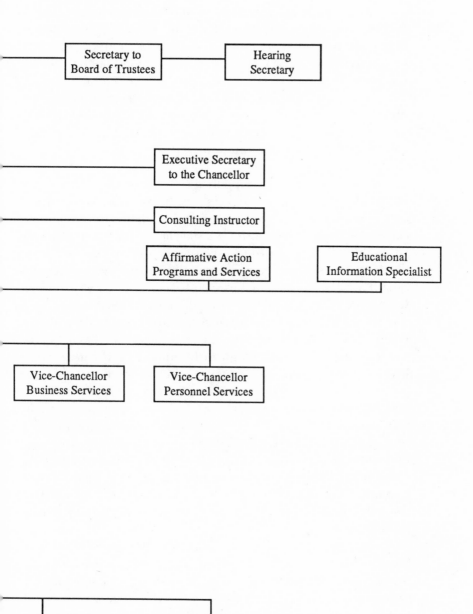

the campus heads, it has been difficult to maintain a decentralized decision-making process when nearly all the factors affecting any unit affect them all. As an example, in nearly all multiunit districts, budget requests may be generated on each campus, but only within the guidelines and limitations set down by the central authority. The central district offices often also maintain separate legal affairs offices to ensure that all decisions on personnel selection and assignments are made in accordance with the terms of the contracts and laws governing the institution.

The State. Publicly supported colleges are under the control of a single authority in numerous states. In 1965 Blocker, Plummer, and Richardson identified twenty states where the community colleges were under the control of a state board of education and six where the colleges reported to a state department or superintendent of education. Separate state junior college boards or commissions existed in only six states; in thirteen others the colleges were under a state board of higher education or the board of a four-year state university. The trend toward state control accelerated with the Higher Education Amendments of 1972, which led to the creation of commissions to coordinate higher education in each state. By 1980 Kintzer (1980a) found fifteen states with boards responsible for community colleges only, five with a university system including two-year colleges, and ten with boards for all of higher education; in addition, fifteen states had boards coordinating all levels of education. Where the state boards had coordinating authority only, they tended to act primarily in fact-finding and advisory capacities. But where they were legally defined governing boards, they recommended budgets and the allocation of state funds, salary schedules, articulation agreements, and the establishment of new institutions.

In states where the public community colleges are under state board control, decisions of funding and operation have become maximally centralized. Connecticut, Delaware, and Minnesota, for example, seem to have one community college with several branches whose presidents report to the state chancellor. Statewide bargaining and budgeting are the norm, although some autonomy in curriculum planning has been reserved for the individual colleges. Figure 4 shows the organization pattern typical of such states.

In many states a combined state university and community college system has been established in order to implement state-level management. More than one hundred two-year colleges, campuses, or institutes affiliated with state universities have been established in eighteen states. Such institutions are prevalent in Ohio and Wisconsin. All public community colleges in Alaska, Hawaii, Kentucky, and Nevada are under the state university system. The university president is the chief executive officer, and the presidents of the colleges answer to the university executives rather than to their own governing boards (see Figure 5). The university boards of regents establish policy. The University of Wisconsin system operates more like a statewide multicampus district, with a chancellor heading the system and each campus under the direction of a dean.

A single state community college board that can exert influence on the state legislature, compete with the university for funding, ensure quality education and equal treatment of faculty, and coordinate a statewide college development system seems appealing. If the boards responsible for community colleges were also responsible for all of higher education, a thoroughly coordinated, economical, and articulated pattern of higher education for the state might result. Ideal in theory, this practice has not been universally adopted; and where it has, its benefits have not been uniformly realized. Institutional competition for support defies any organizational plan.

Increasingly, state agencies have assumed control over expenditures and program planning and have promulgated rules for nearly all aspects of college functioning, from the employment of personnel to the space a college should allocate for different functions. Nonetheless, it is difficult to make a case for the greater efficiency that a trend toward larger units was supposed to bring. In fact, numerous authors (for example, Darnowski, 1978) have documented complaints about duplication, contradictory regulations, and the mass of approvals that must be garnered from various regulatory agencies before college leaders can make a move.

Figure 4. Organization of a State Community College System.

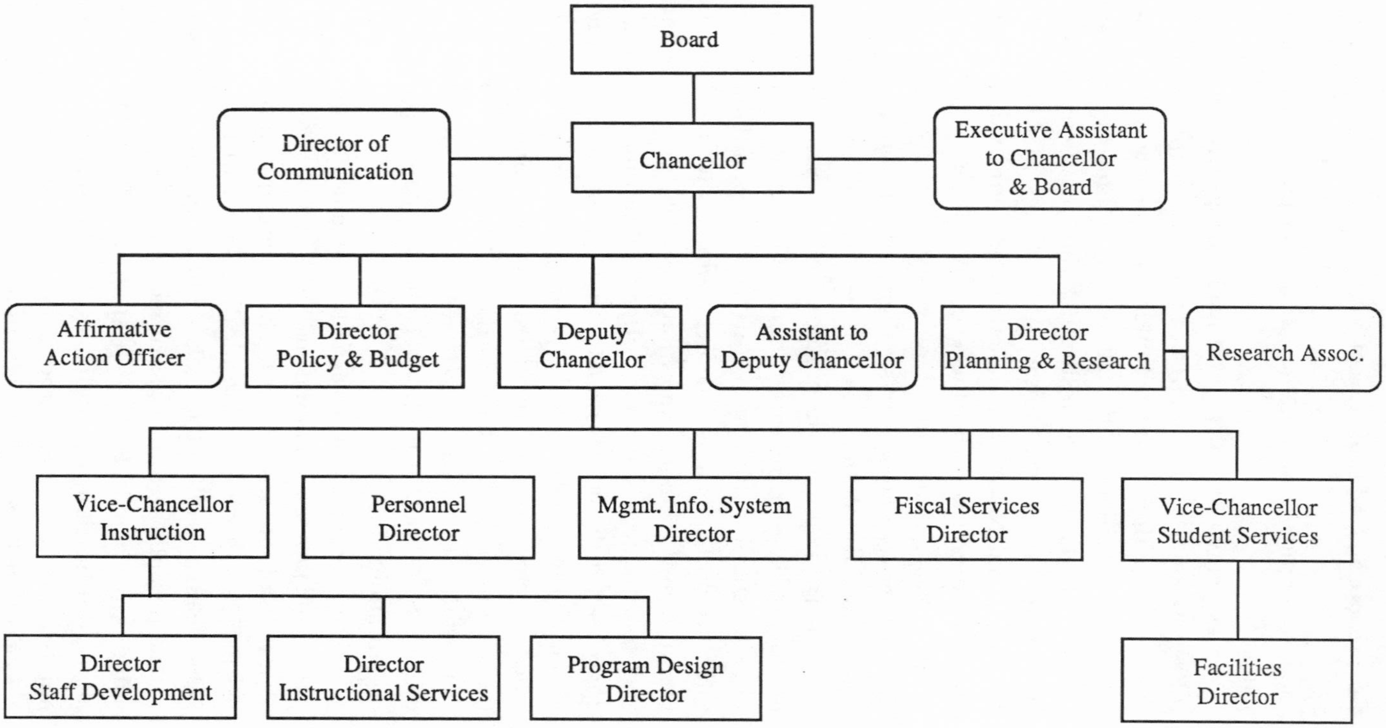

Figure 5. Organization of a University-Controlled Community
College System.

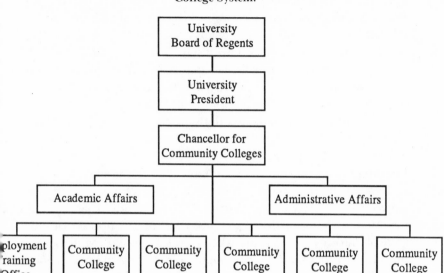

In some states where most of the funds for community colleges are allocated through a state board for community colleges, attempts to retain local autonomy are still being made; but the strains are evident. The problem, however, is not merely one of decision-making authority shared between the local governing board and the state board; it relates also to other state agencies. The state of Washington, for example, has a state board and twenty-two district boards. In addition, executive orders from the governor; directives from the Office of Financial Management; and contractual controls, legal opinions, and audits stemming from numerous state agencies—all "must be taken into account in the decision-making process and in the actual operation of the colleges" (Mundt, 1978, p. 51). Information demands alone are high: "Recently the president of Highline Community College . . . found the college was reporting to twenty-nine outside, third-party agencies in one way or another" (p. 53). In Florida numerous state regulations and agencies impinge on the operation of community colleges— including state laws that provide for public hearings to precede any "rule, fee, degree program, or major catalogue change" (Owen, 1978, p. 26). Puyear (1985) has concluded that 80 percent of the state laws affecting community colleges were not drafted with them as the major focus; instead, the laws are directed toward all of postsecondary education or toward state bodies in general.

Most commentators believe that state-level coordination has made the college leaders' job more difficult and the colleges less responsive to their local communities. Tillery and Wattenbarger (1985) summarize these contentions in their review of the long-standing trend toward state control. However, the advantages of greater state-level coordination have also been documented. Funding has been made more equitable than it was when community college districts depended on local tax revenues and the gap between richer and poorer districts was pronounced. Some states have developed sophisticated management information systems and student information systems wherein all colleges provide data in uniform fashion; the data then can be cross-tabulated for the benefit of planners at individual institutions and can be used to generate reports for other state and federal agencies. Articulation between community colleges and public universities in the same state has also been enhanced when statewide coordination is evident. In addition, a state board is more able to speak to the legislature with a single voice.

Kintzer (1980a) has noted the problems that result when increasing state government surveillance is superimposed on organizational structures designed to serve smaller, more autonomous institutions. He has traced the organizational and administrative changes resulting from the power struggles of collective bargaining, the demands for more sophisticated data to be reported to external agencies, the pressures for budget and personnel accountability, and the new forms of services for students who no longer fit the traditional college-going pattern. The decisions to expand or contract, the rules for admission, and the definition of who should be served and in what way have become governed almost entirely by external forces.

The line between statewide coordination and state control is fine. Many educators would prefer that the resources be provided with no strings attached, since state mandates regarding the programs and services to be provided might unduly restrict their efforts to provide the proper services for their constituents. State-level coordination has certainly magnified the sets of regulations under which the community colleges operate, moved decision making to broader political arenas, and fostered the development of administrators whose chief responsibility is to interpret the codes. But it has also yielded more stable funding, more services for certain groups of students, such as the handicapped, and higher standards of operation; and it has helped to minimize program duplication. The question whether it has been of general benefit or detriment cannot be answered. We can say only that it has changed the ground rules for institutional operation, the professional outlook of the staff, and the way the colleges are perceived by the public. One thing has remained constant: the college trustees and administrators raise the specter of state control every time a state board or legislature rules on funding or curriculum in a way that is counter to their preference.

It is easy to overestimate the influence of the state. Each community college is a complex organization, and its operations and products depend much more on its staff, students, and community than on state policies. For example, most public officials believe that students should progress through the educational system as far as their abilities will take them. Dropout at any level is seen as a waste. However, state policy is not often translated into specific mandates that would enhance the transfer of students from community colleges to universities. A national survey conducted by the Center for the Study of Community Colleges in 1987 found eleven states with projects funded especially to facilitate transfer, seven with legislative mandates, and the majority with various types of negotiated or voluntary agreements between community colleges and state university systems. When state policy is directed toward transfer, significant interventions may be made; in the late 1980s the California legislature made several million dollars available to the community colleges for "transfer centers" and mandated a matriculation plan that sought to identify and place potential transfer students at entry.

Starting a new community college has certainly become a more complex undertaking since state-level coordination became prominent. In the 1920s the local school may have done little more to start a college than to get the state board of education's approval to offer some postsecondary classes. The 1907 California enabling act had stipulated merely that the board of trustees might charge tuition for such classes. Gradually, the criteria expanded to include minimum enrollments, minimum district population, and tax support.

By 1960 the general guidelines for establishing community colleges included "(1) general legislative authorization of two-year colleges, (2) local action by petition, election or action by local board of control, (3) approval by a state agency, (4) a minimum assessed valuation considered adequate for sound fiscal support of the college, (5) a state or local survey to demonstrate the need for the college, (6) a minimum population of school age, (7) a minimum total population of the district, (8) a minimum potential college enrollment, (9) types of educational programs (curricula) to be offered, (10) availability and adequacy of physical facilities, (11) compliance with state operating policies, (12) proximity of other institutions" (Morrison and Martorana, 1960; cited in Blocker, Plummer, and Richardson, 1965, pp. 80-81).

By the 1970s Evans and Neagley (1973) had offered an entire book showing the various patterns of college establishment. They discussed state regulations, local needs studies, and ways of securing local support; spelled out guidelines for appointing and organizing the board of trustees; and presented sample organizational charts and recruiting and selection procedures for staff.

The federal role in community college management has not differed much from its role in all of higher education. The community college sector has taken advantage of federal funding available for certain programs—for example, programs to train technicians, displaced workers, and various categories of underprivileged people. The colleges have eagerly sought these types of funds and built programs accordingly. Federally guaranteed student loans and other categories of financial aid have affected the community colleges less than the higher-cost universities, but they represent an important source of funds for the institutions—survival in the case of proprietary schools. The federal government has insisted that minorities, women, and the handicapped gain access to higher education. As a result, the colleges have had to modify their employment practices in response to affirmative action rulings. However, each state has had a considerably greater influence than the federal government on the policies governing the colleges within its borders.

Nontraditional Organizations

Regardless of the form of institutional control, different organizational patterns have been tried. The "noncampus" college became popular in the 1970s. Because such institutions typically employed few full-time instructors and offered much of their program through reproducible media, often including open-circuit television, their administrative patterns differed. A president would report to a district-wide chancellor, but program directors or associate deans would take responsibility for separate geographical service areas. Further, because of the emphasis on rapid change in course design, instructional planners would be more prominent than department or division chairpersons. Whatcom (Washington), Coastline (California), John Wood (Illinois), Rio Salado (Arizona), and the Community College of Vermont were notable examples of "colleges without walls."

At the other extreme, the continuing search for ways of bringing the decision-making process closer to the faculty and students led to the development of cluster colleges or small, semiautonomous units. The more freedom the smaller unit has to design its own academic program and to set its own rules of conduct for staff and students, the more it fits the ideal of a subcollege operating under the umbrella of a parent organization that provides budgets, legal authority, and general structure. Advocates of cluster colleges have put them forth as the best system for bringing students and staff into the process of making decisions about the types of programs that should be presented. These subcolleges may create their own distinctive patterns—focusing, for example, on the humanities or on a group of related technologies—while sharing access to a central library, auditorium, gymnasium, and general administrative support services.

Cluster units have been organized in approximately twenty-five to thirty colleges. The units in Cypress College and the Indian

Valley Colleges, in California, centered on academic disciplines. At Oakton Community College (Illinois), transfer, occupational, and general education were merged within each cluster. Small units within Los Medanos College (California) were dedicated to a core of general education based on interdisciplinary studies. Management was effected through a coordinating committee, which included a director of learning resources, a business services officer, a director of admissions and records, a public information officer, and a professional development facilitator. Deans of the four major areas in general education (behavioral science, humanities, social science, and natural science) managed the programs in their areas. Traditional academic departments have been conspicuously absent in most cluster college plans. Student services are decentralized, each cluster having its own set of counselors.

Other special organizational forms have included colleges organized for particular purposes—for instance, technical institutes built as separate colleges in multicampus districts. Some of these, such as the Los Angeles Trade and Technical College, have a long history. San Francisco's Community College Centers were formed in 1970 to coordinate all noncredit activities. Miami-Dade's Medical Center is of more recent vintage and is even more highly specialized. Santa Monica's Emeritus College, designed for and operated by senior citizens, is another form of a college within a college.

Governing Boards

The idea of a lay governing board that represents the people is an old concept in American education, and public education has used elected boards to reflect the collective will and wisdom of the people since earliest times. Ideally, the board is the bridge between college and community, translating community needs for education into college policies and protecting the college from untoward external demands. The degree to which boards do so has always been questioned, some observers saying that their composition is too homogeneous. Bernd (1973), for example, has argued that the typical trustee—a Protestant, Republican, business or professional man over age forty-five—cannot represent all his constituents adequately. But such a contention has always been difficult to document.

Governing boards have been studied at some length. Ingram and Henderson (1987) discussed board functions and responsibilities, types of boards, board membership, and the way boards are organized. Chait and his associates (1984) pointed out that boards of trustees should participate in academic program planning and management. Petty (1985) has presented a useful collection of articles that discuss the authority of community college trustees in several areas of institutional management. Bers (1980) has traced the differences in board activities in rural and suburban districts.

Community college boards usually consist of from five to nine members elected from the district at large for four-year terms. They may meet once or twice a month or, in some cases, weekly. According to the Association of Community College Trustees, their responsibilities include selecting, evaluating, and dismissing the president; ensuring professional management of the institution; purchasing, constructing, and maintaining facilities; defining the role and mission of the college; engaging in public relations; preserving institutional independence; evaluating institutional performance; creating a climate for change; insisting on being informed; engaging in planning; and assessing board performance (Potter, 1977).

Because the boards are public corporations, they are legally responsible for all college affairs. This status involves them in legal actions regarding personnel and the purchase of materials (competitive bidding, advertising, special designs). Therefore, as Potter (1976) has shown, a board must have a working knowledge of educational law and be able to recognize potential legal problems before they develop into actual litigation. He offers examples of litigation brought on by students, faculty members, and other parties—for example, suits by students in relation to tuition or over disruptions on campus (which, they contended, interfered with their education) and suits by faculty members, who have usually engaged in litigation because of dismissal from their job.

Governing boards are political entities, and the selection of a trustee may be viewed as a political act in which the appointing authority or the voters weigh costs and benefits. As Goddard and Polk (1976) have indicated, a trustee appointment by a governor may be used to mend political forces, but it may also alienate members of the public who are opposed to the appointees. The elected trustee usually has more power or political independence than the appointed one, but only at the price of the financial and emotional rigors of a political campaign. In instances where the faculty union has contributed heavily to a trustee's election campaign, its influence may be palpable—for example, when the newly elected trustee votes immediately to dismiss a chief executive officer who has fallen out of favor with the union.

State associations for community college presidents and trustees have been prominent in about two-thirds of the states. These voluntary organizations typically coordinate statewide conferences and meetings, conduct professional development workshops for various types of administrators, arrange orientation sessions for newly appointed trustees, prepare and distribute newsletters, and monitor legislation. They provide an avenue for chief administrators and trustees from the colleges within a state to meet and discuss topics of common interest. Active associations that cross state lines, such as the New England Junior College Council, operate in similar fashion. Support for these associations most often comes from members' dues, but some have received funds from the state or a philanthropic institution.

The Association of Community College Trustees (ACCT) has also been active in apprising board members of their need to take a prominent role in college affairs. Since the ACCT was organized in 1972, its publications and conferences have been directed toward moving board members away from a "rubber stamp" mentality that approves everything the college administration presents. It has also stressed the importance of the board's monitoring the college's fiscal affairs and public relations and the necessity of open communication between the board and the college president.

The way that many board members approach their work has changed during the history of the community college. Certainly, the organizations have become more complex, and board members must respond to more initiatives from personnel organizations in the college and from monitoring and controlling agents outside the college. Furthermore, the notion of trustee liability, well documented by Kaplin (1985), has become more pronounced. Less frequently seen in the literature but nonetheless prevalent are contentions that trustees sometimes go too far in their tendencies to manage the colleges. Greater control seems inevitably to follow greater responsibility.

Administration

All colleges must have administration, although the way this function is organized and staffed differs from one college to another. In the medieval university, even though the students were powerful, often fixing tuition charges and determining the curriculum, the faculty was the controlling wheel of the institution. During the nineteenth century a system of centralized control developed in the United States, and faculty power diminished as the administration took over the university. The professors concentrated on their research, scholarship, and teaching, and professional managers controlled the affairs of administration, thus dividing the ranks between administrators and teachers.

With their roots in the secondary schools, the community colleges usually were managed by former instructors who had become first part-time and then full-time administrators. Monroe (1972, p. 305) described many of them as autocrats who had freed "themselves from the control of their superiors and the general public. They assumed a paternalistic, superior attitude toward the teachers. Administrative decisions of the past have often gone unquestioned by governing boards. The members of the boards rubber stamp administrative policies and decisions so that, in practice, the college's administrators become the decision makers of the college." But he was speaking of a time gone by. In the 1970s the all-powerful president had disappeared from all but the smallest colleges, and the governing boards had become ever more intrusive.

The role of the president changed as colleges grew larger. And as faculty and community advocate groups grew stronger, it became ever more circumscribed. Still, the president was the spokesperson for the college, interpreting it to the public on ceremonial occasions. The president was also the scapegoat when staff morale or funds for a favored program diminished. The average presidential tenure has been eight or nine years, shorter than faculty tenure

but certainly sufficiently long to suggest that the job is not particularly precarious.

Primarily, the president carries out general administrative
duties and has periodic meetings with the board and with the heads
of state agencies. To a lesser extent, the president makes decisions
on faculty recruitment and selection; conducts public relations
activities; and coordinates the college program with programs of
other institutions and community groups. Fund raising, always
high on the list of responsibilities assumed by presidents of private
colleges, has recently come to occupy more of the public college
president's time. Wenrich (1980) has enumerated the various roles of
the community college president, and Vaughan (1986) considers
leadership styles along with various personal aspects and professional activities of presidents.

Administrative Patterns. So many administrative patterns
have been advocated that it is impossible to describe an ideal form.
In the line-staff organization recommended by Blocker, Plummer,
and Richardson (1965), the president reports to the board of control,
and a business manager and a director of community relations
report to the president. Underneath the president on the organization chart is a dean of liberal arts and sciences, a dean of technological science, a dean of students for vocational education, and a dean
of continuing education. Under the deans are department or
division chairs and guidance personnel, and under them the faculty.
According to Blocker and his coauthors, such an organization places
more emphasis on college functions than the conventional model,
wherein the dean of student personnel and the business manager
report to the academic dean, who reports to the president.

The college deans are usually line officers in charge of
planning and supervising one or a combination of college programs concerned with instruction, student personnel services,
evening division, or community services. The larger colleges may
also have deans for college development and for admissions, but
deans of men and women, prominent in the early colleges, have
disappeared from the public colleges. Like the president, each dean
becomes involved with legal issues, public relations, intrainstitutional administration and personnel matters, budgeting, and liai-

son with state and federal agencies. Most deans serve as part of a
president's council or cabinet.

Departmental Structure. The academic program in community colleges has usually been provided through departments or
divisions organized around a cluster of academic disciplines or
related teaching fields. The primary objective in creating academic
departments, inherited from the universities, was to create manageable organizational units, not necessarily to interrelate the teaching
of certain subjects or to build interdisciplinary courses. The number
of departments is often related to institutional size; in small colleges
where not more than one or two instructors may be teaching in any
subject field, the combination of teaching fields within a single unit
may be quite broad. But in the larger institutions, the number of
departments has often increased as the number of instructors
teaching a single discipline has grown. As Lombardi (1973a, p. 3)
has noted, "Tradition, pride, logic, and number of instructors are
all factors in determining whether a department comprised of
several disciplines will remain intact or be divided into separate
departments."

The academic department has been a basic building block in
the organizational structure in nearly all community colleges. Its
influence has been quite marked. As an example, the administration
may organize college-wide orientation sessions for new instructors,
but true indoctrination takes place when the neophytes begin
maintaining their offices in the suite assigned to the academic
department of which they are members. And in-service faculty
development workshops conducted on an institution-wide scale
pale in comparison with the influence exerted by a senior departmental colleague's pointed comment, "That's not the way we do it
around here!"

Departments often have responsibility for constructing class
schedules, assigning instructors, allocating funds for auxiliary
employees and services—in short, for acting as miniature governmental units within the larger college structure. For this reason
many senior administrators have sought to retain control by
minimizing departmental power; hence the move toward the larger
organizational unit of the division. Other administrators have

attempted to minimize the power of the department by having faculty members from different departments share office space or otherwise mixing the staff. But the departments have survived in most institutions, probably because the affinity among instructors teaching the same courses or courses in the same academic fields remains strong. Further, some department chairpersons have served the administration well by maintaining certain records, supervising staff, screening applicants for positions, and reconciling conflicts among staff members and between staff members and students that might have been blown out of proportion if they had reached higher levels of arbitration.

Until the spread of collective bargaining in community colleges, the academic department remained the most popular organizational unit. However, as bargaining units were established, the chairpersons with managerial responsibilities were often designated as administrators, and thereby removed from the bargaining unit. At that point the move toward organizing larger units or divisions accelerated, lest a college have thirty or forty administrators, each supervising only a few instructors. However, the distinction was not clear, and department chairpersons were considered faculty members in some contracts, administrators in others.

Lombardi (1974) reports studies showing lengthy lists of responsibilities for department chairpersons: sixty-nine discrete items in one statement, fifty-one in another. However, he suggests that the duty statements appearing in collective bargaining agreements seldom contained more than fifteen items. The essential minimum seemed to be providing orientation for new faculty members, involving faculty members in making departmental decisions, encouraging faculty participation in professional activities, reporting departmental accomplishments, developing long-range departmental goals, ascertaining the needs for equipment, preparing the department budget and overseeing the allocation of funds, planning curriculum changes with the faculty, reviewing trends in student characteristics, and reviewing new developments in similar departments in other community colleges.

Patterns of evaluating department and division chairpersons also reveal their duties. Hammons and Thomas (1980) have reviewed these evaluation systems, and McCombs (1980) has provided evaluation forms and instruments in such areas as instructional leadership, professional traits, management of departmental finances, and student recruitment. In a national survey of department chairpersons in community colleges, Thomas (1980) found that most of them wanted to be evaluated on the basis of results, whereas senior administrators most commonly used a rating scale method.

Management and the Administrators

The chief executive officer's role has become increasingly complex. Evaluation of senior administrators has always been a responsibility of the governing board, although recently the faculty have participated by voting "no confidence" when an administrator falls out of their favor. These votes are usually not binding on the board, but that body cannot afford to ignore them. Miller (1988) found that senior administrators are most often evaluated by committees of peers and other staff members.

Walker (1979) has characterized the less effective administrators as those who need to "defend the sanctity of their office" and who react with "counteraggressive behavior when under attack." They believe that they are supposed to make decisions, even unpopular ones, and to see that their orders are obeyed and the rules enforced. "They view decision making as a series of personal acts of courage, will, and purpose. . . . Over a period of time, because faculty members and students entertain a different notion of leadership, their activities come to be regarded by the administrator as perverse" (pp. 2-3).

The more effective administrators are those who "accept the privileges and status of their office, but wear them lightly. They separate themselves, as individuals, from their office. . . . They regard themselves as working with faculty colleagues who deserve respect as fellow professionals" (p. 4). They work to reconcile the differences among the constituencies on campus, and they may even consider themselves expendable if the welfare of the institution requires that they leave. They consider administration a process, not a series of discrete events, and they tend to be good politicians.

"Their assurance apparently derives from an intuitive knowledge of
the organization and appropriate administrative roles rather than
from naked self-confidence in the egotistical sense" (p. 5). The
personality of the administrator still seems the most important
ingredient. Some administrators have succeeded admirably, others
failed terribly, even while adhering to ostensibly similar administrative styles in the same type of organization.

College administration is not a responsibility assigned to a
faculty member temporarily on leave from teaching responsibilities;
it is more akin to the management of a large business corporation—
which indeed the community college is. As Friedenberg (1965, p. 92)
said of secondary school administrators, they are "not professional
educators in the sense that a physician, an attorney, [and] a tax
accountant are professionals. . . . They are specialists in keeping an
essentially political enterprise from being strangled by conflicting
community attitudes and pressures."

The changes assailing community college administrators
seem to have accelerated. Koltai (1980, p. 1) has noted: "The luxury
of long-range planning is simply not available to us. . . . The status
quo is no longer an option." As the 1980s began, more frequent
accommodation was demanded of community colleges than at any
other period in their history: "Enrollment slumps, collective
bargaining agreements, redefined taxpayer priorities, legislative
scrutiny, declining academic performance, and the advent of
student consumerism" (p. 1) were contributing to the pace of
change. More recently, several new circumstances have contrived to
change the dynamics of college management. In order to ascertain
compliance with state and federal regulations, the college counsel
has become central to decision making. Where a bargaining unit
exists, the union must be consulted on all but the most trivial
decisions. The organization chart may show a staff pattern, but the
lines of authority do not follow the boxes and arrows. State-level
associations of deans, faculty members, and various college officers
often take positions on legislation affecting the colleges that may
run counter to the position that a member's home institution would
prefer. Even though the conferees are staff members at locally
governed colleges, they exert a form of state-level management. A
shadow government has reduced the local districts' powers.

Collective Bargaining

Collective bargaining swept into higher education on the coattails of legislation authorizing public employees to negotiate. As these laws were passed in various states in the 1960s and 1970s, employee groups ranging from refuse collectors to prison guards gained union representation and began negotiating contracts. Within education, elementary and secondary school teachers were first to take advantage of the legislation—possibly because they were the furthest from professional autonomy (Kemerer and Baldridge, 1975). Community college faculties were next most likely to be represented by a bargaining agent, with the National Education Association and the American Federation of Teachers their two most prominent agents. By 1980 authorizing legislation had been passed in half of the states. The spread of collective bargaining slowed notably in the 1980s as only two additional states passed authorizing legislation, but by mid-decade over two-thirds of the full-time instructors in public community colleges were working under contracts negotiated collectively. The 295 contracts noted in Table 13 actually covered the faculty in over 60 percent of the colleges because many involved multicollege systems.

The expansion of collective bargaining brought about a shift in administrative roles. In general, it marked the demise of the

Table 13. Number of Faculty Collective Bargaining Contracts
at Two-Year Colleges by Agents, 1966-1987.

Year	National Education Association	American Federation of Teachers	American Association of University Professors	Independent	Combination of Major Unions	Total
1966	1	1	0	0	0	2
1970	6	3	1	10	7	27
1975	71	52	3	23	1	150
1980	141	72	5	16	2	236
1985	171	82	4	25	4	286
1987	172	84	4	27	8	295

Sources: Hankin, 1975; National Center for the Study of Collective Bargaining in Higher Education and the Professions, Directories, Vols. 1–14.

concept of paternalism, with the president as authority figure, and opened an era of political accommodation among contending forces. These changes were difficult for many administrators, whose experience had not prepared them for their different roles, but the realities of management within the confines of a negotiated contract so confronted them that they either learned to live with the restrictions or they left the practice.

The scope of the contracts suggests the magnitude of their effect. Contract coverage includes contract management procedures; rights of bargaining agents; governance items, such as personnel policies and grievance procedures; academic items, such as class size and textbook selection; economic benefits; and working conditions, such as parking facilities and office space (Ernst, 1985). Under these broad headings practically everything concerning institutional functioning is negotiable.

Collective bargaining drew a legal line between members of the bargaining unit and those outside it—between faculty, on the one side, and administrators and trustees, on the other. It also expanded the number of detailed rules of procedure. It prevented administrators from making ad hoc decisions about class size or scheduling, faculty assignments, committee structures, budget allocations, funding of special projects, and a myriad of other matters, both great and small. It forced a more formalized, impersonal pattern of interaction, denying whatever vestige of collegiality the staff in community colleges might have aspired to. It brought the role of the legal expert to the fore and magnified the number of people who must be consulted each time a decision is considered.

Swift (1979) studied the effects of the negotiated contract on Minnesota community colleges and found that, although job security and fringe benefits were enhanced, managerial authority, campus communication, and faculty involvement in institutional decision making were impaired. At a California community college, according to a report by Armstrong (1978), administrators felt that collective bargaining had reduced their flexibility in assigning tasks. Ernst (1985) also pointed out that the faculty collectively had gained power in governance but individually had lost freedom in defining their own work roles.

Still, as evidenced by bargaining-unit elections, most instructors prefer unionization because, as Andrew and Henry (1983) reported, faculty at colleges with unions earn higher salaries and teach fewer students than their counterparts in similar institutions without unions. And more money and fewer students are among the highest of all faculty-held values. Unionization must also be credited with the tendency of the faculty in some states to create stronger statewide organizations and gain a greater voice in legislative halls. In this context the observation that "the poverty of scholars is of inestimable worth in this money-getting nation," made by the president of Harvard in 1869, sounds ever more quaint (Eliot, [1869] 1978, p. 571).

Collective bargaining seems also to have accelerated a move to larger institutional units. In multicampus districts where the faculty bargains as a district-wide unit, the district-level administration aggregates power, weakening the autonomy of the individual campuses. Kintzer (1984) found bargaining to be the only activity that administrators in multicollege districts consistently regarded as the prime responsibility of the district central office. In states where the faculty bargaining unit negotiates a master contract for all the colleges, power gravitates toward the state level. At best, this concentration of power may result in a federal system, in which certain powers are reserved for the individual colleges; at worst, the colleges become single statewide institutions, with branch campuses in the different localities.

Lombardi (1979a), who traced the effects of collective bargaining on administrators, showed that most accepted it reluctantly, recognizing that it reduced them to ministerial functionaries carrying out the decisions made during the negotiations. Other administrators, however, actually welcomed collective bargaining— some because it enabled them to join forces with the union bureaucracy in controlling the faculty; some because it gave them the opportunity to avoid responsibility for their decisions. It has also increased the administrators' reliance on attorneys whose role is to interpret the contracts.

Under collective bargaining the faculty gained prerogatives in establishing the conditions of the workplace, up to and including a say in institutional governance. Administrators lost the freedom to act according to general principles and were forced to attend to the procedures specified in the contracts. Both parties were restrained from reaching private agreements. In general, an informal relationship of faculty and administration as unequal parties became a formal compact of near equals. And governance and management patterns shifted notably as union representatives, administrators, and various committees and associations composed of people from within and outside the college district made more of the decisions affecting college operations.

Attempts at Efficiency

Various efforts to make community colleges more efficient have been undertaken, in order to increase student learning and, at the same time, maintain cost-effectiveness. Attempts have been made to lower costs, increase staff efficiency, make the college accessible to more students, cut student attrition, and manage the physical plant more effectively. However, increased productivity in one area might lead to a decrease in another; for example, success in attracting different types of students to community colleges might increase the costs of instruction. Further, measuring productivity by the number of students processed through a class in a given time equates the outputs of education with those of a factory. And indeed, using that definition, studies such as one conducted by Berchin (1972) did find productivity related in large measure to class size and to reproducible media.

The concept of management by objectives (MBO), first popularized by Drucker (1954), has made inroads in college administration. The advantages of MBO seemed to center on its demanding that all staff members define in measurable terms what they intended to accomplish. It thus formed a base for staff accountability and helped the staff coordinate their activities around common goals. Critics of MBO found it too time consuming and too mechanistic, but its proponents concluded that it brought college processes out from behind what the public perceived as a curtain of secrecy designed to conceal waste and inefficiency.

The changes in student composition occasioned by the reduced traditional college-age population led to the introduction of marketing. Always alert to new programs to attract different types of students, administrators in many colleges began accelerating their promotional activities and coordinating them with particular programs. These administrators advanced a number of arguments to explain their actions. For example, they contended that the college was best serving its community by extensively promoting its wares. They also noted that college officials must protect their programs against the incursions of senior colleges and proprietary schools, which themselves had stepped up efforts to attract students long considered the proper clients for the community colleges. Johnson (1979) defined marketing as an integration of promotional activities with programs designed particularly for certain population segments and offered at times and places convenient to those groups. He considered it important for college managers to understand marketing, convince other staff members of its importance, and put all elements of the college into a marketing stance, and he advocated organizing marketing task forces to work with instructors and other staff members in devising and promoting new programs. By 1988 a sizable percentage of the nation's community colleges had organized marketing divisions (Bogart and Galbraith, 1988).

Institutional Research

Every increase in federal- and state-level categorical programs has led to an increased need for data to be provided by the campuses. In many cases responsibility for gathering the data has been assigned to the offices of admissions and records, but because of the flood of requests, institutional research received a boost. As extramural grants and contracts were opened to community colleges, institutional research offices became more involved in proposal writing. And as the computer became ubiquitous, more sophisticated data tabulations could be made.

A study coordinated by the ERIC Clearinghouse for Junior Colleges at UCLA (Roueche and Boggs, 1968) assessed the status of institutional research in community colleges in the 1960s, tracing its scope, the number and type of studies completed, and the number of institutions with research coordinators. Full-time research coordinators were found in only about one in five community colleges, usually the larger institutions. In two of five colleges, responsibility for institutional research was assigned to an administrator who also had other duties, and in two of five, no regular staff member had responsibility for coordinating institutional studies. Institutional research studies addressed students, programs, and institutional operations, with a few studies of faculty and student personnel services also under way. The authors concluded that the key to running a successful research office was a commitment by the president, who insisted on good data on which to base educational decisions.

Subsequent studies of institutional research in community colleges revealed that institutional research offices were established in increasing proportion during the 1970s but that they operated on small budgets, in no case exceeding 1 percent of the total operating budget. Knapp (1979) found institutional research offices typically staffed with only one or two persons. Those offices were seen as arms of the administration, providing data to the top administrators while conducting few, if any, studies on behalf of the faculty. Chalker (1981) found that most rural college presidents viewed the function of institutional research as limited to the compilation of reports.

The highest priority for institutional research has been topics concerned with students, including enrollment trends, student characteristics, and follow-up studies. According to Wattenbarger (Educational Testing Service, 1976), data gathering can be properly focused if college staff members ask certain questions—for example, "What effect does probation status have on students? What teaching procedures are most cost-effective? What schedule provides the most effective use of facilities?" Wattenbarger recommended that institutional research responsibilities be assigned to one person, who would coordinate all the college's research activities. He also recommended that administrators establish an institution-wide advisory committee; provide adequate financial support for the research office; urge instructors to participate by suggesting studies and taking an active role in collecting and interpreting data; encourage research coordinators to meet with their counterparts in other institutions; maintain proper filing systems; publish and distribute findings; and enlist the aid of as many people as possible in interpreting and acting on the results. However, few colleges have attended to these recommendations. In 1987 the community colleges of Southern California averaged only .67 FTE institutional researcher each—hardly enough to fill out the data request forms that flowed in from governmental agencies (Wilcox, 1987).

Losak (1986) has presented a more realistic view of institutional research, demonstrating that it follows institutional priorities and concerns. As enrollments decrease, much research is devoted to tracing sources of students and to determining ways of retaining them in the institution. As calls for institutional accountability come to the fore, research seeks information on student outcomes, such as transfer rates and job getting. Institutional research has become integral to the college's marketing efforts.

Some commentators have spoken in favor of statewide coordination of community college institutional research, so that uniform data will be made available. Statewide coordination seems likely, as several states are building student and management information systems using common data drawn from all institutions; Illinois, Hawaii, Washington, and Maryland offer the best examples of statewide information systems.

The recent demands for outcomes assessment could enhance institutional research at the local level if all studies of institutional impact were coordinated through the institutional research (IR) office. Most current attempts at demonstrating institutional effect are crude: here a methodologically suspect accounting of the fiscal contribution a college makes to its region, there a report of the number of people showing up for community service classes or tuning in to the college's television channel. But follow-up surveys of former students, the earliest form of institutional assessment, are still popular, particularly among managers of occupational programs; it is rare to find the head of a nursing program who cannot tell exactly the number of former students who passed the state licensure examination and who are working in the region, the salaries they are earning, and their satisfaction with their job and with the preparation for it that they received. Other institution or program-level follow-up studies address transfer and job-getting rates. These studies could be coordinated with assessments of student learning, and periodic reports of college effects could be issued. Only in the rare institution, though, has this role been assumed by the IR office. In most, the reports on outcomes are provided sporadically and inconsistently.

Issues

Several issues swirl around the concepts of governance and administration. What elements of control should be maintained by state agencies? What should be reserved for the local institutions? Is multicollege or multicampus the better form?

The college as a learning enterprise does not operate well when it is managed as a factory with inputs, process, and outputs as the model. Can the anarchical elements of collegiality coexist with contracts negotiated by distant representatives? Is management by objectives feasible? Vague and often conflicting aspirations affect every classroom and administrative office.

How can the college maintain consistent direction when numerous organized groups within and outside the institution all demand to participate in governance? Will the local district become a hollow shell as informal organizations exert greater influence?

Issues of productivity and accountability have been raised continually. How can staff members be held responsible for their actions when most of the decisions that affect them are beyond their control? Does the larger bureaucracy protect the staff from external scrutiny? Do formalized grievance procedures enhance or retard individual responsibility and creativity?

Institutional research coordinators spend most of their time gathering data to fill out reports requested by external agencies. How can they expand their efforts to serve the college by gathering information necessary for program construction, accurate enroll-ment projections, and college efficiency and accountability?

As the colleges have grown larger and more complex, administrators, faculty members, and trustees all have had to adjust. The only certainty is that, regardless of the form of governance and the models of administration adopted, these adjustments will have to be made with increasing frequency.

Five

―――――――――――

Finances:
Sustaining and Allocating Resources

Trends in financing community colleges have followed shifts in institutional purpose and mode of organization. The colleges have expanded so that they enroll half of the people who begin college; they can no longer be considered merely alternative institutions for students who do not wish to leave their hometown to go to a university. They have become large enterprises, some with budgets exceeding the $100 million mark.

When the colleges were small, they made modest demands on public funds. Few people outside the institutions cared where the colleges' money came from or how they spent it. But when they and their budgets grew large and began competing for sizable funds with other public agencies, they became much more prominent. And when inflation and rapidly increasing enrollments drove costs upward at a phenomenal rate, the colleges' support base came under ever-increasing legislative scrutiny.

The public colleges have always had to operate in a political arena. Since 1907, when the first junior college enabling legislation was passed in California, there has been continual legislative activity on their behalf. The colleges had been organized as extensions of the secondary schools, deriving their support through the public school budgets, but that changed as soon as independent community college districts were organized. Even so, their support continued to come predominantly from local tax funds. The usual

127

pattern was for the local district to provide a fixed sum of money per student in attendance, with state aid minimizing the differences among districts of varying wealth. The proportion of state aid was quite small: Augenblick (1978) reported it at an average of less than 5 percent of all public college revenues in the 1920s. During most of the pre–World War II era, student tuition and fees provided more funds to the community colleges than the states did. Richardson and Leslie (1980) noted that in 1934 local districts provided 84 percent of the colleges' support, with student fees accounting for most of the remainder. But even in those early years, there was much variation among states: Eells (1931) showed that student tuition made up 77 percent of the financial support for the Texas colleges, whereas in California taxpayers from the students' home districts provided the colleges with 81 percent of their operating funds.

Over the years community college funding has been marked by shifting proportions coming from tuition, local taxes, and state revenues. However, as shown in Table 14, the trend has been for the states to pick up an increasingly larger share than the local districts. This trend was furthered in the late 1970s, when California's Proposition 13 limited the property tax to 1 percent of the 1975–76 assessed valuation, with a maximum of a 2 percent annual increase. Local community college districts found their major sources of

Table 14. Percentages of Income from Various Sources
for Public Two-Year Colleges, 1918–1986.

Source	Year							
	1918[a]	1930[a]	1942[a]	1950[a]	1959	1965	1975	1986
Tuition and fees	6	14	11	9	11	13	15	16
Federal aid	0	0	2	1	1	4	8	10
State aid	0	0	28	26	29	34	45	47
Local aid	94	85	57	49	44	33	24	17
Private gifts and grants	0	0	0	0	0	3	1	1
Auxiliary services	NA	NA	NA	NA	12	6	6	6
Other	0	2	2	2	2	7	1	3

[a]Includes local junior colleges only.
Sources: Starrak and Hughes, 1954, p. 28; Medsker and Tillery, 1971, p. 11!; National Center for Education Statistics, Current Funds, Revenues, and Expenditures . . . 1988.

funds effectually capped and were forced suddenly to look to the state for their funds. Within two years the state's share of community college revenues increased from 42 to nearly 80 percent. Several other states—notably, Arizona, Colorado, Hawaii, Illinois, and Washington—passed legislation similar to California's Proposition 13.

There is considerable variation in support patterns among the states. For example, community colleges in Texas receive more than half of their money from the state, 15 percent from the local district. Among other states with well-developed community college systems, Illinois receives roughly one-third state, one-third local funding; Arizona receives one-fourth state, one-half local funding; and Missouri receives slightly less than half from the state and slightly less than one-third from local sources. Community colleges in Delaware, Utah, and Washington receive more than 80 percent of their funding from the state, while those in Kansas and Wisconsin receive less than 30 percent from that source. Although tuition charges accounted for around one-sixth of the colleges' operating budgets nationwide, the colleges in several states derived more than one-fourth of their revenue from their students, whereas students in California paid a token $100—hardly more than it cost the colleges to collect it. Most of the recent increase in federal support comes in the form of direct aid to students.

In 1984 community colleges in ten states received smaller increases in state appropriations than the universities in those states; colleges in another ten states received larger increases; in the remaining states the colleges and universities had about the same rate of increase or decrease. Some of the differences, though, were quite marked. For example, the California community colleges' state appropriation increased by 3 percent, whereas the appropriation for the state's universities went up by more than 20 percent. On the other hand, in Pennsylvania, while the community colleges' appropriations increased by 49 percent, those for the public universities in the state went up by only around 10 percent ("State Appropriations for Higher Education," 1984). In states where the colleges receive no funds from local taxing districts, the state appropriations increased by 14 percent on average between 1985 and 1987 and by 12 percent between 1986 and 1988. In states where the colleges are funded by a combination of state and local sources, the increase in state funds averaged 11 percent between the two former years and 7 percent between the latter (Hines and Pruyne, 1988).

Wattenbarger and Vader (1986), in their summary of recent trends in community college funding, noted that the "expansionist 60s" had given way to a "gradual erosion" of the colleges' finances in the 1970s. In the 1980s the colleges made up for the shortfall by increasing the percentage of the operating budget contributed by tuition and by increasing the funds derived from various individual efforts, such as selling services or renting out land. Local funds were decreasing, and state funds, although increasing, had decreased as a percentage of the total operating budget. By way of compensation, the colleges tended to decrease current expenditures by deferring maintenance and equipment purchases, freezing new employment, reassigning staff, and increasing the use of part-time faculty.

Capital-outlay projects have usually been funded differently from operating budgets. Some states require the colleges to present long-term plans on the need for buildings and facilities, plans that have been difficult to defend in an era of rapidly shifting enrollments. And when appropriations become hard to obtain, capital-outlay projects are among the first to be curtailed. Some states require a bond issue to finance college buildings. Although the community colleges in many states occupy handsome quarters, their policies of reaching out to offer classes in a variety of off-campus localities have reduced their need for new buildings for traditional instruction. However, special-purpose buildings, especially for newly evolving technical programs, are in high demand.

Funding Patterns

Increased complexity in patterns of state reimbursement has accompanied the increased proportion of funds coming from the state. Wattenbarger and Starnes (1976) listed four typical models for state support: negotiated budget, unit-rate formula, minimum foundation, and cost-based program funding. Negotiated budget funding is arranged annually with the state legislature or a state board. Used especially in states where all or nearly all the community college funds come from the state, negotiated budgets demand a high level of institutional accountability for funds expended. Budgets tend to be incremental; one year's support reflects the prior year's, with increments or reductions based on funds available, changing costs, and the introduction or suspension of various programs.

Under the unit-rate formula, the state allocates funds to colleges on the basis of a formula that specifies a certain number of dollars per unit of measure. The unit of measure may be a full-time-student equivalent (FTSE), the number of students in certain programs, the credit hours generated, or some combination of measures.

The minimum foundation plan is a modification of the unit-rate formula. State allocations are made at a variable rate that depends on the amount of local tax funding available to the institution. The allocation may be expressed either as a set dollar amount minus the local funds available per student or as a proportion of the approved district budget minus the amount provided by the local contributions. In either case the intent is to provide more state funds to colleges where local support is less. Inequities in local support among community college districts are smaller than those among lower-school districts because community college districts tend to be larger, and therefore more likely to include both wealthy and poor neighborhoods, and their students come from a broader range of the population. Still, considerable variation exists because community college attendance is not mandatory, so that districts can differ widely in the proportion of the population they serve.

The cost-based funding model provides state allocations based on actual expenditures. In this model state funds are allocated on the basis of program functions, specifically budgeted objectives, and detailed instructional categories. Local tax funds may or may not be factored into the formulas, and the appropriations vary greatly among institutions, depending on the costs of the programs they offer.

The funding formulas are often complex, and whatever formula is adopted benefits certain institutions, certain programs, and certain classes of students while penalizing others. The common practice of reimbursing colleges on the basis of FTSEs may penalize institutions with higher proportions of part-timers. Although reimbursement for occupational students is made at a different rate than for those enrolled in the lower-cost academic programs, costs vary among all the programs. And because of the differences in facilities used, staff salaries, types of students enrolled, and so on, absolute parity among institutions can never be achieved.

There is no consistent pattern in state funding for special student groups or for students in particular curricula. Some states run support to the colleges according to enrollment in several different curriculum categories, each carrying a different reimbursement formula, and provide additional funds for particular groups of students as well. In twenty-three states senior citizens are given waivers of tuition or fees, and displaced homemakers or displaced workers in twenty states get various types of aid. Unemployed students receive aid in fourteen states, and prisoners receive aid in eleven states (Center for the Study of Community Colleges, 1987). These inconsistencies make generalizing about funding a complicated exercise. Categories of curriculum and students qualifying for various levels of aid shift continually.

Over the years the community college funding agents have attempted to solve several complex problems. The first is for state aid to be equalized, so that colleges in the districts with less of a local tax base do not suffer excessively from lower funding. Various formulas have been derived, with the result that the proportion of state aid going to the wealthier districts is reduced and that to the poorer districts increased. One solution has been to recommend full state funding, giving all colleges an equal proportion regardless of the local wealth.

Differential program payments point up another dilemma. Some programs are of most public benefit and therefore worthy of the highest support. General education, a low-cost program, falls in this category. The highest-cost programs, such as some of the technician-training curricula, demand more money per student, but their benefit may be more for the individual than for the public. The continual budget formula adjustments in every state point up the impossibility of reconciling that issue.

Another major issue in funding is the linkage between funding and enrollment. An enrollment-based funding pattern calculates allocations by using student head count or full-time-student equivalent to appropriate funds. Many efforts have been made to separate funding from this pattern, because costs of instruction—which are nearly all based on academic staff salaries, libraries, and maintenance—are constant, whereas enrollments fluctuate. If each year's appropriations are based on student enrollment, great distortions in revenues calculated against expenditures can result. However, alternative patterns of funding, such as a certain base rate calculated according to overall district population regardless of enrollment, have never succeeded. The proponents of decoupling, as that is called, have argued that expenditures for the various categories of activities may not be related to enrollments. For example, the expenditures on physical plant depend more on the age of the buildings than on the number of students occupying them. The net result, however, is that the formulas for funding become more complex (Fonte, 1985).

Breneman and Nelson (1981) examined community college funding patterns from the point of view of the economist and concluded that no one system can possibly accommodate all purposes. They found that the various taxonomies purporting to describe community college funding patterns were not based on mutually exclusive categories. They categorized the several choices that must be made in defining financing plans: funding from the state only or a combination of state and local funding; tuition as a fixed percentage of costs or on some other basis; budgets negotiated or following statutory formulas; financing credit courses only or funds for noncredit; treating community colleges in isolation or making their support relative to other segments of higher education; deriving a proper formula based on recovery costs, average daily attendance, student credit hours, or other measures.

Breneman and Nelson summarized their conclusions as follows: Remedial education should be tuition-free because it is a true extension of lower-school work, which is tuition-free; occupational programs providing training for particular industries should receive at least partial support from the industries that benefit; community education primarily for personal enrichment should be self-supporting; community college students do not necessarily receive less support than their counterparts in public universities, because university costs for lower-division instruction alone cannot be accurately calculated; student aid should be restricted to students enrolled at least half-time; and finance formulas should be devised to reflect differences in program costs and differences in unit costs associated with college size.

Tuition and Student Aid

Questions of the proper balance between local and state funding are no more controversial than the issues surrounding the tuition and fees paid by students. Many two-year-college leaders have advocated a no-tuition or a low-tuition policy for their institutions, which they felt were natural extensions of the free public schools. However, their views were not shared by many outside the institutions. Even in California, where no tuition was charged until the mid-1980s, only 56 percent of the respondents to a 1979 survey of the public were aware that credit courses could be taken free (Field Research Corporation, 1979, p. 20).

After studying the history of tuition charges, Lombardi (1976) concluded that the issue was not whether tuition should be charged but how much. He reported a 1941 survey of a national sample of educators, editors, and other officials that found only a small majority affirming free tuition for public junior colleges. And although the 1947 President's Commission on Higher Education stressed the importance of making public education free through grade 14, nearly all the community colleges organized in the 1950s and 1960s charged tuition. In 1970 the Carnegie Commission on Higher Education urged that students pay a larger share of instructional costs as a way of saving the private sector of higher education. As Lombardi (1976) put it, the concept of no tuition was destined to abort early in its development. Perhaps Eells (1931) anticipated what was coming when he quoted a speaker at the 1928 annual meeting of the American Association of Junior Colleges, who said, "Many people, including those who are careful students of education finance, share the opinion that when the student has monetary investment, he is going to attack the problem of education more seriously than . . . when it is handed to him for the asking" (p. 123).

Well into the 1930s the difference between tuition costs in two-year colleges and in public universities was not large. Between 28 and 37 percent of two-year colleges were charging less than $50 tuition during the 1920s and 1930s, and most others charged less than $150; the highest was $200. During the 1970s a student in the typical state saved only around $200–$400 in tuition per year by attending a community college rather than a state university. The greater savings accrued to the students who commuted, living at home and working part-time.

In the public sector, community college tuition recently has increased at a higher annual rate than tuition at four-year colleges. By the end of the 1970s, tuition at two-year colleges averaged around 60 percent of the tuition charged in four-year colleges. And whereas the median tuition stayed under $100 from the beginnings of the community colleges through the 1950s, it moved to $100–$199 in the 1960s and $200–$299 in the 1970s. By the end of the decade, it was over $300, and by 1987 it had leaped to nearly $700.

The pressure for increasing tuition has usually come from state legislators seeking ways of holding down appropriations. Their arguments have been that the people who benefit from going to college should pay and that students will take their education more seriously if their own money is at stake. The counterarguments are that the entire population benefits when more of its members have been educated and that equity demands that low-income students not be forced to pay the same tuition as the sons and daughters of wealthy parents, because such charges represent a higher percentage of family income for the former group.

The most common type of tuition is a fixed rate for full-time students and a uniform credit-hour rate for all others. When full-time rates are charged, they act as an incentive for students to enroll in more courses per term. Where rates per credit hour are charged, they usually eventuate in the part-timers paying a higher per-course rate.

Whereas tuition usually represents a portion of the costs of instruction, student fees are for special services that may not be required for all students. Optional fees may include use of laboratories or special equipment for certain courses, parking fees, library fines, and special fees for late registration or for changes of program. Some states limit the total amount or the types of fees that colleges may charge, but in others the colleges attempt to collect reimbursements for a wide array of services.

Variations in tuition are wide, depending on the college, the state, and the classification of student; in 1986–87 they ranged from $100 in California to $1,785 in Vermont (Palmer, 1987b). Colleges that derive much of their support locally are usually permitted to establish their own tuition, within certain limits. Out-of-state and foreign students usually pay at a higher rate, as do certain categories of part-time, adult, and evening-division students. In some states at least a minimum tuition must be charged; in others the legislature establishes a maximum. But state policy almost invariably fixes community college tuition at a lower rate than for the public senior institutions because legislators usually want the community colleges to serve as a low-cost alternative for beginning college students.

In the early years tuition and fees represented a major source of institutional income. They declined as a percentage of total revenues in the 1950s, but then began a steady rise. They have provided a conduit for federal aid that might not otherwise run to the community college. And even though mechanisms for distributing state financial aid to students are imperfect because of the limitations on part-time attendance, problems of assessing the financial condition of students' families, and the difficulty in accommodating adult, independent students—all three conditions more prevalent in community colleges than in other sectors—the states have been able to enhance equity by providing funds to the lower-income groups. This has proved a significant method of equalizing opportunity.

By the mid-1980s federal and state aid to students had become a foundation stone of college funding. Around $18 billion was being advanced to higher education in the form of grants to special categories of students and loans to students from middle-income as well as low-income families. Table 15 depicts the proportions going to each sector of institutions, showing the dramatic increase in the proportion going to the proprietary schools. The national community college associations were united in their support of student aid programs, even though the funds were a mixed blessing because

Table 15. Shares of Pell Grants by Sectors, 1973-1987.

Year	Two-Year Colleges		Four-Year Colleges		
	Public	Private	Public	Private	Proprietary
1973-74	24.8	4.0	41.4	22.0	7.4
1975-76	26.1	3.0	39.0	21.9	9.0
1977-78	24.3	2.4	42.8	20.9	8.9
1979-80	21.8	2.8	39.6	25.3	10.5
1981-82	18.7	2.7	40.7	24.4	13.5
1983-84	18.5	2.8	38.0	21.8	18.8
1985-86	18.8	2.5	37.0	19.5	22.1
1986-87	18.7	2.3	35.7	18.5	24.8

Sources: Gillespie and Carlson, 1983; Lewis and Merisotis, 1987.

they enabled potential students to matriculate at the higher-cost universities and proprietary vocational schools. Without the availability of aid, the latter group, the fastest-growing sector and the colleges' main competition in many areas, would close their doors.

In reviewing the issues of equity and efficiency in tuition charges, Breneman and Nelson (1981) argue for higher-tuition/higher-aid strategy. It is possible for colleges to set tuition at a level that reflects the balance between private and public benefits and still maintain equity by running financial aid to low-income students. The problem of aid systems that penalize students who enroll for only one or two courses can be offset by a state's paying the tuition for anyone taking a course considered of prime use—for example, a person on welfare who takes a course in an occupational program. Increased student aid should properly be used for tuition payments lest the incentive for students to enroll in college and receive financial aid to pay living costs lead to the system's being viewed as an adjunct to welfare. Breneman and Nelson believe that community college students receive adequate aid, since more of them live at home and work while attending school and hence their overall costs are much lower.

Richardson and Leslie (1980) recommend that different tuition rates be charged for different programs, since students in the high-cost, high-demand programs (such as the allied health fields) should pay more. This would not discriminate against low-income

groups, since full-time students receive assistance based on the costs
of the programs they attend. Richardson and Leslie also recommend
tuition waivers for needy students who are ineligible for outside aid
and the elimination of tuition waivers for "the more affluent senior
citizen who takes advantage of continuing education or community
services" (p. 40).

Problems in Funding

The increases in tuition and financial aid to students and the
shifting of the major source of support from local to state tax
revenues were the most dramatic, but not the only, problems
affecting community college finance. Sizable salary gains were
made by instructors working under negotiated contracts, but staff
productivity, by any measure, did not increase. This was no surprise
to students of educational structures; in fact, Coombs (1968) had
outlined an impending educational crisis worldwide because, since
teachers' productivity does not rise along with their salaries, the
costs per student must rise. Hence, each year an educational system
needs more finances simply to accomplish the same results as the
previous year. As he put it, "To assume that costs per student will be
held at a standstill by far-reaching, economy-producing innovations still to be introduced is to indulge in fantasy" (p. 51). No
innovation can rescue educational systems from serious financial
difficulty as costs accelerate in what he called one of the last
handicraft industries.

The fiscal problems were accentuated by the different types of
students. Many observers had applauded the institutions' attempts
to reach "new students," but few considered the added costs that
came along with them. "New or expanded functions of the colleges
such as community services, career education programs, special
programs for disadvantaged and minority students, financial aid,
health services, and counseling accompany the increases in
enrollment. Instructional innovation generates experiments, new
teaching methods, and technical devices that often cost more money
and usually increase the unit cost of education" (Lombardi, 1973b,
p. 13). The extra costs of campus law enforcement, utilities, and
theft that resulted from offering night classes for part-timers were

rarely calculated. And few colleges could properly fund the small classes and personal attention necessary to teach the less well-prepared students who had so swelled enrollments since the 1960s. Even extramurally funded programs added to costs when additional people had to be employed to administer them.

Although transferring costs from the local districts to the states seemed merely to shift the problems, not to solve them, some benefits did accrue. As Breneman (1979) noted, because the proportion of school-age children in the population was declining and the proportion of older people increasing, and because state and local governments traditionally have had responsibility for the support of their younger rather than their older citizens, state and local governments would probably be in a better cash position in coming years. Nonetheless, senior institutions had begun competing for lower-income students who brought financial aid with them and for occupationally directed students who found programs of their choice as the universities expanded their career education efforts.

Controlling expenditures has been difficult because education is labor-intensive, but it is not impossible. If it were, expenditures would not differ from college to college as much as they do. The per capita cost, the most common measure, is generally derived by dividing the total cost of operation of a college by the number of full-time-student equivalents. Sometimes it is determined by cost per credit hour—that is, total cost divided by the number of credit hours taken by students. This concept of per capita costs nearly always refers to current expense of education and rarely to capital-outlay expenditures. The cost per student varies according to the mix of programs that a college offers; some courses cost more than others. Another element of per capita costs is the price of the instructors. Instructors with long tenure and doctorates cost more than those with shorter tenure and without the doctorate.

Bowen (1981) reported considerably less difference in expenditures per student among types of institutions than among different institutions of the same type. Using data from 268 institutions sampled from among those that had reported in the Higher Education General Information Survey in 1976-77, he showed that the median expenditure per full-time freshman or

sophomore student equivalent was $2,020 at public research univer-
sities, $2,025 at comprehensive universities and colleges, $1,959 at
two-year colleges. But the range for public two-year colleges was
from $1,102 to $4,150. Data from each state also revealed wide
disparities, although the range within states was not nearly as great.
Bowen ascribed these differences among community colleges to
variance in the relative emphasis on expensive occupational
programs and less costly academic programs.

Where does the money go? Half is devoted to instruction and
instructional support services. This is a higher proportion than the
42 percent that the universities spend on instruction. As shown in
Table 16, the proportions shifted somewhat between 1977 and 1986;
but, because of continual changes in federal data collection definitions and categories, the shift may be more apparent than real.

Solving the Problems

In order to balance budgets, the colleges have given financial
planning a more prominent role and have instituted hiring freezes

Table 16. Index of Expenditures (in Constant Dollars)
per Full-Time Student Equivalent at Public Two-Year Colleges, 1977–1986.

Year	Instruction	Administrative	Libraries	Plant Operation and Maintenance	Scholarships	Total
			Categories of Expenditures			
1977	$1,653	$ 961	$113	$363	$94	$3,18
	52%	30%	4%	11%	3%	
1980	1,588	980	101	371	73	3,11
	51%	31%	3%	12%	2%	
1982	1,538	942	102	371	62	3,01
	51%	31%	3%	12%	2%	
1984	1,521	961	88	363	60	2,99
	51%	32%	3%	12%	2%	
1986	1,753	1,163	101	418	77	3,51
	50%	33%	3%	12%	2%	

Source: Recalculated data from Stern and Chandler, 1988, p. 100; Grant ar
Snyder, 1986, p. 168.

and made selective cuts in personnel, equipment, courses, activities, and services. Cuts in personnel are the most difficult to effect because of contracts, tenure, and seniority, to say nothing of the personal upheaval they entail. The colleges have tried to foster managerial efficiency by employing efficiency experts and training staff members in budget management. They also have responded to fiscal exigencies by making more effective use of physical facilities, including year-round use of buildings, scheduling patterns that distribute class offerings over more of the day, and the use of rented space.

Placing faculty members in contact with more students through larger classes or increased teaching hours has been a favored method of increasing faculty productivity, but that has not been an easily implemented reform because of the tradition equating low teaching load with quality. Similarly, the economies desired by introducing reproducible media for instruction have not been readily seen. Some economy in instruction has been effected where faculty members have begun awarding credit for prior experience; the appeal of assessing what students know rather than the time they have spent in the classroom lies in the savings in instructor salaries and cost of facilities.

Several commentators, including Lombardi (1973b, 1979c), Sussman (1978), and Wattenbarger (1978), have listed these and other ways to control expenditures through better planning and, specifically, by reducing the number of low-enrollment classes, restricting staff leaves and travel, employing more hourly-rate faculty members, offering courses in rented facilities off campus, using reproducible media, encouraging early retirement of staff, reducing student support services, such as tutoring, counseling, athletics, and placement, freezing orders for supplies and equipment, and offering credit for experience. Campbell (1985) has shown that colleges are holding costs down by better managing their finances. But collective bargaining and the demographics of aging (and therefore higher-paid) faculty are inexorable in increasing college costs.

One of the more effective, rapidly expanding ways that colleges are offsetting increasing costs is to sell their services. Contract education with local businesses, the leasing of college land

and buildings, and cooperative ventures with private entrepreneurs have become prominent. In addition, numerous colleges have established their own foundations to serve as vehicles through which to receive funds from alumni, other donors, and philanthropic agencies. Bailey (1986) estimated that, as of the beginning of 1986, 730 community colleges had established foundations, up from 546 in 1978. According to Robison (1982), these organizations are usually holding corporations, which possess and manage assets as their only activity; personality or "old buddies" foundations, which act almost as the personal charity of a community and social leader and his or her friends; structural agents or operating foundations, which, acting as separate legal entities, conduct financial transactions not permitted within public school budgets; special-purpose foundations, which solicit, manage, and disburse funds for a single cause, such as a scholarship fund; or comprehensive foundations, which may encompass features of the other four models. Because the foundation is legally and organizationally independent of the college, it is able to promote the well-being of the college without the statutory limits placed on the college's governing board and staff. Banks and Mabry (1988), Kopecek (1982–83), and Duffy (1980) have detailed the growth, functions, and characteristics of these agencies. Pabst (1989) has reviewed the various uses to which the colleges put foundation money, including, among others, student scholarships, equipment, special-purpose buildings, and endowed chairs for faculty.

Justifying the Costs

Periodically, after they have exhausted their efforts to reduce expenditures, colleges are forced to make policy changes. For example, the colleges' tradition of taking all who applied and keeping them as long as they wanted to stay has come under attack. First of all, state legislatures threatened to impose enrollment ceilings if costs per student were not reduced. In addition, many colleges have been required to tighten their standards for academic progress. Gradually, community college advocates have realized that their proudly voiced claims of unlimited enrollment growth have become passé. As Richardson and Leslie (1980, p. 37) stated,

"The current practice of accepting all who apply regardless of the funding authorized conveys several messages to legislators, all of them undesirable. The first message is that quality is not an important concern of the community college. . . . A second . . . is that very little relationship exists between the amounts appropriated and the numbers of students served." Richardson and Leslie recommended that college administrators gain prior state approval for specific curricula and services and that they introduce first-come, first-served enrollment procedures—in short, maintaining the open door only to the extent that resources permit and ensuring that quality be a hallmark.

It did seem that enrollment caps would spread. Lower schools had no choice in the number of students they admitted; every child not only had a right but by law was required to attend school. Community colleges were different; they could restrict their enrollments by cutting the variety of programs offered, by "marketing" less vigorously, and through numerous other stratagems, including dismissing students who were not making satisfactory progress toward completing a program. The only question was whether colleges would do so voluntarily or wait until the legislatures mandated the changes.

Some college leaders have recognized that, as Nelson (1980) recounted, political factors are more important than economic factors in determining community college financing. (Echoes of William Allen White's admonition to the farmers of the 1930s: "Raise less corn and more hell!"?) It does seem that the colleges will have to cooperate with other sectors of higher education in order to maintain a united front in the state capitols. That is, they must remain part of higher education and not try to go it alone, because—for the remainder of this century at least—there will be more graduates of the University of California than of Los Angeles City College in Sacramento, more graduates of the University of Florida than of Miami-Dade Community College in Tallahassee.

Issues of efficiency and equity arise in any discussion of financing. Efficiency relates to the ratio between the benefits deriving from some good or service and the costs of producing it. Equity relates to the extent to which different members of society attain like benefits from public expenditures. In publicly supported education the two obviously overlap: A highly efficient institution would spend its dollars only on the people who would use their training to make substantially greater incomes, thus paying back significantly more in taxes than their education cost. But such an institution would be inequitable because the members of certain social groups would not receive any of its educational benefits.

How do the community colleges fit in? Economists often categorize school expenditures as investments in general human capital, in specific human capital, and in consumption benefits with little investment value. The classifications "academic," "occupational," and "community service" fit these respective categories rather well. Compensatory programs help people become productive members of society and thus benefit the public by reducing transfer payments. However, the cost is high because of the high-risk nature of the students. Career programs benefit society because of the increased productivity of the labor force, the higher probability of students' going to work after graduation, and the aid to industries that will stay in an area where a trained work force is available. Thus, although students benefit individually from occupational training, substantial public benefits are also present. Community services are most likely to be of the consumer education sort, with benefits accruing only to the individual, not to the public. Accordingly, following the practice in university extension divisions, community colleges should charge the consumers for the full cost of providing these services. However, certain types of community service or noncredit courses, such as courses on child care, family nutrition, or energy efficiency, seem to slide over into the category of public benefits.

Aside from the general issues of efficiency and equity, the schools have always had difficulty in determining how well they do when their actual output is measured against their professed aims. Part of the problem has been their inability, or at least their unwillingness, to set their priorities in operational terms. If they were judged solely by the size of enrollments, the criterion used by many advocates, questions of content and quality would not arise. But the legislator, the economist, and the lay citizen might question what the students have been learning, how much, how well, and how fast. And even then an institution may be at once good and bad:

good when judged by internal criteria, such as student performance on examinations; bad when judged by relevance to the needs of its surrounding community.

Some attempts have been made to demonstrate more direct economic effects. Bess and others (1980) studied the economic impact of six Illinois community colleges by tabulating college-related business volume, value of local business property because of college-related business, expansion of local bank credit base resulting from college-related deposits, college-related revenues received by local governments, cost of local government services attributed to college-related influences, and number of local jobs and personal income of local citizens from college-related activities. They found a sizable positive effect on all indicators and estimated the difference between the positive impact and the costs to local government of supporting the college and its staff as at least $850 million, projected statewide for fiscal 1978. The greatest effects were in business volume created by the expenditures of the college and in the expansion of bank deposits. The difference among colleges in impact per dollar expended was attributed to the percentage of staff members living in the district, amount of salaries spent within the district, amount of college funds spent in the district, percentage of student body that attended full-time, and amount of funds deposited in banks in the district.

Despite the importance of doing so, colleges have rarely attempted to document their accomplishments. The reasons are not clear, but perhaps during periods of rapidly expanding budgets and enrollments, college managers believe that the increases themselves speak for the worth of the enterprise; and during periods of decline, they have used marketing techniques and political persuasion in attempts to reverse the trend. Carefully controlled studies of institutional efficiency and outcome seem to fall between the planks of advertising, on the one side, and lobbying, on the other.

The world of politics, public relations, and illusion surrounds all public educators, who recognize the importance of maintaining an institutional image of fiscal prudence. But a public agency must spend all the money available to it; therefore, an educational system will be as inefficient in its use of resources as it is allowed to be, because efficiency leads to reduction in funding.

College managers who learned their craft in an era when those statements were true find it difficult to shift away from that concept, the bedrock of public agency maintenance. If cuts become necessary, managers try to keep all programs, services, and functions intact in order to avoid the difficult decisions to drop any of them. If further cuts become necessary, they are made where they will be most visible. And larger units, such as multicampus districts, may give the appearance of fiscal prudence because they have fewer top-line administrators, even though the infrastructure may in fact be more expensive.

Issues

College leaders will be forced to face several issues regarding finance in coming years.

What are the inequities among community college districts where the local taxpayers bear a large share of the financial burden? Should stricter limitations be placed on the amount that wealthier districts spend on their community colleges?

How can costs be managed in a labor-intensive enterprise? Bargaining units will restrict the savings that managers formerly gained by employing part-time faculty members and by increasing class size. Reproducible media demand sizable start-up costs and have yet to yield far-reaching financial benefits.

How can accounting procedures document the additional costs to the institution engendered by categorical aid and demands for special programs stemming from external agencies? More broadly, on what grounds can an institution that has prided itself on offering something for everyone refuse to begin a new service even when the costs of providing it exceed the revenues it brings?

Can sufficient funds be generated locally to maintain community education programs? Can a convincing justification be made for switching the funding of community education to the state level? If so, can equitable formulas be found? More broadly stated, what concepts, standards, and definitions actually differentiate between credit and noncredit education?

Does low tuition make sense in the light of substantial student aid? At what point does tuition without offsetting financial aid reduce equity? What are the actual, as opposed to the conceptual, relations between levels of tuition and institutional efficiency? In brief, can benefits be run to one group without offsetting losses to another?

Compensatory studies and high school completion courses seem destined to occupy a major portion of the community college effort. A plausible case can be made for reorganizing many of them along the lines of the 6-4-4 plan that was in effect in some districts in the early years. How can colleges obtain funds to teach the basic education that was supposed to have been completed in the lower schools?

Those portions of career education that benefit certain industries are difficult to justify on the grounds of efficiency. How can the colleges expand the targeted portions of their occupational education and defray the costs by effecting greater numbers of contracts without irreparably damaging the integrity of a publicly supported institution?

What measures of institutional productivity can be introduced so that increased costs can be justified? Answers to that question depend on the effects the institution is trying to achieve. Can education be defended in its own right, or must the criterion always be the financial return to the students and the community?

Difficult questions all, but the college administrator who would be an educational leader would see them as a challenge and set to them with vigor.

Six

Instruction:
Methods, Media, and Effects

The importance of good teaching has been emphasized since the earliest days of the community colleges. College planners never envisioned these institutions as the homes of research scholars. The community colleges could not reasonably expect to influence total student development, because few of them built residence halls and commuter institutions have minimal environmental impact on students. Nor did custodial care of the young, a major feature of the lower schools, become significant, because attendance was not required in the community colleges. Classroom teaching was the hallmark.

Observers of the community college have reported unanimously that teaching was its raison d'être. Eells (1931, p. 389) called the junior college "a teaching institution *par excellence*." Thornton (1972) proclaimed instruction the prime function, saying that it had to be better in the two-year college than in the university because the students covered a broader range of abilities and their prior academic records tended to be undistinguished: "It is fair to say that most community college students are able to learn but are relatively unpracticed. Under good instruction they can succeed admirably, whereas pedestrian teaching is more likely to discourage and defeat them than it would the more highly motivated freshmen and sophomores in the universities" (p. 42).

Most writers followed their exhortations regarding good teaching with the observation that it was indeed to be found in the two-year colleges. Although rarely heard since the colleges grew large, the pronouncement that instruction was better because of the small classes was often voiced in an earlier time. In addition, junior college instructors were considered to be better than those in the universities because their responsibilities were only to teach, not to conduct research; their pedagogical preparation was more evident; and they were bona fide instructors, not teaching assistants. Koos (1924) reported that "*classroom procedure* in junior colleges is assuredly on at least as high a plane as is instruction of freshmen and sophomores in colleges and universities" (p. 219). He pointed to the "superiority of teaching skill" found among instructors at two-year colleges because most of them came from the ranks of high school teachers and had their training in pedagogy, unlike their counterparts at the universities (p. 201).

The way the colleges are organized suggests a commitment to teaching. An administrator, usually a dean of instruction or a vice-president for instruction, has oversight for the formal educational program. This administrator usually chairs a curriculum and instruction committee responsible for all major changes in those areas. The committee comprises program heads, department chairpersons, and representatives of the library and counseling services. This assigning of instructional leadership to the administrators has enabled them to coordinate the work of several faculty members and offer incentives through instructional development grants, sabbaticals, and released time to develop new techniques. The evolution of the library into a learning resource center and the widespread use of tutors and reproducible media also attest to an orientation to teaching.

Instructional Techniques

This instructional emphasis has stimulated a continuing interest in various instructional techniques. Johnson (1969), who surveyed community colleges around the country, tabulated the incidence of cooperative work-study education, programmed instruction, audiotutorial teaching, television, dial-access audio systems, instruction by telephone, multistudent response systems, the use of film and radio, gaming and simulation, computer-assisted instruction, and a host of other techniques ranging from electronic pianos to a classroom in the sky. Hardly an instructional medium could be identified that was not in place at some community college.

The trend has continued. By 1985 the Wisconsin State Board of Vocational, Technical, and Adult Education (VTAE) was able to report seventy-eight electronic technologies in use in twelve VTAE districts. Writing across the curriculum, cognitive-style mapping, and other techniques also have found favor periodically.

Television. Television has been one of the most generally adopted teaching tools. Programs have been presented on closed circuit for students in the classrooms and through open circuit for the benefit of the public. Many of the open-circuit televised courses can be taken for college credit, and some institutions generate a sizable proportion of their course enrollments through the use of that medium. Enrollments in the televised courses presented by the Dallas County Community College District alone rose from their beginnings in 1972 to over 10,000 per academic year in eighteen courses in 1978 (Dallas County Community College District, 1979). The City Colleges of Chicago organized a TV College in the 1950s, and several other community colleges also received licenses for the cultural enrichment and entertainment of the public as well as for credit-course instruction.

The community colleges' interest in television led many to develop their own materials. Video production facilities were constructed in most of the larger institutions, and numerous staff members were involved in program generation. By 1980 two-thirds of the instructors nationwide had access to media production facilities. A few college districts—most notably, Miami-Dade (Florida), Coastline (California), Chicago, and Dallas—have become widely recognized for the sophistication of their programming. (Interestingly, whereas a university's prestige often rests on its faculty's scholarship and research discoveries, the export of high-quality television programs provides one of the few ways that a community college can gain a reputation beyond its own district's boundaries.) Interdistrict cooperation in production and distribution of televised courses became common, and several consortia were developed to share programs and production costs.

The use of televised instruction grew steadily throughout the 1980s, with open-circuit courses offered for college credit one of the more popular options. Various surveys found consistently that telecourse students were more likely to be women and older than their counterparts taking courses on campus (Brey and Grigsby, 1984; Clagett, 1983). Students were taking the classes because they did not have time for regular attendance on campus, although their purposes for taking the course were similar to those who took regular classes. Most of them learned about the courses through mailings or newspaper advertisements. Televised instruction had become well established.

Computers. The advent of the computer gave the colleges another opportunity for instructional innovation. A Washington State report on the use of computers in instruction (Howard and others, 1978) divided patterns of use into (1) computer-based instruction, the use of specialized computer programs, such as models and simulators, in the teaching of economics, business, and engineering; (2) computer-managed instruction, which supports teaching by maintaining student records, administering tests, generating progress reports, and prescribing the most suitable types of instruction; and (3) computer-assisted instruction, the presentation of linear and branching instructional programs. In the 1980s the personalized computer gave considerable impetus to this form of education.

Some form of computer-assisted or computer-managed instruction has been adopted in practically every institution. The PLATO (Programmed Logic for Automatic Teaching Operations) system, originated at the University of Illinois, has maintained its popularity; for example, Cuyahoga Community College (Ohio) introduced it as a supplement to remedial English and mathematics courses (Smith and others, 1981). A Time-Shared Interactive Computer-Controlled Information by Television System, installed at Northern Virginia Community College in 1974, has been used to present the entire course material for college grammar, basic algebra, English composition, and certain mathematics courses while scoring tests, presenting instructional modules, and maintaining records of grades (Sasscer, 1977). The computer at the Community College of the Air Force has been used to maintain a file of student characteristics, aptitude scores, indexes of reading ability, and educational background; select and present the best course material for each student, record student responses, and administer tests and supplemental training; predict students' completion dates; and evaluate and revise the course materials (Campbell, 1977). This form of combining diagnostics, instruction, and testing has emerged as a frequent application of computer-managed learning.

Miami-Dade combined computer-managed and computer-assisted instruction. Its Open College allowed students to enroll in classes, buy course materials, and go through the course work at their own pace without going to the campus except for examinations. Interaction between instructor and student was handled through the computer; information was transmitted through television. The system evolved to include a Response System with Variable Prescription (RSVP), a sophisticated mode of individualizing instruction and record keeping. The RSVP package maintained students' records and their responses to various surveys and exams, printed reports informing students of their progress, and provided information to instructors about student performance and collective class data. The RSVP also delivered personalized letters to students, prodding them to maintain progress. The program was used to diagnose student writing and to provide corrective prescriptions for various types of errors and explanations of basic writing concepts (Miami-Dade Community College, 1979; Emerson, 1978; Kelly and Anandam, 1977).

As with all forms of instruction, the use of the computer promotes student learning to a greater or lesser degree, depending on the application. A review of only a few of the many assessments that have been conducted reveals varied results. Computer-assisted instruction in English grammar was less effective than a programmed text method (Lundgren, 1985); more effective than traditional instruction in business organization classes (Brum, 1983); less effective in developmental reading (Taylor and Rosecrans, 1986); no different in an air conditioning/refrigeration program (Houston Community College System, 1986); led to greater improvement in reading skills but higher dropout rates (Kester, 1982); or produced higher grade point averages and higher course completion rates (Penisten, 1981). Most of the applications of computer-assisted instruction continued to be supplemental to the basic classroom structure; although the faculty in nearly all colleges had free access to computers, only a minority of them used it as a substitute for or even as an adjunct to their own teaching (Saunders, 1986). The computer was more widely used in specialized situations—for example, in classes for remedial or learning-disabled students— than in the traditional college-credit classes. Its most effective applications were in combining instruction with testing, providing rapid feedback to students regarding their progress, and, in general, managing the flow of students through the colleges' programs.

Cognitive-Style Mapping. Some colleges have used cognitive-style mapping as a device for determining students' best mode of learning, so that they could be placed in courses and with teachers that fit. The Myers-Briggs Type Indicator was a favored tool. It was used to identify a student's personality type, relate it to the student's preferred learning style, and match the student with instructors or classroom-learning situations that would be most accommodative (Fish and McKeen, 1985; Ritchie, 1975; Roberts, 1975). Much of this cognitive-style mapping was based on the work pioneered by Joseph Hill at Oakland Community College (Michigan) early in the 1970s, and it continued to be done well into the 1980s. Mountain View College (Texas) designed a cognitive-style program to determine preferred learning styles for the students and aid them in selecting appropriate courses (Ehrhardt, 1980). Funds from the Elementary and Secondary Education Act and the Vocational Education Act were used to bring information on cognitive styles to community colleges in New York, show instructors how to use it, and arrange programs for cognitive-style mapping for the colleges in that state (Martens, 1975; Rotundo, 1976).

The idea that people learn in different ways and that these ways can be guides to instructional practice is an elusive yet enduring notion. The concept of learning style considers personality, information processing, and social interaction—all with the intention of forming instructional methods that will enhance the learning for people whose style matches the classroom emphasis. Knowledge of learning style is also presumed helpful in selecting approaches to use in counseling students. Claxton and Murrell (1987) summarized many of the studies that have sought ways of classifying and identifying learning styles, the instruments that have been employed, and the results obtained. Villa and Lukes (1980) found that cognitive mapping yielded greater retention, higher grades, and student satisfaction. Some success in arranging college teaching to accommodate students' learning styles has been noted, but the concept has not taken hold as a major determinant of teaching method. It is used in limited applications in classroom experiments by instructors and student services staff members who are intrigued with the concept.

Writing Across the Curriculum. In the belief that practice in writing should not be emphasized solely in English composition classes, a number of colleges have attempted to stimulate instructors in other disciplines to require writing. This concept achieved some popularity in the 1980s. Adams and his associates (1985) described writing across the curriculum at Somerset County College (New Jersey); Walter (1984) discussed the approach at Sinclair Community College (Ohio), Preston (1982) at Miami-Dade Community College (Florida), and Landsburg and Witt (1984) at Pima Community College (Arizona). This instructional methodology has students developing writing assignments in specific classes. In some applications the papers are submitted to a writing instructor, who assists in evaluating the products; in others the students in composition classes work on papers that are related to the content of their subject-specific classes. Attempts have also been made to integrate writing instruction into occupational programs; Pollack and Godwin (1983) described such an effort at Orange County Community College (New York).

Supplemental Instruction. Supplemental instruction uses course content as the basis for skills instruction. Pioneered at the University of Missouri at Kansas City, it is designed to teach students to read the texts and interpret the tests used in the academic classes they are taking. In these programs students work with tutors outside of class. A leader coordinates the work of the tutors with that of the instructors who have agreed to participate by encouraging their students to take advantage of the tutoring. The concept has spread to many colleges where dropout and failure rates in basic, introductory academic courses have been unconscionably high. Wolfe (1987) has described its application and the results obtained in a history class at Anne Arundel Community College (Maryland). Its uses in natural and social science courses at various colleges have been summarized by Friedlander (1982a). In California state funds are available for tutors, but only if the additional instruction is mandatory for everyone enrolled in the class. Supplemental instruction shows promise because it provides community college students with what they most need—additional time spent on learning the skills they must have if they are to succeed in the classes they must take.

Resistance to Innovation

It is reasonable to assume that in an institution dedicated since its inception to "good teaching," new instructional forms will be tried. However, despite the spread of reproducible media, traditional methods of instruction still flourish. Visitors to a campus might be shown the mathematics laboratories, the media production facilities, and the computer-assisted instructional programs. But on the way to those installations, they will pass dozens of classrooms with instructors lecturing and conducting discussions just as they and their predecessors have been doing for decades.

Findings from the CSCC studies in the 1970s and 1980s showed widespread use of reproducible media, but they were being used as adjuncts to traditional instructional methods. Over half of the instructors reported that they had their students view or listen to filmed or taped media at least part of the time, but lecturing was the most prevalent teaching form, and class discussion ranked second. The textbook was, of course, the most frequently used reading material. Student grades were based, for the most part, on examinations and written papers. Quick-score or objective tests accounted for a sizable portion of student grades in about half of the classes, and essay exams were a prime determinant of grades in slightly under half. Detailed information on the use of instructional media is shown in Table 17. Information for each academic discipline is presented in *The Collegiate Function of Community Colleges* (Cohen and Brawer, 1987).

For several reasons, although many instructors have adopted the new media, more have not. Many faculty members continue to believe that close personal contact with students is the most valuable,

Table 17. Percentage of Classes Using Instructional Media.

Medium	Humanities		Science/ Social Science	
	Frequently	Never	Frequently	Never
Films	13	22	9	44
Single-concept film loops	1	65	1	68
Filmstrips	6	40	3	64
Slides	12	34	8	54
Audiotape/slide/film combinations	5	45	3	62
Overhead projected transparencies	11	45	20	39
Audiotapes, cassettes, records	18	26	3	62
Videotapes	4	46	3	63
Television (broadcast/closed-circuit)	2	55	1	72
Maps, charts, illustrations, displays	36	13	20	31
Three-dimensional models	2	60	10	47
Scientific instruments	NA	NA	18	44
Natural preserved or living specimens	NA	NA	9	64
Lecture or demonstration experiments involving chemical reagents or physical apparatus	NA	NA	10	54
Other	5	0	6	1

Sources: Cohen, 1978; Cohen and Hill, 1978.

flexible instructional form that can be developed. Purdy's (1973) in-depth study of the faculty at a college widely known for its audiotutorial laboratories, computer-programmed course segments, videocassettes, and other reproducible media (a national magazine dubbed it "Electronic U") revealed a sizable group resistant to all those media.

Media-based techniques are not the only instructional forms that meet resistance. Why don't the faculty require more writing? Many reasons can be advanced, but the one that the faculty often give is that they have too many students in their classes, that if they require their students to write more, then they (the teachers) are required to read more. In most classes too few papers are assigned because the instructors cannot accept alternatives to their reading them. Either outside readers are not available to them, or they do not trust anyone but themselves to read their students' written work—probably some combination of both. Nor have the faculty ever accepted the notion that student writing can be sampled, with only every second or third paper read or each paper read only for certain restricted characteristics. They still act as though every practice session must be critiqued, whether the student is practicing the piano, hitting baseballs, or writing compositions.

Anything that lessens direct contact with students or that demands more of the instructors' time stands a good chance of meeting resistance. The ad hoc lecture requires the least preparation time. And innovators must prove the positive effects of their techniques, while traditionalists can usually go their way without question. Teaching as a profession has not developed to the point at which proper conduct in the instructional process can be defined and enforced in the face of individual deviation. Hence, whereas lower teaching loads would allow more time for instructional reform, they would not be sufficient to revise instruction; merely giving people more time to do what they are bent to do does not change the perception of their role.

Moreover, not all innovations in instruction have met with success. Some were greeted with apathy by the faculty at large, and when the initiators tired of them, the innovations died. Others were promoted by administrators who wished to give their colleges an image as forward-moving structures but were unable to persuade the faculty to use the hardware. In some institutions the faculty blamed the administrators for everything from a film projector that broke down to a television studio constructed with funds that faculty members felt belonged in their salaries. Other innovations were dropped because of the expenses involved; instructional programs presented through reproducible media have never been as economical to prepare and maintain as some of their promoters claimed they would be.

Some innovations, such as allowing students to drop out of class without penalty, had untoward consequences. Nonpunitive grading (that is, the substitution of "Withdrawn" or "No Credit" for a failing grade) was adopted widely in the 1970s, but the practice fostered grade inflation and distortion in transferring credits between institutions. It may also have contributed to the students' taking a casual approach to their studies. How do people respond when they may drop in and out of an institution, a program, or a course at will, making no advance commitment, receiving no penalty for failure to complete anything? Might students not respond with "Well, if it doesn't matter to them when or whether I complete this course, why should it matter to me?" By the mid-1980s policies allowing students to withdraw at any time had become much less prevalent.

Learning Resource Centers

The community college library has long been recognized as an important instructional service. Johnson (1939) called it the heart of the college and recommended numerous ways it might become central to the instructional process. Although none of the libraries developed collections of research materials, they did provide books and periodicals sufficient for a textbook-oriented institution. Table 18 presents data on the libraries in the seven largest community college states in the 1970s. Although the overall numbers have since changed, the average holdings per student have not. The community college library is among the features that most differentiate that institution from the university. It is much less likely to be a resource for independent research and is much more

Table 18. Library Holdings and Average Holdings Per Student
at Public Two-Year Colleges in Selected States, 1975.

State	Number of Colleges	Avg. No. Students per College	Holdings			Avg. Holdings per Student
			High	Low	Average	
California	98	9,643	155,587	505	56,912	5.9
Florida	28	5,331	254,121	11,294	60,595	11.4
Illinois	48	4,861	80,866	8,979	34,739	7.1
Michigan	30	5,514	158,940	10,000	45,428	8.2
New York	44	5,662	119,662	21,552	54,028	9.5
Texas	54	3,580	144,459	2,928	36,119	10.1
Washington	27	4,220	58,316	4,750	31,106	7.4

Sources: National Center for Education Statistics, *Library Statistics for Colleges nd Universities*, 1975; American Association of Community and Junior Colleges, *Community, Junior, and Technical College Directory*, 1976, 1979.

likely to be an adjunct to classroom teaching and the home of other instructional forms, such as programmed and tutorial instruction.

Evidencing these tendencies, many community college libraries underwent a major transformation during the 1960s and 1970s, when they became learning resource centers (LRCs). In some colleges the library remained intact, but facilities were added for individual study through the use of self-instructional programs. But in many colleges totally new LRCs were built to encompass a library; a learning assistance center; audio and video learning laboratories; a center for the distribution of audiovisual materials; and centers for tutorial services, graphic and photographic reproduction, and video production. About one-third of the LRCs also had career information centers and computer-assisted-instruction terminals. Table 19 shows the services offered as the LRCs were organized.

Problems of converting libraries to learning resource centers, in order to provide not only materials but also instructional services, were exacerbated by the expansion of courses offered off campus and in satellite centers. Coupled with the general move toward the use of reproducible media in community colleges, this extension of the instructional program to numerous localities in the district led to an increase in the percentage of the operating budget

Table 19. Services Offered in New Learning Centers at
Two-Year Colleges, 1973–1983 (*N* = 238).

	Number of Centers	Percentage
Library	222	93
Audiovisual distribution	223	94
Audio learning laboratory[a]	138	80
Graphic and photographic production	171	72
Audio/video production	192	81
Tutorial services[b]	96	55
Skills/learning assistance center	138	58
Video learning laboratory[b]	105	61
Reprography (other than copy machine)	104	44
Career information center[c]	94	39
Computer-aided instruction[d]	28	29

[a]Category combined in 1978–79 from two former categories.
[b]Information not available for 1978–1983.
[c]New category in 1977–78.
[d]New category in 1978–79.
Sources: Henderson and Schick, 1973, 1977, 1978; Bock, 1979, 1984.

devoted to the LRC. By the early 1980s the median library operating budget was just under $185,000, and 10 percent of the libraries had expenditures of $500,000 or more. The median number of titles held exceeded 30,000 (National Center for Education Statistics, *College and University Libraries,* 1987). The LRCs also were deeply into cooperative ventures with libraries and other agencies, such as museums and governmental units, in their region (Person, 1984).

The Technology of Instruction

One of the most persistent ideas in education is that individualization must be the goal in every instructional program. Numerous articles have begun with the statement "Let's assume that the best ratio of teachers to learners is one to one" and then gone on to explain how one or another instructional strategy might be tailored to fit each student. The most extreme version of individualization was realized when colleges began granting credit for experience gained anywhere. Core courses taught in singular fashion and required of everyone were at an opposite extreme. Each had its proponents and both were seen, often in the same institutions.

A technology of instruction in which goals are specified and a variety of learning paths designed so that most students may reach those goals offered a compromise. A variety of learning outcomes and instructional strategies allowed students to decide whether they wanted to be involved in the programs and, at the same time, enhanced the credibility of the institutions as teaching and learning enterprises. Throughout the 1980s the policies in many community colleges were modified so that students who did not make steady progress toward completing a program might be dropped from the rolls. The colleges also developed a variety of instructional strategies to accommodate different types of learners.

A technology of instruction has made some inroads, but progress has been slow. The definitions of *instruction* in use offer a clue. *Instruction* may be defined simply as "an activity that implements the curriculum." This definition assumes a sequence of courses that must be brought to the students. Another definition of *instruction* is "a sequence of events organized deliberately so that learning occurs." This definition does not depend on a curriculum, but it does include the word *learning,* and it implies a process leading to an outcome. But most instructors seemed still to define *instruction* not as a process but as a set of activities (lecturing, conducting discussions, cajoling, and so on) in which teachers typically engage. Such a definition removes both the courses and the learners from the enterprise.

Regardless of the medium employed, the basic model of instructional technology includes clearly specified learning outcomes or objectives, content deployed in relatively small portions, learning tasks arrayed in sequence, a variety of modes of presenting information, frequent feedback on student performance, and criterion tests at the ends of instructional units. The instructors are part of the technology of instruction when they define the objectives, write the tests, select and/or present the media, and, in general, connect the student to the learning tasks.

The technology of instruction has been important for two-year colleges, typically commuter institutions, in which the environment of a learning community is not available to exercise its subtle, yet powerful, influence on the students. The tools basic to an instructional technology have been available ever since words were first put on paper. The expansion in variety and use of other forms of reproducible media made additional sets of tools available. However, the concepts of instructional technology have been less widely adopted. It is as though new types of hammers, saws, and trowels had been taken up by artisans unaware of the shape of the houses they were attempting to construct.

The beginnings of a technology of instruction have been realized in the institutions that have adopted competency-based education and its companion form, mastery learning. In both of these strategies, the learning desired of the students must be converted into specific abilities or tasks that they can demonstrate at the conclusion of the sequences. A notable effort on behalf of both strategies was made during the 1970s, when the Fund for the Improvement of Post-Secondary Education sponsored a Competency-Based Undergraduate Education Project. It built on decades of efforts to define the competencies to be exhibited by the graduates of academic programs. The occupational programs rarely had difficulty in specifying the accuracy with which a student was expected to caulk a pipe or type a letter.

However, specifying tangible, desired outcomes has often been perceived as a precarious exercise. The span from broadly stated college goals to tasks to be performed by students at the end of a portion of a course is long, and the connections may be difficult to make. The links between "Making people better," "Helping them cope with society," "Training them for jobs," "Preparing them for clerical positions," and "Students will type 70 words per minute" may be too tenuous. A technology of instruction puts responsibility for learning jointly in the hands of instructors and students; both must participate. Perhaps educators despair of being called to account if they fail. Teaching is not like building a wall; the chances are good that a brick will remain in place, whereas the influences on students, the myriad impressions they receive in addition to their instruction, the predispositions they bring to the task—all can change program results.

Yet the search for a technology of instruction applicable to an institution with a heterogeneity of students has continued, and with good reason. As Drucker (1969, p. 338) has said, "Teaching is the only major occupation of man for which we have not yet developed tools that make an average person capable of competency and performance." He was concerned about the perennial search for "better teachers," saying that we cannot hope to get them in quantity: "In no area of human endeavor have we ever been able to upgrade the human race. We get better results by giving the same people the right tools and by organizing their work properly" (p. 338). Drucker's plea was for a technology of instruction that would improve teaching by making it depend more on better techniques than on better people.

Some of the most far-reaching applications of instructional technology have been undertaken by the instructors of remedial courses and the managers of learning resource centers. During the 1970s and 1980s, this group moved steadily from the periphery of the educational establishment toward the mainstream. They became not only teachers of remedial classes but also managers of student flow, and their learning resource centers became more nearly integral parts of the instructional programs. They expanded their provision of academic support services to instructors in the academic and occupational areas, and they became more deeply involved in measuring instructional outcomes. Because they were not expected to perform traditional classroom instruction, and because remedial classes frequently were assigned to them, they were able to develop different instructional forms. Some of them built programs based on mastery learning (Campbell, 1983), while others focused on computer-managed instruction (Havlicek and Coulter, 1982). They became considerably more aware as a professional group; and this awareness was reflected in their participation in vigorously functioning professional associations: the National Association for Developmental Education, the Western College Reading and Learning Association, and the Illinois Association for Personalized Learning Programs. Conceptually, they coalesced around instruction as a discipline. Many of them had begun as teachers of reading, English, mathematics, or psychology; but as they became deeply involved in the learning resource centers and the remedial programs, their connections with their academic disciplines weakened, and they became much more concerned with the technology of instruction.

Mastery Learning. Mastery learning, a technology of instruction in itself, was described and advocated by several educators, especially by Benjamin Bloom of the University of Chicago (see Bloom, 1973). The intent of mastery learning is to lead all students to specified competencies (as opposed to programs that have the effect of sorting students along a continuum of individual ability). In a mastery learning plan, competencies are specified in the form of learning objectives. Practice tests, corrective feedback, additional learning time for those who need it, and a variety of instructional techniques are provided to ensure that all, or at least most, of the students attain mastery of the concepts or skills at the prescribed standard.

Proponents of mastery learning have pointed to sizable cognitive and affective gains made by students—gains on test scores and in personal development—when this strategy has been used. The gains have been attributed to any or all of the following: more focused teaching; cooperation instead of competitiveness among students; the definition of specific learning objectives; the amount of class time actually spent in learning; practice and feedback before the graded examinations; and teachers' expectations that most students will attain mastery.

Mastery learning procedures have been adopted in some community college courses and programs, even becoming prominent for a while at City Colleges of Chicago (Shabat and others, 1981), but the concept has not swept the field. Many reasons can be advanced for the failure of this technology of instruction to become more prevalent. Faculty members and administrators who have shied away from mastery learning offer several: It costs too much to develop and operate programs with a sufficient variety of instructional forms; it takes too much of teachers' and tutors' time; outcomes for most courses cannot be defined or specified in advance; allowing students time to complete course objectives interferes with school calendars; students may not be motivated if they are not in competition with their fellows for grades; employers and the public expect the college to sort students, not to pass them all through at prescribed levels of competency; accrediting agencies and other overseers demand differential grades. Froh and Muraki (1980) interviewed 40 of the 200 instructors who had been introduced to mastery learning strategies at workshops sponsored by the University of Chicago and the City Colleges of Chicago. About one-third of these instructors said that they had modified or abandoned the components because it was too time-consuming to construct program specifications and tests and to give necessary feedback to the students.

Regardless of the validity of the arguments set forth by proponents and by antagonists of mastery learning, the concept would seem to have a firm place in a teaching institution. If mastery learning can bring most students to the criterion levels, as specified in learning objectives, why should it not be installed? The answer may be that many people within the community colleges see themselves as gatekeepers for the universities and the employers, denying certification to many in order to accredit the few who will achieve at the succeeding institution or place of work. This attitude runs deep in an institution that for most of its history has had to defend itself against charges that it was not a true college. "Haven't the best colleges always sorted their students so that only the brightest went on to the most prominent careers? What would happen to our students if we did not prepare them for the competitiveness that exists in universities where mastery learning is not in place? How would our students fare in the competitive world of work?" So run the objections.

Competency-Based Education. Another technology, competency-based education, has also made inroads in community colleges. Competency-based education depends also on the specification of desired competencies to be exhibited by the students, but it does not include all the specific instructional strategies of mastery learning. The Competency-Based Undergraduate Education Project wrestled with defining the outcomes of liberal education. Ewens (1977) found a paradox in attempting to convert liberal education to competencies. It was the seemingly insoluble dilemma of converting higher education from an ideal-referenced standard to criterion-referenced or norm-referenced standards. "Ideal-referenced judgments presuppose some notion of the good, the excellent, the higher, the best," but most education now deals with minimal competencies, functioning in an environment, meeting acceptable standards of behavior (p. 19). There is no room for the ideal when we ask "What is a competent person?" The dilemma appears with force in the tendency of all education to teach job-related skills. One's job is what one *does*; one's work is what one *is*. If education teaches for jobs, ignoring what the person is, it runs the risk of creating a corps of dissatisfied graduates when they find that a job is not enough for a satisfactory life—not to mention the issue of whether they find jobs at a level for which they were trained.

The most successful adoptions of competency-based education have been in occupational studies, especially nursing education and business education, where the performance objectives reflect tasks that must be actually done in a particular job. At institutions such as Gateway Technical Institute (Wisconsin), competency-based education is used in all the classes (Kaprelian and Perona, 1981). It has also been used as a basis for articulating secondary school occupational programs with their community college counterparts (Doty, 1985). And it has been employed in high school completion programs (Singer, 1986). Competency-based education has not been widely adopted in general education or liberal arts programs. When it has been adopted for this purpose, it has been most successful at small institutions, where working face to face is feasible for a critical number of the entire staff—that is, small colleges such as Kirkwood Community College (Iowa), where competency-based education has become the foundation of the liberal arts program.

The Possibilities for Instructional Technology. For a variety of reasons, efforts to build instructional technology into the college system have enjoyed little success. During the 1960s the fantasy of automated instructional systems that would take students from one point of measured learning to another was popular (see, for example, Leonard, 1968). This fantasy subsided in the 1970s as institutional inertia proved too great and as institutional purposes other than effecting student learning became too prominent. The students themselves subtly undermined the installation of instructional systems as they came to the colleges seeking what Green (1980, p. 47) has called "second-order educational benefits"—such as certificates, diplomas, and licenses that could be used to enhance their occupational opportunities and income. The classroom with one faculty member and a group of students in attendance remained the dominant instructional model. Fashions in instruction— writing across the curriculum, critical thinking in every classroom, and the visionary search for students' learning style, to name but a few—came and went; the basic structure remained the same.

The most successful programs have several elements in common, even when they are not based on a technology of instruction. Many of the career programs include programmatic funding from outside the college; examinations administered by an external licensing bureau; criterion-based achievement examinations designed and administered by the faculty; follow-up surveys of student job entry, success, and attitudes toward the program; special admissions requirements; entrance and diagnostic examinations; sequenced courses required of all matriculants; and staff identification with the program. These components are usually combined in a program administered by a specially designated coordinator or chairperson. The instructors associated with such a program work together as a unit, often in specially designed facilities. And the more successful the program, the more the program head and the instructors are in control of its various components: student recruitment, admissions, and job placement; course content; selection of instructional technologies; relations with licensing and accrediting agencies; and budgetary expenditures.

These program components are more a function of organization than of different forms of instruction. Yet in combination they exert a powerful influence on their staff and students. By contrast, it is difficult to counsel students into a curriculum when it is in fact a set of separate courses; to select or mandate particular instructional forms when the outcomes desired for the curriculum are vaguely stated; or to manage such a program when a request from a dean or a chairperson can be rejected by the instructor, who is actually the arbiter of the course. Courses for the baccalaureate-bound students are more often than not discrete, each with its own goals, media, and standards. The collegiate curriculum is more a myriad of miniature curricula than a program. The technology of instruction in community colleges rests more on the form of a program's organization than on the teaching devices it employs.

Nonetheless, judging from the spread of learning resource centers and instructional laboratories, instruction seems still a major concern. The drawbacks of further development of instructional technologies relate to both staff predilections and program organization. The inducements stem from the instructors and administrators alike who appreciate the significance of the felicitous description that Thornton (1972, p. 42) applied to the community college: "Either it teaches excellently, or it fails completely."

Assessing Instructional Effects

No type of instructional technology has been sufficiently powerful to overcome the traditional educational forms against which it has been pitted. With rare exceptions an institution-wide commitment to demonstrable learning outcomes has foundered on the rocks of inertia and on an inability to demonstrate that it is worth the effort it entails. However, assessing student learning is as important a component of instruction as any other aspect of the process.

Is the community college the home of "good teaching"? Information on the effects of instruction is always hard to obtain because of the number of variables that must be controlled in any study: the entering abilities of the students, the criterion tests and instructional procedures used, and the level of the course or learning unit, to name only a few. Comparative studies are especially difficult because of the unfeasibility of matching student groups and instructional presentations (are any two lecture sessions really the same?). Rather than try to compare learning attained, many studies have used student and instructor preferences as the dependent variable. Researchers have measured the value of computer-assisted instruction by asking students whether they preferred it to live lectures. The reports usually indicated that many students prefer the interpersonal contact with instructors, while many others do quite well with the instructional programs presented through the computer. But pre- and postinstructional assessments of student learning rarely yield significant differences between treatments, and few researchers in community colleges report this type of study.

In the 1980s new efforts were made to assess institutional effects broadly—for example, by measuring student learning through statewide, interinstitutional, and institution-wide studies. Even though such studies are common in most other countries, they are alien to American higher education (where the responsibility for measuring cognitive change in students has been relegated to classroom instructors). Therefore, the efforts to institute such studies have been greeted with little enthusiasm. The leaders in many institutions have given lip service to the importance of student outcomes measurement, but, beyond a flurry of study groups and the usual skittishness displayed by educators who are faced with a potential change in their routine, little has been effected.

In a few states, however, the colleges have been encouraged or mandated to install institution-wide testing programs. Sometimes the encouragement includes a budget supplement. Tennessee has authorized up to 5 percent in additional appropriations to each college that provides information on student learning in general education or in the area of the student's major, or data on the number of students passing licensure examinations. Supplemental funds are also available to colleges that use data from surveys of current students, alumni, and dropouts to improve college programs and services. Other states have used the stick instead of the carrot. In Florida students must pass an externally designed College Level Academic Skills Test (CLAST) before they can receive an associate degree and/or enter the junior year at a publicly supported university. Georgia and Texas have similar programs. Outcomes assessment in those states has been connected with student progress—a significant departure from the more typical practice of assigning places in higher classes primarily on the basis of student interest, course-taking pattern, and grades received.

Little coordinated measurement of student learning has been effected elsewhere. In a 1987 study Boyer found that nine states required placement examinations for freshmen but only three required a degree-qualifying test—and, in one of those states (California), the requirement did not apply to community colleges.

Four states were conducting alumni and follow-up studies. The institution-wide assessment activities most often found were placement tests in the three Rs. Pre- and posttests applied in remedial programs were also popular. Externally imposed assessment was an actuality in only a few states, but the threat was there. According to El-Khawas (1987), 85 percent of the community college administrators who were surveyed felt that some form of assessment would be likely in the next few years, but they seemed to have no clear sense of what to assess or what instruments they could apply to their programs.

The press for assessment continued. Alarmed at the rapid increase in per-student cost, especially since the public pays most of it, and prodded by constituents who deplored the low success rates for minority students, the legislatures and appointed officials in many states insisted on more direct measures of college outcomes. What proportion of the matriculants obtain degrees? How many pass licensure examinations? How many are employed in areas for which they were trained? And—most disturbing of all for a professional group that has taken pride in its vaguely defined goals and processes—how much did the students learn? For the faculty especially, this last query could not be set aside as beyond their purview. Influential outsiders were demanding to know just what was happening as a result of their ministrations.

New Jersey's College Outcomes Evaluation Program offers an example of the direction that assessment was taking. The program was created by the Board of Higher Education in 1985. An advisory committee was appointed to develop a comprehensive assessment program with emphasis on "a sophomore test in verbal skills, quantitative reasoning, and critical thinking" (New Jersey Advisory Committee . . . , 1987, p. iii). The board's action followed from various statewide testing initiatives, especially a basic skills assessment program that had been installed for entering freshmen several years earlier. The New Jersey Advisory Committee recommended that several types of assessment be undertaken, some within the colleges and others external to them. The internal measures were to be the outcomes of general education, student learning in each major course, and retention and completion rates—the standard variables in assessing student progress. The main external measure was to be a "common statewide assessment of general intellectual skills." The program was to coordinate these efforts, "oversee the collection and analysis of the information, and report regularly to the Board of Higher Education" (pp. iv–v). Questions of enforcement and sanctions for noncompliance were not settled.

The New Jersey plan touched the community colleges just as the Florida College Level Academic Skills Program had. Collecting student retention and follow-up data was one thing, but a test of student knowledge administered at the conclusion of the sophomore year was quite another. Complaints about outside control of the curriculum, the demise of academic freedom, and similar lamentations were heard. Examinations that reveal student learning to people outside the confines of the single classroom have been anathema in academe. Few within the colleges had any notion of how to construct them. Except in rare instances the staff had made no effort to collect and use such information until the state legislatures tied the process to college funding or to student access.

The Pros and Cons of Assessment

Most staff members in most colleges are resistant to outcomes assessment mainly because colleges are organized in such a way that academic departments and courses reflecting subject-area content are dominant. Students are supposed to learn history, music, and mathematics in separate enclaves. Some students learn more efficiently than others, and classroom tests have always been used to determine which students are better than their fellows. The national testing organizations that offer subject tests from biology to sociology, used to determine which students deserve entry to further school programs, play into this form of normative measurement. It works well when the purpose is to spread individuals along a continuum, because it emphasizes variation in student ability. This variation is so strong that the difference in scores made by students in a single course will often be as great as the difference between the class average and the scores made by another group of students who have never taken the course.

This normative model, useful for assigning places in a

program or grade marks to students within it, is different from the criterion-referenced measures usually employed when a program or an institution is being assessed. Criterion-referenced measurement refers to the learning obtained by individuals as measured against a standard. If all students answer all questions correctly, then the entire group has learned everything that the test asked; and if the test was designed as a sample of all knowledge to be gained in a course, program, or institution, then the instructional unit has been a total success. However, applying criterion-referenced analysis in an institution with a history of normative-referenced testing requires a complete shift in the way that the staff view their work. Easy to conceptualize, that form of outcomes assessment bogs down in practice. Rare is the institutional leader with sufficient patience or skill to turn the group away from its traditional way of looking at student-learning measures. Rare is the leader who can explain the value and purposes of population sampling and test development that demands items that are not course specific.

Unfamiliarity with assessment is a central issue even though much information is available. Ewell (1987) has discussed many of these problems in implementing assessment programs, showing that often no one on campus knows what assessment is for or what its consequences will be. He has also noted the organizational problem of assessment, which, like any innovation, may disturb many long-standing formal and informal relationships. Adelman's (1986) collection of essays on the assessment of college students' learning includes arguments for and against assessment in higher education, descriptions of practices, and critiques of instruments and techniques. Harris (1986) has prepared a useful paper showing where additional information on ways of assessing outcomes may be obtained. Miller (1979) places assessment in a broader context, considering everything from institutional objectives and the operation of the governing board to student learning and faculty effectiveness. And detailed information for evaluating career programs is provided by Warmbrod and Persavich (1981). Forms, questions, sample surveys, and full sets of instructions are included.

Many other reasons why assessment has not been widely adopted have been advanced, including the feasibility of measuring important outcomes, the time or money available to implement a testing program, the tendency for the faculty to teach primarily what the test will measure, the risk of outsiders' misusing the information gained, and the students' unwillingness to cooperate in a process that has no relevance to them. But all these objections can be overcome if an institution's leaders and at least a proportion of its faculty want to pursue the process.

Why should the staff members in any institution measure the learning attained by their students? Such measurement in the abstract is an exercise not likely to gain much staff support. The colleges are not funded according to student learning; budgets are fixed in a political arena. The data can be used for institutional public relations, but only if a skilled leader knows how to weave them into statements of institutional worth. Appeals to professionalism are of little use because the staff perceive information on student learning gathered by outsiders as peripheral to them. Information on student outcomes might be used to bolster staff morale, but only if sizable learning gains are demonstrated; like the children of Lake Wobegon, all one's students must be above average. Attempts to feed student-learning data back to instructors, so that classroom practices can be improved, probably will prove futile because most instructors will not accept data about their students from anyone else.

Even so, assessment can be used for several purposes. Students can be tested at entry so that they can be directed into proper courses. The scores can be used to establish a baseline against which students' learning can be measured periodically as they progress through the programs in which they are enrolled. Students' achievement on licensure examinations, their rate of placement in jobs, their graduation success, and their movement into further education can also be measured, along with their satisfaction with the education that they received. Any type of standardized or locally developed instrument may be applied.

A longitudinal study can be initiated, with the entire cohort of students entering for the first time in any term as its subjects. However, this procedure is limited because of the magnitude of the data that must be collected. It works best where a percentage of students is sampled. Each term these students can be asked about their aspirations and course-taking patterns. Different forms of the placement exam or other measures can be used to test the students at entry and at various points along the way. When a small group is sampled, follow-up becomes much more feasible.

An alternative form of outcomes assessment is based on a cross-sectional model, where content measures are included with items asking about student satisfaction, course-taking behavior, use of support services, and other information about intrainstitutional concerns. An item bank can be developed, with items categorized by skills, such as critical thinking, reading, and writing; by content, such as history, chemistry, and mathematics; and by response type, including multiple and free response. The items can be as specific or as general as desired. Tests can be constructed and administered to students in classes, and certain demographic information can be solicited at the same time. After the tests have been taken, groups of students can be classified according to aspiration, number of units taken, prior school experience, or any other measure that seems of interest.

The longitudinal model works best in a college where the students matriculate with the intention of participating in programs organized sequentially and where the college's processes are designed to ensure that they do. The cross-sectional model should be used if the college leaders are serious about providing an institution where students can drop in and out at will, the lifelong learning ideal. It skirts the problem of student retention and the difficulty of follow-up because it generates new cohorts each time it is administered. The level of knowledge displayed by the students *collectively* at entrance, after they have completed a certain number of units, and at graduation can be compared. Any available demographic information can be used to make further differentiations.

Regardless of the impetus for assessment or the model that is pursued, certain principles should apply:

- The results of an examination should not be tied to a single course or instructor; causal inferences should not be sought, nor should the findings be used to judge an instructor, a department, or a discipline.

- The items used must not be course specific but should cover concepts that might have been learned anywhere.
- Scores on the examination should not be made a condition of graduation for the students.
- The student population should be sampled; universal assessment systems are too cumbersome for most colleges to manage.
- Alternate forms of the numerous entrance examinations should be used as measures of student knowledge at the completion of certain numbers of units.
- The faculty must be involved as much as possible in test selection, design, item construction, and test scoring, but installation of the process should not be delayed until all are in accord.
- Testing specialists who are sensitive to the staff should be employed, with the understanding that, although assessing is a group effort, staff members will not be forced to participate.
- No one set of measures should be used to provide data for different evaluations. Different measures should be used, for example, to evaluate student progress, college processes, and the college's contribution to its community.
- Measures of student achievement need not be restricted to learning but may also include assessment of employment, transfer, satisfaction with the institution, and retention; measures that relate to academic knowledge are of considerably more interest to educators than they are to legislators or members of the lay public.
- A belief in the value of individualization need not extend to variant curricular objectives for everyone; if shared understandings and values contribute to social cohesion, then some consistency in college goals and in measures of college outcomes should be maintained.

Issues

The major issues in instruction center on the extent to which a technology of instruction will progress. Will more instructors adopt instruction as a process instead of an activity? What types of instructional leadership can best effect this change?

Assessing instructional outcomes is an integral part of instructional technology. Will the persistent calls for mandatory assessment enhance the development of a technology of instruction?

Low-cost personal computers have become widespread. How has their use affected the students' writing and computational skills? How has it affected the teaching of those skills?

Will administrator-dominated instructional management evolve? How much responsibility should the director of the learning resource center have for the entire instructional program? Will instructors gain control over more of the essential elements of instruction?

The consequences of a turn away from print as the primary mode of information transmission have not yet been fully realized. What impact on instruction will be made by students who have gained much of their prior knowledge through nonprint sources? Does an instructional program centered on teachers in classrooms best accommodate them?

Mastery learning has been effected in compensatory and career education. Can it spread to the collegiate function?

Although each new instructional medium, from the radio to the computer, has forced educators to examine their teaching practices, none alone has revolutionized teaching. A general acceptance of instruction as a process that must, by definition, lead to learning might do more in actualizing the prime function of the community colleges.

Seven

Student Services:
Supporting Educational Objectives

Direct classroom or laboratory-based instruction is only part of what colleges offer their students. They also provide services such as registration, advising, extracurricular activities, job placement, orientation, financial aid, and activities that assist students in negotiating their way through the college. The category "student services" covers all these activities.

Student Personnel Services

The rationale for student personnel services stemmed originally from the institution's need to regulate its clients' activities. According to O'Banion (1971, p. 8), "One of the historical models for the student personnel worker is that of regulator or repressor. The student personnel profession came into being largely because the president needed help in regulating student behavior." In other words, students need to be controlled for the sake of institutional order, a rationale underlying not only the counseling of students into the proper programs but also the registration, student activities, orientation, student government, and record-keeping functions.

However, the rationale evolved so that the student personnel services were presumed to be more positively supportive of student development. Reporting findings of the Committee on Appraisal and Development of Junior College Student Personnel Programs, Collins (1967, p. 13) wrote, "The student personnel program should be the pivot, the hub, the core around which the whole enterprise moves. It provides the structure and creates the pervasive atmosphere which prompts the junior college to label itself as student-centered." Surveying the programs in 123 colleges, the committee identified twenty-one "essential student personnel functions" that should be provided if the colleges were to fulfill their mission of teaching and directing their vast array of students. The functions were categorized as *orientation* (precollege information, student induction, group orientation, career information), *appraisal* (personnel records, educational testing, applicant appraisal, health appraisal), *consultation* (student counseling, student advisement, applicant counseling), *participation* (cocurricular activities, student self-government), *regulation* (student registration, academic regulation, social regulation), *service* (financial aid, placement), and *organizational* (program articulation, in-service education, program evaluation).

Several similar listings of student services have been published. Humphreys (1952) offered six major categories; Thornton (1972) divided the services into five categories; and a manual for student services issued by the Washington State Board for Community College Education (Heiner and Nelson, 1977) offered ideal philosophies, goals, objectives, functions, and staffing patterns for the administration of student services, dividing them into eight areas.

A more recent statement, issued by the League for Innovation in the Community College, outlined a revised set of concepts regarding student development. Thirty-one directives organized under seven major headings instructed student development professionals to design processes that would smooth student entry and placement, enhance student interaction with college staff and functions, assist students in gaining support from all types of college services, ensure student learning and development, coordinate with other organizations, maintain student records, and assist in selecting college staff members (Doucette and Dayton, 1989).

Recruitment and Retention. Services to students begin even before they arrive at the institution. Because of the community colleges' commitment to serve as many members of the community as feasible, they have frequently engaged in extensive recruitment activities. These activities, which accelerated as the population of eighteen-year-olds declined after peaking in the late 1970s, have been especially vigorous in communities where the percentage of high school students beginning college has decreased.

All but one of the thirty-four community colleges in six of the largest districts in the nation had procedures linking the college with its surrounding high schools (Dallas, 1982). The faculty in the technical and occupational programs carried out recruiting activities for their areas, but the counseling staff were responsible for recruitment in general. These activities included administering tests to high school students and then helping them and their parents interpret the results; providing campus facilities for activities attracting high school students; presenting videotaped and personal recruitment promotions; offering advanced-placement classes to qualified students; and disseminating radio, television, and mailed information to potential students (not only high school students but also members of the broader community), advising them of campus events.

The drive to attract students coincided with attempts to retain them, propelled by the quite reasonable notion that it is more feasible to keep the students enrolled than to continually seek new matriculants. One aspect of retention depended on placing the students in programs commensurate with their interest and abilities. Accordingly, members of the student personnel staff were involved in admissions testing and cooperated with the instructional staff in using the results of those tests to place students in courses. The literature is filled with accounts of efforts to counsel students into the proper courses. In California, for example, 65 percent of the community colleges require that all students take tests at admission, and around one-fourth use tests of basic skills as prerequisites for entry to occupational or academic transfer-credit classes (Kangas, 1985). These activities were accelerated in the 1980s as several states began urging the colleges to reduce their dropout rates and increase the number of students satisfactorily completing programs and going on to employment or to further education. The

Florida State Department of Education developed a manual replete with ideas for retaining students (Farmer, 1980).

Student retention has broad appeal because of its importance to staff members and funding agents. Retention was central to an interinstitutional study undertaken by twenty-nine California community colleges. This Learning Assessment Retention Consortium tested and administered surveys to students in remedial English classes and tracked retention along with student success in subsequent classes and student self-assessment (Slark and others, 1987). The effort was similar to a student-tracking study conducted in a set of fourteen California community colleges in the late 1970s. These types of interinstitutional measurement efforts have several benefits; for example, they encourage skilled staff members to share their expertise, and they help to mitigate intrainstitutional concerns about the dire uses to which the data might be put.

Counseling and Guidance. Counseling and guidance have been at the core of student services since the earliest years. Eells (1931) gave guidance a status equal to the "popularizing," "preparatory," and "terminal" functions in his list of the junior college's main activities. The contention has been that community college students need help in moving into the college and out again into careers and other schools, and that individualized instruction through counseling and other non-classroom-based activities is essential.

Guidance has always been intended to match applicants to the programs best suited to their own goals and abilities. Medsker (1960) emphasized the necessity of placing students in the programs that are best suited for them. According to Thornton (1972, p. 269), the purpose of guidance is "to help each student to know, to accept, and to respect his own abilities, so that he may match them with realistic educational and occupational goals." Riesman (1981) asserted that guidance is essential for students who may want to attend further school but are terrified at the idea of going to "college."

The belief that these students deserve more than cognitive development in a rigid environment has also guided practitioners. The expressions "treating the student as a whole" and "assuming

responsibility for the full intellectual, social, and personal development of students" are frequently seen in the student personnel
literature. By definition, these professionals try to effect student
development in psychic, moral, and physical, as well as intellectual,
realms. To student personnel advocates, students are not minds
apart from their bodies and emotions; they are whole people, and
the college should treat them as such.

As the key element in student development, counseling must
be integrated with other campus activities; must maximize students'
chances to reach their potential; must focus on educational, personal, social, and vocational development; and, being student-
centered, must take into account students' interests, aptitudes,
needs, values, and potential. Comprehensive counseling should
include goal setting, personal assessment, development of change
strategies, strategy implementation, evaluation, and recycling of the
whole process for each student.

This therapeutic view affirms the belief that the best way to
educate people is to integrate all their objectives and all their ways
of functioning—cognitive, affective, and psychomotor. It holds that
students are active and responsible participants in their educational
growth and process, that with help and support students must make
decisions affecting their lives and must deal with the consequences
of their decisions, and that all professionals on the campus must
work collaboratively toward greater integration of their services and
their professions. In this approach counseling is not imposed on
students but is initiated and determined by them. It works in
partnership with classroom instruction and cocurricular activities.
In this student development process, goals are set, the individual's
current position in relation to these goals is assessed, and the best
change strategy or a combination of strategies is implemented. The
strategy's effectiveness in meeting the individual's goals is then
evaluated; new goals are set; and the process begins all over again.

Assessments of student services' effects are sometimes based
on this holistic development model. Measures based on psychological constructs have been applied, and the level of satisfaction that
students feel has been a favorite measure. College leaders point with
pride to the follow-up studies showing that most students value
their college experiences for their contribution to self-understand-

ing, further schooling, social interaction, and job skill training. However, personality development concepts are more applicable in institutions that control most aspects of the person's life. Apparent change in the developing personality is more likely to be revealed in a four-year, residential college than in a commuter institution where most students attend part-time.

Regardless of the concepts undergirding their efforts, counselors face unremitting conflict between guiding students into the programs most consonant with their abilities and allowing them to reach for their own preferred goals. Many students have wanted to go in one direction but seemed best qualified to go in another. Guidance counselors have devised procedures for ascertaining student goals and assessing student qualifications, trying all the while to strike the proper balance between goals and abilities. But when students appear without distinct career or study goals, when their goals do not match their abilities, or when the testing instruments do not adequately assess them (and all three often come into play at the same time), the role of the counselor has been blurred. When students have decried discrimination and demanded the right to enter any program, the guidance function has staggered. And when institutional policies allow most students access to all but the programs with limited space or limitations imposed by external accrediting agencies, guidance workers have to adjust.

Some critics have taken guidance counselors to task on broader issues. Gay (1977), for example, argued that "while student personnel workers have professed themselves to be educators and to be interested in the whole student, they have served essentially as housekeepers, guardians of the status quo, and have been seen by many in the postsecondary education arena as petty administrators or 'those people who sit in their office and give warm strokes to students who complain about the system, particularly the teacher.' . . . In their present capacities, student affairs workers are clearly providing services, needed services, which contribute to student mobility; but whether or not some of the mundane tasks necessary to the services now rendered are wise use of the skills and talents of counselors and other specialists of student affairs is another question" (p. 18). And Brick (1972, p. 677) questioned whether psychological counseling is "an educational function which should be implemented by an educational institution, or . . . a public health function which should be implemented by a public health agency?"

Still, counseling and guidance services have been maintained. They are less likely to be questioned now because of their presumed usefulness in maintaining student flow into the programs for which they are best suited and on through to successful program completion. Faculty advisers cannot reasonably be expected to carry the entire burden; in fact, one study found that 21 percent of the students whom the faculty had advised to take certain courses had not met the prerequisites for those courses (Heard, 1987). However, student development theory has become considerably less applicable to the counseling situation because of the high proportion of part-time students who use the college as only one resource in their environment and because of the wide range of student age. It is difficult to apply concepts of adolescent development when at least half of the students are age twenty-five or older. In addition, many of the eighteen- to twenty-five-year-olds are responsible for their own behavior and often for that of their dependents. Guidance activities also must be structured differently for the high proportion of part-time students who have been involved in the work force or in other areas of higher education.

Orientation. Student personnel workers also plan and operate student orientation programs. Tang (1981) described orientation as but one part of recruitment and retention efforts. Sessions offered during the summer preceding the term, in one- or two-day sessions at the beginning of the term, in classes meeting throughout the first term, and in seminars for special groups of students have all been popular. One college offered a three-day retreat for the first 150 freshmen to sign up with faculty members, who helped in leading the activities. Another maintained a series of lectures on issues of concern to students each week throughout the term. Orientation in many colleges was the responsibility of the counselors, who set up small sessions to inform students of college policies. Some colleges had orientation committees composed of faculty members, students, and student personnel administrators, who planned various events for beginning students.

Frequently, student orientation accompanies a psychology course for which credit is awarded. Counselors and instructors often participate jointly in these courses, teaching study skills, career exploration, individual goal orientation, and various strategies for "surviving" in college. They may also use psychological test batteries designed to apprise the students of their own personality profiles. There have been fewer mass sessions at which new students are welcomed to the college by the president, board members, and other dignitaries and given directions and a listing of the college rules. Session planners have come to realize that such occasions are more ceremonial than instructive.

Specialized orientation programs frequently are offered in the summer before classes begin. Queensborough Community College (New York) has operated such a program successfully, finding that students who participate are only about half as likely to drop out of school and are more likely to make better grades (Miller, 1987). Specialty orientation sessions also deal with test-anxiety reduction; at these sessions numerous types of aptitude, achievement, and interest instruments are administered. A study of California community colleges found that orientation was required or recommended for at least some students in nearly all the institutions (Rounds and Andersen, 1985).

Programmed instruction booklets have proved useful in helping students plan their course work; the efficacy of orientation through a self-paced instruction book was demonstrated at Mississippi Gulf Coast Junior College, where students learned more about the college though using those materials than comparable students in orientation lectures (Fisher, 1975). However, no single orientation method has proved uniformly satisfactory, and one college often adopts a procedure just as another is abandoning it.

Extracurricular Activities. Various types of extracurricular activities for students have been in place in community colleges since the earliest institutions organized student clubs and athletic events. Eells (1931) listed numerous student activities in the junior colleges of the 1920s, mentioning in particular Pasadena Junior College (California), in which seventy clubs were active. The most popular were athletic clubs, with literary groups, musical activities, and religious and moral organizations following. Science organizations were most common in the public institutions, but camera clubs, pep clubs, honor clubs, and so on, operated throughout the colleges of the day.

Although all colleges have had student clubs and extracurricular activities, few of them developed programs in which sizable percentages of the students participated. A survey at Johnson County Community College (Kansas) found that students recognized the importance of student activities but did not participate because of lack of time and interest (Tolbert, 1971). Fewer than half of the students in the Los Angeles Community College District expressed any interest at all in extracurricular activities (Weiser, 1977). Students enrolled in off-campus centers of Prince George's Community College (Maryland) were even less likely to want to take part in extracurricular events (Larkin, 1977). Students who do participate usually benefit. Those involved in major student activities are more likely to stay in school even through their grade point averages are comparable to those of the noninvolved students (Pankanin and Lucas, 1981; Rinck, 1979). The Study Group on the Conditions of Excellence in American Higher Education (1984) contends that the more that students are involved in a full range of campus activities, the more they gain from their college experience.

For a number of reasons, student activities programs are difficult to organize in community colleges: Freshmen and sophomores lack the leadership experience of university upper-division students; many students work part-time; few reside on campus; only two years are available to develop student leaders; and many high school leaders elect to attend universities instead of community colleges. Clearly, the full effect of a campus environment is not available to students who spend little more than an hour or two a day in class. Such students often spend more time working and commuting than full-time students in residential colleges spend on class preparation. Moreover, because commuter students spend most of their time away from the campus, other attractions, especially jobs and noncampus activities, make great claims on their time and interests. It is difficult to entice them to participate in activities or attend events other than those that coincide with the time they would be on campus for classes anyway. Community program a success if only as many as 10 percent of the students participate.

In spite of these handicaps, there have been some vigorous attempts to build student activities programs: providing student leadership-training programs, with workshops on group dynamics and communications skills; involving students as full voting members of faculty committees; assigning greater responsibilities to student government organizations, including their legal incorporation; assigning faculty members to student associations as consultants rather than as advisers; instructing student government representatives in procedures for polling student opinion on pertinent issues; requiring orientation courses with emphasis on student activities; developing a strong college art collection and sponsoring frequent, well-publicized exhibitions; and involving students in encounter-group sessions with faculty members and administrators. Many extracurricular activities have been developed especially for high-ability students in colleges that were unable to mount full sequences of honors courses. Bishara (1986) described these programs in rural Virginia, Friedlander (1982b) traced them in urban community colleges, and Farnsworth (1981) analyzed them in a college in Iowa.

As a way of involving more students, some commentators have called for student activities and organizations centering on academic departments. Goldberg (1973) proposed that, instead of charging the students a fee, colleges should allocate a portion of each department's budget for activities other than classroom instruction. This arrangement would involve instructors in publicizing the speakers, seminars, and concerts and in tying the events to the course work. Such a plan would seem to have merit; most of the respondents to the Center for the Study of Community Colleges' surveys of the faculty indicated that there were too few humanities-related colloquia, seminars, lectures, exhibitions, or concerts and recitals offered outside class; few instructors required attendance at out-of-class activities. Departmentally sponsored events would undoubtedly attract more student and faculty interest.

Studies of student athletic activities have found wide variance in the emphasis given to intercollegiate athletics and, indeed, to in the emphasis given to intercollegiate athletics and, indeed, to physical education in general. During the 1970s most institutions continued offering intramural team sports for interested students, but as the colleges increased their percentages of older, part-time students, these activities declined. Student activities began centering less on team sports and more on individual pursuits. Clubs and ad hoc groups organized to engage in hiking, cycling, scuba diving, backpacking, and jogging became widespread. Exercise classes open to staff members as well as students also sprang up as the concern for physical fitness grew among people of all ages. The 1980s saw this trend continuing, with aerobic dancing, swimming, and weight lifting gaining in popularity. However, since many of these activities were offered as credit or noncredit classes, they were not under the jurisdiction of the student services staff.

Residence Halls. Although the community college residence hall became rarer as the institutions grew in urban areas, it has persisted, with dormitories found in at least a few colleges in most states. In 1977 all public junior colleges in Mississippi except one had dormitories, and 14 percent of the students lived on campus (Moody and Busby, 1978). Richardson and Leslie (1980) recommended a return to residence halls as a way of coping with the growing costs of commuting.

Conceptually, housing students on campus has been identified as a key element in reducing attrition. Tinto's (1975) model of student involvement makes a strong case for on-campus residence, and Astin (1986) has noted that campus living increases students' involvement with the process of learning and development. But there has been no move to build residence halls at community colleges, and those who would enhance student involvement have been forced to attempt instead to increase faculty contact with students outside of class, to encourage students to form student clubs, and to schedule special events that would keep students on campus beyond class hours. Even providing opportunities for students to work on campus has proved considerably less widespread than providing direct financial aid, although students with campus jobs are certainly more likely to maintain their involvement.

Financial Aid. Financial aid for students has become an outstanding feature in higher education. Federal and state funds administered through Pell Grants, Supplemental Educational Opportunity Grants, Guaranteed Student Loans, College Work-Study aid, and State Student Incentive Grants, to name only some of the programs, have grown so that any shift in their availability has an immediately discernible impact on enrollments. Aid is so much a part of the college system that when the California legislature mandated a $100 per year fee to be paid by community college students, it made $52.5 million dollars available as student aid in the same bill (California State Postsecondary Education Commission, 1984).

Federal financial aid to students began with the Servicemen's Readjustment Act (GI Bill) in 1944 and was expanded with the National Defense Education Act (NDEA) in 1958; but the community colleges were slow to seek these funds. Not until after the passage of the Basic Educational Opportunity Grant program in 1972 (now called Pell Grants) did the majority of community colleges organize financial aid offices. Even then, according to Nelson (1976), the presidents of very few institutions felt that they had adequate staff to cover the responsibilities of student aid; some aid officers deliberately understated their requests for aid funds because they felt that it would add to an impossible work load.

One reason for the slow start was the misperception that, because of the comparatively low cost of community college education, students did not need financial assistance. However, students still had to spend money to live, still commuted to classes, and, by attending school, were forgoing income that they could otherwise have earned. Furthermore, since community college students were typically from lower-income groups, their needs were greater even though the cost of college going was less. By the 1980s the financial aid offices in most community colleges had gained the ability to direct grants and loans to students who needed them; one campus office at Northern Virginia Community College was making and maintaining more than 1,500 award packages each year (Archer and Archer, 1985).

Still, because of the relatively low tuition costs and because of various aid program restrictions, such as discrimination against part-time or non-degree-credit attendees, community college students have not received their proportionate share of financial aid. From the mid-1970s through the mid-1980s, the federal scholarship and fellowship funds received by community college students remained at around 16 percent of the total awards, if the proprietary schools were not included, even though the colleges enrolled over 25 percent of all full-time students and an even higher percentage of the part-timers. This proportion varied greatly between states, depending on the percentage of a state's students enrolled in community colleges and on the relative level of tuition charged. Students in community colleges in Arizona, Florida, Mississippi, and Oregon received more than 25 percent of the scholarship funds going to college students in those states, while community college students in Maine, New Hampshire, Louisiana, and South Dakota received less than 5 percent of the grant monies (National Center for Education Statistics, 1986b). Students in Maryland community colleges were receiving 21 percent of the total aid awarded to undergraduates in the state; Illinois students received 17 percent of the aid distributed in that state; Texas students received 13 percent. However, the figures for those three states are low compared to the percentage of the students enrolled in community colleges in those states.

Student abuse of the financial aid system has been a persistent problem. The charge has been made that many students enroll merely for the funds available to them and that student aid thus represents another form of welfare payment. City Colleges of Chicago (1984) took steps to mitigate abuse by insisting that class attendance, grades awarded, course repetitions, and numerous records reflecting academic progress be carefully watched, so that students receiving financial aid would maintain the proper enrollment status. Default rates on student loan repayment have grown along with the increased number of students receiving them; by 1988, 33 percent of the Guaranteed Student Loans in California were in default (California Community Colleges, 1989).

Financial aid availability affects student decisions both in enrolling initially and in maintaining continuing attendance. A series of studies done in California after a mandatory fee was imposed for the first time concluded that the fee contributed to a 7 percent enrollment loss statewide in 1984. Enrollment declines were greatest in districts with the lowest-income populations, but after financial aid procedures were strengthened and publicized, the low-income students returned (California Community Colleges, 1986, 1987b; Field Research Corporation, 1986). A Montgomery College (Maryland) study found that the local unemployment rate and consumer price index and the difference in tuition between the college and the University of Maryland did not significantly account for student enrollment variability but that financial aid awards were positively correlated with both initial enrollments and returning students in all age groups (Montgomery College, 1983). Murdock (1987) analyzed the data from several studies and found that financial aid had a slightly greater effect on persistence among community college students than among students at four-year colleges. In summary, financial aid is important to community college students, who seem to be receiving their share of financial aid if they attend on a full-time basis; and the typical aid recipient is older than the usual college student, more likely to be self-supporting, and more likely to be a member of a minority group (S. E. Miller, 1985).

Articulation

Program articulation refers to the movement of students—or, more precisely, the students' academic credits—from one school to another. Articulation is not a linear sequencing or progression from one point to another. It covers students going from high school to college; from two-year colleges to universities and vice versa; the double-reverse transfer students, who go from the two-year college to the university and then back again; and the people seeking credit for experiential learning as a basis for college or university credit. The concept includes admission, exclusion, readmission, advising, counseling, planning, curriculum, and course and credit evaluation.

Until recently articulation with the universities has been largely a one-way situation, a series of policies and procedures dictated by senior institutions. Before 1960 coordinated efforts to improve the plight of the transfer student were "almost nonexistent.

While articulation agreements between senior colleges and universities and high schools were generally well developed, programs centering attention on the two-year college graduate were scarce" (Kintzer, 1973, p. 5). Three styles of articulation agreements operate in the fifty states: formal and legal policies; state-system policies, in which the state tends to be the controlling agency; and voluntary agreements among institutions, whose main features are cooperation and negotiation rather than unilateral declaration or legislative statute.

Because the purposes of articulation are to facilitate the flow of students, coordinate programs among institutions, and minimize course duplication and overlap, nearly everyone in the college community is affected. Most of the problems in articulation have centered on the questions "Who decides?" "What shall be the criteria?" and "Who shall have the ultimate authority?" As community colleges have drawn an increasing proportion of entering freshmen, the problems have grown more complex.

Knoell and Medsker (1965) urged the development of master plans at the state level to define institutional roles and plan coordinated curricula because, in their view, the proper matching of transfer student and institution is probably more important than the matching of freshman student and institution.

Wattenbarger and Kintzer, who have individually and together studied issues in articulation, believe that articulation is essential but that community colleges should not be bound by university dictates. They found that transfer students usually perform in a manner similar to their past patterns of accomplishment but that various senior institution policies discriminate against students who transfer. They noted that little progress had been made in smoothing transfer relations in the years prior to 1985 and concluded that "At least half of the 50 states continue transfer negotiations interinstitutionally, most on a case-by-case basis" (Kintzer and Wattenbarger, 1985, p. 40). Problems were typically related to the types of courses for which transfer credit should be given, the students' finding openings in the academic major field of their choice, and the fact that in most cases the university staff insisted that the evaluation of community college credit should be made by the baccalaureate-granting institution. The spread of specialized career programs in the community colleges and of associate degree-granting proprietary schools has further accentuated articulation difficulties.

Where formalized articulation agreements were in place, they were usually brought about through the intervention of state boards of higher education. In states where upper-division universities had been built, articulation agreements spelling out roles of each institution in facilitating transfer were an obvious necessity. Agreements on a common core of general education courses were negotiated between the community colleges and universities in several states, but periodic negotiation was necessary to keep them current. Despite many efforts to involve faculty members from community colleges and universities in curriculum articulation, the student personnel staff typically contributed the lion's share of the effort—with counselors, admissions and records officers, transcript analysts, and articulation officers doing nearly all the work. It was one thing to make high-level pronouncements on the importance of articulation, quite another to negotiate the details.

Educators concerned with articulation have also had to consider reverse transfers, a large and growing group. Figures for 1986 reported by the Center for the Study of Community Colleges show that 25 percent of the students in community colleges had attended a four-year college or university; 10 percent had at least a bachelor's degree and were returning to take classes either for their own interest or to gain occupational skills. But many of the others had not succeeded at the senior schools. Grafton and Roy (1980) analyzed the effectiveness of community colleges in aiding students who had transferred to a senior institution, failed academically, returned to the community college, and then reentered the senior institution. They found that the students were more successful the second time around. Temple (1978) has argued that the two-year college's contribution to the achievement of reverse transfer students is greater than the university's and hence that the senior institutions must bend their efforts toward making their curricula compatible.

Problems of articulation between community colleges and secondary schools have never been as difficult as between community colleges and universities. Nonetheless, as the pool of high school graduates shrank in the 1980s, the community colleges worked to smooth the flow. Sacramento City College (California) issued a report pointing out how community colleges could develop or expand articulation programs with local high schools (Carey, Wark, and Wellsfry, 1986). Various computer-assisted guidance models have been developed so that secondary school counselors can direct students to proper community college programs (Lockett, 1981).

The major efforts in articulation took place between community colleges and universities, stimulated by the figures on the percentages of ethnic minority students transferring. With a combination of pride and deference, community college practitioners became much more aware that they were now the dominant force in mass education, and they deplored the university's lethargy in program articulation. They felt more like equal partners and were less willing to be dictated to by academic specialists in senior institutions, whose failures returned to community colleges for successful experiences. But problems of articulation seemed to rise more quickly than interinstitutional committees and state coordinating boards could resolve them, and the universities typically retained the upper hand in deciding who would be admitted.

In a pioneering move to stabilize community college entrance and to smooth the way for ultimate transfer, Miami-Dade Community College developed a comprehensive program to screen students into certain courses at entry and to monitor their progress throughout their tenure at the college (Harper and others, 1981; Kelly, 1981). Previous institutional practices had allowed students to take any courses and to stay at the institution indefinitely, whether or not they were proceeding toward program completion. In the new plan students were advised of the requirements both for graduation from the college and for transfer to various programs in Florida's universities. The system was mandatory; everyone who matriculated, except those who already had degrees and were taking courses for personal interest, was included in it.

Some internal resistance to the plan came initially from those who feared that enrollment would decline. And as soon as the strict probation and suspension rules were adopted, Miami-Dade dropped from its rolls several thousand students who were not making satisfactory progress (McCabe, 1981). It cost the institution about 5 percent of its students, or 700 FTSEs annually, after the number of students who were advised to drop out and the increased loads taken by students who remained in the system were balanced off. But although some students were dropped, many more were helped.

The system added measurably to the counseling load, but it also tended to get the faculty back into the academic advisement process. It made registration less easy; no longer could a student merely drop in and take a course. It did not discriminate against minority students; indeed, completion rates for those groups were improved measurably. As an example, 17 percent of the students and 14 percent of the graduates were black, suggesting that the black students, who began at a lower level of prior academic achievement, were being pulled up.

The Florida experience was repeated in other states. In California, for example, various efforts to identify and assist transfer students were funded. Several of the state's community colleges built Transfer Centers to coordinate information about transfer policies and to smooth course articulation, especially for minority and other underrepresented students. Similar centers were built elsewhere—for example, at Cuyahoga Community College (Ohio). These efforts to enhance transfer rates were stimulated not only by state agencies but also by various philanthropic foundations— notably the Ford Foundation, which funded an Urban Community College Transfer Opportunities Program.

Funding and Effect

Student services to various groups of nontraditional students have expanded. Child care services became widespread, and offices were opened to assist students with various types of handicaps. Job placement services, always a feature in community colleges, grew as the proportion of students seeking immediate job entry rose. Student services also were extended as entrance testing became widespread.

Funds to support these augmented services were derived from a variety of sources. In some cases special state funds were made available. In others Vocational Education Act funds, Title III monies, Educational Opportunities Programs and Services funds, and various state and federal programs supporting handicapped students and those in other special categories were used. Thus, although the student affairs division might be organized on a line-and-staff basis, as detailed in Deegan's (1982) monograph, the subordinate offices might expand or contract with the availability of funds to support them. For the first time in the history of the community college, the 1980s saw a trend toward funding student services on soft money—that is, extracurricular funds targeted to assist certain types of students.

The effectiveness of student services was a perennial issue. In many colleges evaluation depended on reports from students about how well they perceived the usefulness of one or another aspect of student services. As an example, students at Thomas Nelson Community College (Virginia) were highly critical of student activities, indicating that programs were not very good (McLean, 1986). Students at Howard Community College (Maryland) rated all services except student activities and transfer evaluations as very useful (Nespoli and Radcliffe, 1982). Students also typically rated job placement services as not very useful. However, there were efforts at more sophisticated evaluations, particularly attempts to determine how student retention and achievement were affected. Counseling and orientation activities were frequently assessed for their contribution to retention. Most students found that preregistration counseling and orientation sessions were effective in enhancing performance and increasing retention (Brophy, 1984; Lowe, 1983; Stupka, 1986). Richards (1986) found that Colorado community college students who followed the advice that counselors gave them regarding courses to take were considerably more likely to stay in school and succeed in their classes.

The effects of the many efforts to stimulate articulation and transfer are difficult to discern. Reliable data are unavailable. The research officers and student services personnel in many colleges conduct follow-up studies of students, but response rates are typically poor, and the universities in the region are often uncooperative about sending reports back to the colleges. In some states the student follow-up studies are conducted by central agencies. Since 1967 the Illinois Community College Board has sent names of all community college alumni who have appeared in the state's universities to the community colleges, which, in return, report institutional data on them back to the board. The California State Postsecondary Education Commission has engaged in a similar activity since 1978. The Washington State Board for Community College Education conducts annual student transfer surveys, and since 1976 the Maryland State Board has coordinated student follow-up surveys in cooperation with the community college institutional researchers. But relating student progress to the efforts of student service activities is precarious.

Issues

As a whole, the college's services to students have grown faster than the instructional activities, but the various services have shown different patterns. Counseling and guidance declined early in the 1970s in response to students' demands to be admitted to courses of their choice and to the increase in part-time students, but these services increased in the 1980s as tight budgets and competition from other schools forced community colleges into streamlining their procedures for guiding students through the system. Recruitment and retention also became prominent concerns of the student personnel staff, who gradually adopted concepts other than those set down by theorists whose model was the full-time resident student. Articulation has become more important as coordination of all education in each state has developed.

However, not all student services have expanded. Student activities supporters have not been able to convert their programs to fit commuting students, and much of what they formerly did has been adopted by community service directors, a trend in keeping with the expansion of the colleges from campus to community.

The challenge for college leaders has been to maintain a balance among all services and coordinate them with the formal instructional program. But issues of educational philosophy swirl around the questions of student personnel work. How much responsibility does the college have for the lives of its students? How personalized can an institution dedicated to mass education afford to get?

Although between-sector comparisons are precarious because

of differences in institutional mission, the question whether community college students receive as much aid as their university counterparts has not been resolved.

Program articulation with the secondary schools will have to be expanded. Can the articulation committee members eventually realize that fitting the college's courses to the senior institution's requirements is not the most important, and certainly not the only, job they must do?

Student personnel workers still need to explain the implications of the changed student body to the faculty. How can they educate the faculty more effectively? As an example, how can they assist the faculty in making the instructional modifications necessary to accommodate the increasing numbers of handicapped students?

University training programs for community college student personnel workers have rarely fit the realities of the institutions in which the trainees will work. How can the programs be modified? To what extent can the community colleges train their own staff?

The concepts underlying student activities stem from an era long past. How can programs be restructured to fit the adult, part-time, nonresident student body that predominates in community colleges?

Answers to these questions will determine the future course of student services in the community colleges. As with all other questions about the types of services that community colleges provide, the answers rest on the energy and political skills of the advocates of one or another activity. And that, above all, is why the services vary as much as they do in colleges across the country.

Eight

Career Education:
Occupational Entry,
Change, and Development

A group of prominent citizens called together by the American Association of Junior Colleges (AAJC) in 1964 to serve as a National Advisory Committee on the Junior College concluded that "the two-year college offers unparalleled promise for expanding educational opportunity through the provision of comprehensive programs embracing job training as well as traditional liberal arts and general education" (American Association of Junior Colleges, 1964, p. 14). The committee recommended that "immediate steps be taken to reinforce occupational education efforts" (p. 1), a statement similar to those emanating from many other commissions and advisory groups, including the AAJC's own Commission on Terminal Education a quarter century earlier. Its words were notable only because they came at a time when the floodgates had just opened and a tide of career education programs was beginning to inundate the two-year colleges.

The year 1963 marked the passage of the federal Vocational Education Act, which broadened the criteria for federal aid to the schools. Along with the new criteria, Congress appropriated funds generously—$43 million in 1968, $707 million in 1972, and $981 million in 1974—and these funds were augmented with additional monies for occupational programs for the disadvantaged and for handicapped students. On this surge of monies, occupational education swept into the colleges in a fashion dreamed of and pleaded for but never realized by its advocates.

Early Development

A major impetus to the expansion of higher education early in the century was the drive toward professional status that was made by numerous occupational groups. One of the inputs toward professionalism is the number of years of schooling that a group can require before allowing neophytes to enter their ranks. As the professions developed, a set of auxiliary or support occupations, sometimes called semiprofessional, developed around them. The professional training moved into the university, but the training of the auxiliaries who would support them remained outside. The community colleges grew in part because some of their earlier proponents recognized the coming need for semiprofessionals and despaired of the universities' adjusting rapidly enough to provide this less-than-baccalaureate education.

Calls for occupational education in the two-year colleges had been made from their earliest days. In 1900 President William Rainey Harper of the University of Chicago had suggested that "many students who might not have the courage to enter upon a course of four years' study would be willing to do the two years of work before entering business or the professional school" (cited in Brick, 1965, p. 18). The founders of the junior colleges in California had postulated that one purpose of their institutions was to provide terminal programs in agriculture, technical studies, manual training, and the domestic arts. Alexis Lange had indicated that the junior colleges would train the technicians occupying the middle ground between manual laborers and professional people. And Koos (1924) described and applauded the occupational curricula in the junior colleges of the early 1920s.

Arguments on behalf of occupational education were raised at the earliest gatherings of the American Association of Junior Colleges. At its organizational meeting in 1920 and at nearly every meeting throughout the 1920s and 1930s, occupational education was on the agenda. Brick traced these discussions and noted that "the AAJC was aware that it had to take a leadership role in directing the movement for terminal education" (p. 120). He quoted C. C. Colvert, president of the association, who, in a 1941 address, had admonished junior college educators for not encouraging the national government to fund occupational education for people of junior college age: "Had not we of the junior college been so busy trying to offer courses which would get our graduates into the senior colleges instead of working and offering appropriate and practical courses—terminal courses—for the vast majority of junior college students, we might have thought to ask for, and as a result of having asked, received the privilege of training these young people" (cited in Brick, 1965, p. 121).

The association itself had been diligent. In 1939 it created a Commission on Junior College Terminal Education, which proceeded to study terminal (primarily occupational) education, hold workshops and conferences on its behalf, and issue three books summarizing junior college efforts in its area of interest. Much had been done, but, as the commission noted, more remained to do: "At the present time probably about one third of all the curricular offerings in the junior colleges of the country are in the nonacademic or terminal fields. Doubtless this situation is far short of the ideal, but it shows a steady and healthy growth in the right direction" (Eells, 1941a, pp. 22–23).

In 1940 terminal programs were offered in about 70 percent of the colleges. The most widely offered included business and secretarial studies, music, teaching, general courses, and home economics. About one-third of the terminal students were in business studies; enrollments in agriculture and home economics were quite low. Tables 20 and 21 present data on the numbers of colleges and programs.

Definitions

The terminology of career education has never been exact: The words *terminal, vocational, technical, semiprofessional, occupational,* and *career* have all been used interchangeably or in combination, as in *vocational-technical.* To the commission and the colleges of 1940, *terminal* meant all studies not applicable to the

Table 20. Percentage of Total Curricular Offerings Classified as
Terminal or Vocational in Junior Colleges, 1917–1937.

Investigator	All Junior Colleges		Public Junior Colleges		Private Junior Colleges	
	Number of Colleges	% of Offerings Terminal	Number of Colleges	% of Offerings Terminal	Number of Colleges	% of Offerings Terminal
Dowell (1917)	47	14	9	18	28	9
⸱s (1921)	58	29	23	31	35	25
⸱lingsworth-Eells ⸱930)	279	32	129	33	150	29
⸱vert (1937)	—	—	195	35	—	—

Source: Eells, 1941a, p. 22.

baccalaureate, but programs designed to lead to employment
dominated the category. Earlier, *vocational* had generally been used
for curricula preparing people for work in agriculture, the trades,
and sales. But because it usually connoted less-than-college-level
studies, most community college educators eschewed the term.
Semiprofessional typically referred to engineering technicians,
general assistants, laboratory technicians, and other people in
manufacturing, business, and service occupations. *Technical* im-
plied preparation for work in scientific and industrial fields.
Occupational seemed to encompass the greatest number of programs and was used most often for all curricula leading to
employment. *Career* education was coined in the 1950s to connote
lower-school efforts at orienting young people toward the workplace. The title was applied to several programs sponsored by the
U.S. Office of Education after Sidney Marland became commissioner in 1970, and it has survived because it is sufficiently broad to
encompass all the other terms.

Although the college-parallel (collegiate) function was
dominant in community colleges until the late 1960s, the structure
for career education had been present from the start. The community college authorization acts in most states had tended to recognize
both. The California District Law of 1921 allowed junior colleges to
provide college preparatory instruction; training for agricultural,
industrial, commercial, homemaking, and other vocations; and

Table 21. Number of Students Enrolled in Each Terminal Field, 1938–39.

Group	Number Enrolled in All Terminal Curricula	Number Enrolled in									
		Gen. Cultural	Agri- culture	Busi- ness	Engi- neering	Fine Arts	Health Services	Home Economics	Jour- nalism	Public Service	Miscel- laneous
All institutions	41,507	6,205	1,673	14,511	4,449	3,406	1,603	1,387	808	6,500	965
Public	30,261	4,724	1,631	11,278	3,915	2,341	1,029	876	673	3,033	761
Private	11,246	1,481	42	3,233	534	1,065	574	511	135	3,467	204

Source: Eells, 1941a, p. 239.

civic and liberal education. The 1937 Colorado act defined a junior college as an institution providing studies beyond the twelfth grade along with vocational education. Mississippi required that the junior college curriculum include agriculture, home economics, commerce, and mechanical arts. By 1940 nearly half of the state junior college laws specifically set forth the terminal functions along with the college-parallel studies. The national and regional accrediting associations of the time also wrote that provision into their rules.

However, student enrollments did not reach parity. Well into the 1950s, occupational program enrollments accounted for only one-fourth or less of the whole. In 1929, 20 percent of the students in California and 23 percent in Texas were in terminal programs (Eells, 1941a, p. 24), and not all of those were in occupational studies; the figures include high school postgraduate courses for "civic responsibility." Eells reported 35 percent in terminal curricula in 1938, but when nonvocational terminal curricula are excluded, the percentage drops to less than 25, a figure that held constant until 1960. Although 75 percent of students entering junior college as freshmen did not continue beyond the sophomore year and hence were terminal students by definition, only about one-third of them were enrolled in terminal curricula. "The difference of these two figures shows that *more than 40 percent of all junior college students are enrolled in curricula which are not planned primarily to best meet their needs*" (Eells, 1941a, p. 59).

Limitations

Why did the career programs fail to flourish before the 1960s? First, their terminal nature was emphasized, and that tended to turn potential students away; few wanted to foreclose their option for further studies. For most students, going to college meant striving for the baccalaureate, the "legitimate" degree. That concept of collegiate education had been firmly established.

Another handicap to the growth of career programs was the small size of the colleges. Average enrollment remained below 1,000 until 1946. Colleges with low enrollments could not offer many occupational courses; the costs were too high. Eells (1941a) reported a direct relation between size and occupational enrollments. Small colleges (up to 99 students) had 10 percent in terminal curricula; medium colleges (100–499 students), 32 percent; large colleges (500–999), 34 percent; and very large colleges (1,000 and over), 38 percent.

A third reason for limited terminal offerings was the association of many early junior colleges with high schools. In these colleges administrators favored collegiate courses because they were more attractive to high school students than vocational courses, they entailed no new facilities or equipment, they could be combined with fourth-year high school courses in order to bolster enrollments, and they would not require the hiring of new teachers.

The prestige factor was important. Most of the new junior colleges were opened in cities and towns where no college had existed before. Citizens and educators alike wanted theirs to be a "real college." If it could not itself offer the bachelor's degree, it could at least provide the first two years of study leading toward one. In the eyes of the public, a college was not a manual-training shop. Well into the 1960s, college presidents reported with pride the percentage of their faculty holding doctoral degrees.

Costs were an important factor. Many career programs used expensive, special facilities: clinics, machine tools, automotive repair shops, welding equipment. By comparison, collegiate studies were cheap. The transfer courses had always been taught in interchangeable classrooms. The same chairs and chalkboards, and often the same teachers, can be used for English, history, or mathematics.

And last, the secondary schools of the 1920s and 1930s provided education in shop trades, agriculture, secretarial skills, bookkeeping, and salesmanship. Career education in community colleges could not grow until employers in these fields began demanding some postsecondary experiences and until the health, engineering, and electronic technologies gained prominence.

For all these reasons, and despite the efforts of Eells and his commission and subsequent AAJC activities, college leaders did not rally around the calls for terminal occupational studies. In some states—Mississippi, for example, where occupational education was a requisite, and California, where the institutions were large enough to mount comprehensive programs in both occupational and collegiate studies—occupational education did well. But in the smaller institutions in states where the popularizing function, the function of promoting higher education, was dominant, sizable career programs were not developed.

Calls for change continued. In 1944 the Educational Policies Commission of the National Education Association published a report, *Education for All American Youth*, stressing the desirability of one or two years of occupational education. In 1947 the President's Commission on Higher Education recommended an increase in the number of community colleges, so that students who might not benefit from a full four-year course of studies could attain an education enabling them to take their place in the American work force. The commission recommended the expansion of terminal programs for civic and social responsibility and occupational programs that would prepare skilled, semiprofessional, and technical workers.

The AAJC-affiliated advocates of occupational education pressed unrelentingly for more vocational curricula and courses and for greater efforts to encourage students to enroll in them. For example, in the chapter "Development of the Junior College Movement" in the second edition of *American Junior Colleges*, Ward (1948) devoted twelve lines to the college transfer function but more than a page and a half to the status of technical education. She observed that despite the growing interest in and "the overwhelming need for terminal education . . . the development of these courses generally has been very slow" (p. 15). In fact, she felt it safe to generalize "that effective terminal courses have never been offered in sufficient numbers to meet the need for them—that is, terminal courses which provide education both for an occupation and for personal adequacy" (p. 14). Jesse Bogue, executive secretary of the AAJC, urged the colleges to "strike out boldly, demonstrate that they are not bound by tradition or the desire to ape senior colleges for the sake of a totally false notion of academic respectability." He warned educators that, unless they acted, legislatures would follow Texas's example of setting a minimum of "40 percent of programs . . . in so-called terminal fields [to] qualify for state aid" (1950, p. 313).

Growth

Career education enrollments began growing at a rate greater than liberal arts enrollments in the 1960s and have continued to do so for twenty years. This rise is attributable to many causes: the legacy left by early leaders of the junior college movement and the importunities, goadings, and sometimes barbs of later leaders; the Vocational Education Act of 1963 and the later amendments; the increase in the size of public two-year colleges; the increase in part-time, women, disadvantaged, handicapped, and older students; the community colleges' absorption of adult education programs and postsecondary occupational programs formerly operated by the secondary schools; and the changing shape of the labor market.

The Vocational Education Act was not the first to run federal funds to two-year colleges. The 1939 Commission on Junior College Terminal Education noted that at least sixty-two junior colleges in fourteen states were receiving federal funds that had been appropriated under the 1917 Smith-Hughes Act and the 1937 George-Deen Act. The federal monies were earmarked for institutions where the education was less than college grade: "It does not mean that the *institution* must be of less than college grade—only that the particular *work offered,* for which federal aid is received, must be of less than college grade" (Eells, 1941a, p. 29). The U.S. Office of Education called programs of trade and industrial education less than college grade if college entrance requirements were not prerequisites for admission, the objective was to prepare for employment in industry, the program did not lead to a degree, the program was not required to conform to conditions governing a regular college course, and the instructors qualified under state plans. According to Dougherty (1988), as early as 1937 the AAJC was lobbying for the repeal of the provision restricting support to programs of less than college grade.

The 1963 Vocational Education Act and the amendments of 1968 and 1972 vastly augmented the federal funds available to community colleges. The Carl D. Perkins Vocational Education Act of 1984 modified the guidelines further, primarily to determine the state responsibilities for administering the funds and to expand the programs directed to handicapped and disadvantaged students. By 1985 the community colleges were receiving around 22 percent of the $791 million allotted under Perkins. Enrollments had increased, especially among students from the special groups named in the legislation (State University of New York, 1987; McKinney and

Davis, 1988). And for every federal dollar appropriated, state governments and local districts provided five to ten more.

These augmented funds came initially at a time when the colleges were increasing in size, a condition conducive to the growth of occupational programs. Between 1960 and 1965 the number of public two-year institutions increased from 405 to 503, but enrollments doubled. By 1969 there were 794 colleges, with enrollments averaging over 2,000; in the 1980s the average was over 2,500.

As enrollments increased, so did the occupational programs. In Illinois, where many of the new districts were formed on the promise to the electorate of having more than 50 percent of the programs in career education, 1,871 curricula, or 66 percent of all curricula, were occupational (Illinois Community College Board, 1976). In Florida associate degree and certificate occupational programs exceeded 200. The small Hawaii system offered 80 different programs (Career Information Center, 1974).

Although many individual colleges offered 100 or more different occupational programs, those that led to the greatest variety of career options were the most popular. Programs in business drew the most students because of the breadth of options they presented. The health professions and the engineering technologies drew large numbers of students because of the expanding base of the professions in those areas and the ever-growing need for support staff. Computer science became popular in the 1980s because of the rapidly expanding applications of computers in all career fields. Other programs ebbed and flowed depending on job markets. These enrollment trends have been corroborated in numerous statewide studies—for example, in Connecticut (Connecticut State Board of Trustees for State Technical Colleges, 1987), Wisconsin (Redovich, 1987), and Illinois (Illinois Community College Board, 1985).

The growth in part-time, women, disadvantaged, handicapped, and older students also reflected the rise in occupational enrollments. Bushnell (1973) pointed out that although 40 percent of all students enrolled in career programs, only 25 percent of full-time students did so. The proportion of women who chose career programs was 35 percent, while among men it was only 17 percent. Disadvantaged and handicapped students were encouraged to enroll in occupational programs through special grants. Occupational enrollments were weighted toward the older, part-time students.

Some of the enrollment increases resulted from the upgrading of institutions and the transfer to the community colleges of functions formerly performed by other segments of education: secondary and adult schools, technical institutes, and area vocational schools or centers. This trend has been most marked in Florida, where fourteen of the twenty-eight community colleges had a department designated as an area vocational education school, and others had cooperative agreements with school boards that operate area vocational-technical centers; in Iowa, where all the public community colleges were merged with area schools; in Nebraska, where the state was divided into technical community college areas; and in North Carolina, where the technical institutes were part of the community college system (Lombardi, 1975). In some states (California, for example) community colleges have expanded their occupational offerings with and without formal agreements with other institutions. Nearly all the publicly supported occupational education in Long Beach, San Diego, and San Francisco was offered by the community college districts. Similarly, in Chicago the adult and vocational education programs were transferred from the city schools to the community college system.

The combination of these forces has counteracted to a considerable degree those open and subtle forces that caused students and their parents to value the baccalaureate over the occupational programs. In its statewide master plan for 1978 to 1987, the Maryland State Board for Community Colleges (1977, p. 34) reported that the "increasing emphasis on occupational programs reflects changing values and attitudes among students and their families as to the level of education required to qualify for desirable employment opportunities. This shift is reflected in national projections predicting that throughout the next decade, 80 percent of available jobs will require less than the bachelor's degree." U.S. Department of Labor data listed as the main areas of job openings in the 1980s retail salesclerks, cashiers, stock handlers, and similar jobs for which a bachelor's degree is not required; "Managers and Administrators" was the only job category in the top fifteen to suggest baccaulareate training. Projections for 1990

were that "the U.S. will require 125,000 more computer programmers and 125,000 more electrical engineers . . . but it will
require 3 million more secretaries and office clerks" (Kuttner, 1983,
p. 62).

Stability

The growth in occupational enrollments that began in the
second half of the 1960s is revealed in the enrollment figures shown
in Tables 22 and 23. It is reflected also in the figures on degrees
awarded (Table 24). Obviously, this percentage increase could not
continue indefinitely, and it began leveling off in the 1980s. The
1986 CSCC survey found 38 percent of the students nationwide in
career programs. Enrollment in career programs in Illinois stabilized
at 34 percent of the head count in 1983, 33 percent in 1987; an
additional 9 percent, practically all of them part-timers, were in "Vocational Skills" classes (Illinois Community College Board, 1987c).
Wisconsin Vocational, Technical, and Adult Education District
enrollments declined 10 percent from 1983 to 1986 (Redovich, 1987).
Vocational course enrollments in Washington's community colleges

Table 22. Enrollments in Community College Career
Programs as a Percentage of
Total Enrollment in Selected States.

State	Year	Percentage Career Enrollments
Arizona	1972	31
	1986	43
California	1965	13
	1983	35
Illinois	1969	26
	1986	34
Washington	1957	27
	1985	42

Sources: Lombardi, 1978b; Arizona State Board of
Directors for Community Colleges, 1987; Illinois Community
College Board, 1987c; Washington State Board for Community College Education, 1985; CARVELL Education Management Planning, Inc., 1986.

Table 23. Enrollments in Terminal-Occupational Programs in
Two-Year Colleges as a Percentage of Total Enrollments, 1963-1975.

Year	Total Enrollments	Terminal-Occupational Program Enrollments	Percentage of Total
1963	847,572	219,766	26
1965	1,176,852	331,608	28
1969	1,981,150	448,229	23
1970	2,227,214	593,226	27
1971	2,491,420	760,590	31
1972	2,670,934	873,933	33
1973	3,033,761	1,020,183	34
1974	3,428,642	1,134,896	33
1975	4,001,970	1,389,516	35

Source: National Center for Education Statistics, *Opening (Fall) Enrollments in Higher Education*, 1963-1975.

Table 24. Associate Degrees Conferred by Institutions of Higher Education
by Type of Curriculum, 1970-71 to 1984-85.

Year	All Curricula	Arts & Sciences or General Programs	Percentage of Total	Occupational Curricula	Percentage of Total
1970-71	253,635	145,473	57	108,162	43
1973-74	347,173	165,520	48	181,653	52
1976-77	409,942	172,631	42	237,311	58
1979-80	405,378	152,169	38	253,209	63
1982-83	456,441	133,917	29	322,524	71
1983-84	452,416	128,766	29	323,650	72
1984-85	454,712	127,387	28	327,325	72

Sources: Stern and Chandler, 1987, p. 102; Snyder, 1987.

declined from 43 percent of the total FTSE in 1983 to 38 percent in 1987 because many programs "were reduced or eliminated due to low employment demand" (Washington State Board for Community College Education, 1988, p. 20). The 1985 figures for Maryland (44 percent), Minnesota (20 percent), and Florida (24 percent) showed little change over the prior few years.

Because of frequent changes in ways of classifying programs and enrollments, it is perilous to compare data between states or even in the same state in successive years. For that reason the national data shown in Table 23 cannot reasonably be updated beyond 1975. The percentage jump in degrees awarded between 1979-80 and 1982-83 shown in Table 24 is in large measure related to the National Center for Education Statistics' changing its classifications between those years. The wide variation among states results partly because of varying community college missions and partly because enrollment data are not reported uniformly between states: the unit of measurement—head count, FTSE—varies; and some reports indicate opening fall enrollments, whereas others report fiscal year enrollments.

The data have been unstable also because the higher funding patterns for vocational education encouraged colleges to classify as vocational many programs that had been classified as general education or liberal arts. In order to show high enrollment in career programs, educators also may have classified as occupational students those who took one occupational course, even though they were actually majoring in a liberal arts transfer program. Several efforts to refine the data were made in response to criticism of these practices. California, for example, developed a Student Account-ability Model (SAM), a "uniform method for classifying occupational courses and identifying occupational majors" (Gold and Morris, 1977, preface). Under the SAM guidelines an occupational course is defined as one that is intended to develop skills and related knowledge needed for job performance, is part of the course sequence of an occupational program offered by the college, and is designed primarily for job preparation and/or job upgrading or updating and not for general education purposes. As a result of a similar redefinition of classifications of courses in the state of Washington, academic enrollments increased by 4 percent and vocational enrollments decreased by 4 percent (E. F. Price, Washington State Board for Community College Education, personal communication, Nov. 3, 1977).

Regardless of data reliability, there is little question of the general popularity of career education. The national figures on the percentages of community college students enrolled in and graduating from career programs are reflected in surveys at individual institutions. Career program enrollees tend to graduate at a rate approximately equivalent to their representation in the student body.

Program Success

Career programs are established with the intention of serving students by preparing them for employment and serving industries by supplying them with trained workers. The college staff presumably initiate programs by perusing employment trends in the local area and by surveying employers there. Program coordinators are appointed and advisory committees composed of trade and employer representatives established. Funds are often secured through priorities set down by state and federal agencies. The entire process suggests rational program planning. Nonetheless, questions have been raised about the appropriateness of certain programs and whether the matriculants are well served, and much research on program effects has been conducted.

Most students in occupational programs seem satisfied with the training they receive. Follow-up studies routinely find 80 to 90 percent of the program graduates saying that they were helped and that they would recommend the program to others. Among the students who do not complete the program, a sizable number usually indicate that they dropped out because they received the training they needed in the courses they took, not because they were dissatisfied with the program.

Students have been less sanguine about the help they received in obtaining jobs. Graduates of a Maryland college listed the weakness of college job placement services as a problem area (Gell and Armstrong, 1977), and similar comments were received in surveys of students in a Pennsylvania community college (Selgas, 1977). Career program graduates from North Carolina's community colleges rated job placement services poorest among all the services provided by the institutions (Hammond and Porter, 1984). Such assistance seemed to be given through the occupational programs themselves rather than through a college-wide job placement service.

Career students' relative success in finding and maintaining jobs in the areas for which they were trained has always been a controversial topic. Depending on the data obtained and the criteria for defining success, different researchers reach different conclusions. Noeth and Hanson (1976) studied a sample of 4,350 students who had been surveyed at 110 community colleges and technical schools in 1970. The students were enrolled in business and marketing, accounting, science, social science, arts and humanities, electrical engineering technology, auto mechanics, and nursing programs. The jobs they held five years after the testing date showed a continuation of their interests in the fields in which they had been enrolled. Half of the graduates and dropouts from the business and marketing programs held business contact jobs (for example, meeting customers and selling products), and a large number held business detail jobs (office work). All who had completed the registered nursing programs were working in nursing, students from accounting programs held business detail jobs and business contact jobs, and so on through the programs, with those from the technology programs holding technology jobs and those from the auto mechanics programs holding trades jobs.

Several more recent statewide data sets are available. Students who graduated from forty career programs in Florida in 1983–84 obtained employment in their major field in varying rates. Those in the health fields, who comprised nearly half of the graduates, tended to be employed at rates of 85 percent or greater, whereas some of the other fields, such as office work and real estate, showed only around 50 percent employment (Baldwin, 1986). Of the 998 graduates from the New Hampshire Technical Institute and Vocational-Technical Colleges in 1987, 81 percent were employed—96 percent of them in their college major or a related field (New Hampshire State Department of Postsecondary Vocational-Technical Education, 1988). Seventy-one percent of the career program graduates in the North Carolina community colleges were working in the field for which they had been prepared (Hammond and Porter, 1984). Seventy-five percent of the Illinois career program graduates were employed, 83 percent of them in related fields. A follow-up survey of graduates of the Wisconsin system found 93 percent employed after three years, 78 percent in a field related to their training (Wisconsin State Board of Vocational, Technical, and Adult Education, 1985). Fifty-eight percent of Maryland's career program graduates were employed full-time in their area of training (Maryland State Board for Community Colleges, 1987).

Single-college studies show similar findings. A follow-up of graduates of career programs at William Rainey Harper College (Illinois) found 87 percent of them working, 70 percent in a field related to their major (Lucas, 1988). And 70 percent of the graduates of the career programs in Los Rios Community College District (California) were working in a job related to their program (Lee, 1984). The programs were obviously keyed to the employment fields.

Wilms and Hansell (1980) studied graduates and dropouts from both community college and proprietary school programs in San Francisco, Chicago, Boston, and Miami. The programs were designed to train people for jobs as accountants, computer programmers, electronics technicians, secretaries, dental assistants, and cosmetologists. Wilms and Hansell found that few students obtained professional, managerial, technical, or sales jobs; most graduates and dropouts from the accounting, computer, and electronics programs obtained clerical or lower-level jobs. Students from the secretarial, dental assistant, and cosmetology programs did better in obtaining the jobs for which they had been trained.

Pincus (1980) took the occupational programs to task, arguing that no one seems to know whether terminal vocational education programs are effective. He deplored the lack of data on unemployment rates and incomes of recent graduates and nongraduates of community college vocational programs, compared with such figures for recent high school graduates, graduates of four-year colleges, and so on, with statistical controls for age, sex, race, and other variables. Although he rejected the inconsistent methodology in the various studies cited, he erected a table and calculated an average showing that "unemployment rates among former vocational students are high" (p. 349). He noted that vocational graduates are less likely to be unemployed than high school graduates but may be no more employable than college graduates: "The best that can be said is that vocational graduates are no more likely to be unemployed than college graduates" (pp. 349-350). He later reiterated his contentions: "By and large, there is no good evidence that vocational education in community colleges delivers on the promises of secure employment, decent pay, and ample career opportunities" (Pincus, 1986, p. 49).

Obviously, the data can be interpreted in many ways. The number of students who are already employed and enter career programs only to get additional skills must be factored in, just as the students who obtain job certification but find no jobs available to them must be considered. Students who leave programs before graduation and enter employment in the field for which they are prepared must be considered as program successes. Students who graduate but do not obtain employment because they have entered related baccalaureate programs should not be counted among the unemployed. And it is misleading to categorize career programs as a unitary group, because there are high- and low-status programs; and there are programs preparing people for areas of high demand, such as health care and electronics technology, and programs in areas for which the market is not as distinct, such as real estate or data processing. Much depends also on the time that has elapsed since the students were enrolled; the ordinary drift of careers suggests that fewer students will be employed in jobs related to their program several years after they have left the college.

Some critics of career education are concerned that the programs do little in equalizing status and salaries among types of jobs. They view with alarm the high dropout rates without realizing that *program completion is an institutional artifact.* Even though the AACJC mounted an "Associate Degree Preferred" campaign in the mid-1980s, urging employers to give preference to graduates, the degree is not as important as the skills that the applicant manifests. To the student who seeks a job in the field, completing the program becomes irrelevant as soon as a job is available. The categories "graduate" and "dropout" lose much of their force when viewed in this light. This phenomenon is not peculiar to community colleges; generations of young women participated in teacher-training programs in universities even though few of them expected to teach more than a few years and fewer than half entered teaching at all. If one merely surveys the career program graduates who are working in that area or places graduates in one category and dropouts in another, the true services rendered by those programs may be lost.

Few critics of career education acknowledge that questions

about its value are much more complex than simplistic data on job entry and first salary earned can answer. What is the value of an occupational education program when an enrollee hears about an available job, obtains it, and leaves after two weeks? In that case the program has served as an employment agency of sorts. What is the value of a program in which a person who already has a job spends a few weeks learning some new skills and then receives a better job in the same company? There the program has served as a step on a career ladder. What of the person who enrolls to sharpen skills and gain confidence to apply for a job doing essentially the same work but for a different company? And what of the students who enter occupational programs but then transfer from them to other programs in the same or a different college?

A curriculum is a conduit through which people move in order to prepare themselves to do or be something other than when they began. Yet for some people the curriculum has served an essential purpose if it but allows them to matriculate and be put in touch with those who know where jobs may be obtained. At the other extreme are the students who go all the way through the curriculum, learn the skills, but either fail to obtain jobs in the field for which they were trained or, having attained them, find them unsatisfying. For them the institution has been a failure. The critics cannot seem to accommodate the fact that for many dropouts the program has succeeded, while for many of its graduates it has failed.

Success may be measured in many ways. A few studies of both graduates and nongraduates of career programs have shown that, although most enrolled to obtain job entry skills, many sought advancement in jobs they already held. Around two-thirds of the respondents to a survey of career students in a Kansas community college gave "job entry skill" as their reason (Quanty, 1977; Tatham, 1978), but around one-third had enrolled primarily for advancement. A somewhat smaller percentage of students enrolled in career programs in California community colleges (34 percent) reported that they sought to prepare for jobs; 11 percent of that group had enrolled to improve skills for their present job (Hunter and Sheldon, 1980). Nearly half of the students in the CSCC's 1986 national survey had occupational intent, and those seeking job entry skills outnumbered those seeking to upgrade themselves in a job they already had by only two to one. Such data often fall between the planks when program follow-up studies or comparative wage studies are made.

Another important finding in studies of graduates and current enrollees in career programs is the sizable number who plan to transfer to four-year colleges and who do eventually transfer. Few institutions or state systems collect these data routinely, but where they are available, the relationship between career programs and further education is well established. In a California statewide study, 25 percent of students enrolled in career curricula said that they intended to transfer (Hunter and Sheldon, 1980), and national data compiled by CSCC in 1986 yielded a similar figure (Palmer, 1987a, p. 134). Regardless of their intentions when they enrolled, 40 percent of the Los Rios Community College District (California) career program graduates transferred (Lee, 1984); 36 percent of the William Rainey Harper College (Illinois) career alumni (Lucas, 1988); 11 percent of the graduates of the technical institute and the six vocational-technical colleges in New Hampshire (New Hampshire State Department of Postsecondary Vocational-Technical Education, 1988); 14 percent of the career program graduates in Illinois (Illinois Community College Board, 1987c); and 27 percent of the career program graduates in Maryland (Maryland State Board for Community Colleges, 1988). Many of the graduates were employed in their field of study and pursuing further education simultaneously.

The Broader Implications

Career education has other implications: To what degree *should* the schools be in the business of providing trained workers for the nation's industries? None, say the academic purists; totally, say many community college leaders. A lengthy list of commentators and educational philosophers would argue that the preparation of people specifically to work in certain industries is not the school's purpose because the school should have broader social aims and because the industries can do the particular job training much more efficiently. And those who take this approach are not necessarily those who plead for a return to an era when higher education was for providing gentlemen with distinctive sets of manners.

Is career education primarily an individual or a social benefit? The individuals gain skills that make them more employable and at higher rates of pay; society gains skilled workers for the nation's businesses and technologies. Solmon (1976) argues that community colleges can and should work closely with employers to facilitate students' passage through to the labor market. To the extent that they do, everyone benefits: students, their families, the colleges, business, and the general public. Solmon contends that the costs must be maintained by all. Students forgo earnings while they are in school for the gain of ultimate entry into the labor force with greater skills. Although employers must provide expensive apprenticeships, they can benefit by using cooperative programs to identify students whom they would like to retain. The colleges lose some control over their students when business firms decide whom to involve in cooperative programs and when those programs become more susceptible to external evaluation. However, they gain by doing a better, more direct job for students and by keeping them enrolled longer.

Nevertheless, other writers in education, and certainly the majority of those who comment on the role of the community colleges, suggest that education is an essential expenditure for economic growth and is not merely a nonproductive sector of the economy, a form of consumption. To the extent that the schools are viewed as investments of this type, educators can make a more effective claim on national budgets. To justify this claim, the schools must be brought in line with the goals of society; if they are to foster economic growth, they must provide trained workers, and the more they provide trained workers, the more they will be looked upon to fit those trainees to the jobs that are available. Hence, they can be criticized to the extent that their graduates do not obtain jobs or are not able to function effectively in the jobs they get. And thus the term *overeducated* can be used to describe those who are prepared for nonexistent jobs or who have jobs to which they do not apply the type of education they received.

Should the colleges get paid on some pro rata basis only when the trainees have been employed? The proponents of payment only for training that results in jobs argue that it would free the public school sector to provide education in the broad sense, leaving job training to the proprietary schools (Wilms, 1987). The notion is seductive but fraught with problems. First, the institutions' managers might be tempted to select at entry only those people who are likely to be employable, leaving behind the difficult ones. Second, depending on the institution to provide data about who is employed and for how long before funds are released begs creative data reporting. Third, employers prefer a larger pool of potential employees rather than the smaller pool that this type of contracting for performance would effect.

Eells (1941a) deplored the fact that 66 percent of the students were enrolled in programs designed primarily to prepare them for what 25 percent would do—transfer to the upper division. At the time he was writing, there was no great difference between the public and the private junior colleges: "The problem is essentially the same for both types of institutions" (p. 63). However, Eells also noted that "of all groups, only the private junior colleges of the New England states and the public junior colleges for blacks report an enrollment in terminal curricula which even approximates the proportion of terminal students" (p. 59). Now, there were colleges that knew what they were doing! The private junior colleges of New England could fit the girls for homemaking, sales, and secretarial work, and the public junior colleges for blacks in the South could prepare their students for the manual trades.

Recently the urge to completely vocationalize the community colleges has been strong among college managers, who are aware of the sizable funds and handsome political support attendant on career education. Their arguments sound plausible: Since many students neither transfer nor get an associate degree, they should stop trying to compete academically and obtain a marketable skill before leaving the educational system; Parnell (1985) has detailed this argument. Nevertheless, there are risks, too. Breneman (1979) has pointed out that emphasizing the financial return for undergraduate education proved a disservice to the colleges, not because the analysis was wrong but because educational leaders accepted the economists' determination that people who go to college earn more in their lifetime than those who do not, and they used this argument in their presentations to legislatures and the public.

The idea of career education reflects a belief that separate curricular tracks are the best way to accommodate the varying educational objectives and characteristics of the students. However, Palmer (1987a) suggests that the organization of career education as a separate curricular track stems from several viewpoints other than student intentions. First is a "political agenda" held by state legislators and college planners. According to this agenda, occupational programs are supposed to serve students whose primary educational objective is to gain skills allowing them to enter the work force. Second is the "terminal education" agenda, which sees occupational studies as a way of serving academically less able students, who are not likely to obtain the baccalaureate. Third is the "economic agenda," which holds that occupational studies improve the economy through labor force development and thus serve society. These three agendas, embedded in the history of the community college, have been put forth by AACJC leaders from Eells (1941a, 1941b) to Parnell (1985). A fourth, the "hidden agenda," has been postulated by other commentators, who charge that occupational programs channel low-income and minority students away from academic studies and the upward social mobility attendant thereon.

Palmer's study demonstrates that the career programs in community colleges may have been furthered by leaders who subscribe to those beliefs but that the "agendas" do not accurately reflect what the curricula do. Occupational studies actually serve a much broader diversity of students, students with a wide range of abilities and goals. The programs are not exclusively related to the work force or the economy; they also serve individuals wishing to obtain skills for their personal interest, students who take vocational classes "for their intrinsic value and not necessarily for their vocational import" (p. 291). Palmer based his assertions on the 1986 CSCC survey of students enrolled in all types of classes in community colleges nationwide. In that survey 16 percent of the students in occupational classes indicated that they were *not* enrolled in an occupational program, and 26 percent of the students who *were* in occupational classes or programs said that they intended to transfer.

He rejects the charge that community college students are counseled into career programs on the basis of their academic ability and hence their socioeconomic status. His analysis shows that the enrollment patterns in high-status and low-status occupational classes deviate considerably from what would be expected if curricular tracking were efficiently carried out. Low-income students enroll in high-status and low-status program areas in almost equal numbers; and highly self-confident students equally tend to enroll in low-status program areas, just as students with below-average self-ratings of ability are as likely to enroll in high-status programs. "Many students clearly go their own way, regardless of whether counselors try to track students by ability" (p. 305).

In summation, an oversimplified view of career education as a track leading away from the baccalaureate gives ground to several errors. It neglects the extent to which occupational classes serve avocational or community service functions. It enhances the confusion of curricular content with student intentions. It suggests that career education serves an ever-changing middle-level portion of the job market, which supposedly requires some college study but not the baccalaureate, thus ignoring the high transfer rates exhibited by career program graduates. And it perpetuates the myth that career studies are the exclusive domain of the low-ability or low-income students.

Whether or not career education is useful or proper, it has certainly captured the community colleges. Its advocates have increased, and more of them are being appointed to administrative positions, mostly in vocational areas but occasionally in positions involving academic program supervision. Upgrading of instructors, which started in the 1950s, was supported by the enlarged appropriations for staff development programs and encouraged by salary schedules that provided incentives for academic degrees. Many of the instructors who formerly had only trade experience have acquired bachelor's and master's degrees, removing one of the most potent symbols of inferiority in the academic community.

All these factors—the 1960s to 1980s enrollment surge; staff upgrading; and financial support from business, industry, and government—have given occupational educators a buoyancy that shows up in new courses, programs, teaching strategies. They have a large reservoir of funds, mostly public but some private and foundation, to undertake studies on every aspect of occupational education: preparing model courses and programs, conducting follow-up studies of graduates, assessing employment trends, establishing guidelines for choosing new courses and curricula, and developing criteria for weeding out the obsolescent and the weak courses and programs or for upgrading others to conform to new job specifications. They have been flattered that four-year colleges and universities have been showing greater interest in two-year occupational courses and programs, but they are concerned about losing enrollment to the four-year colleges as well as to the proprietary vocational schools. They worry also about losing the programs themselves if the baccalaureate becomes the requisite degree, as it has become for registered nurses in many states.

Many liberal arts advocates have become understandably apprehensive about the future of their area, fearful that the higher favor enjoyed by career education will mean the further slighting of their disciplines. Instructors have watched their once-popular classes fade, but they have not been able to counter the attrition. In contrast, college leaders who subscribe to the marketplace as the prime determinant of the curriculum accept career education, just as they accepted the transfer function of an earlier day. For them, the enrollments are the measure of all value.

Regardless of the curriculum favored, many college leaders view with concern the growth of the proprietary or for-profit schools. This group, the fastest-growing sector of postsecondary education in the 1980s, includes cosmetology and barber colleges, trade schools, and business and secretarial institutes, along with several other less populous categories. According to the Association of Independent Colleges and Schools (1988), they were growing both in the number of students served and the number of institutions. In 1988, 92 colleges and business schools belonging to the association offered Associate in Arts or Science degrees, up from 62 only a year earlier. And 144 additional institutions offered specialized associate degrees in occupational studies, applied sciences, and business, up from 119 in 1987. Supported in the main by students who were receiving federal and state aid with which to pay their tuition, this group was proving a most effective set of competitors in the market to provide vocational training.

Merging Academic and Occupational Studies

The separation between the career and collegiate functions is more organizationally then conceptually inspired. Consider the statement "Students will learn to plan more efficient use of time, analyze written communcations, understand interpersonal relations, respond appropriately to verbal directives, evolve alternative solutions, maintain involvement with tasks until resolution, communicate effectively verbally." Are those goals related to occupational or to baccalaureate studies? They are as likely to appear in course syllabi from either area.

Some eloquent pleas for merging career and liberal studies have been made. Solmon (1977), who has conducted several studies on the relations between college going and the kinds of jobs that graduates get and the extent to which they are satisfied with those jobs, points to several commonly held misconceptions: that job preparation in college is antithetical to short-term enjoyment of being in college or preparation for citizenship or appreciation of the arts; that students tend to get jobs for which they were specifically trained in a major field or in a job-related training program; and that the more education one receives, the greater the chances of getting a good job. On surveying numerous graduates of all types of programs several years out of college, he found them wishing they had had more preparation in English, psychology, and ways of understanding interpersonal relations. He recommended breadth in studies in all programs.

Feldman (1967) has said that the schools can best serve their students by supplying them with access to open-ended jobs, jobs that make enhanced responsibility, salary, and advancement available to them: "Merely to offer blind-alley employment and obsolescing trades to youngsters in a dynamic technological society is to exchange one kind of subservience and dependence for another" (p. 2). In an argument for career education, he pointed out that the work world is a valid component of educational content. "The most glaring defect in the present piecemeal, ill-coordinated effort to develop manpower at the fringes of society's mainstream is the separation between educational and occupational skill development" (p. 4).

Harris and Grede (1977) discussed career potential for the liberal arts in the context of "the hopeless job prospects of two-year college graduates in liberal arts and general studies" (p. 227). The common purpose of liberal education in all ages is that it must prepare people for the type of life they will lead. At one time only those who were educated were preparing for leisure or for directing people in other classes. More recently, liberal education has meant preparing for work. Because all people are free and all people work, a truly liberal education for a free person must include a work component. In that sense all education is vocational education.

Harris and Grede predicted a breakdown in the rigid dichotomy between liberal arts and vocational curricula or between transfer and nontransfer curricula in community colleges and foresaw a time when teachers of the liberal arts would recognize the importance of career education, and teachers of vocations the importance of the liberal learning. However, this prediction has not come to pass, not least because of the rigidity of the separate funding channels through which support flows into the career and the collegiate courses. At most, courses in some colleges have been designed so that they incorporate elements of both the liberal arts and career studies. At a California community college, for example, a "Living with Technology" course is conducted by faculty from various vocational areas who provide an introduction to the history and concepts of technology; at an Oregon community college, a multidisciplinary course called "Oceans" bridges humanities, technology, and science and is required for students in all occupational fields; and at an Illinois community college, a set of one-credit courses in the liberal arts includes "The Worker in America," "The Individual and Technology," and "Modern Business Ethics." As long as career programs lead to the associate degree, the proponents of the liberal arts will be able to sustain their courses as program requirements.

Of itself, occupational training involves a higher risk for the student than liberal arts education. The costs in tuition and forgone earnings may be the same for both, but occupational training is almost entirely wasted if there is no job at the end. The liberal arts at least hold the person's options open, a perception certainly accounting for at least some of the liberal arts' continuing popularity among students. Since it seems impossible to predict with much accuracy the types of jobs that will be available by the time an entering student leaves school, the problem can be accommodated in two ways. First, the educational system can be made open enough that people may return successively for retraining throughout life. Second, the initial training can be made sufficiently broad that the skills learned are applicable to a variety of situations. The argument can be made that all contemporary education is vocational, since it is designed for people who will one day work. Furthermore, the concept of work is sufficiently broad to accommodate people who are less interested in doing or making things than they are in maintaining jobs for their status, social connection, and the human interaction they provide. Many people define themselves by their role but not by their work; it is easier for them to say that they are the assistant manager of something than it is for them to recount exactly what it is they do.

Occupational education has become the major function in most community colleges, but the high growth rates of the 1960s and 1970s have stabilized. Unless more community colleges become exclusively vocational-technical postsecondary institutions—as at least 15 percent of them were by 1980—or unless more proprietary schools are defined as community colleges, enrollments in the career programs will probably remain under 50 percent of the total credit-course enrollment. But this percentage will depend in large measure on the way programs are classified.

The major change in recent years has been that career programs in community colleges increasingly became feeders to senior institutions, which were undergoing their own form of vocationalization. Students were finding that many of the credits they earned in their two-year occupational programs were acceptable for transfer. Thus, the categories "occupational" and "transfer" became inadequate to describe the realities of the community colleges, and "terminal" certainly became obsolete. Sizable percentages of the transfer students sought leisure-time pursuits; sizable percentages of the occupational students desired certification for transfer. A view of the community colleges as terminal institutions and of the universities as institutions for students interested in the liberal arts is woefully inaccurate.

Because many career programs are serving as the first two years of a baccalaureate program, the community colleges must articulate those programs with the programs at senior institutions. They are much more likely to do that than to support program separation or to concentrate on the occupations that do not require the baccalaureate, such as secretarial skills or construction trades. Competition from the proprietary schools for programs in these areas is too great, and, to the extent that the community colleges emphasize such trades areas, they become vulnerable to the charge that they channel their clients into low-status occupations.

In his book *The Two Cultures,* the English writer C. P. Snow (1959) posed a distinction between the humanities and the sciences. The scientific culture attempts to describe laws of the natural world and is optimistic that problems can be solved. The other culture, the literary world, is pessimistic about the likelihood of solving major problems and regards members of the scientific culture as barbarians. According to Snow, the literary intellectuals or artists lack foresight, are unconcerned about their fellow humans, and do not understand what science can do. The scientists regard the artists as lacking precision in thought and action, as speaking in phrases capable of a myriad of interpretations.

However, the two cultures can be presented another way. Perhaps on one side are those who have a vision of the future; who work with discipline, pride, and rigor; who articulate their ideas through language that has consistent meaning; who value the intellect. On the other side are those who demand quick gratification; who refuse to be told what to do or what to study; who are antiliterate, rejecting language; who deal with feeling, not thinking, with emotions, not intellect. If these are the two cultures, the split is not between the liberal arts, on the one hand, and career education, on the other. That argument is passé, even though community colleges are still organized as though the real distinction were between people who were going to work and those who were not. Work in the sense of vocation demands commitment, planning, delay of gratification, application of intelligence, acceptance of responsibility, a sense of present and future time. As such, it differs less from the concepts surrounding the liberal arts than it does from the antiliterate, language-rejecting, stultified group, who cannot understand themselves or their environment in terms that have common reference.

As though it anticipated later developments, the AAJC's 1964 National Advisory Committee concluded, "Time must be provided, even in a two-year curriculum, for at least basic courses in languages, arts, and social sciences. The technicians of the future must be inoculated against the malady of overspecialization. . . . They must not be forced to concentrate so narrowly on technology that they cannot be useful citizens or cannot accommodate changes in their own specialties" (American Association of Junior Colleges, 1964, p. 14). Nearly a quarter century later, an AACJC-sponsored group reiterated a concern for combining career and general education: "Many students come to the community college with narrow backgrounds, and, for them, career education may mean only gaining skills for a specific job. . . . Through lack of attention to general education, community colleges often exacerbate this tendency toward narrowness. . . . We recommend that the core curriculum be integrated into technical and career programs" (American Association of Community and Junior Colleges, 1988, pp. 17–19). Some things don't change very much.

Issues

Career education's phenomenal growth in the 1960s and 1970s stabilized in the 1980s. Will its 40 to 50 percent enrollment share continue? How much will competition from the proprietary schools affect it?

Can career education be effectively merged with the collegiate function? Few prior attempts to integrate esthetic appreciation, rationality, ethics, and other elements of the higher learning with programs training people for particular jobs have met with success. Can the staff itself do it? Does the community college leadership want it?

The lines between career and collegiate education have become blurred since more students began transferring to universities from community college career programs than from the so-called transfer programs. Questions of the conceptual differences between occupational and liberal studies have often been raised, but the answers have yielded little to influence program design in the community colleges. What type of staff training, program reorganization, or external incentives might be provided to encourage faculties and administrators to reexamine both programs in the light of the practicalities of their own institutions?

Much of the value in career education programs derives from their connecting students with jobs. Can the colleges demonstrate this value? How can they capitalize on it?

Programs designed to prepare students to work in particular industries should be supported, at least in part, by those industries; and many examples of this type of support have been set in place. But how can industry be assigned its proportionate share of all training costs? What channels can be opened to merge public and private funds so that an equitable share is borne by each?

Career education remained a subordinate function throughout the first fifty years of community college development, until federal funding moved it to the fore. Will the separate funding channels be maintained? How will they change if the programs preparing people in the high-level technologies move to the universities?

The full effects of career education as the prime function have yet to be discerned. The public's view of community colleges as agents of upward mobility for individuals seems to be shifting toward a view of the institutions as occupational training centers. This narrowing of the colleges' comprehensiveness could lead to a shift in the pattern of support.

Nine

Compensatory Education:
Enhancing Literacy and Basic Skills

Nothing is easier to decry than the ineffectiveness of the schools. One observer of American education noted, "Paradoxical as it may seem, the diffusion of education and intelligence is at present acting against the free development of the highest education and intelligence. Many have hoped and still hope that by giving a partial teaching to great numbers of persons, a stimulus would be applied to the best minds among them, and a thirst for knowledge awakened which would lead to high results; but thus far these results have not equaled the expectation. There has been a vast expenditure . . . for educational purposes . . . but the system of competitive cramming in our schools has not borne fruits on which we have much cause to congratulate ourselves." The sentiments in this passage, written *in 1869* by the American historian Francis Parkman (p. 560), have been echoed countless times since.

Numerous critics have taken the position that the schools may teach people to read and write, but they fail to teach them to think. Parkman himself felt that the school "has produced an immense number of readers; but what thinkers are to be found may be said to exist in spite of it" (p. 560). One hundred years later, the American poet and critic John Ciardi complained that "the American school system has dedicated itself to universal subliteracy. It has encouraged the assumption that a clod trained to lip-read a sports page is able to read anything. It has become the whole point of the

school system to keep the ignorant from realizing their own
ignorance. . . . An illiterate must at least know that he cannot read
and that the world of books is closed to him" (Ciardi, 1971, p. 48).
Similarly, H. L. Mencken asserted that "the great majority of
American high school pupils, when they put their thoughts on
paper, produce only a mass of confused puerile nonsense. . . . They
express themselves so clumsily that it is often quite impossible to
understand them at all" (cited in Lyons, 1976, p. 33). And a more
contemporary writer, the novelist Walker Percy, has offered this
devastating critique: "Our civilization has achieved a distinction of
sorts. It will be remembered not for its technology nor even its wars
but for its novel ethos. Ours is the only civilization in history which
has enshrined mediocrity as its national ideal" (Percy, 1980, p. 177).

The charge has been raised that students not only fail to
become well educated but also do not learn even the rudiments of
reading, writing, and arithmetic. The title of Copperman's 1978
book reflects one indictment: *The Literacy Hoax: The Decline of
Reading, Writing, and Learning in the Public Schools and What
We Can Do About It.* Copperman reports studies showing that over
20 million American adults, one in every five, are functionally
illiterate—that is, incapable of understanding basic written and
arithmetic communication to a degree that they can maneuver
satisfactorily in contemporary society. The popular press has
repeatedly carried articles about the tens of millions of adult
Americans who cannot read or write well enough to perform the
basic requirements of everyday life or who are only marginally
competent. Not all commentators blame the schools alone. However, although each generation's cohort of criers-with-alarm has
had its favorite target, most of them eventually disparage the public
schools.

Decline in Literacy

Broad-scale denunciations are one thing, accurate data quite
another. Information on the literacy of the American population
over the decades is difficult to compile, even though data on the
number of people completing so many years of schooling have been
collected by the Bureau of the Census for well over 100 years. One

reason that intergenerational comparisons are imprecise is that different percentages of the population have gone to school at different periods in the nation's history. A century ago only the upper socioeconomic classes completed secondary school or enrolled in higher education. Further, the United States does not have a uniform system of educational evaluation. Nonetheless, the available evidence suggests that the academic achievement of students in schools and colleges registered a gradual improvement between 1900 and the mid-1950s, an accelerated improvement between the mid-1950s and the mid-1960s, and a precipitous, widespread decline between then and the late 1970s before stabilizing in the early 1980s. The Scholastic Aptitude Test taken by high school seniors showed mathematical ability at 494 in 1952, 502 in 1963, 470 in 1977, and 476 in 1988; verbal ability went from 476 in 1952 to 478 in 1963 and dropped in 1977 to 429, where it stabilized: it was 430 in 1986 and 428 in 1988. The scores made by entering community college freshmen who participated in the American College Testing Program also declined notably between the mid-1960s and the later 1970s, before leveling off in the 1980s (Table 25).

Reports emanating from community colleges and universities alike confirm the slide. In various surveys instructors have indicated that they deplore their students' lack of preparation (Brawer and Friedlander, 1979). Boyer (1987) compared the Carnegie surveys of faculty in 1976 and 1984. In 1984 a higher percentage of instructors in all types of institutions felt that their students were

**Table 25. Mean ACT Scores for Freshmen at
Two-Year Colleges, 1964–1986.**

Year	English	Math	Social Science	Natural Science	Composite
1964	17.6	17.4	18.2	18.5	18.0
1970	17.2	17.7	18.0	19.0	18.1
1975	15.8	14.9	15.2	18.9	16.3
1979	15.8	13.9	14.4	18.4	15.8
1982	15.7	13.3	14.5	18.4	15.6
1986	16.3	13.5	14.9	18.7	16.0

Source: American College Testing Program, *College Student Profiles*, 1966, 1972, 1976–77, 1978–79, 1982–83, 1987–88.

not well prepared. The Educational Testing Service (1978, p. 1) noted: "At the University of California at Berkeley, where students come from the top eighth of California high school graduates, nearly half of the freshmen in recent years have been so deficient in writing ability that they needed a remedial course they themselves call 'bonehead English.'" More recently, H. Astin (1985) reported similar figures for the University of California at Los Angeles. Other studies also have revealed the decline in basic skills among students in all higher education institutions: "We are led to the inescapable conclusion that far too many of today's students lack a solid academic foundation—not just in their command of English, but in general education—and these deficiencies prove to be a serious barrier to academic progress" (Boyer, 1987, p. 76).

No one can say with assurance which social or educational condition was primarily responsible for the decline in student abilities that apparently began in the mid-1960s and accelerated throughout the 1970s. Suffice it to say that numerous events came together: the coming of age of the first generation reared on television; a breakdown in respect for authority and the professions; a pervasive attitude that the written word is not as important as it once was; the imposition of various other-than-academic expectations on the public schools; and a decline in academic requirements and expectations at all levels of schooling. This last is worthy of elaboration because it is the only one that is within the power of the schools to change directly.

Several premises underlie schooling—for example, that students tend to learn what is taught; that the more time they spend on a task, the more they learn; that they will take the courses required for completion of their programs. Hence, when expectations, time in school, and number of academic requirements are reduced, student achievement, however measured, seems certain to drop as well. In its 1978 report on *The Concern for Writing*, the Educational Testing Service noted: "The nub of the matter is that writing is a complex skill mastered only through lengthy, arduous effort. It is a participatory endeavor, not a spectator sport. And most high school students do not get enough practice to become competent writers" (p. 4). In the 1960s and 1970s, the schools put less emphasis on composition, and even in the composition courses, "creative expression" was treated at a higher level than were grammar and the other tools of the writer's trade.

Copperman (1978) recounted the depressing statistics regarding the deterioration of the secondary school curriculum. Specifically, the percentage of ninth- through twelfth-grade students enrolled in academic courses dropped between 1960 and 1972: from 95 to 71 percent in English courses and proportionate drops in social studies, science, and mathematics. In other words, the average high school graduate had taken four years of English in 1960 and only three years in 1972. And the curriculum in English shifted from sequential courses to electives chosen from courses in creative writing, journalism, public speaking, classical literature, science fiction, advanced folklore, composition, mass media, poetry, and a host of other options. Not only were students taking less science, math, English, and history, but in the academic classes they did take, the amount of work assigned and the standard to which it was held deteriorated as well.

Further, the texts used in secondary schools and two-year colleges became more simplistic, written at a level that the average twelve-year-old could understand. Richardson, Fisk, and Okun (1983) showed how the requirements for reading and writing in all courses, including general education and the liberal arts, had been reduced in one representative community college. Students were expected to read little but the textbook; and even in that, they were reading not for content or ideas but only for the minimal amount of information needed to pass quick-score examinations. The expectations for student writing had dropped so that students wrote at most a few pages in any course.

In an effort to stem the decline, several states introduced competency or high school completion tests in the 1970s, and the movement spread in the 1980s. Students were expected to pass a test of achievement before a high school diploma would be awarded. Even that did not suffice: In 1980 at Miami-Dade Community College, 50 percent of the matriculants were below the eleventh-grade level on reading and writing, 60 percent were below on mathematics, and most felt that their high schools had expected too little of them (Losak, Schwartz, and Morris, 1982). The high school competency test apparently could be passed at a level far below a pattern of literacy that would enable a student to enter college-level studies with any hope of success. One commentator reported, "In New York, the test . . . has—shockingly, albeit unsurprisingly—elicited tremendous opposition. Even though its demands seem to me very far from draconian, it is being denounced as a fiendish tool for depriving countless innocent young people from advancement in life" (Simon, 1979, p. 16).

But none of this is really new. Comments on students' lack of preparation for college-level studies may be found as early as the beginnings of the colleges in colonial America. Rudolph (1977) noted, "Because the colonial colleges were founded before there existed any network of grammar schools . . . most entering students were prepared privately, often by studying with the local minister" (p. 52). And so many colleges were built in the first three decades of the nineteenth century that they could not find enough students who were prepared for the higher learning. Hence, "college authorities, defining their own course of study, learned to restrain their expectations in deference to the preparation of the students who came their way" (p. 60).

College Admissions

Because each college set its own standards, and because the founding of colleges preceded the development of a widespread secondary school system, the early colleges displayed a wide variety of admission requirements. By the latter part of the nineteenth century, most of them were operating their own compensatory education programs. In 1895, 40 percent of entering students were drawn from the preparatory programs operated by the colleges and universities themselves (Rudolph, 1977, p. 158).

Numerous attempts to stabilize college admissions have been made. In 1892 the National Education Association organized a Committee on Secondary School Studies, known as the Committee of Ten, which was to recommend and approve the secondary school curriculum for college matriculation. In 1900 the College Entrance Examination Board began offering a common examination for college admission. Nonetheless, the wide variety in types and quality of colleges in America made it impossible to devise uniform admission standards. There has never been a standard of admission to all colleges in the United States. The Educational Testing Service and the American College Testing Program offer uniform examinations across the country, but each college is free to admit students regardless of where they place on those examinations.

Of all postsecondary educational structures in America, the public community colleges have borne the brunt of the poorly prepared students in the twentieth century. When sizable cohorts of well-prepared students were clamoring for higher education, as in the 1950s and early 1960s, the community colleges received a large share of them. But when the college-age group declined and the universities became more competitive for students, the proportion of academically well-prepared students going to community colleges shrank. Thus, the colleges were dealt a multiple blow: relaxed admission requirements and the availability of financial aid at the more prestigious universities; a severe decline in the scholastic abilities of high school graduates; and a greater percentage of applicants who had taken fewer academic courses.

Comparisons of entering students who need remedial help in their studies suggest these different patterns. Of the students entering New Jersey county (community) colleges in 1985, 45 percent were identified as needing remediation in verbal skill, 58 percent in computation, and 77 percent in algebra. Not surprisingly, these percentages were considerably higher than comparable figures for those entering the state colleges or the state university (New Jersey State Department of Higher Education, 1986). Well over half of the students entering community colleges in Washington were deficient in English, reading, and/or mathematics (Washington State Board for Community College Education, 1985).

The community colleges responded by accommodating the different types of students without turning anyone away. They have always tended to let everyone in but have then guided students to programs which fit their aspirations and in which they had some chance to succeed. Students who qualified for transfer programs were never a serious problem; they were given courses similar to those they would find in the lower division of the four-year colleges and universities. Technical and occupational aspirants were not a problem either; career programs were organized for them. Internal selectivity was the norm; failing certain prerequisites, applicants were barred from the health professions and technology programs. And the students who wanted a course or two for their own personal interest found them both in the departments of continuing education and in the transfer programs.

The residue, the poorly prepared group of high school pass-throughs, has been the concern. What should the colleges do with marginally literate people who want to be in college but do not know why? How should they deal with someone who aspires to be an attorney but who is reading at the fifth-grade level? Shunting these students to the trades programs was a favored ploy, giving rise to Clark's (1960) cooling-out thesis. Another ploy was to offer a smattering of remedial courses where students would be prepared, more or less successfully, to enter the transfer courses—or entertained until they drifted away. But the decline in achievement exhibited by secondary school graduates—and dropouts—in the 1970s hit the colleges with full force. The problem of the marginal student became central to instructional planning.

How to guide and teach students who are unprepared for traditional college-level studies is the thorniest single problem for community colleges. Some institutions seem to have given up, as evidenced by their tendencies to award certificates and degrees for any combination of courses, units, or credits—in effect, sending the students away with the illusion of having had a successful college career. Others have mounted massive instructional and counseling services especially for the lower-ability students, stratagems designed to puncture the balloon of prior school failure. But in most programs in most institutions, expectations for student achievement have declined. The weight of the low-ability student hangs like an anchor on the community colleges.

Enrollments in Remedial Studies

Remedial, compensatory, and *developmental* are the most widespread terms for courses designed to teach literacy—the basics of reading, writing, and arithmetic. Compensatory education is not new to the community colleges, but until recently it was composed almost exclusively of disparate courses designed to prepare students to enter the college transfer program. Students were placed in the courses on the basis of entrance tests or prior school achievement. The courses were usually not accepted for credit toward an academic degree. All public two-year colleges have had developmental, preparatory, or remedial courses. Morrison and Ferrante (1973) estimated that, by 1970, 99 percent of the colleges had remedial courses, a figure corroborated by the College Entrance Examination Board (1986). The Center for the Study of Community Colleges (1978b) tallied the sections offered in a national sample of public and private colleges in 1977–78 and found that about three in eight English classes were presented at below college level (Table 26); in nearly one in three mathematics classes, arithmetic was taught at a level lower than college algebra; and remedial classes accounted for 13 percent of the enrollments in chemistry. Roueche, Baker, and Roueche (1984) further documented the problems of literacy among community college students and the institutions' efforts to deal with it.

Even though the decline in student ability stabilized in the 1980s, compensatory education grew. The rise in remedial course enrollment occurred because student ability had sunk so low that college staff members, legislators, and the staff of the universities to which the students transfer had had enough. The dropout and failure rates were unconscionably high. When the population was

Table 26. Level of English Class Sections Offered in 129 Community Colleges, 1977–78 (Percentages).

Level	Percentage
Remedial/developmental	36.9
Composition	17.3
Reading	19.6
College-level	63.1
Composition	56.9
Reading	6.2
Total	100.0

Source: Center for the Study of Community Colleges, 1978b.

expanding and an ever-increasing number of new students showed up each year, the problem was not as acute and few colleges did anything about coordinating compensatory education. In the late 1970s, however, the attitude shifted as the college staff realized that it was more feasible, not to say socially and educationally defensible, to keep the students enrolled than to let them drop out as a result of academic failure.

Increased enrollments in remedial courses and programs were the result. In 1987, 13 percent of the credit-course enrollment in Illinois community colleges was in remedial courses (Illinois Community College Board, 1988). In Washington the figure was 14 percent (Washington State Board for Community College Education, 1988) and in Kansas, 16 percent (Gainous and others, 1986). The funding for these courses sometimes came through the regular academic instructional budget, as in Austin Community College (Texas), where one-third of all state-reimbursed funds were allocated to remedial instruction (D. Angel, personal communication, Jan. 20, 1989). And special funds were often available, some from federal programs to assist disadvantaged students or developing institutions, some from special state appropriations, such as a "Literacy Tutor Coordination Program" in Washington (Carbone, 1987).

Revised Practices

Compensatory courses and programs can be built within the colleges, but several questions remain: Is compensatory education effective? How does it affect the college staff? How can it be conducted in the context of an open-admissions institution without jeopardizing the college's standards and its legitimacy in higher education? How can the segregated compensatory education programs respond to the charges of racism and class-based tracking? How many times should the public pay the schools to try to teach the same competencies to the same people?

Placement testing and integrated compensatory education services have dominated the recent efforts in remedial studies. Beginning in the late 1970s, the nation's community colleges moved toward a system of placement testing, restricted admissions to many courses and programs, integrated remedial programs complete with counseling and tutorial services, and assessment of the efficacy of these procedures. In the 1980s state-mandated placement testing was installed, first in Florida and Georgia and subsequently in numerous other states (Blumenstyk, 1988). These requirements affected all the publicly supported institutions. In California's colleges assessment was not mandated by the state, but two-thirds of the colleges required it. In a nationwide study conducted in 1985, over 90 percent of the community colleges indicated that they used tests for course placement, but only a few of them used the test results to deny admissions to even minimally prepared students. Most of the colleges maintained open-door admissions and used the tests as diagnostic instruments to advise students to enroll in remedial and other program areas. However, around one-fourth of the institutions indicated that all first-time students were required to take a test, and many more felt that testing would be required in the future (Woods, 1985).

Another prominent development in compensatory education has been the integrated program combining instruction in the three Rs with counseling, tutoring, study skills seminars, and a variety of special interventions. Students participate voluntarily or, more often, are placed in the program on the basis of scores made on an entrance test. Special counseling procedures are established, and each student's attendance and progress are monitored. The courses may include developmental reading and writing, and adjunct classes centering on certain content areas also may be provided. The students may be tutored individually by professionals or peers. The programs frequently include reproducible instructional sequences presented through learning laboratories. In some of the more sophisticated compensatory programs, remedial classes are offered through the English and mathematics departments, adjunct courses or study programs are offered through the learning resource center, study skills activities are presented by members of the counseling staff, and tutorials are coordinated by any of the aforementioned divisions. The intent of all the compensatory activities is to keep the students in school and to help them improve their basic skills so that they can complete an academic or a vocational program satisfactorily.

Some compensatory education programs have been designed, often in conjunction with other agencies, for people who were not regularly enrolled at the college. For example, programs have been established for Navajo Indians (Smith, 1979) and for inner-city adults working in construction jobs (Howard, 1976). Compensatory education thus involves the colleges not only with the students who come to the campus seeking academic programs, degrees, and certificates but also with adult basic education. The adult studies are often funded and organized separately. Sometimes, especially where the colleges are responsible for adult education in their district, adult programs lead to entirely separate structures, such as the Community College Centers maintained under the egis of the San Francisco Community College District. These structures take some of the pressure for compensatory education away from the colleges' regular programs.

Program Effects

Hundreds of studies reported in the published literature and in the ERIC files suggest that, even though reliable data are not readily available, the student placement procedures seem valid and that the students learn to read and write in the remedial classes. In a study of remedial English classes in fourteen community colleges, the students' writing ability at the end of the courses was found to be, on the average, equivalent to the writing ability of the students who were beginning the regular college English classes (Cohen, 1973a). Students enrolled in remedial English classes in twenty-nine California community colleges showed gains on a pretest and posttest of writing skills, suggesting that, on average, they were prepared for entry into college-level English (Slark and others, 1987).

The integrated compensatory education programs, designed to effect retention as well as learning, similarly show positive results. Between 8 percent and 20 percent of Miami-Dade's under-prepared students graduate from the college within two years. That may seem a low figure, but such students would not have been admitted into any of the state's universities; hence, any of the students who graduate represent a net plus. Of all the students graduating in 1983–84, 34 percent had taken at least one developmental class, and almost one-third of the students who entered the college in 1981 and were identified as needing remediation subsequently passed all four subtests on the statewide College Level Academic Skills Test (Miami-Dade Community College, 1985). These effects are not surprising. When staff members are involved in a comprehensive program, they pay closer attention to the students, integrate teaching with counseling, provide a greater variety of learning materials than ordinary students receive, and motivate their enrollees to devote more time to their studies. In short, when special treatment is applied, when students are given supplemental counseling, tutoring, and learning aids, when they are singled out for additional work, they tend to remain in school. Special treatment of any sort yields special results.

The relationship between student self-concept and instructors' perceptions of student abilities has been studied. In the Los Angeles Community College District, a much greater percentage of students than instructors reported that the students could learn independently (63 percent versus 29 percent), express themselves in writing (54 percent versus 24 percent), and solve arithmetic problems (62 percent versus 42 percent) (Friedlander, 1981a). The relationship between student self-concept and achievement has also been studied. No significant relationship between student attitudes and grades was found in a study of mathematics courses in the College of DuPage (Illinois) (Eldersveld and Baughman, 1986), but other studies have found student self-rating quite reliable in predicting the scores that students make on tests in basic skills (Greenan, 1983; Palmer, 1984a).

How do college faculty members who face the students daily feel about the massive compensatory education efforts and the poorly prepared students in their classes? The students' abilities exert the single most powerful influence on the level, quality, type, and standard of curriculum and instruction offered in every program in every school. Other influences—instructors' tendencies, externally administered examinations and licensure requirements, the entry levels imposed by succeeding courses in the same and other institutions—pale in comparison. Nothing that is too distant from the students' comprehension can be taught successfully. All questions of academic standards, college-level and remedial courses, textbook readability and coverage, course pacing and sequence come to that.

The students are part of the instructors' working conditions. Except for faculty members recruited especially to staff the compensatory programs, most feel that their environment would be improved if their students were more able. In the CSCC's 1977 national survey of science instructors at two-year colleges, respondents were asked "What would it take to make yours a better course?" Over half of them noted, "Students better prepared to handle course requirements" (Brawer and Friedlander, 1979, p. 32). That choice far outranked all others in a list of sixteen.

If students cannot be more able, at least they might be more alike, so that instruction can be more precisely focused. Teaching groups of students whose reading or computational abilities range from the third to the thirteenth grade is demoralizing; everything is more difficult, from writing examinations to showing group progress—hence the unremitting pressure for ability grouping, remedial courses, learning laboratories that serve to remove the poorer students from the classrooms.

Thus, compensatory education affects the staff in several ways. The traditional faculty members remember their college in the 1950s and early 1960s, when they had well-prepared students. They may feel nostalgic, perhaps even betrayed, because the conditions under which they entered the colleges have changed so substantially. At the same time, they may be pleased that the segregated compensatory education programs remove the poorest students from their own classes.

As integrated compensatory programs grew in the 1980s, separate divisions combining faculty members, counselors, and support staff were formed to accommodate them. This separation of the compensatory education staff from the academic discipline-centered faculty has led to an increased level of professional consciousness among members of the former group. The teachers of remedial courses, managers of learning resource centers, directors of testing centers, and staff members in charge of various tutorial, orientation, and counseling activities for academically disadvantaged students have formed their own professional associations.

They publish their own journals, which carry articles on peer tutoring, the pros and cons of mandatory testing, ways of organizing reading and writing laboratories, and the various treatments they apply to students who come within their purview. Their instructional efforts are outcome oriented; they are considerably more likely than their academic discipline–based colleagues to subscribe to mastery learning concepts, particularly the notion that instructors should measure student learning before and after instruction and make decisions based on the findings. In some colleges the academic instructors treat them as pariahs, but they have their own colleagues and support groups.

The compensatory educators are responsible for a sizable proportion of the studies conducted on the effects of various instructional treatments. Baker (1982) compared the effectiveness of remedial classes with that of traditional courses by examining students in the two groups according to the scores they made on standardized writing tests. Suter (1983) and Johnson (1985) compared grades earned in other classes and retention rates for students who had been through a developmental studies program. Marcotte (1986) used graduation rates as the dependent variable and tracked the students who graduated back through the developmental education program to determine its effects. All these studies and many more that might be cited describe the treatments applied and track their effect on student learning as measured by grades earned in other classes, persistence and graduation rates, and scores made on various testing instruments. A new discipline of organized knowledge based on instructional treatments and effects seems nascent.

Legitimacy

The question of legitimacy is one of image in the eyes of the public, the potential students, the funding agents, and the other sectors of education. Like any other public agency, an educational institution must maintain its legitimacy. The community colleges have strived to maintain their claim to a position in the postsecondary sector through numerous stratagems. In the 1950s and 1960s, for example, they sought people with doctoral degrees to serve as staff

members and rewarded current staff members when they obtained
the higher degree, even though possession of a doctorate bore little
or no relation to a faculty member's professional activities. The
doctorate was a way of saying "We are as good as the senior
institutions." Similarly, they segregated their compensatory
programs in an attempt to regain the legitimacy lost when the
colleges accepted adult basic studies and job-training programs that
could in no measure be considered college level.

Actually, a school's legitimacy rests on its academic standards and the definition of its guiding principles. Academic standards certify that a student holding a certificate or degree has met
the requirement for employment or for further study at another
college; they are the basis for the reputation of institutions and the
people who work in them. Even though community colleges
typically maintain open-admissions policies, they must still attend
to these concerns. Their students must be certified; their instructional programs, testing and counseling services, course content,
and course requirements must all relate to a shared vision of desired
competencies and outcomes. Their certificates or degrees must
evidence some set of proficiencies achieved at some minimum level.

What are the standards in compensatory education? Here the
special programs exhibit several problems in common with the
traditional. One of the main problems is the difficulty in setting
fixed *exit* criteria (grading standards) for courses and programs that
have no set *entry* requirements. If anyone may enroll regardless of
ability, a wide range of students will be attracted. Accordingly,
either the exit criteria must be fluid, with a different standard for
each student, or the time and type of instruction must be greatly
varied, or the instructors must maintain exceedingly modest expectations. All three options are at play in practically all programs.

Standardized expectations of accomplishment, or exit criteria, suggest social norms as contrasted with standards for individuals. Social norms suggest that people who would function
adequately in particular social settings (the workplace, school) must
act to a certain standard. The alternative, relating accomplishment
to the desires or entering abilities of individuals, suggests that any
accomplishment is satisfactory and that the institution has succeeded if any gain in individual ability can be shown. This conflict

between social and individual standards is an issue of the absolute versus the relative, and it strikes at the heart of compensatory education.

Different groups take different positions on the issue. Community college instructors tend to argue in favor of absolute standards. The Academic Senate for California Community Colleges (1977) has studied the problem extensively, surveying its members and sponsoring state conferences on the issue. The ASCCC deplored some of the pressures to lower standards: students entering the college with inadequate basic skills but with expectation of passing the courses, as they have done throughout their prior school careers; ill-prepared students insisting on enrolling in transfer courses rather than remedial courses; the virtual elimination of *D* and *F* grades and concomitant wider use of passing grades; reduction in the number of required subjects; and the cult of growth afflicting community colleges, as evidenced by aggressive student recruiting drives. The ASCCC Academic Standards Committee recommended that standards should be maintained through the use of diagnostic and placement testing, directive counseling, academic prerequisites for courses, and proficiency testing before awarding academic degrees. These recommendations were in no small measure responsible for California's adopting matriculation standards in the 1980s.

Advocates of the concept of lifelong learning often provide an opposing view. To them, any seeker of knowledge should find the institution a resource to be used for an infinite variety of purposes. Cross (1978, pp. 19–20), for example, has argued that substantial changes in school forms are needed, so that anyone may learn anything at any time: "My concern is that in our exuberance for recruiting adults and certifying that *their* learning projects meet *our* standards, we will corrupt independent, self-directed learners into learners dependent on someone else to determine where, when, and how people should learn. Visions of a learning society with people of all ages enthusiastically pursuing learning that interests them could so easily turn into a joyless learning society with people grimly fulfilling requirements and seeking legitimacy for every conceivable variety of learning."

These opposed positions suggest differing views of present

and potential students. Some see them as lethargic illiterates; others, as humanistic knowledge seekers.

The Dilemma of Tracking

Segregating the less well-prepared students has much appeal. Classes can be made more homogeneous; the bright students are not forced to wait for the less able to catch up; and, most important, the instructors whose classes have been relieved of the poorer students can regain the attitude that they are teaching in a true college. However, the practice of shunting students to remedial classes is based on tenuous assumptions, especially the assumption that student performance standards are immutable when nearly all school programs are actually based on shifting norms. The concept of functional literacy provides an example.

Definitions of Functional Literacy. One definition of functional literacy is "the level of reading, writing, and calculating ability that people need to succeed in the public realm in which they choose to operate." Under this definition the level of literacy required to function as a citizen, taxpayer, or homemaker or merely "on the street" serves as a criterion. A second definition is "the level of reading, writing, and ability to send and receive messages that it takes to obtain and maintain a job." And, obviously, different levels of literacy are required for performance in different types of jobs. A third definition of functional literacy is "the level required to perform successfully in a college program." Here again, different types of programs require different levels of competency. All these definitions, then, can be subsumed under the statement "Functional literacy is the ability to communicate in the symbolic language of reading, writing, and speaking that is adequate for people to maintain themselves in the context of particular situations," or, as the National Assessment of Educational Progress defines it, "using printed and written information to function in society, to achieve one's goals, and to develop one's knowledge and potential" (Kirsch and Jungeblut, 1986, p. 3).

So defined, functional literacy is related to the milieu in which people find themselves. It is relative; there are no absolute minimum standards of competence. A functionally literate person in some school settings may be functionally illiterate in certain jobs. And a person who is quite able to communicate within the confines of certain jobs may be functionally illiterate for purposes of a college program.

Hence a dilemma. Institutional legitimacy and faculty predilections rest on standards, defined outcomes, and certifiable results. But the definitions guiding staff efforts and the precepts of continuing education or lifelong learning are relative. Each person brings idiosyncratic backgrounds and aspirations to the institution; each finds a separate set of experiences. How can the two be reconciled in an open-admissions institution? The question is not limited to compensatory education, but the influx of students with low academic ability brought it to the fore. In addition to providing a more useful learning experience for the poorly prepared students, many of the compensatory education programs have segregated them into separate enclaves, thus protecting, at least temporarily, the legitimacy of the other portions of the college.

Segregation and Tracking. Issues of minority student segregation and tracking are not so easily submerged. Compensatory education is designed to do what its name suggests—to compensate for deficiences. These deficiencies are not merely those occasioned by failures of the lower schools; they relate also to cultural differences. For example, in families from the lower classes, where obtaining food, clothing, and shelter is a matter of daily concern, a tendency toward immediate gratification is built in. Where the necessities of life are not cause for daily concern, aspects of family life will allow for deferred gratification, and the norms guiding child rearing will include using formal education as a means of reaching for rewards to be obtained later. The idea of using the school as an avenue for potential advancement in the culture may be alien to people from the lower classes. Instead, if school is to be used as an avenue of advancement in any realm, it is toward higher-status employment. Yet their tendencies toward immediate gratification make it difficult for members of these groups to accept the regimen of years of study needed before one obtains certification.

Morrison and Ferrante (1973) commented on the impact of cultural differences among community college students. In their view, the term *disadvantaged* means that students have been socialized into attitudes, values, and norms that inhibit their advancement into the mainstream of society; therefore, "disadvantaged" is synonymous with "culturally different" (p. 5). Weis (1985) studied the students in a community college that enrolls a high proportion of ethnic minorities and found distinct cultural differences affecting student attendance, tardiness, achievement, and peer-group relations. The relative unimportance that the students attached to prompt, regular attendance continually ran afoul of college policies. The students who missed school because of problems with transportation or baby-sitters could not understand why their progress in the classes was invariably impeded.

Commentary on disadvantaged or culturally different students is pertinent in a discussion of compensatory education because those terms are applied most frequently to ethnic minority students, who are overrepresented in compensatory education programs. For example, in 1985 in Illinois, 27 percent of the Asian students, 24 percent of the blacks, 58 percent of the Hispanics, and less than 6 percent of the white students were taking remedial classes (Illinois Community College Board, 1986b). Much of the federal and state aid available to community colleges is targeted toward their providing special instructional and counseling services for the minorities.

Thus, the establishment and operation of segregated compensatory education programs become freighted with overtones of racism. Because requiring a literacy test for admission to college transfer programs tends to discriminate against members of the ethnic minorities, who may have been less well prepared in the lower schools, the compensatory programs take on the appearance of programs for the culturally different, giving rise to charges that reading tests are culturally biased and that writing tests discriminate unfairly against those whose native language is other than English.

As long as the colleges admit everyone but maintain certain admissions requirements for different programs, the controversy will continue. Selective admission to any program is as discriminatory as it is justifiable. Regardless of the yardstick applied, the people who are shut out of the programs in which they wanted to enroll have been discriminated against. And yet, with accrediting agencies, state licensing boards, and senior institutions looking in, program directors feel justified in admitting only a select few, particularly if the field of endeavor for which the program prepares people can take only so many graduates or if college facilities allow for only so many matriculants.

Should the colleges restrict admissions to certain programs? If some applicants cannot gain admission to a program because their level of literacy is lower than a cutting score, the issue is resolved for them. But if applicants *are* admitted to the program, then program operators have the responsibility to teach the students the skills required for them to succeed in it. The pattern of allowing all to enter and using the program itself to screen out the unworthy should be discounted—first, because one cannot at the same time teach and judge; second, because it is too expensive, in terms of concern for humans, to allow sizable numbers to enroll with the expectation that many of them will not complete the course of study.

The pressures for selective admission to various programs have grown in recent years. In the 1950s most colleges screened students into remedial programs if their prior high school grades or their scores on entrance tests suggested that they might not be able to succeed in the transfer programs. In the 1960s the pressure to allow anyone to enter a transfer program grew, the reason being that remedial programs were seen as catchalls for the less worthy, as holding tanks for students who must be "cooled out" of higher education. In the 1970s the pendulum swung back, with many institutions building compensatory programs, screening students into them, moving away from the attitude of letting students try everything and fail if they must. And that trend accelerated in the 1980s.

However, it is quite possible to teach functional literacy in the transfer program. Some notable efforts at mainstreaming—that is, allowing lower-ability students to take the regular college classes even while they are being assisted supplementally—have been made. Many of these efforts involve the use of learning laboratories. As examples, in the Developmental Studies Program at Penn Valley

Community College (Missouri), the Learning Skills Laboratory (LSL) was used as an extension of the math and English classroom. Students could complete LSL instructional activities, as prescribed by faculty members, before progressing to the course or concurrently with it (Ford, 1976). Sacramento City College (California) initiated a Higher Education Learning Package (HELP) to promote the success and retention of students with basic skill deficiencies while mainstreaming them into regular courses. Students who were reading at a sixth-grade level worked with instructors and tutors in small groups and on a one-to-one basis (Bohr and Bray, 1979). Introducing concepts of mastery learning into the regular courses in City Colleges of Chicago resulted in student achievement and retention superior to those obtained in remedial courses or in the regular courses taught in nonmastery fashion (Chausow, 1979). A series of one-hour study skills courses coordinated with the regular academic courses in Dutchess Community College (New York) led to better grades and retention not only in the related courses but also in other classes (Weeks, 1987). Thus, remediation does not have to come in the form of segregated remedial courses.

It is likely that most students can succeed in the collegiate and occupational programs if they are required to supplement their courses with tutorials, learning labs, special counseling, peer-group assistance, and/or a variety of other aids. "Required" is a key word in the foregoing sentence; left to their own choice, few students who need assistance will seek it out. Several surveys of students have found that, of their own volition, students tend not to take advantage of the support services that the college provides for them. Yet mandating support services means that additional funds must be found. The question is how much effort the colleges are willing to put into the extra treatment required by students who enter programs they are not capable of coping with. Given a choice between an admissions screen to keep students out of the programs and the allocation of sizable funds to ensure students' success if they are admitted, many institutional managers faced with static budgets opt to keep the less well-prepared students out of the transfer courses by placing them in remedial courses or segregated compensatory education programs.

But denying students admission to programs of their choice

is difficult to justify. The open-door philosophy of the community college implies that these students should not be denied. The fact that some can succeed suggests that they should not be denied. And the fact that students who are denied access to the collegiate programs are typically denied exposure to the humanistic and scientific thought on which these areas are based mandates that they must not be denied. Community colleges have succeeded in opening access to all; if that access is limited to a compensatory program that offers primarily the same type of basic education that failed the students in the lower schools, then students have been cruelly denied access to the higher learning. The colleges cannot afford to operate separate programs for the less qualified unless those programs are verifiably supportive of the collegiate and career programs.

Teaching the basic skills to people who failed to learn them in the lower schools is expensive. Questions of impact on college staff and image pale before the issue of cost. No form of teaching is cheaper than a course for self-directed learners; the teacher-student ratio is limited only by the size of the lecture hall. None, not even education in the higher technologies, is more expensive than the varied media and close monitoring demanded by slow learners. Until recently, many college leaders have been reluctant to publicize the extent of their compensatory education programs. They feared that their funding would be threatened by legislators and members of the public, who might raise embarrassing questions about paying several times over for education that was supposed to be provided in the lower schools.

Those who would impose standards for programs at any level face difficulties stemming from lack of consensus on institutional purpose, antagonism to the idea of group norms, and, in secondary schools and community colleges, the inability to impose entrance requirements. Selective screening into the collegiate programs could not be maintained in an earlier era because students demanded and got the right to fail, and that contributed to the unconscionable attrition figures of the 1970s. Selective admission into the collegiate programs has been tried again because it is easier to screen students out *en bloc* than to establish criteria for functional literacy course by course. And yet, unless those criteria are defined, selective admissions will again be unsuccessful. Even though it is impossible to bring all students to the point at which they can succeed in the courses and programs of their choice, the community colleges must continue trying. As the Commission on the Future of Community Colleges pointed out, "Literacy is essential both for the individual and society. . . . Community colleges must make a commitment, without apology, to help students overcome academic deficiencies and acquire the skills they need to become effective, independent learners" (American Association of Community and Junior Colleges, 1988, pp. 16-17).

Reconciling the Dilemma

Three options are available to colleges that would reconcile the conflict between maintaining standards and allowing all students to enter the programs of their choice. First, they can define the specific competencies required to enter and succeed in each course. "College level," "program proficiency," and "academic standards" are not sufficiently precise. There is too much variation among courses in the same program—indeed, among sections of the same course—for these criteria to hold. Standards are too often relative instead of absolute. Screening tests can be used at the point of entry to each class. And precise exit criteria—also known as specific, measurable objectives—can be set.

The second option is to allow all students to enroll in any course but to limit the number of courses that poorly prepared students can take in any term and require that those students take advantage of the available support services. Thus, students might take only one course at a time and participate in tutorial and learning-laboratory sessions on the basis of three hours for each credit hour attempted.

The third option is for the colleges to abandon the pretext that they offer freshman- and sophomore-level studies. They could enroll high school dropouts, adult basic education students, job seekers, and job upgraders, offering them the services they need outside the "credit hour" structure.

All three options are now in play to some extent. The colleges that are involved in mastery learning and other techniques that rely on precisely specified measures of student progress have built their programs on absolute standards. Those that monitor student progress and insist that students participate in the auxiliary instructional efforts have moved well toward building the kinds of college-wide instructional effort that teaching poorly prepared students demands. And those that have erected separate institutes that concentrate exclusively on adult basic education and career-related studies have abandoned collegiate studies de facto.

At least two options are *not* acceptable: allowing sizable percentages of students to fail and reducing academic standards so that those who do get through have not been sufficiently well prepared to succeed in the workplace or in further education. The high failure rates have led to numerous charges that the community colleges are a dead end for many of their matriculants, especially the minority students. By reducing standards, as detailed by Richardson, Fisk, and Okun (1983), the colleges were merely pushing the problem off to the students' employers or to the academic institutions in which they subsequently enrolled. In the 1980s the numerous state mandates designed to improve student progress reflect a decided unwillingness to allow either of those options to continue.

As community colleges become involved more heavily in compensatory education, they will have to reconcile their relations with the secondary schools, from which they broke away. Education at any level depends on prior preparation of the students. The decline in the secondary schools during the 1970s was one of the most notable events of the decade in education. Why it happened is not relevant to this discussion; reduced school budgets, the coming of age of a generation reared on television, the assigning of noneducative tasks to the schools, and numerous other causes have been cited. But much of the blame can be placed at the colleges' doors. The dearth of communication between college and secondary school staff members, the lack of articulation in curriculum, the failure to share teaching materials except on the basis of a random encounter—all must be mentioned. Concerns for social equity replaced a prior concern for admission standards. In their haste to expand access, the colleges neglected to assist the secondary schools in preparing the people who would be coming to them and even, in many cases, to recommend the secondary school courses that the students should take. Reconciling the dilemma will force them to rectify this omission.

Issues

Whether or not the community colleges pick up the seventeen-year-olds who have left high school early, and whether or not they serve as a bridge between schooling and work for their older students, compensatory education fits within their mission of connecting people with opportunities. They will be involved in compensatory education in one form or another, and their career education programs have already enrolled half of their students. Linking the two may be a natural next step. Can the colleges do it?

The colleges need more information about the effects of the compensatory education in which they are so heavily engaged. Do segregated compensatory programs lead to higher standards in other courses? Do the faculty members outside the programs add content to the courses from which the lesser-ability students have been removed? Do they pass students through the courses more rapidly when they are relieved from having to wait for the slower students? If so, all these results should be tabulated as benefits of the separate programs. If not, the better students have not gained from the absence of the poorer ones. So far, studies of these effects have been almost nonexistent.

Several attempts to engage instructors in defining the outcomes of their courses in specific, measurable terms have failed. What forms of staff development would be successful? What incentives could be used?

Would allowing the instructors to test the students who sought entry to their classes and bar those who did not pass the test suffice to encourage them to become accountable for passing a specified percentage? No moves in this direction are apparent.

Required support services increase instructional costs. Can the colleges find sufficient funds for the necessary tutors, counselors, learning-laboratory technicians, and paraprofessional instructional aides? Can the faculty be encouraged to work with these aides, so that classroom and auxiliary instruction lead to parallel objectives?

What patterns of learning are demanded of students in the courses currently in place? Finding answers to that question demands analyses of classroom tests and teaching techniques, a form of research rarely seen in the contemporary college. Will the faculty and administrators demand it?

The overriding issue is whether community colleges can maintain their credibility as institutions of higher education even while they enroll the increasingly less well-prepared students. If they can, they will fulfill the promises of their earliest proponents.

Ten

Community Education:
Extending College Services and Training

Community education, the broadest of all community college functions, embraces adult education, adult basic education, continuing education, contract training, community services, and community-based education. Found in the earliest community colleges, these activities were carried along for decades on the periphery of the career and collegiate functions. They expanded greatly in the 1970s, but the rate of expansion slowed in the 1980s as college services came under closer scrutiny from external budget allocators.

Community education covers a wide range. It may take the form of classes for credit or not for credit, varying in duration from one hour to a weekend, several days, or an entire school term. Community education may be sponsored by the college, by some other agency using college facilities, or jointly by the college and some outside group. It may be provided on campus, off campus, or through television, the newspapers, or radio. It may center on education or recreation, on programs for personal interest or for the good of the entire community.

The various forms of community education usually are fully supported by participant fees, grants, or contracts with external organizations. The participants tend to have short-term goals rather than degree or certificate objectives. They are usually older than the traditional eighteen- to twenty-one-year-old students, and their range of prior school achievement is more varied: many of them already hold baccalaureate or graduate degrees; many more have never completed high school. They usually attend the course or activities intermittently and part-time. They have their own reasons for attending, and the program managers design activities accordingly.

Rationale

Beginning with Jesse Bogue, who popularized the term *community college* in the 1950s, and culminating with the Commission on the Future of Community Colleges' report, *Building Communities* (American Association of Community and Junior Colleges, 1988), the leaders of the AACJC have been vigorous in their support for community education. Edmund J. Gleazer, Jr., president of the association from 1958 until 1981, wrote extensively in favor of education for direct community development, the expansion of the colleges beyond their role in postsecondary education, and continuing education as the main purpose. He emphasized the "community," rather than the "college," in the institution's title. To him, the institution was a resource to be used by individuals throughout their lifetime and by the general public as an agency assisting with community issues.

One of Gleazer's prime contentions was that "the community college is uniquely qualified to become the *nexus* of a community learning system, relating organizations with educational functions into a complex sufficient to respond to the population's learning needs" (1980, p. 10). He thought the institution capable of serving as a connector by virtue of its students and staff members, who frequently work at other jobs in the community. The college would be a link among all community organizations that provide learning activities. "Among these are radio and television stations, newspapers, libraries, museums, schools, colleges, theaters, parks, orchestras, dance groups, unions, and clubs" (p. 10). As for the money to pay for all this, Gleazer made repeated calls for fiscal formulas that would recognize the diverse programs presented by community colleges. However, he recognized that "a kind of riptide exists between the interest in lifelong education and the apparently limited financial resources available for conventional education for traditional students" (1976, p. 6).

Numerous other commentators have favored community education as a dominant function for community colleges. Myran (1978) traced the community education concept through university extension services and the adult and continuing education that has been offered by the public schools for the past century. These institutions were thereby able to provide educational services to individuals and groups without being wed to traditional academic forms, such as credits, semesters, and grades. In Myran's view, the community-based college is eminently equipped to provide such services because of its ability "to coordinate planning with other community agencies, its interest in participatory learning experiences as well as cognitive ones, the wide range of ages and life goals represented in its student body, and the alternative instructional approaches it arranges to make learning accessible to various community groups" (p. 5). Martorana and Piland (1984) similarly promoted the concept; Cross has furthered it in many of her writings, such as *Adults as Learners* (1981); and it is thematic in the numerous issues of *Community Services Catalyst,* published since 1970.

Its intentions are noble. Harlacher and Gollattscheck (1978, p. 7) recommended a college that would be a "vital participant in the total renewal process of the community . . . dedicated to the continual growth and development of its citizens and its social institutions." Such a college would offer the kinds of education community members want, not the kind that pedagogues think is good for them, at locations where the learners are, not where the college says they should be. Harlacher and Gollattscheck urged community colleges to cooperate with social, governmental, professional, educational, and neighborhood agencies in mutually supportive advisory relationships and in joint ventures.

Most recently, the AACJC-sponsored Commission on the Future of Community Colleges has urged the colleges to coalesce around the community education concept: "The community college, at its best, can be a center for problem-solving in adult illiteracy or the education of the disabled. It can be a center for leadership training, too. It can also be the place where education and business leaders meet to talk about the problems of displaced workers. It can bring together agencies to strengthen services for minorities, working women, single parent heads of households, and unwed teenage parents. It can coordinate efforts to provide day care, transportation, and financial aid. The community college can take the lead in long-range planning for community development. And it can serve as the focal point for improving the quality of life in the inner city" (American Association of Community and Junior Colleges, 1988, p. 35). This seems a large order, but the commission is dedicated to fostering the colleges as centers of community life. Its report begins with the premise that "The term *community* should be defined not only as a region to be served, but also as a climate to be created" (p. 3), and many of its seventy-seven recommendations follow from that theme.

What has stimulated these calls for completely revised structures? What has made these advocates so concerned with community building and noncampus forms? One clue is provided by the nature of community colleges' political and fiscal support. The colleges draw minuscule funds from private donors and have few foundation-supported research contracts. Instead, they depend almost entirely on public monies awarded in a political arena. And here they have difficulty competing with the more prestigious universities for support in legislatures dominated by state university alumni. They seem to be turning to their local constituents, seeking links with taxpayers at the grass roots—seeking support from the business community, for example, by providing customized job-training services for local employers.

Community education proponents foster activities different from the traditional courses taught by regular faculty members, saying that these are archaic, restrictive, discriminatory, and narrowly focused. They seem to feel that doing away with the traditional forms in which education has been conducted will necessarily lead to a higher quality of service. In their desire to eschew elitism, they articulate populist, egalitarian goals. The more diverse the population served, the less traditionally based the program, the better. The National Community Education Association sees community education as an opportunity for local citizens, community schools, and institutions to become partners in actively addressing educational and community concerns. The association's purpose is to bring community members together to identify and link community needs and resources, so that people are helped to help themselves. Its members believe that education is a lifelong process, in which everyone in the community shares responsibility, and that citizens should be involved in deciding the community's needs and linking those needs to available resources.

The overarching concept of community education is certainly justifiable; few would quibble with the intent of an institution to upgrade its entire community rather than merely to provide a limited array of courses for people aged eighteen to twenty-one. However, the total seems less than the sum of its parts. The components of community education must be addressed separately in order to understand its scope and effect. Are all segments of equal value? Who decides what shall be presented and who shall pay for it?

Categories

Brawer (1980a) has listed the terms most commonly used in definitions of community education: (1) *adult education*—instruction designed for people who are beyond the age of compulsory school attendance and who have either completed or interrupted their formal education; (2) *continuing education*—the learning effort undertaken by people whose principal occupations are no longer as students, those who regard learning as a means of developing their potential or resolving their problems; (3) *lifelong learning*—intermittent education, whether or not undertaken in school settings; (4) *community services* (the broadest term)—whatever services an institution provides that are acceptable to the people in its service area; (5) *community-based education*—programs designed by the people served and developed for the good of the community. Respondents to a nationwide survey of directors of continuing education defined it as "courses and activities for credit or noncredit, formal classroom or nontraditional programs, cultural, recreational offerings specifically designed to meet the needs of the surrounding community and using school, college, and other facilities" (Fletcher and others, 1977, p. 12). "Community-based" education was more related to community problem-solving activities.

Not content with a definition centering on the participants' age, the proponents of adult and continuing education refer to it as learner-centered education, with the learners participating "actively at every stage of the educational process. . . . The content and the methodologies should draw heavily upon the learner's life and work experience." The instructors are "facilitators of learning," concerned more with process than with content (Freedman, 1987, p. 63). As with most concepts in education, continuing education is more an ideology than a theory.

Conceptually, community education includes elements of career, compensatory, and collegiate education. Career education is organized around programs that prepare people for the job market, whereas community education includes short courses offered for occupational upgrading or relicensure. Collegiate education is directed toward preparing people for academic degrees, whereas community education may include regular college courses taken by adults, the awarding of college credit for experience, and noncredit courses actually taught at the college level—for example, conversational foreign languages. Compensatory education is designed to remedy the defects in student learning occasioned by prior school failure, whereas community education may include adult basic studies that focus on literacy, high school completion, and general education development. Some elements of community education— programs for the handicapped and for prison inmates, for example—may cut across all three of the other functions. However, other elements in community education relate more to providing noneducative services to the community than they do to the educational dimension itself. In this category would fall the opening of college facilities for public functions and a variety of recreational services, the community service notion.

Practically, the source of funds tends to divide community education from the other functions. Community education activities are more likely to be self-supporting, fully funded through tuition or with money provided by an outside agency on the basis of a contract for services rendered. State and federal funds earmarked for special groups are often used in community education programs. In some cases local tax monies and categorical grants are used for community education, whereas career and collegiate education are funded by the states through various formulas, usually based on student enrollment or credit hours generated.

Enrollments

The variations in definition make it difficult to estimate the magnitude of community education. Enrollment figures, especially, are unreliable; they are usually understated except when being pronounced by advocates intent on showing that the colleges serve nearly everyone in their district. Because degree-credit courses are funded at a higher, more consistent level than most of community education, the tendency is to classify as much as possible as degree credit, thus inflating those numbers at the expense of community education enrollment figures. Actually, the total would far exceed the combined enrollment in the career certificate and collegiate degree programs if people enrolled in college credit classes but without degree aspirations were classified instead as adult basic education students, enrollees in short courses offered in continuing education programs, and participants in community service activities.

The enrollment figures that are available are worth recounting. Community education enrollments (in service, recreational, and life enrichment programs that are not part of for-credit, academic programs) were reported in the AACJC *Directory* between 1974-75, when they were 3,259,972, and 1984-85, when they totaled 3,651,225. For the decade they ranged between 3 and 4 million. However, the introduction to the 1980 *Directory* states that "because these programs vary in length, with no clearly defined registration periods, it is difficult to get a clear picture. . . . Some institutions do not routinely collect enrollment figures from community education students" (p. 3). Extrapolating from the 877 institutions that did report student head count in noncredit activities in 1984-85, the compilers of the *Directory* estimated that 4,848,065 participated nationwide, with 99.3 percent of them in public colleges. The AACJC has since stopped reporting these data in its *Directory* because of the imprecision of the figures.

Data difficulties make it impossible to compare community education enrollments between states as well. Some state reports include adult basic education and/or participation in recreational activities and others do not. Further, head-count enrollments in community education usually include duplicate enrollments occasioned when the same person participates in more than one noncredit course or activity during the year. Nonetheless, state enrollments are useful as an estimate of the magnitude and types of functions included in the community education definition.

For example, the AACJC *Directory* reported 153,086 participants in community education in 1979 in California, compared with a total enrollment of 1,101,648 students in degree-credit programs. This relatively low ratio reflects the predominance of the California secondary schools in adult education. In the three community college districts that had jurisdiction over adult education, more than half of the students were classified as adults. Community education enrollments in California plummeted after the passage of Proposition 13 in 1978 cut off the local funding base for community services, but enrollments rose again when the courses were reinstated on a student-fee basis.

In Florida the community colleges have major responsibility for offering courses to individuals aged sixteen and older who had legally left the lower schools. In 1985-86, 119,936 were enrolled in adult general studies and 122,711 in community instructional services, totals comparable to the enrollments in collegiate and career programs (Florida State Department of Education, 1987). And in Washington, where over 10 percent of the courses offered by community colleges are contractual or fully student funded, all of the growth in enrollment between 1986-87 and 1987-88 was in these two areas (Washington State Board for Community College Education, 1988). However counted, community education represents a sizable proportion of the community college effort.

Scope

The scope of community education is reflected in documents emanating from colleges around the country. Continuing education alone covers a broad area.

Continuing Education. A Ford Foundation Study reported by Gittell (1985) found that many low-income adults are involved in community education and concluded that community-based colleges provide an important option for many people who are not served elsewhere. Whatever the financial circumstances, many groups of people are involved because community education addresses a wide variety of concerns, including child care, substance abuse, senior citizen services, student achievement/school effectiveness, community pride/support for schools, unemployment and underemployment, literacy/diploma and degree completion, and community economic development.

Programs for special groups are provided, usually when special funding can be obtained. Programs for displaced workers (Crist and others, 1985; Charbonneau, 1986), gerontology programs for both the general public and providers of direct services to older adults (Hartmann, 1986; Roche, 1985), women's programs (Trevor and Lucas, 1986), and retired persons' programs (Yoseloff and others, 1987)—all are focused on special groups of people. Programs for single parents/displaced homemakers also became popular (Bromley and Moore, 1987; Gulf Coast Community College, 1987; Hawaii Interviewing, 1986; Lake City Community College, 1987). Community colleges in New York used funds derived from the Carl D. Perkins Vocational Act to offer programs for adults in need of training or retraining or for single parents (State University of New York, 1987). Several hundred community colleges have participated in the Servicemembers' Opportunity College network, which provides tuition reimbursement and other support services for military personnel who enroll in course work that need not be related to their service duties (American Association of Community and Junior Colleges/American Association of State Colleges and Universities, 1974).

Credit for Experience. The awarding of college credit for experience is a component of community education. A survey of Texas community colleges (Golemon, 1979) revealed that 76 percent awarded credits applicable to an associate degree. The learning was validated by examination, a verified experience record, personal interview, or combinations of these and other methods. In Sinclair

Community College's (Ohio) Credit for Lifelong Learning Program, 1,000 people took "Portfolio Development" as a credit course in 1979. The program awarded an average of eighteen hours of credit to each student, nearly all of which was applicable to a degree (B. Heermann, personal communication, Aug. 11, 1981). Whatcom Community College (Washington) developed a handbook for students to help them gain credit for prior learning experiences (Deiro, 1983). Orange Coast College's (California) Assessment of Prior Learning (APL) program includes an assessment procedure used to award credit for demonstrated competencies (Snow and Bruns, 1982). A similar program in Texas is described by Lindahl (1982).

Special Services. Several types of cooperative endeavors between community colleges and other community agencies may be found. The AACJC's Policies for Lifelong Education project surveyed cooperative relationships between colleges and community groups in 1978 and reported an average of fifty-nine cooperative arrangements serving 8,781 people at each of 173 colleges. Arrangements between the colleges and local and state clubs and organizations as well as other educational institutions dominated the list. Cooperative arrangements were also found with county and municipal government agencies and private enterprise, including industrial concerns. These joint ventures ranged from sharing facilities to offering mutually sponsored courses. The majority of funds came from tuition and fees charged participants, but many of the programs were supported by college community service funds, often generated by local taxes (Gilder and Rocha, 1980).

Although not included in the community education figures, the many programs that fine arts and humanities departments sponsor in cooperation with local agencies, such as arts councils and museums, are properly a part of the concept. Some colleges have developed community-based discussion forums in which the participants discuss subjects reported in the local newspaper. And the community forum procedure has been used to bring the humanities to participants through lectures, panels, debates, dramatizations, films, and radio broadcasts. In these forums college humanities instructors work together with citizen groups in planning and presenting the programs.

Community education often involves the community colleges in providing special services to other publicly funded institutions. Several programs operated by community colleges for prison inmates were described by Cohen and his associates (1975). Hagerstown Junior College entered the field of prison education in 1969 at the Maryland Correctional Training Center (Galley and Parsons, 1976). In 1967 thirty-one state correctional systems were providing inmate education in cooperation with postsecondary education in their correctional institutions, and in 1976 forty-five states had such programs. A 1985 survey found more than 260 community colleges providing services to around 26,000 inmates (Wolford and Littlefield, 1985). Community colleges in Canada, too, have been urged to contract with prisons in their areas to provide academic and vocational assessment, diagnostic and remedial programs, and training in languages and life skills for the inmates (Dennison, 1979). Snowden (1986) has described the New Brunswick Community College program in a maximum-security facility.

Many of these programs for prisoners have been expanded, and others have appeared. Since 1984 several New Jersey community colleges have provided basic skills and vocational training to juvenile offenders (Grissom and McMurphy, 1986). The largest inmate education program in Virginia, in existence since 1984, operates through Southern Virginia Community College. Since the program's inception 208 inmates have earned high school diplomas, and in spring 1988 the first student inmate earned an associate degree (Gendron and Cavan, 1988).

Contracted Services. Contract training refers to an arrangement in which a business, a government agency, or a community association contracts directly with a college for the provision of instruction to its employees, clients, or members. The activities include apprenticeship training; contract services for industry; economic development services; Job Training Partnership Act Programs; and faculty "return to industry" programs, in which instructors spend time in industrial plants to gain information about contemporary technologies (Suchorski, 1987). In 1987 community colleges in Illinois provided customized job training for 1,395 companies through 1,954 courses, serving over 37,000 employees (Illinois Community College Board, 1987b).

Ohio State University has issued a guide to help two-year colleges create linkages with business, industry, and labor as well as to offer cooperative training programs (Kalamas and Warmbrod, 1987). El Paso Community College (Texas) developed a Business and Industry Center as a rapid response system for the college and the community. It offers short- and long-term credit and noncredit courses and on- and off-campus services as well as walk-in technical assistance (Troyer, 1985). The National Small Business Training Network (NSBTN) provides a rationale and an outline for program planning and offers a checklist for maintaining NSBTN in local communities (Jellison, 1983). Kopecek and Clarke (1984, p. 1) describe customized training for business as "meeting local and regional needs with uniquely local solutions" and present examples of ways that colleges have organized to operate several types of customized programs.

Community colleges have long taken advantage of various federal programs designed to retrain technologically displaced workers and other unemployed people. They have used funds provided by the Manpower Development Training Act of 1962, the Comprehensive Employment and Training Act of 1973, and the more recent Job Training Partnership Act of 1983. These programs assisted the colleges in designing activities in accordance with local job needs and in cooperation with employers in their region. In 1985 the Sears-Roebuck Foundation gave a sizable award to enhance collaboration between community colleges and local employers. Through the award the AACJC and the Association of Community College Trustees established a Keeping America Working project (American Association of Community and Junior Colleges, 1986).

Labor union leaders also have supported community education programs—for example, by negotiating tuition aid packages with employers, serving on advisory committees for the colleges' occupational programs, and helping to establish cooperative apprenticeship training programs and programs to assist union members in studying leadership roles. Some union-sponsored activities assist members in studying the liberal arts (Berger, 1988). Others are designed to help working people deal with personal problems or problems with employers.

In sum, because the concept of community education describes an area of service that knows no limits on client age, prior educational attainment, interest, or intent, the scope of offerings is limited only by staff energies and imagination and by the funds available. According to Coastline Community College (California) administrators, "The community is its campus, both physically and philosophically. The college nurtures the community and is, in turn, sustained by it. . . . Virtually any course may be offered if it is approved by the state, can attract sufficient enrollees to make it cost-effective, and if suitable instruction is available. Considerable latitude in programming decisions devolves upon the college, which, as a result, is encouraged to adopt a fairly aggressive marketing posture" (Luskin and Small, 1980-81, pp. 25-27).

Effectiveness

Are the programs effective? Assessing the outcomes of community education is difficult because, with the entire community as the client, effects are diffuse and subject to contamination from innumerable sources. A favorite way of measuring the effect of continuing education courses has been to ask the participants how they liked them. Nickens (1977) coordinated such a study, with the results indicated in Table 27. The Maryland State Board for Community Colleges (1988) has specified that continuing education courses, in order to be eligible for state funding, "must illustrate the skill or knowledge to be developed and the student outcomes expected" (p. 13). McGuire (1988) has provided a set of criteria by which entire community-based programs might be measured. But these again are process criteria: the extent to which community members were involved in program planning, the linkages that were built between the college and other community agencies, the feedback received from community leaders and clients, and similar subjective measures that are dependent on an observer's interpretation. All of community education seems to be assessed as though it were continuing education for individuals raised to the level of the

Table 27. Students' Reasons for Enrolling in Community Service
Courses and Extent to Which Their Expectations Were Met
in Ten Florida Community Colleges (*N* = 4,631).

Reason for Taking Community Service Courses	Percentage of Enrollment	Percentage Expectation Met
To learn skills for a sport or game	14.1	86.8
To improve my citizenship skills	12.8	83.3
To prepare for my retirement	16.4	83.6
To improve my reading skills	5.5	60.7
To help me understand alternate life-styles and how to cope with them	20.5	85.5
To help with an alcohol- or drug-related problem	1.9	40.0
To improve my financial planning abilities	28.7	87.6
To improve my consumer skills	21.0	85.8
To learn about family planning	3.4	55.6
To learn how I might adjust to a major change in the family (birth, death, marriage, divorce, loss of job, promotion, and so on)	14.8	81.0
To learn a certain hobby	33.5	90.2
To further my cultural or social development	38.7	92.6
To learn skills for effective membership and participation in clubs and organizations	12.7	80.7
To learn health maintenance skills	17.3	85.1
To learn homemaking skills	10.5	76.8
Because it was aimed at improving communication and understanding between the different ethnic groups in the community	9.6	83.1
To learn more about my cultural heritage	4.5	64.7
To improve my chances of employment	42.1	90.0
To learn job-getting skills like résumé writing and interview technique	6.7	59.3
To improve my teaching skills and/or learn how to deal with a particular teaching problem	8.7	73.5
As a part of an in-service training program organized by my employers and the college	11.9	75.9
Other	27.4	89.6

Source: Nickens, 1977, pp. 16–17.

broader group. If the clients define the goals and the processes, success is measured by their saying that they achieved those goals. Independent ratings based on measurable change seem as scarce as is the advance determination of the change to be effected.

Organization and Funding

The organization of Coastline Community College in California, as a noncampus institution devoted primarily to community education, and similar institutions in Arizona and Washington stimulated the development of a new form of professional community college educator. The managers of these institutions not only must be curriculum and instructional designers, the role played by practitioners in all colleges, but also must interact with community advisory committees, find agencies to bear the cost of their programs, advertise for students, employ part-time staff members continually, produce varieties of new instructional media, and resolve jurisdictional disputes with other agencies. Even though such roles are not as well defined in the more conventional community colleges, those with sizable community education efforts have, of necessity, a number of people acting in those capacities.

Separate administrative entities have also been organized in several individual community colleges. Valencia Community College (Florida) began an Open Campus in 1974 to coordinate all continuing education, community services, and functions that the college was providing away from the campus. Headed by a provost reporting directly to the president, the Open Campus was organized as a unit equal in autonomy to the other branch campuses of the college (St. John, 1977). The off-campus learning center operated by Lansing Community College (Michigan) included a director of continuing education, a formal contract between the college and the local school districts, a broad selection of courses, and the same basic support services that were provided at the central campus (Herder and Standridge, 1980). The Extended Learning Institute at John Tyler Community College (Virginia) uses television, radio, and newspapers as media for the instruction of a wide variety of students in its district (Adams, 1986). The Adult Basic Education Program at Rio Salado Community College (Arizona) provided services to more than 5,700 students in numerous locations in 1987 (Vanis and Mills, 1987). These types of organizations—which coordinate the noncredit courses, distance learning, and related community education activities—have been built in many colleges.

They typically have their own staff, budget lines, and funding sources.

Myran (1969) identified five organizational patterns for community service programs operating within traditional college structures. In the *departmental extension* pattern, community service programs are located in and generated through the departmental structure. The other four patterns consist of differentiated administrative structures. In the *college centralized* pattern, professional community service staff members divide their time between assessing community needs and coordinating programs. They are located in a separate department or division. Staff members in the *community specialist* model are located in the community rather than on the campus. In addition to semipermanent advisory committees that may be coordinated by a college staff member, the *community advisory group* arrangement includes ad hoc committees dealing with critical issues. Administrators in the *college affiliate* pattern have direct responsibility to organizations in the community and an affiliate relationship with the college.

The ways that community education has been funded reflect its growth and variety. Some community education activities receive no direct aid; all expenses are borne by the participants themselves or by an agency with which the institution has a contract. Others are funded by enrollment formulas that tend to be lower than the formulas used for the career and collegiate courses. Funding for the recreational and avocational activities within the community education definition is the most difficult to obtain because those activities seem least justifiable for support at taxpayer expense.

Evans (1973) surveyed funding patterns in the seven states with the most widely developed community college systems and concluded that community service advocates needed to continually justify their programs and to be ever more resourceful in obtaining funds. In Washington community services were self-supporting; in other states the support from fees charged to participants ranged from 74 percent in Texas to around 5 percent in California, before Proposition 13. Roed's (1977) survey revealed that no state funding was provided for community services in ten states; in eight others, only partial funding was forthcoming. Support by participants' fees and local taxes was typical.

The activities other than community services conducted within the community education definition have fared better. Some states have funded adult basic education at the same rate as career and collegiate programs. Others have funded them well but under different formulas. In Florida developmental and community instructional services received nearly as much state money per full-time-student equivalent as the career and collegiate functions. However, continuing education courses in Iowa were not eligible for state aid. Oregon reimbursed colleges for remedial and continuing education courses at approximately the same level as for collegiate and career programs. Maryland funded continuing education courses that met certain criteria, especially if they focused on occupational, developmental, and consumer education; recreational courses were not eligible for reimbursement (Maryland State Board for Community Colleges, 1988). Once again, it is important to note that between-state comparisons cannot accurately be made because the definitions of the courses and programs included in the different categories vary widely.

There is no best plan for financing community colleges in every state, and disputes over financing often disguise disagreements over the community college mission. In this context Breneman and Nelson (1981) point out that community college leaders who try to convert their institutions into lifelong learning centers are gambling that political and financial support for such programs will grow. However, state officials seem less likely to accord high priority to financial support of these programs, compared with the traditional academic and occupational functions. Historically, community services have been funded more by local sources, and as community college finance shifts toward the state level, funding becomes more precarious. Martorana (1978) also alluded to the problems in funding the community-based mission with state funds, saying that the concept had not been sufficiently well defined, interpreted to the public, or accepted by the educators to warrant its being seen as a major shift in institutional direction.

The precarious base of funding for community education was revealed during the 1978-1981 period, when tax-limitation legislation was passed in several states and a national administration pledged to reduce taxes was elected. Soon after the 1978 passage of Proposition 13 in California, the average community services budget was cut by at least 50 percent. These cuts resulted in a 76 percent increase in courses for which fees were charged and a 24 percent decrease in courses funded through college budgets (Ireland, 1979). Kintzer (1980b) detailed the cuts, showing that 20 percent of the 4,600 noncredit courses were eliminated and 10 percent were placed on a fee basis. Recreational noncredit classes were reduced by 60 percent, and senior citizen programs were halved statewide as twenty-one colleges deleted their community service budgets. Overall, since Proposition 13 "eliminated the five-cent permissive property tax that had protected community services activities, including programs, personnel, and some capital construction, for nearly fifteen years, the fiscal basis for this function was destroyed" (p. 7).

However, the programs not only survived but actually expanded. In 69 percent of the colleges surveyed by Harlacher and Ireland (1988), the community services directors said that "the status of their community services and continuing education programs had increased during the past five years. Another 21 percent said that the status had been maintained" (p. 3). The prime programmatic emphasis was on work-force training and retraining, with leisure-time education and economic development the secondary areas of emphasis. Despite the strength of these programs, Harlacher and Ireland noted that the growing mandate for self-support by community services and continuing education programs posed a major threat to their continued expansion. The regulations most commonly cited by their respondents were state rules regarding self-support for noncredit offerings, community instructional service, and leisure-time courses. Other notable threats to expansion were lack of instructional support and integration, and competition from the private sector and community-based organizations.

Much of community education transfers the cost of certain programs from one public agency to another. The training programs conducted by community colleges on behalf of police and fire departments that are too small to operate their own academies offer an example. Where the departments pay the college to do the training, little changes except that the college coordinates the training. But in some instances law enforcement programs are converted to degree- or certificate-credit programs, thus qualifying them for support through the state's educational funds. The cost of these programs is therefore transferred from the local to the state government budget. Similarly, some industries contract with community colleges to train their workers, paying for the services. But in numerous instances such specifically targeted training programs are given for credit, thus shifting the cost from the industrial concern to the state budget.

College managers tread carefully when developing training programs for the employees of local industries. The programs are often presented at the plant site, using the company's equipment. There is no problem if the company pays all expenses, including the instructors' salaries, on a flat rate or cost per head. But if the programs are offered for college credit and the usual state reimbursement procedures are in effect, they must be open to all applicants, thus potentially compromising the company's work rules. In many cases existing courses offered at the college have been modified to fit a major employer's requirements, thereby maintaining intact the faculty contracts and preexisting course accreditation. The company may provide new equipment, paying in kind for the special service. Program development costs may also be charged to the company, but the accounting procedures occasioned by the charge-back can be difficult to effect.

Contracts to train military personnel are particularly intricate. They specify the site, the curriculum, and the tuition that may be charged. They are overseen not only by the college accrediting agency but also by the military officials, the Veterans Administration, and other federal agencies. Difficulties arise when, for example, the college faculty is covered by a union contract but the military does not recognize union membership for its employees. Such involvements also add greatly to the college's administrative costs because of the complexities of arranging the contracts and maintaining elaborate files for the auditors.

In sum, the variety of activities within the scope of community education provides an opportunity not only for serving new clients but also for manipulating the funding to the institution's advantage. If a course can be designated as a degree-credit course and thus become eligible for state aid, it may be moved to that category. If a program can be offered on a contractual basis, with a different government agency or a private industrial concern paying for it, it may be so arranged and thus not drain the college's operating funds. Although administrative costs may be high, community education offers the opportunity for creativity in program planning and staff deployment to college managers who find their efforts in the traditional programs hamstrung by external licensing bureaus and negotiated contracts with the faculty.

Program Validity

Advocates answer questions of validity by saying that through community education they can serve the entire populace rather than just the relatively few people of traditional college age. To them, community education is a natural extension of the open-door policy and the egalitarian impulses that gave rise to community colleges in the first place. Instead of serving only the children of the middle classes, they now include among their clients the minorities, the physically and mentally disadvantaged, adults of all ages, institutionalized people, and job seekers, along with the children of the poor.

The idea of community uplift has also been presented as a main purpose for community education. To those subscribing to that idea, the development of a sense of community is the goal. The college serves as the focal point for community pride. The events that it sponsors enhance a sense of community in the district; the act of planning, teaching, and participating in recreational programs and personal-help workshops fosters community spirit. By this line of reasoning, any activity that brings people together—health fair, senior citizens' day, hobby course offered in a convalescent home, or college-sponsored trip to a foreign country—will suffice.

Less noble, but nonetheless prevalent, is the intent to aggrandize the institutions or at least to maintain their current size. Decline is painful. College leaders who peruse the demography charts, consider the competing institutions in their area, and study the potential market for their own programs may wonder about sources of students. As Aslanian (1986) has pointed out, the enrollment of older students enabled the colleges to avoid severe declines when the population of eighteen-year-olds dropped in the 1980s. Much of community education acts as a marketing device, not only for the activities offered within it but also for the traditional college programs. The awarding of credit for experience offers a prime example. As many as 80 percent of the people who receive such credit go on to take additional courses at the college. The term *changing markets* is frequently used by those who exhort the institutions to move into new service areas lest they suffer the fate of once-prosperous industries that failed to adapt to changing conditions.

Community education seems also a way of blunting charges of failure in other areas. In the 1950s and 1960s there were widespread contentions that community colleges would enable the disadvantaged to move upward on the socioeconomic ladder and would teach skills of citizenship and literacy to people whom the lower schools had failed. College spokespersons also promised to provide an avenue to the baccalaureate for students of lesser ability and lower income. All these goals prove more elusive than their proponents expected. It is easier to propose new roles for the colleges than to explain away their inability to fulfill old ones.

The issue of institutional credibility must also be addressed. Is the community college a true college? Most community education advocates and most of those who make fervent calls for a "new mission" make light of that question, but it has been posed both by members of the public and by professional educators. Faculty members trying to maintain collegiate standards in their courses certainly take a dim view of most community education activities. Correspondingly, most community education proponents find little place for the regular faculty members in their programs, preferring instead to staff them with part-timers working ad hoc with little or no commitment to the institution itself. Community education has thus fostered internal dissension. Administrators may perceive the traditional faculty members as anchors dragging at an institution that would propel itself into a new era; the faculty tend to cast a jaundiced eye on the recreational activities and the contract programs that use instructors as interchangeable parts to be dismissed when the particular programs for which they were employed have ended.

To those whose memories of college center on courses in the liberal arts taught on a campus, community education threatens to debase the institution. Their perception of college is as a place of mobility for individuals who, through exposure to the higher learning, take their place as productive members of society. To them, community uplift is an alien dimension; its aspects seem to be frills or peripheral functions at best, anti-intellectual at worst. They question the standards in the noncredit, open-circuit, and continuing education programs; and they wonder about quality control in an institution lacking a corps of full-time professional scholars. They reject contentions that an institution serving up a pastiche of uncoordinated functions to the masses bears any relation to an institution of higher learning. Community education advocates may try to dismiss these critics as anachronisms nostalgic for the ivy-covered college for an elite group, but the ranks of the critics include sizable percentages of the public, who want their community college to serve as an avenue of mobility for their children, not as a purveyor of circuses and illusions.

Future Development

The future for community education rests on its funding base and the way it is organized within the colleges. The people served through community education do not fit typical student categories. They do not enroll in programs leading to degrees; they may not even be enrolled in formally structured courses but, instead, may be participating in events especially tailored for their interests. Therefore, any attempt to fund community education on the basis of average daily attendance, full-time-student equivalent, or some other category that suggests students attending courses leading to degrees or certificates on a campus is at variance with the intent of the program and the pattern of student participation.

To the extent that community education activities are merged even conceptually with the collegiate and career education functions, they all are weakened. Community service activities cannot flourish when they are presented by people with traditional views of instruction and when they are funded ad hoc. The collegiate function is weakened when it coexists with community service activities in which people get college transfer credit for participating in courses and events even when they are not intending to gain degrees. And the career education function suffers when the figures on the number of people gaining employment in the areas for which they were trained are reduced by the number of students upgrading their skills in jobs they already hold or transferring to senior institutions instead of going to work.

Community colleges that want to maintain successful community education operations should be reorganized. Ideally, community education would be funded programatically; that is, a college would be awarded a fixed sum each year to provide cultural, occupational upgrade, recreation, personal interest, community health, and semiprofessional retraining programs to the people of its district. Or the colleges could maintain their open-access policies—with students taking courses that may or may not lead to degrees—but should build a transfer or honors college within such a structure. The main funding pattern would be for individuals participating in courses with reimbursement on an attendance basis; but the transfer or honors college would be operated separately, with a variety of especially funded enrichment opportunities and work assistance or scholarship monies made available. Another way of separating community education efforts might be to maintain the college's collegiate and career functions but to offer all the community education services through an extension division, as many universities have done. This would put all community education on a self-sustaining basis, since those who take the short courses or participate in the activities offered would pay for them ad hoc. Still another way of maintaining the traditional college with a community education component would be to place the community service work, along with the remedial and adult basic education function, in a separate center, where staff members might not have credentials. Unlike the regular faculty, who are paid on a class-hour basis, they would be paid for working a forty-hour week. None of these models is likely to enjoy widespread adoption. Community education will continue as adjunctive, supported by participant fees, contracted services, and special-purpose grants.

The education of youth aged sixteen to twenty may well be a fruitful area for expanding community education services. In the late 1970s the Carnegie Council on Policy Studies in Higher Education conducted several studies pointing to the importance of revised educational forms encompassing both schooling and work for sizable percentages of youth. This area of study was pursued in the 1980s by the U.S. Department of Education, which published several reports on the topic—for example, *Education and Training of 16- to 19-Year-Olds After Compulsory Schooling in the United States* (Stacey, Alsalam, Gilmore, and To, 1988). Special funds from state and federal governments and philanthropic foundations will be run to this area in increasing volume.

Expansion of community colleges' activities to include special services for youth would be consistent with their tradition. Throughout their history they have been the recipients of technical and vocational functions that previously had been assigned to trade schools affiliated with the public school districts; the flowering of career education in the community colleges was merely the most recent development in that trend. The increasing number of arrangements whereby the colleges take responsibility for high school graduates at grade 11 suggests a move in that direction. Lieberman (1988) details many such programs.

Adult basic education is another area for the possible expansion of community education. In almost every state special funds have been made available for literacy training for adults, and in many states this responsibility has been shifted from the lower-school districts to the community colleges.

It seems, then, that the areas of community education most promising for further development are those that have taken the community colleges away from their higher education affiliation. But this redefinition in the direction of career and literacy training differs markedly from the idea of the community college as an agency of direct community uplift. It is the community college as latter-day secondary school, not as social welfare bureau. It is the community college as educational structure rather than as purveyor of recreational activities and quasi-educative services.

The prognosis for other forms of continuing education is less clear. It is certain to vary in different institutions, depending mainly on the directors' vigor in attracting funds and publicizing offerings. The large market frequently noted by proponents of lifelong learning is composed, in the main, of people teaching themselves to play tennis, make furniture, cope with their families, understand their own physiology, and deal with cyclical changes in their lives. Those who need the discipline afforded by structured, institutionally sanctioned activities may be enticed away from their self-help books and informal study groups. But it is doubtful that they will greet eagerly the intervention of an agency that would coordinate all their learning efforts.

The issue of social versus individual benefits looms large in connection with community education. Most economic theorists would contend that funds collected from the taxpayers at large should be used to benefit society; hence, if a program is more beneficial to the individual than to the broader community, the person receiving that benefit should bear the cost. This is the basis for the legislative antagonism toward supporting courses in macramé and ceramics. And, indeed, many community education advocates were caught with their premises down when those human "needs" for activities that were provided by the college during the period of liberal funding dried up as the recreational programs were put on a pay-as-you-go basis, and enrollments declined to the extent that tuition advanced.

However, much of community education cannot be neatly categorized into services that benefit individuals rather than the broader society. When people complete a program in nursing at public expense and go on to work as trained nurses in the community, who benefits more, society or the individuals? Society gains trained nurses; the individuals gain access to a profession in which they can earn many more dollars than they could without the training. At the farther extreme are those forms of community education that assist society most clearly. One example is provided by community forums that explore patterns of energy use, quality of life, the effects of zoning, and the environment in the local community. Citizens are provided with information important to their making decisions within the social unit.

Those who would expand community education might do well to articulate and adhere to certain principles underlying its structure. The programs most defensibly supported by public funds are, first, those that are more toward the socially useful, as opposed to the individually beneficial, end of the continuum—for example, the forums instead of the self-help programs. Second, they are the verifiably educative programs, as opposed to those which are predominantly recreational, which provide credentials offering the illusion of learning, or which are thinly disguised contributors to transfer payments. Third, they are programs that provide services which are not readily available elsewhere for members of the population served by them. Thus, the better-integrated businesses would manage their own employee training programs while the colleges concentrated on assisting workers in less well-organized industries, such as restaurant workers in their area, who might benefit from periodic refresher courses in health care and sanitation. Heretofore, members of these latter groups have been the least likely to participate in education of their own volition, but the true community service institution would bend all effort to serve them. Unfortunately for the concept of social utility, programs in which the colleges effect training relationships with *Fortune* 500 companies are much more common than those that support farm workers or the homeless.

The advocates might also reduce their claims that community education has the potential for solving community problems. As Talbott (1976) observed, the college is confusing its ability to take on the whole community as its province with its ability to take on and solve all of the community's problems: "To take on the role of an omniscient social welfare agency strains the credibility as well as the resources of the college. It is not set up to revamp the courts, to change the traffic pattern, to purify the water, to clean the air of smog" (p. 89).

Gottschalk (1978) also noted the dissimilarities between serving individuals and society by differentiating between problems and issues. Problems are individual; issues are broad enough to affect the community. Individuals who are unemployed have problems that the community college can mitigate by training them sufficiently so that each may obtain paid employment. But massive unemployment is a community issue, over which the college has little control. Attempting to solve community issues would require political action, which the colleges cannot afford to undertake because the risk of offending important public support groups is too great. The colleges sometimes get involved in low-risk community issues, offering forums on safe topics such as energy conservation. But a forum on the history of a local labor dispute would be risky. Most college leaders opt for the safe course. The local arts council may often meet in a college building that is never made available as a dormitory for the homeless.

Several prominent spokespersons for community colleges have urged institutional leaders to direct their efforts beyond the campus-based career and collegiate education activities, despite the dim view of this expansion of services taken by most local community college staff members. But community education has not reached parity with degree- and certificate-credit programs either in funding or in internal and external perceptions of the college's main mission. For the foreseeable future, the community college as nexus for all the area's educational forms is an even less likely eventuality.

Issues

Funding is a major issue in all college programs, but the fiscal aspects of community education are particularly tenuous. How can an institution funded predominantly by the state respond appropriately to local needs?

How can noncredit courses that may be every bit as valuable as credit courses be funded equitably?

Cultural and recreational activities conducted as part of community service programs have declined in the face of limited budgets and concomitant conversion of these functions to a self-sustaining basis. Should colleges try to maintain their recreational functions? Can cultural presentations be offered as part of the regular humanities programs and thus absorbed into their funding packages?

Should colleges expand their efforts at educational brokering? Who benefits? Who should pay?

Should colleges seek additional contracts to provide educational services to industries and government agencies? How can the costs of these services be distributed equitably?

How can quality be controlled in community education

programs that do not come under the scrutiny of any outside agency or under internal curriculum review?

Any public agency ultimately can be supported only as long as the public perceives its value. The educative aspects of community education—its short courses, courses for institutionalized populations, and courses offered on job sites—are the colleges' strengths. Each noneducative function may have a debilitating long-term effect, because it diffuses the college mission. Each time the colleges act as social welfare agencies or modern Chautauquas, they run the risk of reducing the support they must have if they are to pursue their main purpose.

Eleven

Collegiate Function:
Transfer and
the Liberal Arts

The collegiate function encompasses two concepts: student flow and the liberal arts curriculum. Student flow refers to the providing of education at the thirteenth-and fourteenth-grade levels for students who are moving through the American educational system, which reaches from kindergarten through graduate school. The liberal arts curriculum includes education based on the humanities, science, and social science.

Liberal Arts

Originally, the liberal arts embodied the collegiate function. They were the main and, in some cases, the only curriculum in the early American colleges. Codified in the medieval European universities, they were brought into the colleges as reflecting the best in human thought. From the ancient grammar, rhetoric, logic, music, astronomy, geometry, and arithmetic considered essential for the learned person, they gradually came to include the classical languages, philosophy, and natural science. By the end of the nineteenth century, the physical and social sciences had also shouldered their way into this curriculum.

In the late nineteenth century, the universities gained dominance over the liberal arts colleges and, together with them, assumed responsibility for defining the educated person. Before that time people studying the liberal arts were as likely to do so in their own home, in a society of amateurs, in a church or monastic setting, or in an independent laboratory as within a school. But the universities institutionalized the teaching of science and those aspects of the humanities that had not theretofore been part of the curriculum—modern foreign languages, literary criticism, art, and history—and made the study of them tantamount to being educated.

This institutionally based definition of education was fostered by an intramural revolution: the ascendancy of scholarship. The universities were grounded on the assumption that they would sustain the work of contemplative scholars advancing the frontiers of knowledge. For their part, the scholars felt they could best pursue their work by organizing themselves into academic disciplines. Thus, along with all other areas of intellectual endeavor considered worthy of inclusion in the higher learning, the liberal arts took disciplinary form. One who would be ennobled by them studied them from the viewpoint of the disciplines as defined by the scholars. The organization of the curriculum became ineluctably associated with the form of the discipline.

This conversion of the liberal arts predated the advent of the community colleges. By the time these new institutions came on the scene, the collegiate function had already been so codified in terms of the academic disciplines that no college, no legislature, no educator's call for a "student-centered curriculum," no student's cry for "relevance" could shake it. All attempts to tailor the students' studies to their own interests produced little more than rearranging the number or sequence of courses required for graduation, wide varieties of course distribution requirements, or laissez-faire elective systems. The liberal arts were captives of the disciplines; the disciplines dictated the structure of the courses; the courses encompassed the collegiate function.

Ideally, the liberal arts provide contexts for understanding, rather than the knowledge that some bit of esoterica is true or false. If the definition of education depended on knowledge of certain data, facts, or the modes of discourse in any academic discipline, then no one prior to the nineteenth century was liberally educated, because the concept of the academic discipline did not exist. The liberal arts can be useful only as they help people evaluate their society and gain a sense of what is right and what is important. This sense is not inborn; it is nourished through studies in which the relations among forms and ideas are explicated, the "general education" ideal. The conversion of the liberal arts from these precepts to the academic disciplines reflected a major shift away from the individual to the organization as the arbiter of learning.

Transfer Courses

Thus structured, the collegiate function was adopted in toto by the community colleges. In their drive for acceptance as full partners in the higher learning, with their faculty trained in university departments, they arranged their curricula in the university image. The terms *college parallel, college transfer,* and *college equivalent* were (and are) used to describe their academic programs. Their collegiate function, their part in the acculturation of the young, was embodied in the transfer courses. The more closely those courses resembled university courses, the higher their status.

The most pervasive and long-lived issue in community colleges is the extent to which their courses are accepted by the universities. Articulation agreements (sometimes written into state education codes), interinstitutional standing committees, and policy statements that date from the earliest years of the community colleges to the most recent—all attest to the importance of transferability. For all the rhetoric emanating from community colleges about their autonomous curriculum for special students and purposes, the universities have dominated the collegiate function by specifying what they accept for transfer credit, what they require for the baccalaureate degree. Major or sudden changes in certain courses can often be traced to a nearby university's changing its graduation requirements and/or its specifications for the courses that must be on the transcripts of incoming transfer students.

The community colleges rarely articulated their curriculum with that of the secondary schools, where courses in the various disciplines developed inconsistently. United States history, American government, literature, biology, and modern foreign languages were included in the secondary school curriculum; but philosophy, anthropology, art history, Western civilization, religious studies, and interdisciplinary sciences and humanities were rarely seen. Community college practitioners of those disciplines, as well as all the other disciplines in the liberal arts, have looked to the universities for guidance in forming their courses. There has been minimal flow-through from the lower schools and a paucity of give and take of ideas, course patterning, or texts.

In the earliest community colleges, most of the offerings were transfer courses in the liberal arts. Koos (1924) studied the curriculum in fifty-eight public and private junior colleges during 1921 and 1922 and found the liberal arts totaling three-fourths of the offerings. Ancient and modern languages alone accounted for one-fourth of the curriculum. English composition was taught, but literature courses accounted for more than half the courses in English. Agriculture, commerce, education, engineering, and home economics, along with all other occupational studies taken together, came to less than one-fourth of the whole (see Table 28).

Table 28. Average Number of Semester Hours and Percentage of Total Curricular Offerings in Junior Colleges by Subject, 1921–22.

Subject or Subject Group	Number of Semester Hours	Percentage of Total Offering
English	17.1	7.9
Public speaking	2.9	1.4
Ancient languages	16.9	7.9
Modern foreign languages	40.0	18.6
Mathematics	15.9	7.4
Science	29.9	13.9
Social subjects	22.3	10.4
Bible and religion	2.3	1.1
Philosophy	2.1	1.0
Psychology	3.0	1.4
Music	6.2	2.9
Art	4.2	2.0
Physical education	2.5	1.2
Agriculture	3.0	1.4
Commerce	10.9	5.1
Education	7.9	3.7
Engineering and industrial	13.1	6.1
Home economics	12.5	5.8
Other occupational	1.9	0.9

Source: Koos, 1924, p. 29.

This emphasis on the liberal arts continued well into the 1960s. All observers of the community colleges were aware of it. Medsker in 1960 discussed the prestige value of "regular college work." In 1966 Thornton wrote that transfer "is still the function on which the junior colleges expend most effort and in which most of their students express interest" (p. 234). Even after the flowering of career education, Cosand (1979, p. 6) reported, "Community colleges were, are, and will be evaluated to a major degree upon the success of their transfer students to the four-year colleges and universities."

However, the 1970s saw an extreme narrowing of the collegiate curriculum. Except for political science, history, and literature, many two-year associate-degree-granting institutions abandoned the humanities entirely. Cultural geography, religious studies, and ethnic studies were found in fewer than one-third of the colleges. Cultural anthropology, art history and appreciation, interdisciplinary humanities, theater history, and philosophy were offered in one-third to two-thirds of them. The greatest number of humanities courses was seen in the older institutions, a legacy of the days when the colleges fed from one-fourth to one-third of their students into senior colleges. The trend has been decidedly toward introductory courses for the transfer students. Enrollments in specialized courses were dominated by adults taking them for their own interest, not for degree credit.

Table 29 presents total enrollments and average class size in all courses offered in each discipline in the humanities, sciences, and social sciences in 1977–78. Total enrollments are not presented, because the figures represent head counts and the same student may have taken two or more courses. Figures are extrapolated from the 175 colleges sampled by the Center for the Study of Community Colleges to the universe of 1,215 colleges. Laboratory sections in the sciences are not included. Using the same methodology, the CSCC collected information about the liberal arts in 1986. Table 30 shows the percentage of class sections offered in the liberal arts, thereby suggesting enrollment patterns. Tables 31 and 32 display trends in the humanities in recent years. Table 33 offers information about the sciences; and Table 34, about the fine arts and the performing arts. Detailed information about instructional practices in each

Table 29. Total Enrollments and Average Class Size in Community College Humanities and Sciences, 1977–78.

Humanities	Total Enrollment	Average Class Size	Sciences	Total Enrollment	Average Class Size
History	335,000	33	Math/computer science	449,000	28
Political science/government/law	255,000	31	Psychology	225,000	39
Foreign languages	162,000	19	Biology	208,000	39
Literature	132,000	23	Sociology	204,000	35
Interdisciplinary humanities	90,000	37	Engineering/engr. tech.	128,000	24
Philosophy	89,000	27	Economics	103,000	35
Art history and appreciation	60,000	31	Chemistry	73,000	30
Music history and appreciation	46,000	30	Earth and space sciences	66,000	34
Cultural anthropology	36,000	31	Physical anthropology and interdisciplinary social sciences	44,000	30
Religious studies	under 20,000	28	Agriculture	38,000	26
Ethnic studies	under 20,000	22	Physics	35,000	24
Total		28	Total		31

Source: Center for the Study of Community Colleges, 1978b.

**Table 30. Percentage of Sections in Community College
Liberal Arts Classes by Subject Area, 1986 (*N* = 95 Colleges).**

Agriculture	1.2%	History	4.0
Anthropology	0.6	Interdisciplinary social	
Art history	1.0	sciences	0.1
Biology	5.0	Interdisciplinary humanities	0.1
Chemistry	3.0	Literature	2.0
Earth and space	1.0	Mathematics	20.0
Economics	2.5	Music appreciation	0.8
Engineering	5.0	Philosophy	1.0
English	21.0	Physics	2.0
Environment	0.2	Political science	2.0
Fine and performing arts	13.0	Psychology	6.0
Foreign languages	5.0	Sociology	3.0

Source: Cohen and Brawer, 1987, p. 36.

discipline, along with a description of the survey procedures, may be found in *The Collegiate Function of Community Colleges* (Cohen and Brawer, 1987) and in *Art Education in American Community Colleges* (Center for the Study of Community Colleges, 1988).

Beneath the stultifying sameness of a curriculum shrunken to introductory courses, a notable variety can be perceived. Specialized courses flourished where instructors with a bent toward designing and marketing those courses were found. Nearly every college in the CSCC samples had one or a few instructors concerned with presenting something of particular interest, determined to do something different for the different students with whom they were confronted. The oft-heard contention that the curriculum cannot be centered on the collegiate function because the pragmatic students would not attend the courses and because the transferring institutions do not force them to attend did not hold. Exciting, active, lively engagements with ideas, tastes, and values did attract audiences, just as in the broader society the cinema and the stage have survived commercial television. Faculty members who have determined to break away from their transfer-credit, lecture/textbook course offerings have been able to do imaginative college-level work with their students. Unfortunately, their ideas typically

**Table 31. Percentage of Community Colleges Offering
Humanities Courses During Spring Term, by Subject Area.**

Humanities Subject Area	1975 (N = 156)	1977 (N = 178)	1983 (N = 173)	1986 (N = 95)
History	90%	92%	93%	92%
State and local	28	26	31	25
Western world	82	83	76	71
United States	87	88	85	83
Other world regions	28	23	26	25
Special groups	29	30	26	23
Social history	25	28	20	23
Political science	89	94	90	86
American government	75	82	71	75
Local/city/state	40	40	35	40
Comparative	23	20	28	25
Tools and methods	26	26	15	3
Specialized (topical)	18	15	32	26
Jurisprudence	30	34	33	36
Literature	91	92	93	87
Introduction/survey	84	87	80	74
Genre	38	36	35	41
Authors	20	17	24	23
Group	24	22	22	22
Bible	6	6	12	6
Popular	15	16	11	9
Classics	10	9	10	3
Foreign languages	82	80	82	78
French	60	56	57	59
German	40	38	45	41
Italian	11	12	17	16
Russian	9	7	4	5
Spanish	70	68	72	68
Career-related Spanish	6	10	6	1
English as a second language	26	33	27	38
Classics	4	5	5	5
Other	8	11	15	15
Miscellaneous	50	51	61	69
Interdisciplinary/survey	28	28	38	52
Theater	24	26	34	26
Film	12	16	21	17
Specialized	19	18	16	12
Philosophy	66	64	68	76
Introduction/history	56	56	54	58
Ethics	25	23	29	37
Logic	26	26	39	38

Table 31. Percentage of Community Colleges Offering
Humanities Courses During Spring Term, by Subject Area, Cont'd.

Humanities Subject Area	1975 (N = 156)	1977 (N = 178)	1983 (N = 173)	1986 (N = 95)
Religious	21	18	21	34
Specialized	15	19	20	13
Art history/appreciation	70	68	76	76
Introduction/history-appreciation	69	67	84	77
Specialized culture	3	6	6	13
Other specialized art	7	7	12	6
Music history/appreciation	74	70	69	63
Introduction/survey	73	68	75	62
Jazz	3	6	9	8
Specialized	7	7	4	13
Cultural anthropology	44	46	44	48
Introduction/survey	39	42	41	45
American Indian	4	5	8	7
Folklore/magic/mythology	1	2	1	NA
Other specialized	12	11	6	14
Social/ethnic studies	22	21	10	(included
Ethnic	15	15	6	in
Women	3	3	4	history
Individual	1	1	2	and
Other	12	11	4	literature)
Religious studies	26	28	24	
Introduction/survey	12	14	15	(included
Specialized	10	11	8	in
Texts	16	17	12	philosophy)
Cultural geography	26	22	34	NA
Introduction/survey	26	21	32	
Specialized/regional	3	1	5	

Source: Cohen and Brawer, 1987, pp. 37–38.

were uncoordinated and unexported and had to be reinvented afresh by their counterparts in other colleges.

The collegiate function has tended to center on courses based on reading and writing, textbooks and examinations. In the 1970s that function suffered a dual assault from students oriented toward careers and from students who were ill prepared in the lower schools. However, it tended to thrive in the continuing education

Table 32. Percentage of Total Humanities Class Sections
by Subject Area.

Discipline	1977 (N = 178)	1983 (N = 173)	1986 (N = 95)
Cultural anthropology	3.2%	2.1%	2.7%
Art history/appreciation	3.8	4.2	5.7
Foreign languages	20.5	27.7	28.4
History	23.0	19.9	21.5
Interdisciplinary humanities	7.2	7.3	5.7
Literature	11.4	11.2	10.0
Music appreciation	3.3	3.4	4.8
Philosophy	6.4	6.2	7.8
Political science	16.6	14.7	13.5
Religious studies	1.5	1.4	(included in philosophy)
Social and ethnic studies	3.1	1.9	(included in history)

Source: Cohen and Brawer, 1987, p. 38.

Table 33. Science Instruction in the Two-Year Colleges,
1978 (N = 175) and 1986 (N = 95).

	Percentage of Colleges Listing Course in Class Schedule		Percentage of All Science Courses Listed in Schedule	
	1978	1986	1978	1986
Agriculture and natural resources	61%	52%	6%	2%
Biology	100	98	13	11
Engineering	81	72	20	9
Mathematics and computer science	99	100	22	41
Chemistry	97	96	8	5
Earth and space	79	72	5	2
Physics	89	92	6	4
Physical anthropology and interdisciplinary social sciences	67	53	3	2
Psychology	99	100	6	12
Economics	99	97	4	5
Sociology	100	95	4	6

Source: Cohen and Brawer, 1987, p. 35.

Table 34. Percentage of Total Classes Offered
in the Fine and Performing Arts
in 109 Colleges, Spring 1987.

	Percentage of Total Classes Offered
Visual arts	
Design	6%
Graphics	6
Handicrafts	16
Painting/drawing	14
Special projects	1
Dance	6
Music	
Instruments	24
Theory	9
Voice	10
Special projects	1
Theater	
Acting/drama	4
Production/directing/ stagecraft	3
Special projects	1

Source: Center for the Study of Community Colleges, 1988.

component of community education, just as it did in university extension programs within the senior institutions, which themselves faced the same types of shifts in student desires and capabilities. A true picture of the collegiate function is obscured if it is perceived only through the filter of the transfer-credit courses.

Some of the ways that the transfer-credit curriculum has been modified can be discerned. Community colleges offer relatively few courses in the history of any world region other than the United States, comparative or specialized political science, literature of a single author, languages other than Spanish and English as a second language (ESL), ethnic and women's studies, and cultural geography. However, courses in social history, Spanish, film appreciation, and the history of art in certain cultures have increased. Most of these changes have attracted students to areas in which enrollments had been diminishing. A decline in introductory classes in music appreciation has been offset by increased enrollments in jazz and other specialized music forms. Spanish and ESL have expanded, so that, by 1986, those two areas accounted for 72 percent of all the foreign language class sections offered. It is unlikely that those same students would have enrolled in German, Russian, or Italian. And many of the interdisciplinary courses in the humanities and sciences were able to enroll students who might otherwise have shunned specialized courses in those fields.

These changes may be traced through most of the disciplines. Art history instructors capitalized on student interest in certain cultures by presenting the art of Mexico or Asia to students who might not have studied the art of Europe. New courses in folklore, magic, and mythology attracted some students who would not have enrolled in anthropology courses dealing with kinship systems. Students who would not take classes in climatology signed up for "The Living Desert" or "The Tidepools of California." Specialized courses in problems of the city replaced introductory sociology, just as courses in family life took students from introductory psychology. An interest in ecology drew students who were not interested in or qualified for courses in physics or chemistry to "The Oceanic Environment." Although precise figures cannot be obtained, taking all categories of students together, these specialized, current-interest courses accounted for around 20-25 percent of enrollments in the liberal arts.

Although student interest in careers took enrollments away from the traditional transfer programs, the collegiate function was maintained in a different form. Courses in political science and jurisprudence were found in every program for law enforcement officers. Students in social welfare programs took specially modified courses in sociology. The allied health programs in numerous institutions included medical ethics and Spanish. And the faculty in some institutions built such courses as "The Humanities in a Technological Society" for career education students, so that they might meet general education requirements without taking the traditional history and literature courses. There was some overlap, too, in liberal arts course work presented to students who were planning careers in liberal arts–related fields. Although 22 percent of the students in fine and performing arts classes reported that their most important reason for attending college was "to satisfy a personal interest (cultural, social)," 38 percent anticipated that within five years they would be involved in the arts to the extent of making a career and a significant proportion of their income therefrom (Center for the Study of Community Colleges, 1988).

The collegiate function also survived elsewhere than in course formats. In approximately three of every eight colleges, numerous concerts, recitals, and musical events are presented each year, and around one-fourth of the colleges mount art exhibits. The colleges were also deeply involved in theatrical productions, film series, and lectures and seminars open to the public. These events were funded typically by the participants or by the colleges themselves, although a few colleges were successful in obtaining funding from external sources. In many cases the colleges participated with community drama or musical groups, local art councils or museums, and secondary schools in presenting these events.

Articulation Agreements

The tendency of many community colleges to develop a pattern of courses and events tailored particularly for their own students was reflected in the types of articulation agreements maintained between community colleges and the senior institutions in their area. Community college representatives almost invariably tried to encourage the senior institutions to accept for transfer credit the special-interest and interdisciplinary courses designed apart from adherence to traditional concepts of the academic disciplines. Although the changes in university requirements affected enrollments in individual courses in community colleges, their effect on overall enrollments was less clear. Frequently, a community college would respond to a change in, say, history requirements by no longer requiring its own students to take a survey of American history but maintaining a three-hour history requirement for the associate degree and allowing students to choose a course in local history or the history of a particular culture. Private two-year colleges, especially, reported little or no influence on their curriculum from the senior institutions.

Articulation agreements often specified the courses that the two-year colleges could *not* offer, rather than those they must offer;

junior- and senior-level courses offered by the senior institutions, particularly, were out of bounds. In some states articulation boards reviewed noncredit offerings as well as credit courses and acted, for example, to discourage conversational language offerings in two-year colleges' community education programs because those courses were considered the province of the senior institutions.

Paradoxically, the decline in students' literacy and in their interest in the liberal arts has stimulated little articulation between community colleges and secondary schools. Community college instructors rarely spoke to their counterparts in high schools. They tended not to accompany counselors on their annual visits to the high schools to advertise their offerings, and they made little attempt to recruit promising students of the liberal arts from secondary schools. Counselors seemed more inclined to emphasize the job-related features of the community colleges than to advertise the collegiate function as such.

And so the collegiate function weakened. Based on the liberal arts, which themselves were reformed by academic disciplinarians in the universities, it has been maintained predominantly through the traditional transfer courses. Why has it been so attenuated? Can it survive? What forms might it take?

Reasons for Decline in Collegiate Studies

Part of the decline in collegiate studies must be attributed to the decline in confidence in contemporary social institutions. Not only has faith in the schools wavered, but also faith in government, in business corporations, and indeed in the authority of adults. The students' cry of the 1960s "You have no authority to tell me what to study!" was accepted as valid by educators, who themselves were members of a community that had lost faith in its institutions. They had come to expect, even to welcome, corruption in government and business because governments were by definition oppressive and businesses rapacious. The evidence was all around: Nixon's derelictions, congressional peccadilloes, top officials in Reagan's administration shipping arms to Iran clandestinely, corporations bribing government officials. All this was "normal." The crime was in getting caught.

McClintock (1979) traced the decline to a decline in the

purpose of education as preparing people to become members of a free society: "Where people no longer possess the kind of freedom they were presumed to possess in the design of liberal education, that form of education will have no real purpose to serve" (p. 637). In different eras different forms of education would properly be liberal. The free citizen in one society needs different sets of understandings than the free citizen in another. Thus, liberal education might change without declining. "A real decline of liberal education can result only as the purpose that one or another variant of it was designed to serve falls into disuse. A decline of liberal education results from a decline in the freedom and autonomy enjoyed by the persons who receive the education, not from a change in the mode of the education they receive" (p. 637). Unless people perceive themselves "as autonomous participants in a common enterprise, there will be no purpose for liberal education, whatever its program" (p. 638). Given the specialization of function in a corporate society, the best that liberal education can offer is a path to freedom for the individual within the structure. The liberally educated person lives by the maxim "You may bind my actions but not my spirit." This is more than education for leisure-time pursuits; it is education for the life that nearly everyone leads.

But because liberal education as taught in the schools did not make the conversion from education for the polity to education as freedom for people in a society of specialists, many of its recipients now show up as dropouts from the businesses and professional specializations. The manual laborer, tradesman, or assembly-line worker who writes or reads extensively, purchases or creates original art, performs classical music, and attends concerts—the truck driver with a library card—may be a liberally educated person. Such people are relatively free from corporate and governmental restraints, but it is unlikely that they have incorporated their education into their work.

Persistently, the collegiate function has been assailed as being irrelevant to the students. The study of history came under particular attack because many American social institutions and traditions were similarly under attack. The belief in social progress and in a nation that allowed opportunity for all its citizens was weakened. Allegations about racism, sexism, and unjust wars came together as criticisms of American society. Hence, requiring students to study a bland history that emphasized the social justice and democracy of America was condemned. Similar accusations were leveled at literature, fine arts, and the other cornerstones of the liberal arts. Even language symbolized oppression because it denied the person's individuality, and "black English" and bilingual studies received intramural support accordingly.

Because numerous educators agreed that their curriculum was unworthy, the terms *relevance* and *individualism* replaced the calls for teaching values and a common heritage. Accordingly, the supporters of the liberal arts had little defense against the demands for occupational education. Consumerism became the hallmark of education, a consumerism whereby the client-consumers dictated the terms under which they would study, what they would study, and what they expected to obtain from their efforts. Under these conditions an education that demanded commitment, adherence to traditions, the intensity of scholarly inquiry, examination of alternative value systems—the bases of the liberal arts—could not sustain itself. It had few adherents within or outside the academy.

The cult of relevance, of meeting student needs, of allowing every student to define a particularized curriculum came to be considered the highest form of schooling. An institution that could adjust most suitably to an infinite variety of student desires was the ultimate in responsiveness. Relevance was interpreted as providing job skills to the young, who, save for the intervention of the schools, might be unemployed. As Hurn (1979, p. 632) summarized, "Lacking any consensus as to the content of liberal education, and lacking confidence in their prescriptive authority—as the catchphrase puts it, 'to impose their values upon others'—educators were in a weak position to mount a defense of anything other than an educational supermarket, where customer preferences, in the middle and late 1970s at least, were clearly for the more immediately utilitarian and basic items on the shelf."

Attempts were made to sweep the collegiate function out of community colleges. Numerous legislators and institutional trustees were lauding the colleges as places designed to prepare workers, whose training had no space for liberal arts courses. And liberal arts devotees, who remained convinced that the traditional academic transfer courses were the sole vehicle for transmitting the liberal arts, inadvertently fed these contentions. The more successful the colleges became in their mission of providing trained workers for the community, the more precarious became the idea of liberal education within them.

However, reports of the demise of the collegiate function were greatly exaggerated. Enrollments in liberal arts classes stabilized in the 1980s at just over 50 percent of total credit-course enrollments. Granted that a sizable proportion of this enrollment was in science, social science, English, and mathematics courses in service to occupational program areas, and that much of it was directed toward students attending for their personal interest or fulfilling distribution requirements for the associate degree, the collegiate function was tenacious. The basic trend in the 1980s continued in the direction of career education. But—because of the efforts of the community college liberal arts instructors, the effects of state or locally mandated graduation requirements, university transfer expectations, and, in general, the place of the community college in higher education—the collegiate function was proving resilient. By the middle of the decade, there were renewed calls for strengthening that component of the associate degree.

The Faculty as Support Group for Liberal Arts

The collegiate function survives, but any assessment of its future must consider the faculty, who have been its staunchest supporters. When the liberal arts were brought from the universities into the community colleges, the ethos of academic scholarship did not accompany them. The colleges were not supportive of scholarship, and the university training that instructors received was not, in itself, adequate to foster teachers who would attend to the reflections and meanings of their disciplines. Further, too few instructors have banded together to build interdisciplinary courses in the sciences, social sciences, and humanities. The argument that the universities would not accept new types of courses for transfer credit is spurious; practitioners in two-year colleges have not pursued them with sufficient diligence.

The idea that the faculty, as independently functioning

practitioners, should have the power to define the curriculum stems from the turn-of-the-century university model. The concept of academic freedom, of instructors teaching what they want within the confines of their own classrooms, was not accepted by the secondary schools. But the community colleges adopted it even though few of their instructors had become sufficiently profession-alized to develop courses that fit the institutions' broader social purposes. Within the liberal arts especially (but not exclusively), the departmentally designed and administered examination is resisted. Common textbooks for courses taught in multiple sections by different instructors are more the exception than the rule. Although community college instructors ostensibly all work from common syllabi on file in the dean's office for display to visiting accredita-tion teams, those documents rarely give direction to the courses. Any request for uniformity—any request for explanation—is likely as not to be refused.

If the liberal arts exist within an anarchy, if scientists and humanists work within different frameworks of ideas, the curricula that they articulate will be diverse. In universities, however, the expectation is that instructors will be affiliated with the academic disciplines and that the curriculum will reflect the tenets of those disciplines. In community colleges, where disciplinary affiliation is much weaker, the unseen hand of the academic discipline is much less strong as an influence on the form of courses or on instructors' activities. Accordingly, the innovation and flexibility so prized by community college spokespersons derive less from educational philosophy than from the fact that the curriculum is without a rudder. One instructor's whim will change the pattern, emphasis, and direction of a course and hence a curriculum. Whereas the university organizes the intellectual world in a division of *intellec-tual* labor and necessarily accommodates a plurality of diverse intellectual stances, the community college organizes its world in a division of *faculty* labor and necessarily accommodates a plurality of diverse instructor stances. The amorphous, sporadic monitoring of instructors by department chairpersons, deans of instruction, accreditation teams, and peers is of little consequence. Instructors' work is influenced by the writers of textbooks they use, the speakers at conferences they attend, the new information they learn in in-service programs or on their own. But the enterprise is chaotic, directionless.

An example is provided by contrasting the modes of teaching the liberal arts and the occupational courses. Traditionally, the liberal arts have been taught by a teacher in a room equipped with chairs and a chalkboard. Instructors have acted as though contact between themselves and the students is the key element, as though all that is necessary for a person to learn is to engage in dialogue and to read and reflect in a solitary fashion. Career educators, in contrast, have taken the position that they need laboratories, shops, equipment, and links with the business and industry community in order to teach people a trade. They say their students must practice the craft, not merely talk about it.

What if the faculty in the liberal arts took similar views? Music instructors might allege that students cannot properly learn to appreciate music unless the college provides each of them with a compact disc player and a couple of hundred classical recordings. Instructors teaching art appreciation would say that students cannot learn unless they are provided with slide viewers, sets of slides showing all the principal art in the Western world, and funds to travel to museums. Anthropology instructors might insist that students be paid to work at archeological digs, so that they can learn the ways of thinking in earlier cultures. Political science instructors would have students serving as apprentices to politicians and bureaucrats in all types of government agencies, so that they can learn how decisions are really made. And certainly the best way to learn a language is to live in a country where that language is spoken, with the colleges sponsoring such trips. But liberal arts faculty members rarely advocate such views, whereas nursing educators insist that they must have laboratories, equipment, and on-the-job training. It would not occur to them to try to teach nursing in a room equipped with nothing more than chairs and a chalkboard. They get the clinics and the funds they need to maintain their small student-teacher ratios. The liberal arts instructors get chalk dust on their clothing.

These variant attitudes stem from the different ways that the career and collegiate functions were taught before they came into the colleges. Career preparation evolved from a history of apprenticeships in work settings, the traditional mode of learning a trade. The liberal arts were the province of a group inclined toward contemplation. Thus, it costs more to teach the occupations because the workplaces are duplicated or at least simulated on site. Liberal arts educators in community colleges do not even have the benefit of sizable library collections. And they do not act in concert to modify the conditions.

The Weakened Disciplines

The collegiate function in community colleges has been characterized by a reduction in emphasis on the academic disciplines. Community college instructors tend not to conduct scholarly inquiry, not to belong to disciplinary associations, not to be excessively concerned with disciplinary purity. All to the good for faculty members who are instructed to teach in areas of current student interest and who must often cross disciplinary fields; the instructor whose work load comprises one course in anthropology, another in sociology, and two in American history does not have the luxury of maintaining currency in all fields. However, the turn away from disciplinarianism has had some untoward effects. Many courses appeal to immediate relevance and focus excessively on the person. Instructors confront the students with art, music, literature, or current events and ask for personal reactions. "How did you like it?" is the key question, not "What are you seeing? Why is it there? What is the meaning of this? How does this relate to other phenomena?" One test of the level of a course is the degree to which it makes intellectual demands of its students. Many liberal arts courses have strayed far from the collegiate ideal. Under the guise of presenting a student-centered curriculum, courses that reflect the popular literature of self-help books on coping, gaining singular advantage, and other personal concerns are often built within the liberal arts framework.

All curriculum must, in the end, be based on knowledge. No matter what the ultimate intent of a student-centered course, that course cannot maintain its collegiate character unless something is being taught. That something is the subject; that subject stems from the discipline. Without the anchor of the humanistic and scientific disciplines themselves, the basis of the academic tradition, the collegiate function would be adrift. Even if the liberal arts were not a curriculum in themselves, they would still have to be maintained as the foundation of the liberal education that is provided through all the other curricula.

The demise of the academic disciplines as the organizing principle of collegiate courses has both reflected and served to limit faculty members' awareness of recent trends in their academic fields. Such an awareness is important even for such a seemingly simple task as evaluating the new textbooks that appear. But it is important for more than that; the academic disciplines need reconceptualizing to fit compensatory and career education, the institution's dominant functions in addition to transfer. This reconceptualization cannot be made outside the colleges themselves. For the sake of the collegiate function, community college instructors must reify their own disciplines. It is difficult for a group that has severed connection with its disciplinary roots to accomplish that.

Transfer Students

A first requisite for modifying the collegiate function is the recognition that it is not embodied exclusively in the transfer courses. The collegiate function, the higher learning, teaches reflection, use of the intellect. It broadens choices and connects people to their culture and to past and contemporary society. The coincidence of this function with the transfer courses in the liberal arts has made the two seem immutably associated. But the percentage of students transferring to senior institutions has declined, and those who do transfer often take routes other than through the liberal arts.

Since the mid-1970s more students appear to have transferred to universities from career education programs than from college-parallel programs. The transfer function has changed. The students with distinct objectives move through the programs in engineering, forestry, and business and transfer to senior institutions. Those who are less certain of their directions, along with the few who adhere to the ancient view of college as a place for developing self and learning to control one's environment, take the liberal arts classes.

Some of them transfer; most do not. Thus, the link between the collegiate and transfer functions has been weakened.

By equating the collegiate function with transfer courses, its proponents do it a disservice. Few community college matriculants adhere to graduation requirements; few obtain Associate in Arts degrees; few transfer to the universities at all; most are part-time students taking a course or two for personal interest or career education. Many students who do intend to transfer find that they can study the liberal arts in greater breadth and depth at the senior institutions. The transfer function, then, serves as a will-o'-the-wisp, leading liberal arts proponents to rely on it to fill their classes, although at the same time it has changed its character.

The collegiate function cannot be sustained *in its traditional form.* Brann's analysis of collegiate education inadvertently reveals why. Brann (1979) equated *education* and *literacy,* calling them "convertible terms" She confined *education* to reflection on the books and ideas that make up the tradition of the civilization. She rejected an education centered on social problems as though the individual could solve them, as though human affairs were amenable to easy treatment: "It is a faith encouraged by certain academics who . . . want to invest their subject with irresistible urgency" (p. 30). Students need a much better intellectual foundation and some critical independence before they can apply solutions to social ills. This type of education is as portable as books, but it cannot be attained without them. According to Brann, the Western tradition is set down in books and must be apprehended by the study of texts. Therefore, it is not available to the person who cannot or who does not read.

However, those contentions have been challenged on the grounds that reading and writing are as archaic in the twentieth century as study of the classics was in the nineteenth century. Communication through nonprint images is pervasive. The spoken word is carried across distance not by a courier with a packet of letters but through wires and waves. The ubiquitous hand-held calculator has done for arithmetic what the invention of movable type did for story telling. Supermarket checkers rely on bar codes; restaurant cashiers, on pictures of the product superimposed on a register key that records the cost of the item and the amount of change to be tendered. Why, then, should educators be concerned about teaching literacy? Advocates of the collegiate function would argue that the failure to teach literacy only perpetuates social-class divisions and increases the benighted individual's reliance on authority. Any educator with less than a totally cynical view of society would agree.

Effecting a Merger

For the collegiate function to reach its full potential and involve all students, it will have to be fit to the career, compensatory, and community education programs, as well as the degree-credit liberal arts classes. The first issue, though, for those who would pursue the collegiate function in community colleges is whether those institutions are, or properly ought to be, educational structures. If the colleges are only to provide access, a stepping stone to a job or some other school, along with the illusory benefits of credits and degrees, then their status as schools is marginal. The second issue is whether they are properly part of higher education. How much of their efforts is devoted to developing rationality? To leading students to form habits of reflection? Many institutional leaders have seized on the term *postsecondary education* to characterize their colleges' place. To them, the collegiate function is irrelevant.

For the sake of their students and communities, the community colleges should maintain a place in higher education, but a reorientation is required. For example, community colleges might integrate the liberal arts with career education through a merger of principles stemming from both the humanities and the sciences. Technology is ubiquitous; students would have little difficulty understanding generally how the history, politics, ethics, sociology, and philosophy of science and technology affect their world. Those who would be more than mechanics would attend to the fundamental assumptions undergirding what scientists and technologists do. Where the colleges have built courses around such productions as Jacob Bronowski's *Ascent of Man* or James Burke's *Connections,* they have succeeded in emphasizing these principles. In general, literature and art in the community colleges have not dealt sufficiently with technology, but a fully integrated course could be required in all career programs. Similarly, portions of the liberal arts could be designed especially for key courses in the career programs—a pattern described more fully in the next chapter.

The context for the reading and writing courses that make up compensatory education can be the literature that addresses basic human concerns. The courses themselves can be made competency-based, a part of the general curriculum. Their texts can be supplemental to the academic classes. The students can be awarded credit for attending art exhibitions, recitals, forums, and lectures in the same way that credit is given for noncollege experience. Spectator events can be used to encourage reflection.

And it is certainly feasible to maintain the collegiate function in courses for adults who seek an environment and a stimulus for reading, reflecting, and discussing great works and issues. To them, education is not the literate activity of a leisured interlude between childhood and professional training; it is that which takes place when the other requisites of their life have been accommodated. It is utilitarian, not for a living but for living the good life. To participate in liberal education, students must suspend their immediate anxieties about the jobs they will obtain as a result of attending college, must shift from the short-term goals of education to its longer rewards. The young seem unable to do that, but many adults can.

Can It Happen?

The waves of fashion, trends in funding, interests of students, imaginativeness of the faculty—all affect the prognosis for collegiate studies in community colleges. Several trends favor the expansion of these studies. Aspects of finance favor collegiate studies because they are less expensive than the career and compensatory programs. Tradition is on their side; they have been present since the first days of the institutions, and tradition (or inertia) plays an important role in education. Those who would abandon collegiate studies must answer to charges that they are thereby denying opportunity to the great numbers of students who still see the community college as a stepping stone to the higher learning.

Collegiate studies also remain the favorite of many people who already have jobs but who want to attend college for the personal benefits it brings. These students may increase in number. There will be less competition for entry-level jobs as the younger age group decreases as a percentage of the population. Hence, students may be free to study the liberal arts without fear of being closed out of employment. And when the current wave of distrust of social institutions passes, the authority of the school as an arbiter of the curriculum may be reinstated. A sizable percentage of the population seems still to believe that the school has a responsibility to define what its students should study.

But trends suggesting that the collegiate function will weaken can also be identified. Students who demand that the institution provide them with a skill they can sell in the employment marketplace still account for a sizable percentage of all entrants. They may take the collegiate courses, but only if they can be shown the value attendant on such studies. Less easily traced, but certainly influential, is the continuing move away from print as a medium of communication. Students reared on a diet of instant information presented through electronic media may find the reflectiveness and self-discipline basic to the collegiate function difficult to master. Although some imaginative efforts at integrative courses presented through television have been made, the long-term effects of a turn away from print have not yet been fully appreciated. Not least is the idea that the college has no reason for existence other than to serve its students and the business community, no right to a life of its own as an intellectual community. Accordingly, it is easy to reduce the institution's value to the increase in its graduates' income.

The community college faculty's tendency to be translators of ideas rather than seminal thinkers ill serves the collegiate function at a time when it must be reformed for the clients. The disciplinary streams through which the collegiate function has been codified, advanced, studied, and taught are rarely seen in the community colleges. Not only are instructors' disciplinary affiliations weak, but also the purposes and operations of community colleges tend toward areas other than the academic disciplines. The disciplines are useful for training scholars; the community college does not train scholars. The disciplines are useful for learning about a subject in depth; the community colleges tend toward providing knowledge in breadth. Any reformation must be undertaken outside the academic-discipline stream and thus in uncharted waters.

Nonetheless, if such a reformation is to occur, it must be based in the community colleges themselves. There is no external agency organized for the purpose of revising collegiate studies in a manner that would better connect the liberal arts concepts with the students' interests and goals. The best examples of integrated course presentations in the humanities and the sciences have come from those practitioners who have understood the problems of translating the liberal arts for their students and have merged elements from several disciplines into imaginative instructional programs. And they have usually come from the institutions that have the resources to commit to faculty members working in concert and to the reproducible media that frequently form the core of such programs.

For the students who come to an institution asking "What kind of job can I get as a result of my attendance?" the community colleges have many programs. The students rarely ask themselves, "What sort of self am I in the process of making?" The institution has the responsibility of creating that question in the minds of its matriculants, eschewing the facile rejoinder that for community college students individual freedom begins with economic security. The greater service to students may well be to insist on their studying the liberal arts.

The term *overeducated* may prove to be among the most pernicious perversions of the idea of schooling ever set forth. It suggests that one who has broader understandings is ill fitted for work. It glorifies as the finest product of our schools the drone who exists on the fast-food service line without any familial or civic responsibility. It suggests that no learning is of value except that which is of immediate and obvious utility. It denies the essence of humanity and of civilization.

The notion that thought and intelligence must undergird all human activities runs counter to the tendency of many within and outside the academy who extol irrationality, emotion, and hedonism. Practitioners of higher education have been justly accused of overemphasizing the intellect to the exclusion of other dimensions of human life. But because people think, thought being that which differentiates them from the animals, these practitioners believe that reflection on purposes is itself the purpose of human life.

Two-year colleges are not of themselves going to produce reflective human beings; no single institution can claim a monopoly on that strategy. What the colleges can do is to provide some portions of the education for the masses that tends toward encouraging exercise of the intellect. There is no surplus of agencies encouraging that form of reflection in America, certainly not for the community colleges' clients.

Ideally, a liberal education should prepare the individual to be an informed citizen and a participant in civic affairs. That was the rationale for the terminal general education articulated by those early-century community college proponents who saw the institution providing a capstone education for those who would not go on to the specializations of the baccalaureate. That same rationalization will have to be used as the base for the necessary redefinition of the collegiate function.

The argument that community colleges should concentrate on career and compensatory education because they do it better than senior institutions has been articulated by numerous observers. Breneman and Nelson (1981), for example, suggest that the collegiate function is best maintained in senior residential colleges, where students have a better chance of progressing through to the bachelor's degree. Here they are in accord with Astin (1977), who has argued that the residential experience promotes the holistic development of students and helps them maintain their attendance through to the level of the bachelor's. However, these arguments hold to a simplistic view of the college experience, differentiating unnecessarily between the typical undergraduate experience and the best principles of a college education.

The community colleges may be better able than the senior institutions to offer the best form of lower-division studies. Their experiences with compensatory education will help. They certainly have had more experience with it, since from their inception they have been populated by less well-prepared students. The community colleges have an opportunity to reconceptualize their collegiate functions, not by maintaining arbitrary and artificial standards of the senior university type but by building truly integrated general education. Their compensatory education programs should not be limited to adult basic education but should be broadened to include study of science, technology, the humanities, and the broader concepts of the culture. Students formerly pursued such studies in the secondary schools, but the secondary school curriculum is no longer functioning properly. There is room for the collegiate function, but in revised form.

Issues

The overriding issue is whether the community colleges should maintain their position in higher education. If they should not, no deliberate steps are necessary. Continued deterioration in course requirements will suffice. But if they should, what can they do?

Can the collegiate function be expanded beyond the college-parallel courses? Can it be made part of the career programs? What can the liberal arts say to the student who wants nothing more than job upgrading or new skills?

Must the collegiate function decline along with the decline in students' tendency to read and write? Can the liberal arts be offered in a manner that fits less well-prepared students' ways of knowing?

Which elements of collegiate studies are most usefully presented in community education? Will community education directors build components of the higher learning into their programs?

What would stimulate the liberal arts faculty as a group to translate the concepts of their disciplines so that they fit the community colleges' dominant programs?

Advisory committees comprising concerned citizens, labor leaders, and employers have been influential in connecting the career programs to the world of work. Can lay advisory committees for the liberal arts similarly help connect those programs to the broader society?

The collegiate function has many advocates within and outside the colleges. The future of the community college as a comprehensive institution depends on how they articulate its concerns.

Twelve

General Education:
Knowledge for Personal and Civic Life

Confronted on the one side by universities wanting better-prepared students and on the other by secondary schools passing through the marginally literate, captives of their own rhetoric to provide programs to fit anyone's desires, the community colleges erected a curriculum resembling more a smorgasbord than a coherent educational plan. What else could they do? Their policies favored part-time students dropping in and out at will, whose choice of courses was often made more on the basis of convenience in time and place than on content. Their funding agents rewarded career, transfer, and continuing education differentially.

Most colleges responded by abandoning any semblance of curricular integration, taking pride instead in their variety of presentations for all purposes. Except in career programs monitored by external licensing agencies and accreditation societies, the idea of courses to be taken by every student pursuing a degree diminished. The ultimate in rejection of sequence, of the belief that knowledge builds predictably on other knowledge, was reached when the colleges began awarding individualized-studies degrees for any set of courses or experiences that the students offered in evidence.

The disintegration of the sequential curriculum was not confined to community colleges. The universities have been plagued with course proliferation since the turn of the century, and a similar, if less pronounced, phenomenon affected the secondary

312

schools when the number of electives that might be taken to fulfill graduation requirements increased. Yet the belief that some studies are important for all students dies hard. Pleas for core curricula have been sounded from innumerable platforms, where secondary schools and universities alike are chided for allowing students to pass through them without enjoying any experiences in common.

Those who call for an integrated curriculum frequently use the term *general education*. General education is the process of developing a framework on which to place knowledge stemming from various sources, of learning to think critically, develop values, understand traditions, respect diverse cultures and opinions, and, most important, put that knowledge to use. It is holistic, not specialized; integrative, not fractioned; suitable more for action than for contemplation. It thus differs from the ideal of the collegiate function. The liberal arts are education *as;* general education is education *for.*

General education received widespread publicity in 1977, when the Carnegie Foundation for the Advancement of Teaching published a book indicating the imminence of the first curriculum reforms in higher education in thirty years. The Carnegie Foundation said the time was right because the test scores of students entering college were down, and it was obvious that much was wrong in precollegiate education. Further, students seemed to be learning less in college, and even though remedial education had been tried by all types of colleges, it was difficult to show the efficacy of these efforts. The foundation proposed a reform toward integration in a curriculum that had become fractionated, toward education in values in a curriculum that had purported to be value-free. It sought a return to general education.

The Carnegie Foundation report was followed by several reports on the same theme emanating from other agencies. *Involvement in Learning,* a report by the Study Group on the Conditions of Excellence in American Higher Education (1984), formed under National Institute of Education auspices, advocated a liberal education that would enhance shared values and involve students in the learning process. A National Endowment for the Humanities report, *To Reclaim a Legacy* (Bennett, 1984), called for a general education centered on traditional texts and curriculum. Another report, *Integrity in the College Curriculum,* sponsored by the Association of American Colleges (1985), called for a basic curriculum that would teach students to think about subject matter in the manner that academic specialists approach it. And a subsequent Carnegie Foundation report, entitled *College: The Undergraduate Experience in America* (Boyer, 1987), advocated a general education that would extend throughout the college experience and integrate specialized education across disciplinary fields.

So it is one more time around for general education. What happened to it the first time it flourished, in the early nineteenth century? And the second time, between 1920 and 1950?

Background

General education can be traced to the moral philosophy courses found in American colleges during their first 200 years. These integrative experiences usually were taught by the college president and presented to all students. Remnants of the integrated courses pulling together knowledge from several areas may still be seen in the capstone courses required of all students in a few contemporary institutions. However, that type of general education broke apart in most colleges in the second half of the nineteenth century, to be replaced by the free-elective system. No longer were there to be courses that all students would take; no longer would the colleges attempt to bring together threads of all knowledge in a unified theme. Blame the rise of the academic disciplines, the professionalization of the faculty, the broadening of knowledge in all areas, the increased numbers of students, each with his or her own agenda—all these accusations have been made. But, for whatever reason, the elective system took over. The old classical curriculum died out, taking with it the idea of the curriculum as a unified whole to be presented to all students. By the turn of the twentieth century, most American colleges had come down to an irreducible minimum in curriculum: faculty members with academic degrees teaching courses of their choice to those students who elected to study with them or whose goals required that they be there.

All curriculum is, at bottom, a statement a college makes about what it thinks is important. The free-elective system is a philosophical statement quite as much as is a curriculum based on the Great Books or one concerned solely with occupational education. It is an admission that the college no longer has the moral authority to insist on any combination of courses, that it no longer recognizes the validity of sequence or organized principles of curriculum integration. The system was not without its critics. The early-century Carnegie plan—assigning units of credit for hours of study—was introduced in an attempt to bring order out of the free-elective curricular chaos. It had the opposite effect. That is, by ascribing units of credit of apparently equal merit, it snipped to pieces whatever unity was left in the academic subjects themselves. Three credits of algebra had the same meaning as three credits of calculus; a three-credit introductory course in a discipline was of equal value to an advanced seminar in the same field. When a student may accumulate any 120 credit hours and obtain a baccalaureate degree, when all credits are the same, all unity of knowledge falls apart.

The initial reaction against the free-elective system gave rise to distribution requirements—curriculum defined by bureaucratic organization. Groups of courses were specified in a process of political accommodation among academic departments. In order that the history department would vote a six-unit English requirement, the English department was expected to reciprocate by voting a six-unit history requirement. Protecting departmental territory became the curriculum organizer. Placing a disintegrated mass of free-elective courses into a set of distribution requirements gives the appearance of providing the curriculum with a rationale. Thus, the noble truths of general studies arose post hoc to justify the politics of distribution—whence the popular statements that colleges provide a breadth of studies, ensuring that their students leave as well-rounded individuals. In the 1970s the Carnegie Council found that students spend about one-third of their time in undergraduate school taking distribution requirements, the other two-thirds going to the major and to electives. Gaff (1983) found that distribution requirements accounted for half of the units needed to complete an associate degree in the community colleges he studied; the other half went to electives or, especially in occupational programs, to major field requirements. The political accommodations among departments were in equilibrium.

The success of distribution requirements as an organizing principle for curriculum did not stop those who advocated curriculum integration. Their early attempts to return order were founded in survey courses. Columbia University's "Contemporary Civilization" course, first offered in 1919, is usually seen as the prototype. These courses give the overview, the broad sweep, in history, the arts, the sciences, and the social sciences. The academic discipline is the organizing principle of the course, but the course is supposed to show the unity of knowledge, to integrate disparate elements from many disciplines. Survey courses became quite popular during the 1920s and 1930s. Surveys of social sciences, for example, were built into the "Individual in Society" courses. The humanities surveys became "Modern Culture and the Arts." Separate surveys of natural, physical, and biological sciences were also attempted, but with less success.

Advocates of survey courses had constantly to struggle to maintain the integrity of their offerings against the faculty tendency to convert each course into the introduction to a discipline, to teach concepts and terminology in a particular academic specialization as though all students were majors in that field. The faculty objection to the survey courses was that they were superficial, trying to encompass too many different portions of human knowledge. As each course slid away from a true interdisciplinary orientation to become the first course in an academic discipline, it tended to lose its general education characteristics.

Nonetheless, many interdisciplinary courses survived. Much seemed to depend on the level of specialization within the discipline. Social science instructors had little trouble putting together political science, sociology, economics, and anthropology into a general social science survey. Science instructors, however, may have believed that they were teaching a general survey if they integrated molecular and organismic biology into one course. It was difficult for them to include the physical and earth and space sciences. In 1935 most of the college survey courses were in social science, followed by natural science, physical science, and biological science; only a few humanities surveys were offered (Johnson, 1937). However, the humanities courses have fared better recently; in fact, enrollments in integrated humanities courses in community colleges increased recently in the face of a decline in the specific disciplines within the humanities.

General education suffered originally from the free-elective system and the broadening of knowledge that was properly a part of the college curriculum. In his history of the undergraduate curriculum, Rudolph (1977) traced the concept into the 1970s and concluded: "Where highly publicized general education requirements reshaped the course of study in the 1940s and 1950s, less publicized erosion of those requirements took place in the 1960s and 1970s" (p. 253). What happened to it this time? According to Rudolph, general education fell victim to faculty power; lack of student interest; increased demands on faculty time; difficulties in integrating the disciplines; and, most of all, its own lack of demonstrated value and the superficiality of the presentations. General education has remained a noble idea but a practical backwater in most of American higher education.

Definitions

A good part of the difficulty with general education rests with its definition. The term has been in use for more than seventy years and has been defined innumerable times. Sometimes it has been defined narrowly—for instance, as the trivium and quadrivium, the discipline of the medieval scholars; and sometimes broadly—as that education which integrates and unifies all knowledge. It has been confounded with the liberal arts, and it has been connected to the human developmental cycle. It has been defined as what it is not. Following are some of the definitions.

On the side of breadth, the 1939 Yearbook of the National Society for the Study of Education saw general education as concerned with the "widest possible range of basic human activities." It was to guide the student "to the discovery of the best that is currently known and thought." It was "dynamic," "democratic," "systematic." The student was to gain "a real grasp of the most widely ramifying generalized insights—intellectual, ethical, and esthetic" (p. 12). The Harvard "Red Book," *General Education in a Free Society* (Committee on the Objectives of a General Education in a Free Society, 1945), also announced that general education was to bring all knowledge together. Hutchins (1936) defined general education as an interdisciplinary undertaking centered on great books and ideas, and he recommended that high schools and junior colleges devote their curriculum to such studies. (This definition was promulgated fifty years later by William Bennett, then United States secretary of education.)

General education has also been defined as that which everyone should know. The Executive Committee of the Cooperative Study in General Education (1947, p. 17) said that it should provide "the basic understandings and skills which everyone should possess." Mayhew (1960, p. 16) said it should establish "a common universe of discourse—a common heritage." In the proceedings of a 1959 Florida junior college conference on general education (Florida State Department of Education, 1959), the idea of commonality, those learnings that should be possessed by all persons, was articulated repeatedly. Boyer and Kaplan (1977) argued for a common core that should be taught to all students. They spoke of a need for "comprehensive literacy" and "an awareness of symbol systems" that everyone in contemporary society must have (p. 67).

General education has also been defined by what it is not. It is nonspecialized, nonvocational; it is not occupational education; it is not learning to use the tools of a discipline or learning a specialized language. A report of a conference held at a community college in Florida in 1976 offers a wondrous example of definition by exclusion: "At the operational level, general education . . . is not special; that is, it is not designed for specific groups of people or special activities. . . . It is *not* an introduction to disciplines as the first step in specialization. It is *not* content for its own sake. It is *not* the development of skills or the acquisition of knowledge precisely for their applicability to a job, a career, or another specialization. It is *not* a collection of courses. It is *not* simply a rearrangement of content, like an interdisciplinary program or course for the sake of being interdisciplinary. It is *not* so abstract and future-oriented that it can only be hoped for, wished for, or assumed to happen somewhere, sometime. It is *not* merely being able to read, to write, and to do arithmetic" (Tighe, 1977, pp. 13–14).

General education also has been contrasted with liberal education. Educators have always agreed that education should be useful for something (all curricula are justified for their practical value). Apologists for liberal education have held that it frees people from such external tyrannies as caste biases, societal constraints, and professional experts, as well as from the internal tyrannies of ignorance, prejudice, superstition, guilt, and what the Thomists might call "the appetites." Having to do with the virtues, it has been rationalized as affording knowledge for its own sake. In general education, in contrast, knowledge is power—the power of coping, understanding, self-mastery, and social interaction. It must lead to the ability to do, to act; gaining rationality alone is not enough. People who have had a general education are supposed to act intelligently. This view grounds the construct in the everyday affairs of a person: dealing with supervisors and co-workers, choosing associates, coping with family problems, and spending leisure time in socially desirable and personally satisfying ways. To be successful, a general education program not only makes explicit the skills and understandings to be attained but also relates those competencies to external referents, to what people are doing when they have gained them.

According to Miller (1988, p. ix), "It is especially ironic that general education, which was originally formulated as a reaction to what were perceived to be the serious shortcomings of liberal education, should today be confused with the latter. Indeed, the two terms are often used interchangeably, despite the fact that the two forms of education have fundamental conceptual differences." Liberal education is centered in the past, with knowledge historically viewed as an end in itself and the curriculum merely a vehicle for the acquisition of knowledge; general education holds that knowledge is hypothetical and should be regarded as the means to the end of a better personal life and a better society. The generally educated student would use knowledge as needed to solve human problems.

Accordingly, general education is often defined in terms of the competencies to be gained by those whom it touches. A group studying general education in California community colleges in the early 1950s (Johnson, 1952) offered a list of twelve competencies to be exercised by those who are generally educated:

- Exercising the privileges and responsibilities of democratic citizenship.
- Developing a set of sound moral and spiritual values by which the person guides his life.
- Expressing his thoughts clearly in speaking and writing and in reading and listening with understanding.
- Using the basic mathematical and mechanical skills necessary in everyday life.
- Using methods of critical thinking for the solution of problems and for the discrimination among values.
- Understanding his cultural heritage so that he may gain a perspective of his time and place in the world.
- Understanding his interaction with his biological and physical environment so that he may adjust to and improve that environment.
- Maintaining good mental and physical health for himself, his family, and his community.
- Developing a balanced personal and social adjustment.
- Sharing in the development of a satisfactory home and family life.
- Taking part in some form of satisfying creative activity and in appreciating the creative activities of others.

That list, or portions thereof, still appears verbatim in many community college catalogues because it gives the appearance of being competency-based even though it is sufficiently broad to justify any course or program.

The Variant Definitions

Given the plethora of definitions, the failure to maintain general education consistently is easily understood. General education is prey to any group with a strict view of curriculum. Throughout this century the same forces that splintered knowledge into academic disciplines have continued their antagonism to a general or unifying education. The academic profession had become departmentalized in its specializations, thus posing a contradiction for the integration of learning. The academic departments insisted that students pick a major—the earlier the better. Courses were built as introductions to disciplines with their own logic, terminology, goals, organizing principles, and modes of inquiry; adding distribution requirements while leaving the internal organization of the course intact did not enhance knowledge integration, common learnings, or competencies. In short, the academic discipline, with its hold on the faculty and the organization of the college, was the first and most pervasive deterrent to general education.

The definition itself has been part of the problem. If general education is defined by what it is not, instead of what it is, it is open to any type of course or experience. Constantly denying the restrictive organization of occupational and discipline-based education has propelled general education into the areas of unstructured events, counseling activities, courses without content, programs with broad goals impossible of attainment—the anticurriculum.

The breadth of the positive side of the definition hurt too. The most specialized course in Elizabethan literature might lead students to "understand their cultural heritage." The most trivial course in personal habits and grooming might assist students to "maintain good mental and physical health." Guidance and orientation programs could assist students to "develop a balanced personal and social adjustment," and so on throughout the list of competencies and throughout the range of activities and services provided by colleges. Where anything can be related to general education, it falls victim to the whims of students, faculty members, and administrators alike. Positive or negative, none of its goals has been specific enough to have more than rhetorical value. Even when college staff members meeting in conference agree on them, the agreement usually dissipates when each instructor develops course content and methodology to be displayed in an individual classroom.

General education was tainted early on. The phrase *terminal general education* was in use in the 1930s, suggesting that it was an education for the student who would never go on to the higher learning. In some senior institutions, separate colleges were devised as holding tanks for students deemed unqualified to enter the regular programs. Here they would get the last of their formal education, nondisciplinary, nonspecialized, and—according to many professors—of dubious merit. If general education was seen as a curriculum for students unable to do real college work, it was doomed to suffer. Perhaps it was an extension of high school general education, but then what was it doing in a real college? And how could a self-respecting faculty member have anything to do with it? Credit the idea of terminal general education as one of the factors leading to the failure of general education to hold the attention of the academy.

Another clue to the unstable history of general education can be found in its emphasis on individual life adjustment. Early proponents of general education fostered guidance activities. B. Lamar Johnson, a spokesperson for general education during much of his half century in higher education, said in 1937, "Uniformly colleges committed to general education stress guidance. This is reasonable, for if general education aims to help the individual adjust to life, it is essential to recognize that this adjustment is an individual matter—dependent upon individual abilities, interests, and needs. Upon these bases the colleges assist the student to determine his individual objectives and mould a program to attain them" (p. 12). But if the individual is to "mould a program" based on his or her "abilities, interests, and needs," then anything may be seen as general education for that individual. The person may take the most specialized courses or no courses at all. Such a definition dooms the idea of integrated courses—indeed, of all common courses. Thus, general education in the 1930s was so fractionated that it included everything from the Great Books curriculum to life-adjustment courses and student guidance.

The idea that the student should be led to a "satisfactory vocational adjustment" was also common in definitions of general education at midcentury. Occupational education has achieved great success in American colleges and universities but for different reasons. It was built on an alliance of educators seeking support, students seeking jobs, and business people seeking workers trained

at public expense; it has capitalized on legislators who are pleased
to assign schools the task of mitigating unemployment; it has been
enhanced by parents who want the schools to teach their children to
do something productive. It has done well, and if it is a part of
general education, then general education has done well, too. But
when general education is defined as leading students to understand
relationships between themselves and society, gain a sense of values
and an appreciation for cultural diversity, and fulfill the other
broader aims of the program, occupational education is left out.
Credit its inclusion with blurring the image of what general education is or could be.

The expansion of higher education to include more than
three thousand colleges has also added to the difficulties with
general education. Free from the imposition of state-level requirements throughout much of their history, the colleges were able to
develop an indigenous curriculum. When institutions could define
their own patterns of study, it was possible for a strong president to
leave a mark, for an institution to develop its own philosophical set.
Some colleges were reorganized around specific curriculum plans
when their prior offerings proved inadequate to attract a sufficient
number of students to keep the college going. But in nearly all cases,
it was the strong central figure who articulated the philosophy and
used it to install a specialized curriculum and particular course requirements. Rarely did a group of local-campus faculty members and
second-line administrators put together a viable curriculum. Rarely
did a state legislature or a federal agency design integrated general
education programs. At best, the states mandated distribution
requirements, thus ensuring some form of curriculum balance; at
worst, through their reimbursement schedules, they encouraged the
expansion of occupational programs and courses to fit special student
groups, thus stultifying indigenous curriculum development.

Last in this list of contributors to the instability of general
education is the decline in literacy, which forced compensatory
education into the colleges. When faculty members are concerned
with teaching basic reading, composition, and computational
skills, they often think they must abandon instruction in critical
thinking, values, and cultural perspectives. The influx of what were
euphemistically called "nontraditional students" led to a failure of

will even among some of the proponents of general education, who proposed warmth, love, and counseling, instead of curriculum, for that group. General education was shunted aside by those who failed to understand that it could be taught to everyone.

Except for an excessive concern with the academic disciplines, all these problems were more pronounced in community colleges than in universities. The lack of strong educational leadership, a failure to define general education consistently, the rise of occupational education, and adult literacy training affected the community colleges markedly. The colleges were so busy recruiting "new students" that they forgot why they wanted them; the idea that they were to be generally educated was lost. Student demands for relevant or instant education, for something pragmatic or useful, were interpreted as a need for occupational training. And the colleges' place in statewide networks of postsecondary education allowed them to excuse their curricular shortcomings by saying that true general education would not be accredited or would not articulate well with the senior institutions' curriculum.

Still, general education survives. Is it relevant? Pragmatic? Pertinent to community needs? Legitimate in the eyes of the public? General education in community colleges will rise or fall in answer to those questions. It will depend also on the definitions accorded to it and to the terms *education* and *curriculum*.

We define *education* as "the process of learning," of change in attitude or capability. It may take place in school or outside; it may be guided, monitored, or haphazard; but it is something that happens to the individual. *Curriculum* is "any set of courses." This definition excludes those aspects of schooling that take place outside a structured course format. It should not be difficult for community college staff members to accept; as participants in a commuter institution, they have always been uneasy about ascribing value to student activities, clubs, dormitories, and other appurtenances of the residential college. The definitions connect education and curriculum with organized sequences—hour-long, week-long, year-long—designed to lead individuals from one set of abilities or tendencies to another; in short, to instruction.

Why in Community Colleges?

Why general education in community colleges? Statements on its behalf have been advanced not only by educators as far back as the earliest writers on community colleges—Lange, Koos, and Eells—but also by groups outside the academy. In 1947 the President's Commission on Higher Education noted the importance of semiprofessional training but contended that it should be "acquired in an environment that also cultivates general education, thus offering the student 'a combination of social understanding and technical competence' " (Park, 1977, p. 57). Ten years later President Eisenhower's committee (the Committee on Education Beyond High School) also articulated that combination, viewing it as the particular responsibility of the community colleges. Subsequently, an American Council on Education task force recommended that any institution offering an associate degree should attest that its students have become familiar with general areas of knowledge and have gained "competency in analytical, communication, quantitative, and synthesizing skills" ("Flexibility Sought . . . ," 1978). The degree should state not only that the students gained their training in a college but also that the training included a general education component.

These groups see the community colleges as the place where general education should be offered, not only because general education is necessary but also because other types of schools have tended to neglect it. The secondary schools once were repositories of general education, but that function weakened during the 1960s. Boyer (1980) reported on what was left of general education in the secondary schools in 1973 by noting the courses offered by 50 percent or more of the nation's schools:

English I and II	Biology I	Chorus
Public Speaking I	Chemistry I	Art I
General Math	Spanish I	Home Economics I
U.S. History	Driver Education	Typewriting I
Algebra I and II	Band	

"This list—these fourteen courses—represents the closest thing we have to a core curriculum—a list based not on what the students *study* but what most frequently is *offered*" (p. 10).

The community colleges have been caught with some of the same problems. They have taken over much of the basic literacy training for adults as well as remedial education in all areas for high school graduates who failed to learn the first time around. But the organizing principles for these programs are little better developed, and the breakdown in standards of competency that occurred in high schools a generation ago is also endemic. Faced with students of a type they never anticipated and demands for a variety of nontraditional studies to accommodate them, many community college educators have allowed their focus on achievement to be clouded. Further, in the past twenty-five years, the move to career education has led to severe curriculum imbalance. Students graduate from the programs with no core of basic knowledge; the alumni of nursing programs have learned nothing in common with the people who have studied computer data processing. Students learn job entry skills, but they may not learn how to continue to advance within the job. Career educators have also run the risk of frustrating trainees who cannot find the jobs for which they were specifically trained. And they seem contemptuous of their students to the extent that they deny them the joys of learning for the sake of their lives off the job. The career programs are not automatically relevant or valuable; they can be as meretricious as the most esoteric discipline-based course.

Numerous forces prevent excess in any curriculum for too long. Accrediting agencies, student enrollments, institutional funding sources, and the professional intelligence of the staff all act to maintain curriculum balance. The trend in community college curriculum was decidedly toward career and compensatory education in the 1970s; the 1980s saw a cessation of that trend; and succeeding decades may see it swing back toward preparing the generally educated person. Career education can be too specialized; without the breadth that accompanies general education, the colleges would be occupational schools undifferentiated from industrial training enterprises or proprietary schools. Compensatory education is limited in scope because it does not accommodate the human needs for self-expression, social interaction, and understanding of the world. The slogans "salable skills" and "back to basics" are not sufficient for mounting a program in higher education.

Curiously, the idea of lifelong learning, the same phenomenon that excused the abandonment of general education, may be the best argument for maintaining it in community colleges. Hutchins (1937) took issue with the idea of lifelong learning that would train and retrain people for occupations, saying that anything to be taught to young people should be useful to them throughout their lives, that successive, ad hoc retraining in specific skills would not lead them to understand anything of importance about their own lives or the world around them. But it is precisely the older students who perceive the need for general education, even while they seek upgrading within their own careers. They know that employment depends less on skill training than on the ability to communicate and get along with employers and co-workers. They know that a satisfying life demands more than production and consumption. They know that they must understand the ways institutions and individuals interact; that, for the sake of themselves and their progeny, they must understand and act on social issues. They know that they must maintain control over their lives, that what they learn assists them in maintaining individual freedom and dignity against a society that increasingly seeks to "deliver" health care, information, and the presumed benefits of living. That is why they come to the colleges with interest in the arts, general concepts in science, understanding the environment, relations with their fellows, questions of personal life crises and developmental stages— all topics in a true general education curriculum. As Miller (1988, p. 176) concluded, "It may well be that adult or continuing education has already become the cutting edge of general education. Continuing education programs, by force of economics if nothing else, tend to be student centered, future oriented, and change oriented programs. The methods of adult education are especially sympathetic to the goals of general education."

Inherently, the community colleges are neither more nor less able to offer a distribution of courses that would satisfy a general education requirement than are the universities or secondary schools; it is a matter of labeling and packaging. However, their students are less likely to accept distribution requirements because the associate degree has little value in the marketplace and the universities will allow students to transfer without it. Integrated general education courses, however, could find a home in community colleges if faculty members and administrators believed in their value. Instructors are not closely tied to the academic disciplines, nor do they typically engage in research and specialized writing. Many of the colleges have formed divisional instead of departmental structures. The colleges have some advantage, too, in developing problem-centered courses in general education through their ties to the local community.

For which of the many types of students coming to community colleges shall general education be provided? The answer is that the college should provide general education for all its enrollees. The college must guarantee the availability of general education throughout a person's life. Lifelong learning is more than the opportunity for successive retraining as one's job becomes obsolete; it is access to the form of general studies that leads to an understanding of self and society. General education must not be optional, lest the gulf between social classes in America be accentuated as members of the elite group learn to control their environment, while the lower classes are given career education and training in basic skills. The colleges must provide general education for the young students, whether or not they intend to transfer to senior institutions, and for the adults, who see the world changing and want to understand more about their environment.

A key question in general education is "How?" The question must be resolved in the context of the open-access institution. "Open access" means "open exit" as well. If a student may enter and drop at will, the ideal of the curriculum as a set of courses is severely limited. There can be no continuity of curriculum when a student takes one course, goes away for a number of years, and comes back to take one more. This casual approach is unprecedented in higher education and requires special planning if general education is to be effective. At the very least, each course must be considered as a self-contained unity, presented as though the students will never consider its concepts in another course.

Those who would plan general education must take care that they not repeat the cosmic rationalizations offered by early-day apologists for general education, who saw the students becoming imaginative, creative, perceptive, and sensitive to beauty; knowing about nature, humanity, and culture; acting with maturity, balance, and perspective; and so on. The colleges are simply not that influential. However, general education must not be debased by tying the concept exclusively to reading, writing, calculating, operating an automobile, using appliances, consuming products, practicing health, preparing income tax forms, borrowing money, and so on. Important as these tasks are, they can be learned elsewhere.

The rationale for general education in the community college is the freedom enjoyed by the informed citizen. Only when people are able to weigh the arguments of the experts are they truly free. These experts may be discussing issues of the environment, whether to put power plants or oil docks in or near cities. They may be advising on governmental questions. Or they may be telling people who may be born, who has a right to live, what it means to be healthy, and how, where, and when one should die. People need to understand how things work—social systems and persuaders, artists and computers. General education is for the creation of a free citizenry, the Greek ideal of the citizen participating in the polity.

Freedoms gained through a general education extend from the person to the society. The ability to think critically, to place one's own problems in broad perspective, to make informed choices about the conduct of one's own life is the cornerstone of freedom for the individual. The idea of freedom is different now than it was in an earlier era. To be free economically does not mean setting up one's own farm; it means having alternative ways of working within the modern corporate system. To be free politically does not mean going to town meetings and deciding on local issues; it means understanding the consequences of actions taken by bureaucrats and the ways of influencing or countering those actions. Being free morally and personally does not mean abiding by community mores; it means having the ability to understand and predict the consequences of one's actions for self and fellows in the context of a higher order of morality. According to Broudy (1974, pp. 27-28), the form of freedom gained through general education means "that the individual citizen could make up his *own* mind in political affairs, carve his *own* economic career with a minimum of interference, and could shape his *own* decisions by the dictates of his *own* conscience. . . . It is freedom for self-mastery as much as freedom from restraint by others. . . . Knowledge and insight into the principles of the good life are necessary conditions for genuine freedom. . . . That is why throughout the ages, general studies in one form or another have been regarded as the content of liberal education, education for those who would be free."

The cross-currents that affect community colleges generally affect their involvement with general education. It is possible to be optimistic about the future of general education because there is an irreducible minimum in curriculum and instruction below which the college ceases to be. The curriculum must be educative; staff members must act like educators; students must learn. A publicly supported college cannot operate indefinitely with a curriculum perceived as a set of haphazard events; with a corps of part-time instructors who have no commitment to the institution in general, let alone to the planning of curriculum in particular; and with students who drop in casually if they have nothing better to do that week. Such an institution may continue functioning, but it has lost its guiding ethos. A general education that leads to the ways of knowing and the common beliefs and language that bind the society together is offered in every culture through rituals, schools, apprenticeships. The community colleges are responsible for furthering it in the United States.

General Education in Practice

The community colleges have attempted to devise general education patterns. The integrated course has its own history. Medsker (1960) reported the number of these courses offered in seventy-eight colleges in 1956 (see Table 35). Several other descriptions of interdisciplinary survey courses in community colleges have been reported. Course outlines have been reprinted, ways of organizing the courses have been detailed, and problems in maintaining course integrity have been discussed. As an example,

**Table 35. Fields in Which Courses Especially
Designed for General Education Were
Offered in Two-Year Colleges, 1956 (*N* = 78).**

Subject	Percentage of Colleges
Natural science	86
Social science	79
Psychology and personal development	67
Language arts	59
Humanities	51
Fine arts	24
Mathematics	21
Health education	19
Homemaking	14
Preprofessional orientation	13
General studies	12
Occupational orientation	5
Agriculture and conservation	5

Source: Medsker, 1960, p. 60.

interdisciplinary humanities courses have been described by Friedlander and his colleagues (1983), who found that half of the colleges
in the United States offer such courses. Kirkwood Community
College (1986) developed an integrated humanities program to
replace a previously offered set of disconnected courses. Palmer
(1983) describes several other applications.

Interdisciplinary courses in the humanities have been
prominent, but activity in other areas has been undertaken as well.
Courses for general education have been centered on contemporary
problems: race relations, drug use and alcoholism, ecology and the
environment, social controversies, and world peace. In the 1930s
such courses were often built on political problems—at that time
fascism versus democracy; in the 1950s it was communism versus
democracy. In the 1960s political problems gave way to issues
surrounding the individual, and courses on "The Individual and
Society," "Understanding Human Values," and "Intergroup Relations" became more prevalent. But the ideal of education for civic
responsibility would not die. Several colleges—Broome Community
College (New York), for example—continued seeking ways of

educating students for democratic participation (Higginbottom, 1986).

Many colleges that tried such courses subsequently returned to distribution requirements based on a variety of courses. Santa Fe Community College (Florida) opened in 1966 with common courses in science, social science, and humanities. In 1972 the integrated courses were dropped and distribution requirements installed. When Miami-Dade opened in 1960, instructors were hired especially to develop and teach an integrated humanities course. Over the years, however, the course became eight weeks each of art, philosophy, music, literature—a mosaic pattern. The social science course remained integrated but evolved into popular psychology, human relations, and the quest for the self. The college did not build an integrated science course, and by 1977 students could satisfy the general education requirement in science by choosing two courses from a given list, the communications requirement by taking one course in English composition plus a literature elective (Lukenbill and McCabe, 1978). However, the pendulum swung again, and by 1978 Miami-Dade had developed a core of five multidisciplinary courses—"Communications," "The Social Environment," "The Natural Environment," "Humanities," and "The Individual"— which were still viable ten years later (S. Skidmore, personal communication, Sept. 1988).

Some other community colleges have installed integrated courses successfully. Los Medanos College (California) provides one example. In preparing a general education plan for the college in the mid-1970s, the organizers rejected many patterns of general education then existing. They had found that most California colleges were giving general education credit for virtually all academic transfer courses, and some were giving credit for certain vocational or technical courses. Any course that had even a tenuous connection with science, social science, or humanities was being used to satisfy a general education requirement. The organizers rejected those patterns in favor of a core of six generic courses in behavioral, social, biological, and physical sciences and in language arts and humanistic studies. Students were expected to enroll in one or, preferably, two of these courses each semester. The courses emphasized problem areas. The generic course in behavioral sciences was entitled "The Nature of People in Society" and dealt with such topics as variant life-styles, rationalism, and mysticism. The course in humanistic studies, entitled "The Creative Process," considered themes in current literature.

As the Los Medanos plan evolved, a second tier of courses was developed, centering on an interdisciplinary "Societal Issues" course required for all students seeking the associate degree. Subsequently, a third tier—consisting of intensified study of one issue under the instruction of a specialist in the field—was added. There, students selected from a variety of issues courses, such as "Bioethics" or "The Threat of Nuclear War," offered in each of the six curricular areas covered in the first tier. In the third tier students applied methods of ethical analysis to self-directed term projects. The three tiers constituted about half of the total of the sixty units required for the associate degree (Collins and Drexel, 1976; Case, 1988).

The Los Medanos College general education plan is notable less for its content than for the way it was organized. First, there was administrative coordination of the curriculum. Second, each course was required for all degree-seeking students. Third, the college employed a full-time staff development officer to work closely with the faculty in preparing the common course outlines. The result was that about one-third of the college's total enrollments were in the general education basic courses, although by 1988 the percentage had dropped as the college expanded into numerous other curricular areas. All this occurred in a college that draws its student population predominantly from a low-socioeconomic-status community with a high proportion of ethnic minorities.

Various other interdisciplinary combinations have been applied. Valencia Community College (Florida) developed an interdisciplinary studies program centering on a two-year core curriculum organized chronologically (Valencia Community College, 1984). In this program four courses—each including concepts from the arts, philosophy, religion, English, mathematics, social sciences, and physical sciences—were developed; and distinct guidelines for instructional methodologies were provided. Saint Petersburg Junior College (Florida) also established an interdisciplinary studies program incorporating a thirty-six-hour requirement in humanities, history, ethics, composition, speech, American government, and natural science into a comprehensive package (Wiley and Robinson, 1987). Monroe Community College's (New York) interdisciplinary program centered on human ecology (Harrison, 1987).

A few other such efforts might be mentioned, but in most community colleges the pursuit of general education is equated with sets of distribution requirements. In the typical institution students can meet these requirements by taking courses from a list arranged by department or division. The programs in liberal arts, business administration, general science, pre-engineering, accounting, architectural technology, and so on, state various numbers of minimum semester hours to be taken outside the main field. The social science electives may be selected from courses in anthropology, economics, political science, psychology, sociology; the science electives, from courses in physics, chemistry, biology, astronomy; the humanities electives, from courses in music appreciation, art history, literature, philosophy; and the courses in communication, from composition, speech, journalism, or writing. That is the most prevalent pattern. It satisfies the accrediting agencies, comfortable with it because of its familiarity, and the universities because it fits their own curricular mode. Few within the colleges question it. Their rationale is based on freedom of choice for the students. But the result is curricular chaos, mitigated hardly at all by the numerous attempts to specify which courses shall constitute a core of offerings acceptable to the senior institutions in a state. California's efforts are illustrative. The university's Academic Senate approved a "transfer core" curriculum but assured the faculty on each campus that it did "not affect prerequisites for majors, or such upper-division courses as are prescribed by differing campuses or programs" ("'Transfer Core' Curriculum . . . Is Approved by Assembly," 1988, p. 59). This kind of qualifying statement has destroyed general education transfer plans repeatedly in one state after another.

A Model General Education Plan

A general education pattern for all community college students can be devised if the staff adhere to certain premises.

Curriculum is not put together in a vacuum; it is not the responsibility of each professional person acting independently. A general education curriculum needs a faculty working together, a group coordinated by a dean or division head or program manager. This leads to the first premise: *Faculty role definition is essential.* General education cannot be considered only—or even primarily—classroom-centered. The faculty member who wants to hide behind the classroom door and develop courses and instructional strategies independently cannot beneficially participate in a general education program. The part-time instructor with only a casual commitment is of limited value as well. The general education program demands a corps of professional staff members who know how to differentiate their responsibilities.

The leadership for a general education program must come from a staff person whose sole responsibility is to further it. The president can set the tone for general education but is limited in influence on curriculum. Deans of instruction formerly dealt with general education, but in most colleges they have become senior-grade personnel managers. Assigning responsibility to the faculty in general is not sufficient; someone must be in charge. *A general education program must have a program head;* chair, dean, or director—the title is not important.

Third, the general education program should be *vertically integrated:* a program head and faculty members with designated responsibilities. Several technological programs have adopted this model. Wherever there is a program in nursing, for example, there is a director of nursing with staff members who attend to curriculum, student recruiting and admissions, student placement, and the instructional aspects of the program. General education must be similarly organized.

Next, the general education program should be *managed at the campus level.* Strasser (1977) suggested that each campus in his multicampus district should have its own philosophy and operational definition to guide the general education requirements, and he recognized the need for various patterns of general education at the college. He was on target because, apart from the managerial problems in trying to coordinate instructional programs on many campuses from a general office, the same type of program does not fit all campuses within a district. Although powerful forces are leading toward more homogeneity among campuses—and, indeed, among all colleges within a state—this trend can be turned around. But campus instructors and administrators must understand the importance of taking the leadership in curriculum development if they would avert centralized curriculum decision making.

A utopian model for effecting general education is offered here. The faculty would be organized into four divisions: Culture, Communications, Institutions, and Environment. Faculty members in these divisions would separate themselves from their academic departments or the other divisions into which the rest of the faculty was placed. The general education program would have its own budget. The faculty would prepare and operate the integrated courses, course modules, course-exemption examinations, student follow-up studies, and relationships with high schools and senior institutions. Funding such divisions would not be a problem; they would generate enough FTSEs to pay for all their efforts. They would do their own staff development as well.

Although each campus or each college would develop its own programs, it is possible to trace an outline of how the programs would operate. Begin with general education in the career education programs. First, a delegate from each of the four divisions would examine those programs to determine whether intervention might be made. Course modules—portions of courses to be inserted into the occupational programs—would be sought. As an example, in a fashion design program, the faculty from Institutions might prepare a short unit on the role of fashions in society; the Communications staff might do one on advertising copy and another on distribution, ordering, and inventory control; the Culture group would do one on fashion as folk art and another on traditional symbolism in fashion. For the allied health programs, general education modules in the process of grieving around the world and dealing with the terminal patient might be prepared by the Culture faculty; the faculty from Institutions would do a unit on medical ethics. The program in automotive maintenance and transport would be offered modules on energy utilization by the Environment staff; the laws governing highway construction and use, by the Institutions group; the automobile in American culture, by the Culture faculty.

These types of course sections, or modules, would be arranged in consultation with the career program faculty. They might start with one lecture only, tying the occupation to the broader theme, and eventually work into entire courses, depending on the success of the module and the apparent desirability of continuing it. They can attend to the meaning of work, to concepts surrounding the occupation at hand, to the values undergirding particular vocations. They can suggest options for the portion of the students' lives that is not involved with work. And they can expand students' capabilities within the occupation itself by examining the derivation of that function and how it is maintained in other cultures. Some instructors in the health fields have welcomed a unit of a course taught by an anthropologist that considers the puberty rites in various cultures around the world or a unit on the ethics of euthanasia presented by a philosophy teacher. Course modules on the Greek and Latin roots of medical terminology taught by instructors of classical languages have been successfully introduced. Some occupational programs have accepted entire courses in medical ethics or the rise of technology, courses that encompass the dynamics of the occupation and the themes and problems associated with it. Such courses could be pursued vigorously, and the career programs should pay the costs for such courses and course modules.

The four general education divisions would build their own courses for the students enrolled in the collegiate and compensatory programs. Each would do one course only, to be required for every student intending to obtain a certificate or a degree. The courses would be organized around themes, not around academic disciplines. The intent of each would be to point up how contemporary and past, local and distant peoples have dealt with the problems common to all: communications, energy use, social institutions, the search for truth, beauty, and order. The courses would be prepared by the general education staff, specialists in that curriculum form. Their goal: a free people in a free society, thinking critically, appreciating their cultural tradition, understanding their environment and their place within it.

The general education faculty on each campus would build its own four required courses, and, depending on local conditions, there would be great variation among them. The Communications staff might do a course called "How We Communicate," dealing with propaganda, advertising, interpersonal communications, and literary criticism—not criticism of Joyce, Steinbeck, and Salinger but of such contemporary literary forms as the administrative memo, the protest statement, the news release. Students would learn to read the language behind the words.

The Institutions staff might build a course around "People and Their Institutions." This would not be a "Survey of Social Science" or a "History of Western Civilization" course; it would emphasize how people have had to grapple with social institutions throughout the history of civilized society. How did the English kings impinge on the lives of their people? How were the pharaohs able to organize the populace into tremendous labor gangs? What is the grip that modern China has on the minds of its people? How must we deal with our own bureaus and commissions? Here, too, knowledge of the terminology in academic disciplines, the jargon of the specialists, would not be the proper goal.

The Culture staff might do a course on "People and Culture." The theme would be how people have attempted to come to grips with the ultimate questions of all humanity: Who are we? Where did we come from? What mark can we leave? The content would be the types of self-expression through art, music, literature, and dance. Comparative religion would be part of this course only if it were based on the question "Why religion at all?" The way novelists have tried to speak to the human condition would be explored.

The course on "The Environment" could incorporate elements of astronomy, biology, physics—all the earth, life, and physical sciences. It would be concerned with the effects of technology, patterns of energy consumption, shifting concepts in earth and space sciences, how agricultural engineering can be used to solve the problem of famine, what can be known through empirical science and what can be known only through intuition, introspection, or revelation.

The pattern of each faculty group having responsibility for

one large theme-centered course would allow general education to have its own organizing principles. The course would not offer a few weeks of instruction in each academic discipline, lest it fracture along disciplinary lines. If provision were made for a student to exempt or test out of the course, the general education program staff would develop and administer its own examination or other measure of knowledge sufficiency.

Nothing in this type of reorganization would do away with the specialized courses; the college would still teach "Spanish for Correctional Officers," "General Chemistry," "Introduction to Music," and the hundreds of other discipline-based courses that make up a full curriculum. However, the four theme-centered courses might supplant most of the general or introductory courses now offered.

The general education staff would build modules and specifically designed courses for the occupational students, theme-centered courses for the transfer students, and yet another type of course for the large and growing number of continuing education students. These students, attending the institution part-time, picking up courses that strike their fancy because of current interest or because of the social interaction that the college offers, deserve something different. Naturally, they would be invited to enroll in the major theme-centered courses; however, they need special problems courses, an extension of the problems touched on in the broader themes courses.

A model for this group is afforded through current practice in community college adult divisions and university extension divisions, in which around one-fourth of the courses are for general enlightenment. Here is where the specialized course of local interest comes into play. If sufficient interest in the history of a local labor dispute or the latest theories about astronomical black holes can be found, the general education faculty would take part, either by offering such a course or by enlisting the ad hoc assistance of other staff members. The important point is that these courses be offered and their availability advertised. It would be incumbent on the general education faculty to tap community interest in, set up, and promote these courses. The common characteristic of the courses is that they must be educative; they must not be presentations of unknown effect.

The instructional forms used in these courses can be as varied as necessary. Members of a general education faculty of the type described may find that they need to write their own extensive syllabi and text materials. They would probably find it expedient to divide responsibilities, some of them lecturing, others building reproducible media, others writing and administering examinations. But they must stay together as a group organized to provide integrated general education. They will find little difficulty in attaining accreditation of such courses and approval by transferring institutions. The community colleges are in a better position than ever in their history to articulate and defend their general education offerings; the senior institutions cannot be excessively stringent in their interpretation of what shall be qualified for credit at a time when nearly half of the college freshmen begin in two-year institutions.

To conclude, this form of general education can and should be constructed. The greatest impediment to it is within the institution itself. A sufficient number of college leaders—trustees, administrators, and the instructors themselves—must see the urgency of this pattern of curriculum development. The conflict is between pluralism as a goal—every person studying when, how, and where he or she wants—and the use of curriculum as an aid to social integration. If individualism is raised to such heights that the common themes underlying the free person in the free society cannot be perceived, it will be impossible to devise a core curriculum.

Issues

Building a general education program in the community colleges will be no easier in the future than it was in the past. The same centrifugal forces operate to fractionate the curriculum.

How can people trained in a discipline become broad enough to develop interdisciplinary courses? What are the implications for staff development? How are general education leaders trained?

How can the notion of individualism, of every student's right to define his or her own curriculum, be reconciled with requiring certain courses?

Will career education faculty and advisory groups feel that general education requirements have usurped their prerogatives? If so, how can they be convinced that general education benefits their clients?

Can general education courses be credible for university transfer if they enroll all students entering community colleges? Would the universities reject transfers from courses that enrolled the poorly prepared students?

Can the staff in all higher education accept the definition of general education as providing basic understandings for people to act as citizens, rather than as practitioners in narrowly based professions or academic disciplines?

In some states the community colleges have been relegated to a role as career and compensatory education centers. Will this role preclude their offering an appropriate form of general education?

The threat to the academic content of community college education did not come from career education—the technical programs often made rigorous demands on their students. It came from the colleges that offered a few presentations on television, a sizable number of community service programs, and credit courses in hundreds of locations with noncredit options—all with no attempt to ensure that the presentations were educative. The threat came also from the colleges' proudly stated policies that encouraged all to drop in when they want, take what they want, and drop out when they want—the ultimate in curriculum disintegration. A curriculum centered on general education could restore institutional integrity while promoting the form of social cohesion that derives from shared beliefs and people making informed decisions.

Thirteen

The Social Role:

*A Response
to the Critics*

Few serious scholars have been concerned with the community
colleges, even though they enroll more than one-third of all
students in higher education. The scholarly community has tended
to allow institutional spokespersons free rein. Marshall McLuhan is
said to have observed, "If you want to learn about water, don't ask
the fish." Yet people who have wanted to understand the community colleges of America have had little choice; few other than those
within them spoke up.

When the community college is examined by outsiders, the
commentary usually takes the form of criticizing the institution in
its social role or the institution as a school. In the first of these
criticisms, the college is often seen in a negative light. It is an agent
of capitalism, training workers to fit business and industry; it is a
tool of the upper classes, designed to keep the poor in their place by
denying them access to the baccalaureate and, concomitantly, to
higher-status positions in society. When it is criticized as a school,
questions are raised about its success in teaching: do these colleges
really teach the basic skills that the lower schools failed to impart?
Can they provide a foundation for the higher learning? Here, too,
the answers are usually negative; since the community colleges pass
few of their students through to the senior institutions, they are said
to have failed the test.

342

Criticizing the Role

Several distressingly similar papers have taken community colleges to task for their failure to assist in leveling the social-class structure of America. Karabel (1972) asserted that the community college is an element both in educational inflation and in the American system of class-based tracking. The massive community college expansion of the 1950s and 1960s, he said, was due to an increase in the proportion of technical and professional workers in the labor force. This increase caused people who wanted any job other than the lowest-paying to seek postsecondary training, thus contributing to a heightened pressure for admission to higher education in general. Hence educational inflation: an increased percentage of people attending school and staying longer. But the system of social stratification has not changed: "Apparently, the extension of educational opportunity, however much it may have contributed to other spheres such as economic productivity and the general cultural level of the society, has resulted in little or no change in the overall extent of social mobility and economic equality" (pp. 525–526). Students yes, equality no.

Karabel cited data showing that community college students were less likely to be from the higher socioeconomic classes than were students at four-year colleges or universities. They were more likely to be from families whose breadwinner was a skilled or semiskilled worker, had not completed grammar school or had not completed high school, and was not a college graduate. (Not incidentally, these facts had been noted by Koos, the first analyst of junior colleges, fifty years earlier.) Karabel added that most community college students aspired to higher degrees but rarely attained them and that students of lower social-class origins were more likely than others to drop out.

Karabel accepted the notion that lower-class students were tracked into occupational programs as a way of deflecting their aspirations for higher degrees and higher-status employment, noting that the local business people supported this tracking because of their desire for docile workers. Other supporters of community college occupational programs included the federal government through its vocational education funds; the American

Association of Junior Colleges, which, "almost since its founding in 1920, has exerted its influence to encourage the growth of vocational education" (p. 546); and the university, which, "paradoxically, . . . finds itself in a peculiar alliance with industry, foundations, government, and established higher education associations to vocationalize the community college" (p. 547).

Some years later Karabel (1986) argued that the research conducted since he put forth his thesis had confirmed his perspective: "With a far greater body of empirical evidence now available, the fundamental argument may be stated again with even greater confidence: Far from embodying the democratization of higher education and a redistribution of opportunity in the wider society, the expansion of the community college instead heralded the arrival in higher education of a form of class-linked tracking that served to reproduce existing social relations. . . . The overall impact of the community college has been to accentuate rather than reduce prevailing patterns of social and class inequality" (p. 18).

Zwerling (1976) echoed the thesis that the community college plays an essential role in maintaining the pyramid of American social and economic structure: "It has become just one more barrier put between the poor and the disenfranchised and a decent and respectable stake in the social system which they seek" (p. xvii). The chief function of the community college is to "assist in channeling young people to essentially the same relative positions in the social structure that their parents already occupy" (p. 33). The institution controls mobility between classes, keeping higher-class people from dropping down and people in the lower classes from moving up. Zwerling insisted that the community college is remarkably effective at controlling mobility because its students come primarily from the lowest socioeconomic classes of college attenders, its dropout rate is the highest of any college population, and dropouts and graduates alike enter lower-level occupations than the equivalent students who attend higher-status colleges. This dropout rate is "related to a rather deliberate process of channeling students to positions in the social order that are deemed appropriate for them" (p. 35).

Zwerling was consistent. He contended that the expansion of occupational education in the community college was "an ingenious way of providing large numbers of students with *access* to schooling without disturbing the shape of the social structure" (p. 61). He showed that in states where the community colleges were at the bottom tier of the postsecondary education hierarchy, they received less money per student than the senior institutions. Hence, the lowest-income-level students had the least spent on them.

Ten years later Zwerling (1986) extended his argument about the limitations of class mobility, asserting that continuing education also acts as "a regressive force in our society" (p. 55). He found adult education classes populated by the wealthier people, who use them to enhance their employment credentials and to solve individual life crises. In the interests of equity, the colleges should be more accessible to low-income students. Lifelong learning should "contribute to social change and to a society where merit, not privilege, is rewarded" (p. 59).

Pincus, another writer in the same genre, also discussed the community colleges in terms of class conflict, with a particular emphasis on their role as occupational education centers. He traced the development of the occupational function, showing how it fit everyone's needs exactly: "Corporations get the kind of workers they need; four-year colleges do not waste resources on students who will drop out; students get decent jobs; and the political dangers of an excess of college graduates are avoided" (Pincus, 1980, p. 333). And he alleged that "business and government leaders—those at the top of the heap—regard postsecondary vocational education as a means of solving the political and economic problems created by the rising expectations of the working class" (p. 356).

Pincus deplored the unemployment rates for college graduates, saying that "between one fourth and one half of those graduates who found jobs were 'underemployed'; that is, they held jobs that did not require a college degree" (p. 332). And he cited Clark's (1960) cooling-out thesis: "These two-year colleges screen out students who did not have the skills to complete a bachelor's degree and, instead, channel them toward an appropriate vocational program" (p. 333). He showed that nonwhite and low-SES students were more likely to attend community colleges than senior institutions and were more likely to be enrolled in the occupational programs than in the transfer programs. In justice to Pincus, he did conclude that "capitalism in the United States cannot always deliver what it promises. There are a limited number of decent, well-paid jobs, and most working-class and nonwhite young people are not destined to get them. Vocational education does not and cannot change this" (pp. 355–356). His argument, then, was less with the schools than with the system itself.

However, Pincus (1986, p. 49) also concluded that "there is no good evidence that vocational education in community colleges delivers on the promises of secure employment, decent pay, and ample career opportunities." One of his major contentions was that students who enter community college occupational programs are not told the full story about the chances of their obtaining employment in the field for which they are being prepared. If they were, they would probably enter the transfer programs, because the rewards for obtaining the baccalaureate are all out of proportion in comparison to those that a student in a career program might expect.

Other commentators have also contended that the career programs divert students from lower-class backgrounds away from baccalaureate studies. Levine (1986) postulated a cabal, based in the colleges themselves: "Faced with a potential student body increasingly large and diverse in socioeconomic backgrounds and interests, . . . educators encouraged the formation of a new type of postsecondary education devoted to semi-professional vocational training" (p. 183). It was easy for him to conclude, then, that "the interests and needs of the many who attended the junior college to prepare for the university were frustrated by educators' elitist intentions" (p. 184). Richardson and Bender (1987), in their treatise on minority access and achievement, pointed out that, despite increased college attendance rates, "there has been little change in economic and social class mobility for minorities because their curriculum choices have been so concentrated in the career and vocational areas" (p. 1). They argued further that "concentrating occupational offerings on campuses serving the highest proportion of minorities while concurrently permitting transfer programs to decline in availability and quality" leads minority students to "become vocational/technical majors because no viable alternatives are provided to them" (pp. 44–45).

Data to support the arguments regarding class-based tracking are easy to find. After examining patterns of college going in Illinois, Tinto (1973) concluded that low-SES students who go to community colleges are more likely to drop out than their counterparts who attend senior institutions. Katz (1967) studied a California community college and determined that it did not equalize opportunity because it did not provide equal educational outcomes. His conclusion was that the college helped maintain the social-class structure because the lower-class students tended to drop out earlier; the dropout was occasioned because of the economic sacrifice of attending school and because of the middle-class character of the school itself. Using national data, Astin (1977) showed that—even when students were equated for entering ability, parental income, and aspirations—those entering community colleges were more likely to drop out. He concluded, "For the eighteen-year-old pursuing a bachelor's degree, the typical community college offers . . . decreased chances of completing the degree" (p. 255). (However, he subsequently qualified his comment, acknowledging that the regression analysis statistics that he used accounted for only around 25 percent of the variance in degree attainment, with the remainder probably due to some unquantified combination of institutional environment and student characteristics.)

These jeremiads are more politically inspired than empirically founded. At bottom, those who pronounce them are less antagonistic to the community college than they are to what they perceive as a pernicious American social-class system, which they wish were more equitable. The arguments are decades old, different now only in that they name the community college as the villain. Schools at all levels have long been criticized for failing to overturn the social-class system. In 1944 Warner and his colleagues asserted that Americans were not sufficiently conscious of the class structure and the place of the schools in it. They felt that lack of understanding of the class system would lead eventually to a loss of social solidarity. Their concern was for equality of opportunity, for curricular differentiation, and for teaching people to accept the idea of social status.

More recently the belief in the inevitability of the class structure has become less pronounced, confounded now with social justice, equality of opportunity, cultural deprivation, and a determination to correct the abuses historically heaped onto certain peoples. The fact that blacks, Hispanics, and other identifiable ethnic groups tend to be overrepresented in the lower socioeconomic classes has contributed to this confusion. Americans historically have had as a common belief a distinct distrust of anyone who preaches class consciousness. That distrust now is manifested as an abhorrence of anyone who suggests the idea of class, because the suggestion is tantamount to racism. Therefore, those who say that the number of people with qualifications for top jobs is quite small, that by definition not enough high-status jobs are available for everyone, and that people are not born equal but instead have diverse potentialities are termed racists endeavoring to maintain their privileged positions by keeping the lower classes in their place. By extension, an institution that predominantly serves the lower classes becomes a racist institution, a tool of the capitalists.

Criticizing the School

A second set of criticisms pertains to the community colleges as schools. Can they really teach the basic skills that the lower schools failed to impart? Do they provide a foundation for the higher learning? Do their students learn the proper skills and attitudes that will enable them to succeed on jobs or in senior institutions? Stripping away the rhetoric and social implications reduces these questions to the following: How many occupational education students obtain jobs in the field for which they were trained? How many students transfer to the senior colleges? How well have they been prepared for upper-division studies?

Although reliable nationwide data are not available on the degrees of success achieved by students in career programs, some statewide studies have been reported, as noted in Chapter Eight. These studies indicate that most students in most programs obtain employment in the field for which they have been prepared; the better the program is organized and integrated with the local businesses and employers, the more successful its graduates. Placement rates range from 90 percent or more in the health fields down to 50 percent or less in real estate and office work.

Data on the numbers of students who transfer from community colleges to four-year colleges and universities are scattered because the ways of counting transfers vary greatly from system to system and from state to state. Patterns of student flow have never been linear; they swirl, with students dropping in and out of both community colleges and universities, taking courses in both types of institutions concurrently, transferring from one to another frequently. Among the students in junior standing at a university may be included some who took their lower-division work in a community college and in the university concurrently, some who started as freshmen in the university but who dropped out to attend a community college and subsequently returned, some who took summer courses at community colleges, some who attended a community college and failed to enroll in the university until several years later, and some who transferred from the community college to the university in midyear. In some reports *none* of these students would be considered community college transfers; in others *all* of them would.

One certainty about transfer is that it is notably greater wherever a university and the community colleges in its region work closely together. In such cases the university's upper division may have more transfers than native freshmen. Arizona State University and the University of Massachusetts at Boston serve as examples of this pattern. The critics say that the community college is doing a poor job as a feeder institution to the universities, that it serves as grades 13 and 14 for only a small percentage of its matriculants and "cools out" the others. A more accurate interpretation is that community college enrollments in adult education and occupational certificate programs have grown so that they have driven the *percentage* of transfers down to a minuscule level. Although a majority of the graduates of the California State University System have had some community college studies in their background, fewer than 50,000 of the one million students enrolled for credit in California community colleges transfer in any one year.

What happens to the students after they get to the universities? For decades studies found that their grades were lower than those earned by upper-division students who had entered the university as freshmen; that they were less likely to graduate; and that those who did obtain baccalaureate degrees took longer to get them. Menke (1980) reviewed around one hundred studies and found that most of them corroborated the drop in grades suffered by transfers. However, as noted in Chapter Two, more recent data suggest that, although the transfers still take longer to obtain the baccalaureate, the grade differential is negligible.

Responding to the Critics

The community colleges are not selective, residential collegiate institutions. The data about their matriculants may be interpreted in various ways; but it is certain that, *in the aggregate,* students prepared in community college career programs earn less over a lifetime than those who receive baccalaureate or graduate degrees. It is also certain that, *in the aggregate,* students who begin collegiate studies in community colleges are more likely to drop out or, if they do go on to the baccalaureate, to take longer in obtaining it.

What else can we say to the critics? They are on firm ground when they present data showing that relatively small percentages of community college matriculants transfer; that the community colleges enroll sizable percentages of minority students and students from low-SES background; and that, of those students who do transfer, the smallest percentage is among students from the minorities and lower-income groups. But their conclusions are not always warranted. Several of the commentators suggest elevating the class consciousness of community college students so that they become aware of the social trap into which they have been led. Zwerling (1976) recommends that students should be shown how they are being channeled within the social-class structure; they should know that the school is an instrument of power, so that they can act to resist it. Pincus (1980, p. 356) similarly seeks to elevate class consciousness: "If community college educators want to help working-class and minority students, they should provide them with a historical and political context from which to understand the dismal choices they face. Vocational education students might then begin to raise some fundamental questions about the legitimacy of educational, political, and economic institutions in the United States."

Other critics reach different conclusions. Some want to make the community colleges equal to the universities somehow, so that the low-SES students who attend them will have an equal chance at obtaining baccalaureate degrees and higher-status positions. Zwerling (1976) suggests converting all two-year colleges into four-year institutions. Astin (1977) suggests equating funding so that the community colleges and universities get the same number of dollars per student. He goes further and suggests that "states or municipalities that wish to expand opportunities for such students should consider alternatives to building additional community colleges or expanding existing ones. Although community colleges are generally less expensive to construct and operate than four-year colleges, their 'economy' may be somewhat illusory, particularly when measured in terms of the cost of producing each baccalaureate recipient" (p. 55). Karabel (1972) at least acknowledges that increasing the proportion of funds going to community colleges or transforming those institutions into baccalaureate degree–granting structures would not seriously affect the larger pattern of class-based tracking. He admits that the colleges are caught in a dilemma: If they increase their occupational offerings, they increase the likelihood that they will track the lower-class students into lower-class occupations, and if they try to maintain comprehensiveness, they increase the likelihood that their students will drop out without attaining any degree or certificate.

And so the critics skirt the notion of the community college as an agency enhancing equal opportunity. Faced with the unreconcilable problem of social equalization, they present draconian solutions. Suppose all two-year colleges were converted into four-year institutions. Would all colleges and their students then miraculously become equal? There is a pecking order among institutions that even now are ostensibly the same. Harvard and Northeastern University, the University of California and Pepperdine University, the University of Chicago and Northern Illinois University all offer the doctorate. But in the eyes of the public, they are not equivalent. Authorizing the community colleges to offer the bachelor's degree would not change public perceptions of their relative merit; it would merely establish a bottom stratum of former two-year colleges among the senior institutions.

Suppose funding were equalized. Would the colleges then contribute less to the maintenance of a class structure? Perhaps two-year colleges would teach better if sizable funds were diverted from the universities and run to them. Perhaps they would not. But one thing is certain: The major research universities would be crippled. That eventuality might well satisfy those critics who are obsessed with the idea of social class. They would argue that the power of the schools to maintain the social-class structure could be reduced quite as effectively by chopping down the top-rank institutions as by uplifting those serving the lower groups.

One response to the critics might be that the community colleges are no more able to overturn the class structure of the nation than the lower schools have been, that all schools are relatively low-influence environments when compared with other social institutions. But the critics' fundamental flaw is that *they have attempted to shift the meaning of educational equality from individual to group mobility.* If equal opportunity means allowing people from any social, ethnic, or religious group to have the same chance to enter higher education as people from any other group, the goal is both worthy and attainable. And few would question the community colleges' contribution to the breaking down of social, ethnic, financial, and geographical barriers to college attendance. But when that concept is converted to *group* mobility, its meaning changes, and it is put beyond the reach of the schools. Ben-David (1977, pp. 158–159) put it well: "Higher education can make a real contribution to social justice only by effectively educating properly prepared, able, and motivated individuals from all classes and groups. . . . Higher education appears to have been primarily a channel of individual mobility. . . . It can provide equal opportunities to all, and it may be able to help the disadvantaged to overcome inherited educational disabilities. But it cannot ensure the equal distribution of educational success among classes or other politically active groups." In sum, neither the community colleges nor any other form of school can break down class distinctions. They cannot move entire ethnic groups from one social stratum to another. They cannot ensure the equal distribution of educational results.

Suppose the figures on the percentage of students who transfer to universities are incorrect. Certainly, the data are not reliable. Suppose the number of students who transfer short of completing a community college program, or who take only a few courses in the community college prior to or concurrent with their university matriculation, were added in. What if the transfer rate, up in recent years because of tightened matriculation procedures, were doubled? Would it matter to the critics? The colleges still would not be doing their part in the critics' fanciful dream of class leveling. Warner and his associates (1944, p. 145) said: "The decision to be made by those who disapprove of our present inequality and who wish to change it is not between a system of inequality and equality; the choice is among various systems of rank. Efforts to achieve democratic living by abolishing the social system are utopian and not realistic."

Ordinarily, it serves neither education nor society well when the schools are accused of misleading their clients by making promises on which they cannot collect. Such charges can have the effect of generating public disaffection, on the one hand, and, on the other, intemperate reactions by educators. Many commentators, past and present, have been guilty of exaggerated claims that the community college would democratize American society if only all geographical, racial, academic, financial, motivational, and institutional barriers to attendance were removed (witness the title of Medsker and Tillery's 1971 book on the community colleges, *Breaking the Access Barriers*). But criticizing the rhetoric is one thing; criticizing the institution itself is quite another. Although there has been no public outcry against the community colleges, should one arise, it will be difficult to tell whether the reaction is directed against the institution itself or toward the image that its advocates have fostered and the claims they have made.

The critics' conclusions that the community college is the manifestation of an insidious conspiracy against the poor are not warranted. Any student's progress to a baccalaureate is hindered by various processes in the community colleges and the four-year colleges: in the community colleges, by the low academic selectivity and paucity of dormitories and on-campus work opportunities; in the four-year colleges, by the failure to accept credits uniformly, the scarcity of financial aid for transfers, and the unfamiliar environment. Student commitment and persistence interact with those processes in some way that no one has satisfactorily revealed. Dougherty (1988) concluded that it seems more a political question, with the defenders of ethnic minorities arguing that institutional factors are more important and the defenders of the institutions contending that the students' ability and motivations are paramount.

Using the data from the National Longitudinal Study of the High School Graduating Class of 1972 and subsequent surveys sponsored by the U.S. Education Department, some researchers (Velez, 1985; Pascarella, Smart, and Ethington, 1986; Anderson, 1981) have found that where a student begins college has an important effect on baccalaureate attainment and that students who reside or have jobs on campus are much more likely to persist. However, although the conclusions are logical, the statistics are questionable. Putting variables in a regression equation assumes equivalency at the outset. The NLS data assume that all people in the sample had an equivalent chance to enter the university as freshmen, that the universities had classroom space and residence halls available to accommodate everyone—clearly not so.

Students who start at a community college instead of a university are less likely to obtain bachelor's degrees. Much of the difference relates not only to the differing environments but also to the logistics of moving from one institution to another. The phenomenon may be similar to that experienced by people who have to change planes en route to a destination, as compared with those who have nonstop accommodations. Those who must change may miss their connection because of flight delays or cancellations, or they might get diverted because they have met friends in the connecting airport. But no one accuses the airlines of attempting to subvert their clients' intentions. How will the analysts interpret the data regarding the 1988 University of California freshman class? Around 10,000 *qualified* applicants could not be accommodated. Many of them had to begin their higher education careers in one of the state's community colleges. Undoubtedly, for them, baccalaureate attainment will be slightly less likely. Was the selection process the result of an elitists' plot, or was it instituted because of lack of space for a sudden surge of applicants?

The Inevitability of the Allocative Function

Granted that the community colleges are part of an educational system within a larger social system in which numerous institutions sort, certify, ticket, and route people to various stations, what are the options? We could say that society should not be structured along class lines, that it should not support institutions that tend to allocate people to status positions. Those who hold to that view would do well to seek to change the social structure by modifying some considerably more powerful influences—the tax structure, for example. But as long as there are hierarchies of social class (and all societies have them), some social institutions will operate as allocative agencies.

Clark analyzed the allocative function in community colleges and in 1960 applied the term *cooling out* to describe it. He showed that the process began with preentrance testing, shunting the lower-ability students to remedial classes and eventually nudging them out of the transfer track into a terminal curriculum. The crucial components of the process were that alternatives to the person's original aspirations were provided; the aspiration was reduced in a consoling way, encouraging gradual disengagement; and the students were not sent away as failures but were shown the relative values of career and academic choices short of the baccalaureate degree.

Twenty years later Clark (1980) reexamined his thesis, asking whether the cooling-out function might be replaced by some other process and whether the roles of community colleges could be altered so that the process would be unnecessary. He named six options: preselection of students, to take place in the secondary schools or at the door of the community college; transfer-track selection, which would bar the students from enrolling in courses offering transfer credit; open failure, whereby students who did not pass the courses would be required to leave the institution; guaranteed graduation, which would have the effect of passing everyone through and depositing the problem at the doorstep of the next institution in line; reduction of the distinction between transfer and terminal programs, which could be done if the community colleges had no concern about the percentages of their students who succeed in universities; and making the structural changes that would eliminate the two-year colleges' transfer function, convert all two-year institutions into four-year ones, or do away with community colleges entirely.

Clark rejected all those alternatives, saying that preselection "runs against the grain of American populist interpretations of educational justice which equate equity with open doors" (p. 19); limiting the number of people who can take courses for transfer credit would shatter the transfer program at a time when students are in short supply; open failure is too public and is becoming less a feature in four-year colleges as well as in community colleges because it seems inhumane; the dangers of guaranteed graduation have already been realized in the secondary schools ("Everyone is equally entitled to credentials that have lost their value," p. 21); reducing the distinction between transfer and terminal courses "has limits beyond which lies a loss of legitimacy of the community college *qua* college . . . (auto repairing is not on a par with history or calculus as a college course)" (p. 22); and doing away with the community colleges is unlikely because of the reluctance of senior college faculties to esteem two-year programs and because of the continued and growing need for short-cycle courses or courses such as those offered in university extension divisions.

Clark concluded: "The problem that causes colleges to respond with the cooling-out effort is not going to go away by moving it inside of other types of colleges. *Somebody* has to make that effort, or pursue its alternatives" (pp. 23-24). He pointed to examples in other countries, where the longer the higher education system held out against short-cycle institutions and programs, the greater the problem when educators tried to open the system to wide varieties of students coming for numerous purposes. The trend there is toward greater differentiation of types of institutions and degrees, but "the dilemma is still there: Either you keep some aspirants out by selection or you admit everyone and then take your choice between seeing them all through, or flunking out some, or cooling out some" (p. 28). As he put it, "Any system of higher education that has to reconcile such conflicting values as equity, competence, and individual choice—and the advanced democracies are so committed—has to effect compromise procedures that allow for some of each. The cooling-out process is one of the possible compromises, perhaps even a necessary one" (p. 30). In sum, even if the college only matches people with jobs, providing connections, credentials, and short-term, ad hoc learning experiences—even if it is not the gateway to the higher learning for everyone that some commentators wish it were—these functions must be performed by some social agency.

What the Colleges Really Provide

The real benefit of the community college cannot be measured by the extent to which it contributes to the overthrow of the social-class system in America. Nor can it be measured by the extent to which the college changes the mores of its community. It is a system for individuals, and it does what the best educational forms have always done: It helps individuals learn what they need to know to be effective, responsible members of their society. The colleges can and do make it easier for people to move between social classes. And even though they cannot make learned scholars of television-ridden troglodytes, they can and should show their constituents what it means to be involved in a community where learning is the raison d'être. As long as the community college maintains its place in the mainstream of graded education, it provides a channel of upward mobility for individuals of any age. Those who deplore its failure to overturn inequities between classes do a disservice to its main function and tend to confuse the people who have looked on it as the main point of access to, exit from, and reentry to higher education—the lungs of the system.

There is a difference between social equalization and equal access, between overturning the social-class structure and allowing people to move from one stratum to another. The college that teaches best uplifts its community most. People must learn in college, or what is it for? More learning equals a better college; less learning, a poorer college; no learning, no college. The fact that the community colleges serve minority students, marginally capable students, and other groups never before served by the higher education establishment does not mean they have abandoned their commitment to teach.

A person who receives a degree or certificate and who does not work in the field in which that certificate was earned does not represent an institutional indictment unless no other programs were available to the person. If the community college were a participant in an educational system that said to potential matriculants, "You may enter but only if you are particularly qualified and only in *this* program," subsequent failure to obtain employment in that field might be cause for dismay. But the community college does not operate that way; most of its programs are open to all who present themselves. When programs do have selective admissions, as in dental hygiene, nursing, and some of the higher-level technologies, most entrants graduate and obtain positions in the fields for which they were trained. When programs are open to everyone, as in most of the less professionalized trades, the chances that a matriculant will complete the curriculum and begin working in that field are markedly reduced. "Dropout" is a reflection of the structure of a program. An institution, or a program within that institution, that places few barriers to student matriculation cannot expect a high rate of program completion.

For better or worse, the cooling-out function has worked less well in recent years. All the structural components of the cooling-out process are still in place—English placement examinations, career-planning guidance seminars, and so on—but the community college's allocative function is less effective. Clark (1980) has acknowledged that his thesis was tentative and deplores the way that it has been used: "The trouble with the leap to grand theory is that, poorly grounded in empirical research, it is particularly vulnerable to ideology of various persuasions" (p. 30). Palmer's (1987a) work should go a long way toward deflating the notion of cooling out, by showing that the transfer and occupational tracks are less separate than the funding formulas and the way that the curriculum is organized would suggest.

The students use the collegiate and the career programs alike, as though they each were providing a single set of courses that one

may take depending on his or her goals at the time. The community
college now seems to be enhancing lateral career shifts and teaching
current employees skills useful in different jobs within the same
industry, as much as it promotes vertical mobility through progress
toward the baccalaureate. The elitists and conspirators may have
hoped to divert the masses into vocational studies, but the students
are remarkably resilient.

What Are the Alternatives to Community Colleges?

It is possible to sketch the outlines of alternative institutions
that would perform the tasks now performed by community
colleges. Yet there is no point in taking an ahistorical approach to
postsecondary education. Tempting as it is, a view of higher education, of what students need, of what would be good for society,
without a corresponding view of the institutions in their social
context is not very useful. To start with the questions of what
individuals need or what society needs is nice; but, regardless of the
answers, the current institutions will not disappear. Institutional
needs are as real as individual and social needs; in fact, they may be
more valid as beginning points for analysis because they offer
somewhat unified positions that have developed over time, whereas
"individual" and "social" needs are as diverse as anyone cares to
make them. And it is thoroughly out of line to pose a view of society with no educational institutions but with everyone learning
through the mass media and the home computer. The desire for
social interaction is too strong; the demand for certification that
must be awarded by some institution is too great.

Any imagined institution must be postulated totally; that is,
what changes will be made in funding patterns, institutional organization, role of the professionals within the institution, people's
use of their time? The institution's goals must be stated realistically;
we have for too long suffered the open-ended goals of those who
would break all access barriers; would see all citizens enrolled
successively throughout their lifetime; would envisage the community college taking on functions previously performed not only
by the higher and the lower schools but also by welfare agencies,

unemployment bureaus, parks and recreation departments, and community-help organizations.

Can we develop a learning community? Some evidence suggests we can. People are enrolling in university extension and taking classes in the community colleges for their own interest. A sizable cohort will attend school without being compelled. In addition, the number of ways that individuals gain information and that society stores and transmits it has grown enormously.

On the negative side are the individual needs for structured learning situations, the discipline of learning, the sequence that learning demands. Many forms of learning simply do not lend themselves to instant apprehension and immediate applicability; they build one on the other, and a disciplined situation is necessary to hold the learner in the proper mode until the structure is complete. It would also be difficult to fund the infinite variety of learning situations that would be required. Most of the voluntary learning situations now are funded either by the individuals partaking of them or as adjuncts to more structured institutions.

It is possible to pose alternatives to the community college and stay within the context of existing social institutions. In 1968 Devall offered five such alternatives: proprietary trade schools; on-the-job training; universal national service; university extension divisions; and off-campus courses under expanding divisions of continuing education operated by the universities. Certainly, if the community colleges were to lose their funding, most of the services they currently provide could be maintained through expansion of these other agencies. But it is not clear that other agencies could do a better job. Proprietary trade schools do not enjoy a history unmarred by excessive claims, inflated costs, fraudulent advertising, and marginally useful instruction. These schools appear as shining lights only to those who feel that the for-profit sector invariably does a better job than the nonprofit institutions do.

The other options would also lead to unintended consequences. On-the-job training would narrow educational opportunity by focusing the learner's attention solely on the tasks to be performed, and it would shift the burden of payment to business corporations that might not benefit therefrom if the trained workers chose to take positions with competitors. Universal national service suggests compulsion; it would extend the grip that public agencies have on individuals and, in effect, prolong the period of mandatory school attendance. Expansion of university extension divisions would have the effect of turning program monitoring back to the universities. But it would also place the programs on a self-supporting basis and would thus deny participation to people with limited discretionary funds. And expanding the university divisions of continuing education would place adult basic education, literacy training, and similar lower-school functions under the egis of an institution that throughout history has attempted to divest itself of them.

The percentage of community college matriculants who go on to the baccalaureate varies greatly between institutions. It depends on the vigor with which students interested in other outcomes are recruited and on an institution's relations with its neighboring university. And although the colleges provide career, compensatory, and community education, they are certainly not going to surrender the university-parallel portion of their curriculum. If they did, they would be denying access to higher education to those of their students who do go on, particularly to the minorities and other students from families in which college going is not the norm. They would betray their own staff members who entered the institution with the intent of teaching college courses. They would no longer serve as the safety valve for the universities, which can shunt the poorly prepared petitioners for admission to these alternative colleges and which would otherwise be forced to mount massive remedial programs of their own or face the outrage of people denied access.

Some states have multiple college systems and so separate the collegiate from other functions. The Wisconsin Vocational, Technical, and Adult Education Centers perform all community college functions except for the university lower-division courses; Wisconsin has a university-center system with numerous branch campuses of the state university doing the collegiate work. In South Carolina, state technical colleges coexist with branch campuses of the university. The North Carolina system operates both technical institutes and community colleges. These and other alternative structures can also be found in large community college districts. Coast Community College District (California) has two full-service,

comprehensive community colleges along with one institution
devoted exclusively to short-cycle education, open-circuit broadcast-
ing, and community services. In sum, the institutional forms adapt,
but all functions are maintained.

We do not necessarily need new structures. Many forms of
reorganization in our existing community colleges can be made to
accommodate the changing clientele. Some of the more successful
adaptations have been made in occupational programs in which the
liaison occasioned by the use of trades advisory councils and other
connections between the program and the community have fostered
continual modifications in curriculum and instruction. The community service divisions engage in their own forms of modification
by slanting their offerings toward areas in which sizable audiences
can be found. On-campus media forms are introduced to accommodate the different modes of information gathering exhibited by new
groups of students. The list could be extended; the point is that
adaptations within existing forms are continually occurring.

The list of potential changes can also be extended by accommodations that are rarely made. Long overdue is a reconception of
the liberal arts to fit the occupational programs: What portions of
traditional liberal arts studies are most useful for students in
occupational programs, and how might they best be inserted into
those areas? Modular courses have been tried in several institutions,
but much more work needs to be done there to build a bridge
between the necessary discipline of sequential instruction and the
short interest span exhibited by many students. Imaginative ways of
funding community colleges to adopt certain functions abandoned
by secondary schools should be explored. Ways of monitoring
contract relationships between community colleges and other
educational and noneducational institutions could be enhanced.
And the entire area of assessing the worth of the community college
as a social structure needs to be developed.

The community colleges' potential is greater than that of any
other institution in American education because their concern is
with the people most in need of assistance. As Astin (1986) has
noted, if an elite institution reforms itself, it changes little; the same
elite group attains more or different benefits. But if the community
colleges succeed in moving even a slightly greater proportion of

their clients toward what the dominant society regards as achievement, it is as though they changed the world. They are engaged with people on the cusp, people who could enter the mainstream or who could fall back into a cycle of poverty and welfare. That is why they deserve the support of everyone who values societal cohesion and the opportunity for all people to rise to their potential.

Issues

The community college has been criticized for its failure to move sizable proportions of its matriculants to the baccalaureate. But these effects are not uniform. Why do different groups of students go through at different rates? How do institutional and personal factors interact to affect progress?

Even though some of the critics have recommended major changes in institutional structure and functioning, few suggest closing the colleges. However, what would happen to a community if its local college's budget were halved?

A church deals in human hopes, gratification, and superordinate goals. Human satisfaction and assistance with intangible patterns of coping are its stock in trade. To what extent does the community college enhance hope?

Nearly everyone has access to the telephone system. It is a passive, instantly responsive tool that allows people to interact with one another at will. What is the value of the human contact fostered by community colleges?

A television network is another form of passive tool. One turns the television on or off at will, seeking entertainment or diversion. How much is the entertainment provided by the colleges worth?

Museums offer both entertainment and education. A museum may be compared with another museum according to the strength of its collection, the appeal of its exhibitions, and the number of people who participate in its programs. What would be the value of a community college ranking system?

Government agencies are social institutions designed to provide services. They are successful to the extent that they enhance the quality of life in a community by maintaining order and providing public places where people may conduct their own affairs. Can the colleges be so assessed?

If the colleges were funded as the museums and the parks department are funded, they would be on a programmatic basis, receiving money to provide a service. But what could the measures be? The numbers of people who appear? A comparison of the services the colleges provide against those provided by other agencies of the type?

Because few scholars are concerned with community colleges, there is no true forum. The colleges' own spokespersons do not help much. Either they do not know how to examine their own institutions critically, or they are disinclined to do so. They say the colleges strive to meet everyone's educational needs, but they rarely acknowledge the patent illogic of that premise. They say the colleges provide access for all, but they fail to examine the obvious corollary question: Access to what? The true supporters of the community college, those who believe in its ideals, would consider the institution's role on both educational and philosophical grounds. Democracy's College deserves no less.

Fourteen

Toward the Millennium:
Issues and Obligations

Just as historians like to play with the past, educators enjoy speculating on the way the future will affect their institutions. It is tempting to believe that the future is manageable, that an institution can be set on a course that ensures its efficiency, relevance, and importance for the community it will serve.

The imminence of a millennial year stimulated an abundance of commissions organized to assess trends in community college functions and support. State-level groups in Alabama, Connecticut, Maryland, and North Carolina, among others, were active in the 1980s, along with a national Commission on the Future of Community Colleges, empaneled under the auspices of the Carnegie Foundation for the Advancement of Teaching and the AACJC. In several other states the community colleges were considered in the context of public higher education reform. The commissions based their studies on apparent population trends, especially age and ethnicity, and on changes in the economy. Predictions were that the growth of the ethnic minority population would accelerate and the proportion of middle-aged workers would decline as the post–World War II baby boomers aged. The economy would continue shifting away from manufacturing and toward service functions as the dominant form for the United States. This postindustrial or information age would require a more literate work force and fuller participation by groups heretofore excluded or consigned to the no longer prevalent assembly line. Competition from newly industrialized countries would force us to take a global perspective toward production. America would remain a dominant force, but only if we worked more intelligently.

Each of the commissions issued reports predicting the need for enhanced educational services and emphasizing the importance of maintaining comprehensive institutions of high quality that would serve a broad range of clients. Some of the reports were more detailed than others, but all concluded with a set of goals and recommendations for sustaining the community colleges by providing a well-trained, caring staff and adequate fiscal resources. Each was optimistic that these institutions were well suited to act in the best interests of the population. None suggested reducing the scope or size of the colleges. None suggested major departures from contemporary patterns of service.

All the reports—in common with similar studies in prior decades—stressed the importance of career education, open access, partnerships with industry, excellence in teaching, and cooperative relationships with other educational sectors. But a new emphasis on outcomes assessment appeared in these commissions' reports. The importance of valid information on college effects has become so evident that the commissions—which might not have been expected to give more than a passing reference to this issue—put it high on their list of essential institutional and state activities. The idea is certainly not new; calls for more reliable data about college outcomes have been made repeatedly—as, for example, in the 1972 AACJC assembly (Yarrington, 1973). What is new is that groups recommending policies for community colleges have acknowledged the possibility of relating those data to college funding. Whether or not that connection is made, some form of outcomes assessment seems certain to continue being put forward.

This chapter merges information from the commission reports with trend data emanating from other literature to yield a picture of the community colleges as they approach the millennium.

The Students

Any review of the future of the community college must begin with an estimate of the numbers and types of students it will serve. But predicting student numbers is an inexact exercise. Projecting the number of college students in general is precarious because various factors—such as employment possibilities, financial aid availability, and the demands of the military—affect the rate of college going. Estimating the numbers who will attend community colleges is further complicated because of unknowns such as the attractiveness of competing institutions. Even a seemingly straightforward projection of the magnitude of the population in general is subject to variability because of immigration patterns. One factor is certain: as long as the economic benefit of going to college remains high, there will be a demand for collegiate studies. The former predictions of a glut in college-trained people and a marked decrease in the rate of return to a college education did not materialize.

The number of students completing high school has a major effect on rates of college going. Higher education in general expanded capacity in the 1960s and 1970s to accommodate the greater population of high school graduates. As the proportion of students completing high school leveled off, more aggressive recruiting campaigns and the availability of financial aid served to keep enrollments high. The community colleges conducted unceasing campaigns to attract students older than traditional college age, students who may not have considered college but who were enticed to come because of the ease of access and the variety of programs offered. Nonetheless, the modal student is aged nineteen; even though people aged twenty-four or younger comprise less than half of the student head count, that group accounts for 70 percent of the course load. The college-age group is still the most significant factor influencing enrollments.

Trends in the number of eighteen-year-olds in the American population reveal a decline from the high point of nearly 4.5 million in 1979 to around 3.5 million in 1988. As shown in Figure 6, this reduction in eighteen-year-olds has not been steady; it rises somewhat in the late 1980s and bottoms out in 1992. In 1998 the number of eighteen-year-olds in the population will be 20 percent less than it was in 1979, with nearly all of this drop coming in the numbers of Anglos. The decline will be greatest in the Northeast, where the 1998 population will be only 71 percent of the 1979 population. Declines in other regions include the South, where the 1998 eighteen-year-olds will equal 80 percent of the 1979 group; the

North Central region, 81 percent; and the West, where the 1998 figure will be 89 percent of the 1979 figure. To these figures must be added a sizable number, perhaps as much as 10 percent, of additional eighteen-year-olds if immigration continues throughout the century at the 1985 rate. Since most of the foreign immigrants concentrate in a few states, their impact on the number of college-age youths there will be much higher. (Between 1990 and 2010 an average of 110,000 immigrants *per year* will settle in Southern California.)

State-by-state variation is affected notably by the differences in high school graduation rates according to ethnicity. For all eighteen-year-olds, the high school graduation rate remained steady at around 75 percent for the twenty years prior to 1988. However, the graduation rates for black students were 63 percent and for Hispanics, 50 percent. The increase in the number of young people completing high school at an older age is seen in the figures on high school graduation as a proportion of eighteen- to twenty-four-year-olds, a total of around 82 percent. It seems likely that the high school graduation rates of Anglo students will remain steady over the next several years, while those for minorities will rise; the proportion of minorities in the group comprising all eighteen-year-olds also will rise. But here again the variation between states is notable. Florida and Mississippi are at the low end, with 55 to 60 percent high school graduation rates; Minnesota, Nebraska, and Iowa, with graduation rates of approximately 85 percent, are at the upper end.

The rate of college going is less predictable. It remained relatively stable, at just over 45 percent, from the mid-1960s to the mid-1980s; but it varied by ethnicity. In the 1980s around 56 percent of the Anglo high school graduates were entering college, while less than 40 percent of the blacks and 45 of the Hispanics were matriculating. Coupled with the discrepant high school graduation rates for the ethnic groups, these figures indicate that 43 percent of the Anglo eighteen- and nineteen-year-olds entered college, compared with 24 percent of the blacks and 22 percent of the Hispanics in that age group. But members of the ethnic minority groups are more likely to complete high school after the age of eighteen or nineteen; hence, their rate of college going tends to increase after

Figure 6. Eighteen-Year-Olds from 1979 to 1998.

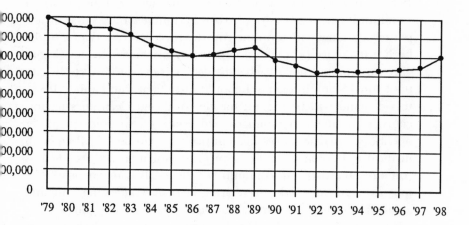

Source: U.S. Bureau of the Census, 1980 Population Census Data, Table 67; reprinted in Solmon and Banks, 1988, p. 8.

members of those groups reach their twenties. (Students of Asian origin are usually not included in the figures on ethnic minorities because their rate of college going is so much at variance. As an example, in California, although 5.1 percent of the college-age population is Asian, students of Asian background account for 10.2 percent of the college enrollments.)

The varying rates of high school graduation and college attendance have a notable effect on the community colleges. Around one-third of the Anglos, blacks, and Asians entering higher education as full-time freshmen in the mid-1980s began in community colleges, but 42 percent of the Hispanic full-time entrants so enrolled. Clearly, since the Hispanic students are overrepresented in community colleges, any increase in their rate of high school graduation or college entry will have an accentuated effect on enrollments, especially in states where the Hispanics comprise a large proportion of the population.

In general, the community colleges will sustain their enrollments because the demand for postsecondary education will remain high. They will continue to get their share of eighteen-year-olds for the same reasons that they have always had: easy access, low cost, and part-time-attendance possibilities. (According to de los Santos, 1989, nearly half of the more than 60,000 students in the Maricopa Community College District [Arizona] complete one course or less per term.) They will continue enrolling job seekers because of the high demand for people in occupations for which some postsecondary training but not a bachelor's degree is expected. According to the United States Bureau of Labor Statistics (cited in Palmer, 1988), this demand will be highest for electrical and electronics technicians, computer programmers, real estate salespeople, computer operators, and data processing equipment repair people, along with medical technologists and certain professional specialists, such as commercial artists. The community colleges also prepare people for jobs as retail salesclerks, secretaries, clerical workers, and nursing aides—all in high demand. The only caveat is that competition with the proprietary schools will intensify as long as their students remain eligible for state and federal financial aid.

Assuming that financial aid availability for middle- and upper-income students does not increase so that tuition differentials are offset, the community colleges will get an even greater share of that group as tuition at four-year colleges and universities continues its rapid rise. Assuming that further limitations are not put on Latino and Asian immigration, college enrollments will benefit from those groups. Even without a change in the rates of high school graduation or college going, enrollments will surpass 6 million before the end of the century—growth that has little to do with new programs or changed curriculum. The students will continue their intermittent attendance patterns. Most students will continue to be employed, and more of them will pursue work and study as parallel activities. The time it takes the median student to gain an associate degree will continue to be from three and a half to four years.

The Faculty

The faculty will be in an ascendant position for the foreseeable future. Everything is going their way. The ratio of full-timers to part-timers has stabilized at just under 40 to 60 and will likely remain there or even increase until the next surge of enrollments makes it necessary to employ sizable numbers of additional staff. The faculty's formal organizations have become more influential in state capitals, taking an active role in shaping legislation affecting community college funding and policies. Within the institutions trends toward professionalization are becoming apparent, especially among those instructors who have taken command of learning resource centers and various curricular projects designed to maximize student learning by combining various instructional and student support services. Opportunities for indigenous research on instruction in academic disciplines have been expanding, as evidenced by an increased number of papers that the faculty have published or presented at professional meetings. The ratio of faculty with doctoral degrees has also increased, and more stringent certification requirements for nonacademic teaching staff have been developed. Miami-Dade, often a bellwether in community college innovation, has introduced a master teacher plan to reward the more involved instructors and have them serve as mentors for the newer ones.

The working conditions of the faculty will not change. The faculty will continue to hold solo practice as their primary code, but in many instances they will band together to make various curricular and student management modifications. An example is afforded by the faculty in the San Diego Community College District, who initiated and managed "Project Success," a multiyear project for modifying patterns of student entry, testing, and placement (San Diego Community College District, 1988). The activity itself was not unusual, but the faculty's conceiving and conducting it was a departure from typical practice.

The faculty could build on these kinds of involvements and take a lead in shaping curriculum, integrating academic support services with instruction, and measuring student learning on a college-wide basis. They could reconceptualize the liberal arts to fit the necessities of career and general education, work as a group with the student services staff to construct academic supports for all students in required courses, and develop testing procedures that will yield information useful in assessing college effects. For assistance in their own classrooms, they could petition for funds to support paraprofessional aides, teaching assistants, and readers; the

time is long past for the faculty to discontinue their prevalent
practice of assigning few papers because they do not have time to
read all of them. Such actions will vary greatly between colleges
because of the variability in faculty leadership.

Faculty hiring practices show little sign of change. Affirmative action programs have been in place in all colleges for many
years, but progress in employing members of minority groups has
been distressingly slow. Nor has there been much progress in
preservice preparation for instructors who are inclined to teach
across disciplinary lines. The number of career-bound students who
take collegiate classes and the number of baccalaureate-bound
students in occupational classes seem destined to force some form of
faculty crossover to accommodate members of both groups. But the
colleges will have to foster their own interdisciplinarians. The
greatest need is for faculty who will become leaders in integrating
curriculum and assessing outcomes. These will come from within
the ranks of the practicing instructors; few people with those skills
can be expected to appear as new employees.

The road to professionalism is a long one, and even though
the faculty have made great strides in extricating themselves from
the administrator-dominated paternalistic situation of a few years
ago, they have far to go. In some institutions they may settle in to an
untoward model: continuing antagonism between them and the
administrators; isolation and solo performance in the classroom;
and periodic battles for smaller classes, augmented salaries, and
more far-reaching fringe benefits. The faculty must take care not to
act too much like other public agency workers in their negotiating
sessions, in the way they seek redress for grievances through legislative action and the courts, and in their inability to police their own
ranks as members of a profession must, lest they be viewed as merely
another category of civil servants.

A more desirable model is a faculty involved with curriculum
planning in the broadest sense: reading and writing in their
disciplines and in the field of education; conducting research on
students' exit and entrance abilities; and becoming program
directors, laboratory managers, or curriculum coordinators managing the paraprofessional aides and part-time instructors who will be
employed as needed. The actuality will be somewhere between the

two extremes. In fact, progress toward both civil service status and professionalism can occur simultaneously. In some districts the faculty champion both a union speaking for wages and welfare and a vigorous academic senate concerning itself with curricular and instructional issues.

Organization and Governance

Few changes in the pattern of organization and governance in community colleges are evident. The number of institutions will change only slightly as new colleges are formed in those states that do not now have an institution within commuting distance of most of their population. But for the most part, branch campuses, satellite centers, and courses offered off campus in rented quarters will accommodate the need for expanded facilities. Many small autonomous centers or specialized units within larger districts will be built. Some of these centers will emphasize career studies and recertification for paraprofessionals; others, operating much like university extension divisions, will offer courses in numerous locations and over open-circuit television. These types of instructional centers have accounted for nearly all the institutional expansion that has occurred since the early 1970s. Few of them have grown into full-service colleges.

Regardless of the calls for expanded functions, the community colleges will still act as schools. The fire department may operate paramedical ambulances, collect food for poor families, and train people in cardiopulmonary resuscitation; but the firefighters had best not forget that their main business is to prevent and extinguish fires. If a building burns to the ground while the department is off performing one of its peripheral functions, heads will roll. Community college leaders may take pride in their role in economic development, but their institution loses its credibility if its students do not become educated there. The colleges' standing outside the mainstream of graded education that reaches from kindergarten to graduate school has allowed them to adjust to their students' changing desires. But they must avoid moving so far outside that they lose credibility. Accreditation, funding formulas, staff predilections, and community perceptions are the anchors holding them in place.

The trend toward greater state-level coordination will continue at a slow pace. As the states become more involved with college policies, gaps in interinstitutional cooperation will be filled, and criteria for student matriculation and progress will be set. The local college districts have retained much power, even though their policies have often been subverted by their own staff members sitting on statewide committees. California's 1988 reforms indicated more authority for the statewide Board of Governors; a renewed emphasis on the basic functions of academic transfer, occupational, and remedial education; and a removal of the instructor certification policies that were a legacy of the colleges' links with the lower school system. Elsewhere, statewide coordination has been emphasized as a means of providing proportionate funding, avoiding curriculum duplication, and easing the flow of students from one sector of public postsecondary education to another. These statewide articulation policies have gradually assumed greater force, and what was once a guideline has in many instances become a mandate.

A few localized organizational changes will occur. In some colleges community services will be offered through separately funded and managed divisions, much the way that university extension divisions have operated. Increased articulation with secondary schools will effect a few shifts. By 1988 the concept of secondary schools operating in close affiliation with community colleges had spread from LaGuardia's Middle College High School prototype to several additional sites in Tennessee, Illinois, Texas, and New Jersey, as well as in New York (Lieberman, 1988). Within the colleges the expanded compensatory education function will elevate the learning resource and tutorial centers to a status and an organizational form approximating the career and collegiate divisions.

A community college network develops by engaging in functions and serving clients not being accommodated by other educational structures. In nations where the university system provides baccalaureate and professional studies, the community colleges may evolve as occupational-training centers. However, as demands for access to higher education grow along with the expansion of common schooling, a system of institutions to provide access is often proposed as a way of taking the pressure off the university. The French Minister for Higher Education and Research proposed such a system to accommodate "an expected enrollment increase in French universities without increasing an already high drop-out rate" (Dickson, 1988, p. A43). Similar systems have been proposed in Italy and other European countries, but the dead hand of tradition makes it difficult for them to be born. They have been established in Canada and Australia, but with nothing like the scope and size of the American community college network. In nations such as China and most of the African countries, where the pressure for university attendance is not as great, the community college takes form as a postsecondary technical-training institute. In nations where the university system has been expanded so that most qualified students can be accommodated—Israel and England, for example—the community college develops more as a lifelong learning institute. Only in the United States has the community college become a combination university access, technical-training, and continuing education enterprise.

The form of the community college will not change. The institution offering career, compensatory, collegiate, and continuing education has become well accepted by the public and by state-level coordinating and funding agencies. The college staff also are comfortable with their institutions' priorities. In a national survey 1,641 instructors, administrators, and counselors in ninety-five colleges ranked the functions in an order corresponding to the purposes for attending that their students named. The only exception was that whereas 15 percent of the students said they were attending for their personal interest, only 3 percent of the staff considered that purpose a top priority (Cohen, 1987a). Modified emphases will occur less rapidly in single institutions than in sets of institutions in states that have differing patterns of higher education. Where the state universities build numerous branch campuses and otherwise make it easy for students to matriculate, the community colleges will emphasize career studies and continuing education. Where the community colleges serve largely as feeders to the universities, the collegiate function will remain strongest. But all current services will continue to be provided, with growth or shifting emphases depending on funding and shifting population bases, not on educational philosophy.

Curriculum and Instruction

Commentators on the community college from the earliest to the most recent have emphasized the value to society of enrolling more students, and institutional funding and philosophy both center on open access. But few have acknowledged the degeneration of curriculum that an open-access institution undergoes. When confronted with it, they say that people should have the opportunity of dropping in or out, studying only what they want when they want, and that prespecified curricula deny free choice. Such statements are based on an unwarranted definition of education, used because it fits what they want the institutions to become: passive lifelong learning centers, responsive to every ad hoc initiative for a new instructional service.

A community college has many purposes. It is a community resource providing short-cycle activities for its constituents' personal interest; cultural upgrading for the community; literacy development, in which it attempts to remedy the failings of other schools; and economic development as it serves as a channel for state development funds and industrial training programs. For most of its students, the college serves as a connector between secondary schools and universities or as a career preparation center assisting them in job entry and job upgrading.

No institution as large as a network of community colleges can rest on a single purpose. The universities provide liberal arts and professional education, along with extension divisions related to their students' personal interests. The liberal arts colleges provide preprofessional training and liberal arts education along with personal guidance. The community colleges provide collegiate studies for students intending on the baccalaureate, along with career and continuing education. The many forces affecting each of these curricular areas ensure that none of them will become the exclusive guiding principle of the institution. Any view of the curriculum must be accommodated to variant social and individual purposes.

As a college evolves, the curriculum develops its own dynamic. Dozens of department chairs, program coordinators, division deans, and directors of evening divisions and off-campus programs forward anticipated course offerings to a central scheduling office. The schedule presents the result of a pastiche of proposals emanating from all those sources. Eventually, an audit is conducted so that reimbursements can be solicited on the basis of credit hours generated. Sections may be added or dropped because of enrollment trends. *But at no time in the process is any common intelligence applied to the entire curriculum.* Instead, the system, the staff's individual preferences, the students' aspirations and abilities, the availability of funds, and, not least, inertia drive the program.

This tendency is not peculiar to community colleges, but for several reasons it is accentuated there. The colleges have allowed, if not encouraged, their students to drop in and out of the institution almost at will, thus making even the most minimal sequencing of curriculum a difficult undertaking. There are few models for teaching general education to students whose background does not include reading, writing, and attendant tendencies toward concept formation. The colleges' staff relations emanate from patterns of free choice for faculty trained according to the university model of disciplinary dominance. There is a paucity of curriculum leadership internally, and the world outside is of little help; the universities judge the colleges' courses according to their own standards.

Curriculum Functions. In spite of the problems noted, an outline of curriculum classified broadly as career, compensatory, community, and collegiate studies can be projected. Career education will remain prominent; there can be no reversing the perception that one of the colleges' prime functions is to train workers, and ample funds are available to support this function. Competition from the universities that develop programs in the technologies and from the proprietary schools and the publicly funded ad hoc job-training programs that teach the more specific skills will not change the central tendency. There is enough demand to keep them all occupied, even as programs within the category rise and fall.

Compensatory education will also be high on the agenda. It has come to the fore after decades of being treated as an embarrassing secret, as something that the colleges did but that their leaders would rather not publicize. The report of the commission planning for the future of the Alabama College System noted that economic development in the state depends in large measure on the colleges' "establishing innovative solutions to chronic illiteracy" (Alabama State Department of Postsecondary Education, 1987, p. 19). The Commission on the Future of the North Carolina Community College System (1989) indicated that the colleges could bring about significant increases in literacy levels by improving the quality of literacy education programs, increasing the number of graduates, and increasing "support among business and government agencies for literacy programs" (p. 20). The Maryland State Board for Community Colleges (1986) and the Board of Trustees of Regional Community Colleges (1989) in Connecticut concluded that community colleges have a primary responsibility to provide remedial education. In California the Joint Committee for Review of the Master Plan for Higher Education (California State Legislature, 1987) elevated compensatory education to a priority second only to transfer and occupational studies. Clearly, compensatory education has come out of the closet.

A sizable amount of basic skill development will continue to be necessary for many years merely to accommodate the backlog of functionally illiterate and non-native-English-speaking people in America. The United States Congress Subcommittee on Select Education (1988) set a goal of "a 90% adult literacy rate nationally" (p. 18). No other postsecondary structure is in a position to provide this essential instruction. The community colleges will not only offer it on their own campuses but will also expand their teaching of literacy in universities, lower schools, and business enterprises. Whether compensatory education is funded separately, or whether its cost is aggregated along with other curricular functions, it will account for one-third of the instructional budget. This amount will vary widely between colleges; it will be highest where the lower schools pass through numbers of marginally literate students, where college going and immigration rates are high, and where matriculation testing and placement are mandated. The not-so-covert elitism manifest in a laissez-faire approach to student success has fallen into the scrap heap of failed ideas in education. Compensatory education has taken its place as a member of the triumvirate of major curricular functions.

Community education expanded dramatically during the 1970s and held its own even in the face of budget reductions in the 1980s. Its proponents have been skilled in effecting cooperative relationships and in securing special funds for it. Nonetheless, its future is not assured, because questions of intent and quality control have not been answered. Nor is it certain how community education affects institutional credibility. But, regardless of the philosophical bases, funding will continue to be the most difficult problem to resolve. Community education advocates grope for ways of financing all the services that fall outside the traditional programs, and they deplore the advantage that funding agencies give to the career and collegiate functions.

Lombardi (1979c) presciently predicted that the financial problem would be partially solved by the imposition of tuition and fees. For some services—hobby courses, for example—the total cost would be borne by the students. Costs of some courses would be borne by firms or public institutions through contractual arrangements. Other services—such as adult basic education for illiterates and non-English-speaking people and special education for the handicapped and for senior citizens—would be funded primarily by the state. Those variant funding arrangements will certainly continue; and, more than any other function, community education's development will depend on the entrepreneurship of its managers.

The prognosis for the collegiate curriculum is good. The universities will develop occupational programs better articulated with those in the community colleges. The linkage aspect of the collegiate function, centering on preparing students to enter junior-level programs leading to bachelor's degrees in health fields, business, technologies, and the professions, will thus thrive because entrance to those programs depends on students' completing courses in the humanities, sciences, social sciences, mathematics, and English usage. The collegiate function will also be affected as the community college leaders strive to maintain their institutions' place in the formal education system. Many of the colleges have stretched the bounds of their legitimacy within the system by overemphasizing community education and by offering certificates that do not fully qualify the recipients for entrance to the next level within the structure, but those tendencies have subsided and are being reversed.

The collegiate function will thrive also as the colleges enroll greater proportions of minority students. Like most students, they want jobs; and, like all students, they need a perspective on the culture, a sense of interpersonal relations, and an ability to analyze situations and to communicate appropriately. Beyond that, students also seek the higher education that they need to progress in the dominant culture: increased literacy, understanding of ethical issues, and realization of past and present time. Some day, readers of the contemporary education literature will react with emotions ranging from curiosity to indignation and shame as they review the allegations that an influx of minority students rationalizes a curriculum centering on the trades, which demand only minimal literacy and manual skills. Should we not teach the humanities to Hispanics? The sciences to blacks? The social sciences to Asians? Which portions of the liberal arts should we drop so that the minorities can concentrate on their hand tools? Which aspects of general education should we deny to them lest they be encouraged to raise their aspirations?

Even though the colleges continually seek adult learners, they will not ignore the students who are new to higher education, those just out of secondary schools seeking entry to the higher learning. The proportion of their offerings that the liberal arts comprise has stabilized at 50 percent. Many of these classes are taken by students seeking job entry skills and by those attending for their personal interest, but much of the enrollment in the liberal arts is composed of baccalaureate-degree aspirants. That group must be served with college-level studies, built in sequence. The heavy hand of the universities will restrict efforts to provide interdisciplinary studies, but the colleges could center their curriculum on general education because of the freedom they enjoy in building academic support services, instructional forms, and course prerequisites. They are not likely to do so, since general education demands continual moves toward integrating academic support services, courses, faculty actions, and college mission. It is a centripetal idea that is constantly subverted by the centrifugal forces of an institution composed of staff members and students with their own agenda.

In the 1970s the colleges' curriculum was designed primarily to accommodate the students' abilities and course-taking behavior. Remedial instruction and English as a second language gained prominence, along with practices allowing students to withdraw from classes without penalty until well into the term. In the 1980s a trend toward enforcing matriculation standards and course prerequisites developed under the impetus of the faculty, who finally made the case that they could not readily teach classes filled with students at every range of ability. The notion of a curriculum that would enable students to complete a program and transfer successfully to a university gained prominence, not least because it became a major cause among the advocates of higher education for members of ethnic minority groups.

These forces driving a curriculum and institutional practices that would enhance student retention and transfer will not soon abate. The links that have been built to enhance transfer between community colleges and universities will strengthen. Faculty interchanges along departmental lines, guaranteed admission at the junior level, a common core of distribution requirements, baccalaureate programs designed for students to complete the first two years at a community college, and state-mandated articulation agreements will become more pronounced. The transfer function does not rest on curriculum alone, but stronger community college programs certainly enhance it.

Fundamental curricular reform occurs very slowly. The clerically dominated classical curriculum was under attack for at least half of the nineteenth century before a secularized curriculum centering on science became the norm. The twentieth century has seen the rise of career education and, most recently, the acceptance of basic studies as a legitimate collegiate function. A mandated, integrative education through which students gain historical per-

spective and a sense of the social and environmental trends that
affect their future has yet to take center stage. In sum, except in the
rare institution, general education will continue being debated in
the context of distribution requirements. It cannot become the
guiding principle of an institution that is less dedicated to societal
benefit than it is to each individual's immediate concerns.

Instruction. It is engaging to reflect on all the media that
were supposed to change the conditions of teaching. To the phono-
graph, telephone, radio, television, and computer have been added
the laser-directed disc, satellites and downlinks, and other electronic
marvels too numerous to be tabulated. These automated media did
indeed change the way that information is transmitted, but not in
the way that the educators had hoped. Their primary application
has not been in socially valuable directions or even in the schools. It
has been in the world of entertainment, where the media have
tended to lure audiences away from the imagery occasioned by
reading, away from reflectiveness, patience, and perseverance. The
dream of students learning on their own while their instructors were
freed from information dispensing to engage in creative interaction
with them has remained just that—a dream from which visitors to
the schools awaken as they walk the corridors and see instructors
and students in classrooms acting quite as they did before the
microchip or, for that matter, the vacuum tube.

Instruction is the process of effecting learning. Learning may
occur in any setting, but instruction involves arranging conditions
so that it is predictable and directed. Those conditions include
access to new information; organization of sequence and content;
and, not least, whatever is necessary to keep the learners attendant
on the task—a condition that requires traditional instruction.
Unlike the automated media, traditional instruction centers on
interaction among people. Would that the drive to learn were so
powerful that all people engaged themselves individually with
learning all they need to know to play valued roles in the society.
Absent that, instruction remains essential.

The efficiency of the process of instruction is frequently
called into question. The first programmed learning texts forced
attention on specific measurable objectives, because it is impossible

to design a deliberate learning sequence unless the form of the intended learning is defined. Some efforts were made to define objectives for classroom instruction and for the various televised and computer-based presentations that have been created, but little progress has been made. Instructional efficiency is defined less often as progress toward specific learning outcomes than as the number of students completing a course as related to the cost of presenting it.

The sporadic attempts at organizing instruction more efficiently for different types of learners led to various testing and instructional and curricular placement activities. If these student-tracking activities derived only from a well-intentioned quest for greater learning for less expenditure of student and staff time, they might be welcome. But in many applications they have been confounded with the pernicious belief that students from different ethnic groups learn differently. Racism dies hard, and it is distressing to hear commentators suggesting special instructional forms for those students they euphemistically call "new."

Student services practitioners have long advocated better integration of their programs with the colleges' instructional efforts; but only rarely have strong links been built between the counseling, tutorial, and orientation efforts, on the one hand, and the instructional programs, on the other. More recently, led by instructional resource center and learning laboratory managers, student services and instruction have come closer together. Laboratory-based activities and supplemental instruction for students in high-risk courses have been mandated. Tutorial centers, staffed by paid, peer tutors, have expanded. The budgetary lines that divide student services from instruction tend to retard the development of this form of integration, but it seems destined to progress nonetheless.

Assessing Outcomes

How might the value of community colleges be assessed? The traditional method of measuring the worth of a school has been to gauge the value it adds to its students. Measures of what the students know when they enter and of what they know when they leave are classic assessment strategies. Single courses, entire programs, entire institutions are measured in this fashion. Value has also been ascribed to increased income, higher-status jobs obtained, or higher degree attainment. But many community college people are convinced that their institution should no longer be assessed in those ways. They believe that they have moved into another sphere, one in which the institution is less concerned with traditional teaching and learning than with coordinating all the community's educational services or uplifting the region's economy. Accordingly, when analysts suggest that the two-year colleges are detrimental to students' passage through the system toward the baccalaureate degree, the college spokespersons react uproariously. For similar reasons the idea of defined outcomes or behavioral objectives has made little headway, because the threat of being held accountable for student learning is too much for most faculty members to endure.

Whether or not pre and post measures of student learning can be applied, the colleges are and will be judged by what their students gain by attending. For those students who enroll in a photography course so that they can have access to the darkroom, in an art course so that they can have their work criticized, in a literature course so that they can find like-minded students with whom to interact, the institution has become a way of gaining "access to tools" (to use Ivan Illich's term for characterizing a useful social institution). The fact that the college classifies those courses in photography, art, and literature as "transfer courses" does not change the reality of the way they are perceived by students. Therefore, measures of the value of that access can and should be applied.

Most of the occupationally oriented courses offered for college credit are organized into programs leading to certificates or degrees. But the students who attend these courses for a short time, learn a few skills (and, more important, learn where the jobs are), and then drop out to go to work have, similarly, gained something of great value. Assessing graduation and placement rates thus misses the colleges' contributions to those students' progress. How valuable has the college been for them?

The classical educational research paradigms apply to the community colleges no less than they do to other forms of schools.

Students attend, learn, and move on to other pursuits. Those outcomes can be assessed—as, indeed, they are in many districts and states. More such studies should be done in individual colleges; but too few institutional research officers are available to coordinate them, too few high-level administrators appreciate their importance, and, when they are conducted, too many well-meaning but futile attempts are made to relate the findings to particular college practices.

The colleges should be assessed on the basis of their success in promoting individual mobility. How many people used them as a step toward the baccalaureate or higher-status jobs? How many broke out of a cycle of family poverty? How many gained rapid access to society by becoming literate? How many learned to put their own lives together? If the goal of individual mobility is not broad enough for those who seek measures of the colleges' contributions, let them look to measures of what the colleges have done for special populations in the aggregate: the aged, disabled, minorities, at-risk youth, or immigrants.

No institution in American education plays a more difficult role than the community college. Its leaders, criticized for their inability to effect miracles with populations that have proved intractable to the ministrations of other schools and social welfare agencies, sometimes propose goals and functions even more unlikely of attainment. They might better concentrate on the social problems that have the most apparent educational components. Functional literacy affords a prime example. It is familiar to the college staff and public alike. It is amenable to intervention. And it enjoys political support second only to reducing unemployment, with which it, in fact, overlaps. The colleges could not only build instructional support systems that would enable them to maintain standards of literacy in all their own classes; they also could reach out by enlisting their own students as trainers of tutors for the primary schools and by organizing literacy sessions in the areas of greatest need in their communities. Measures of success would be apparent.

An intriguing but practically difficult question for assessment is: How much do the colleges contribute to the solution of perennial social issues, such as homelessness, a balanced economy, the armaments race, energy conservation, and white-collar and street crime? The most likely answer is: Very little. The community colleges—all schools—are limited in their ability to take direct action. Staff predilections, the paucity of leadership, and funding priorities internally, along with the externals of public perceptions, community power bases, and the competing influences of the mass media, ensure that the colleges reflect the times more than they lead them. It would be wonderful if, at the millennium, the colleges had reorganized their curriculum and their instructional divisions so that they were providing forms of education that had a direct effect on social problems. But that goal is elusive; all that any school can do is to encourage its students to participate in the polity, to question their own and the community's values, and to consider the consequences of contemporary policies that affect the problems. How much will the colleges contribute to the development of an enlightened citizenry?

No group of educators can agree on what must be known by everyone. But the alternative to a single curriculum is not, therefore, the nihilistic curriculum represented by students attending classes at will. This is chaos, not college. Minimum standards, specific objectives, and enforced prerequisites in curriculum can be sustained, just as students can be directed to matriculate in programs and make steady progress toward completing them. Many contemporary state and local policy trends suggest that such sequences will be enforced; as a consequence, the colleges will gradually but steadily gain additional approbation and respect from their constituents.

Educators do not solve problems or cure ills. But neither do they deliberately sell false dreams or spread bad taste. It is only when they imitate the worst characteristics of business corporations and the mass media that they lose the status the public has granted them. They will not betray the virtues that distinguish their calling.

References

Abraham, A. A. *College-Level Study: What Is It? Variations in College Placement Tests and Standards in the SREB States.* Issues in Higher Education, No. 22. Atlanta: Southern Regional Education Board, 1986. 7 pp. (ED 277 715)

Abraham, A. A. *A Report on College-Level Remedial/Developmental Programs in SREB States.* Atlanta: Southern Regional Education Board, 1987. 78 pp. (ED 280 369)

Academic Senate for California Community Colleges. "Report of the ASCCC Conference on Academic Standards." Unpublished report, Dec. 2, 1977.

Adams, B., Bodino, A., Bissell, O., and Smith, M. "Writing for Learning: How to Achieve a Total College Commitment." Paper presented at annual national convention of the American Association of Community and Junior Colleges, San Diego, Calif., Apr. 14-17, 1985. 38 pp. (ED 258 666)

Adams, J. J., and Roesler, E. D. *A Profile of First-Time Students at Virginia Community Colleges, 1975-76.* Richmond: Virginia State Department of Community Colleges, 1977. 58 pp. (ED 153 694)

Adams, L. *Extended Learning Institute: Policies and Procedures Manual.* Chester, Va.: John Tyler Community College, 1986. 65 pp. (ED 273 313)

Adelman, C. (ed.). *Assessment in American Higher Education: Issues and Contexts.* Washington, D.C.: Office of Educational Research and Improvement, 1986.

Adelman, C. "A Basic Statistical Portrait of American Higher

Education, 1987." Paper prepared for the second Anglo-American Dialogue on Higher Education, 1987.

Adelman, C. "Transfer Rates and the Going Mythologies: A Look at Community College Patterns." *Change*, 1988, *20* (1), 38–41.

Alabama State Department of Postsecondary Education. *Dimensions 2000: A Strategic Plan for Building Alabama's Future.* Montgomery: Alabama State Department of Postsecondary Education, 1987. 34 pp. (ED 295 688)

Al-Sunbul, A. "The Achievement of Two-Year Transfer Students in Four-Year Institutions: A Case Study." *Community/Junior College Quarterly of Research and Practice*, 1987, *11* (1), 1–9.

American Association of Community and Junior Colleges. *Community, Junior, and Technical College Directory.* Washington, D.C.: American Association of Community and Junior Colleges, 1955–present (published annually).

American Association of Community and Junior Colleges. *Responding to the Challenge of a Changing American Economy: 1985 Progress Report on the Sears Partnership Development Fund.* Washington, D.C.: American Association of Community and Junior Colleges, 1986. 20 pp. (ED 270 144)

American Association of Community and Junior Colleges. *Building Communities: A Vision for a New Century. A Report of the Commission on the Future of Community Colleges.* Washington, D.C.: American Association of Community and Junior Colleges, 1988. 58 pp. (ED 293 578)

American Association of Community and Junior Colleges/American Association of State Colleges and Universities. *The Servicemen's Opportunity College: A Network of Colleges and Universities, 1974-75 Catalog.* Washington, D.C.: American Association of Community and Junior Colleges/American Association of State Colleges and Universities, 1974. 83 pp. (ED 093 429)

American Association of Junior Colleges. *A National Resource for Occupational Education.* Washington, D.C.: American Association of Junior Colleges, 1964.

American College Testing Program. *College Student Profiles: Norms for the ACT Assessment.* Iowa City: Research and Development Division, American College Testing Program, 1966–present (published annually).

Anderson, E. F., and others. *Comparison of Transfer and Native Student Progress: University of Illinois at Chicago, Fall 1983 Group.* Research Memorandum 86-9. Chicago: Office of School and College Relations, University of Illinois, 1986. 75 pp. (ED 275 378)

Anderson, K. L. "Post-High School Experiences and College Attrition." *Sociology of Education,* 1981, *54* (1), 1-15.

Andrew, L. D., and Henry, T. A. "A Comparison of Funding Priorities in Two-Year Institutions with and Without Faculty Collective Bargaining." Paper presented at annual meeting of the Association for the Study of Higher Education, Washington, D.C., Mar. 25-26, 1983. 20 pp. (ED 232 609)

Archer, C., and Archer, A. J. "How Successful Financial Aid Outreach Is Developed and Run." Unpublished report, 1985. 15 pp. (ED 284 613)

Arizona State Board of Directors for Community Colleges. *Annual Report to the Governor, 1986-87.* Phoenix: Arizona State Board of Directors for Community Colleges, 1987. 139 pp. (ED 287 549)

Armstrong, C. L. "The Impact of Collective Bargaining at the Rancho Santiago Community College District (Santa Ana College)." Unpublished paper, Pepperdine University (Malibu, Calif.), 1978. 42 pp. (ED 164 043)

Aslanian, C. B. "Mainstreaming of Adults on American Campuses." *Community Services Catalyst,* 1986, *16* (3), 6-10.

Association of American Colleges. *Integrity in the College Curriculum: A Report to the Academic Community. The Findings and Recommendations of the Project on Redefining the Meaning and Purpose of Baccalaureate Degrees.* Washington, D.C.: Association of American Colleges, 1985. 62 pp. (ED 251 059)

Association of Independent Colleges and Schools. *Directory of Educational Institutions, 1988.* Washington, D.C.: Association of Independent Colleges and Schools, 1988.

Astin, A. W. *Four Critical Years: Effects of College on Beliefs, Attitudes, and Knowledge.* San Francisco: Jossey-Bass, 1977.

Astin, A. W. *Minorities in American Higher Education: Recent Trends, Current Prospects, and Recommendations.* San Francisco: Jossey-Bass, 1982.

Astin, A. W. "Student Involvement in Learning." Paper presented at annual conference of the California Community College Trustees, San Diego, Calif., May 24, 1986.

Astin, A. W., and others. *The American Freshman: National Norms.* . . . Los Angeles: Cooperative Institutional Research Program, 1973-present (published annually).

Astin, H. S. "Providing Incentives for Teaching Underprepared Students." *Educational Record,* 1985, *66* (1), 26–29.

Atwood-Canter, C. *Marketing and Public Relations Needs Assessment for Glendale Community College.* Glendale, Ariz.: Glendale Community College, 1985. 30 pp. (ED 278 443)

Augenblick, J. *Issues in Financing Community Colleges.* Denver: Education Finance Center, Education Commission of the States, 1978. 70 pp. (ED 164 020)

Bailey, A. L. "Their Budgets Cut, 2-Year Colleges Turn to Aggressive Fund Raising." *Chronicle of Higher Education,* 1986, *33* (1), 57.

Baker, R. G. "A Comparison of College Freshman Achievement in Remedial English Courses and in Freshman Composition Courses at a Two-Year College." Paper presented at annual meeting of the American Educational Research Association, New York, Mar. 19–23, 1982. 12 pp. (ED 214 615)

Baldridge, J. V. *Power and Conflict in the University.* New York: Wiley, 1971.

Baldwin, A. *Internal Program Review of Associate in Science Programs, 1981–82 Through 1985–86.* Research Report No. 86-83. Miami: Office of Institutional Research, Miami-Dade Community College, 1986. 71 pp. (ED 275 586)

Banks, D., and Mabry, T. *Community College Foundations.* ERIC Digest. Los Angeles: ERIC Clearinghouse for Junior Colleges, 1988.

Bayer, A. E. "Teaching Faculty in Academe: 1972–73." *ACE Research Reports,* 1973, *8* (2), 1–68.

Beavers, J. L. *Follow-Up Study of 1980–81 Graduates and Non-Graduates.* Report No. 82-2. Wytheville, Virginia: Office of Institutional Research, Wytheville Community College, 1982. 27 pp. (ED 231 446)

Ben-David, J. *Centers of Learning: Britain, France, Germany, United States.* New York: McGraw-Hill, 1977.

Bennett, W. J. *To Reclaim a Legacy: A Report on the Humanities in Higher Education.* Washington, D.C.: National Endowment for the Humanities, 1984.

Berchin, A. *Toward Increased Efficiency in Community Junior College Courses: An Exploratory Study.* Los Angeles: League for Innovation in the Community College, 1972. 236 pp. (ED 063 915)

Berger, J. "For Workers, More Paths to Degree." *New York Times,* Mar. 30, 1988, p. B4.

Bernd, C. M. "The Community Junior College Trustee: Some Questions About Representation." Unpublished paper, Gainesville, Fla., 1973. 13 pp. (ED 086 279)

Bers, T. H. "Trustee Characteristics and Decision Making Among Suburban and Rural Community College Trustees." *Community/Junior College Research Quarterly,* 1980, *4* (3), 249-262.

Bess, R., and others. *A Study of the Economic Impact of Six Community Colleges in Illinois.* Springfield: Illinois Community College Board, 1980. 31 pp. (ED 191 516)

Bishara, M. N. *Education for the Gifted in Rural Locations in Virginia: Final Report.* Richlands: Southwest Virginia Community College, 1986. 100 pp. (ED 285 631)

Blocker, C. E. "Are Our Faculties Competent?" *Junior College Journal,* 1965-66, *36* 12-17.

Blocker, C. E., Plummer, W., and Richardson, R. C., Jr. *The Two-Year College: A Social Synthesis.* Englewood Cliffs, N.J.: Prentice-Hall, 1965.

Bloom, B. S. "Recent Developments in Mastery Learning." *Educational Psychologist,* 1973, *10* (2), 53-57.

Blumenstyk, G. "Diversity Is Keynote of States' Efforts to Assess Students' Learning." *Chronicle of Higher Education,* July 20, 1988, *34* (45), A17, 25-26.

Board of Trustees of Regional Community Colleges. *Towards 2000: A Long-Range Plan for the Community Colleges of Connecticut.* Hartford: Board of Trustees of Regional Community Colleges, 1989.

Bock, D. J. "Two-Year College LRC Buildings." *Library Journal,* 1978, *103* (21), 2391-2393.

Bock, D. J. "From Library to LRC." *Community College Frontiers,* 1979, *9* (1), 4-9.

Bock, D. J. "From Libraries to Learning Resources: Six Decades of Progress—And Still Changing." *Community and Junior College Libraries,* 1984, *3* (2), 35-46.

Bogart, Q. J., and Galbraith, J. D. "Marketing America's Community Colleges: An Analysis of National Marketing Efforts of Community Colleges. A Final Report on the MECCA Project to the Council of North Central Community and Junior Colleges." Special condensed summary report presented at annual convention of the American Association of Community and Junior Colleges, Las Vegas, Nev., Apr. 24-27, 1988. 23 pp. (ED 296 771)

Bogue, J. P. *The Community College.* New York: McGraw-Hill, 1950.

Bohr, D. H., and Bray, D. "HELP: A Pilot Program for Community College High-Risk Students." Unpublished paper, Sacramento, Calif., 1979. 12 pp. (ED 168 635)

Bowen, H. R. "Cost Differences: The Amazing Disparity Among Institutions of Higher Education in Educational Costs per Student." *Change,* 1981, *13* (1), 21-27.

Boyer, C. M., Ewell, P. T., Finney, J. E., and Mingle, J. R. *Assessment and Outcomes Measurement—A View from the States: Highlights of a New ECS Survey and Individual State Profiles.* ECS Working Papers, PS-87-1. Washington, D.C.: American Association for Higher Education; Denver: State Higher Education Executive Officers Association, 1987. 63 pp. (ED 282 482)

Boyer, E. L. "Quality and the Campus: The High School/College Connection." *Current Issues in Higher Education,* 1980, *2* (4).

Boyer, E. L. *College: The Undergraduate Experience in America.* New York: Harper & Row, 1987.

Boyer, E. L., and Kaplan, M. *Educating for Survival.* New Rochelle, N.Y.: Change Magazine Press, 1977.

Brann, E. T. H. *Paradoxes of Education in a Republic.* Chicago: University of Chicago Press, 1979.

Brawer, F. B. *New Perspectives on Personality Development in College Students.* San Francisco: Jossey-Bass, 1973.

Brawer, F. B. *Familiar Functions in New Containers: Classifying Community Education.* Topical Paper No. 71. Los Angeles:

ERIC Clearinghouse for Junior Colleges, 1980a. 30 pp. (ED 187 412)

Brawer, F. B. (ed.). *The Humanities and Sciences in Two-Year Colleges.* Los Angeles: Center for the Study of Community Colleges; ERIC Clearinghouse for Junior Colleges, 1980b.

Brawer, F. B., and Friedlander, J. *Science and Social Science in the Two-Year College.* Topical Paper No. 69. Los Angeles: ERIC Clearinghouse for Junior Colleges, 1979. 37 pp. (ED 172 854)

Brawer, M. J. "The Impact of Computer Assisted Instruction as It Relates to Learning Disabled Adults in California Community Colleges." Unpublished bachelor's thesis, University of San Francisco, 1983. 52 pp. (ED 283 509)

Breneman, D. W. "Planning as if People Mattered: The Economy." Presentation to the Society for College and University Planning, Kansas City, Mo., July 1979.

Breneman, D. W., and Nelson, S. C. *Financing Community Colleges: An Economic Perspective.* Washington, D.C.: Brookings Institution, 1981.

Brey, R., and Grigsby, C. *Telecourse Student Survey, 1984.* Washington, D.C.: Instruction Telecommunications Consortium, American Association of Community and Junior Colleges, 1984. 61 pp. (ED 255 258)

Brick, M. *Forum and Focus for the Junior College Movement.* New York: Teachers College Press, 1965.

Brick, M. Review of *Student Development Programs in the Community Junior College.* (T. O'Banion and A. Thurston, eds.) *Journal of Higher Education,* 1972, *43* (8), 675–677.

Bromley, A., and Moore, M. *Focus on Careers: A Program for Single Parents or Homemakers.* Final Report, Project No. 7-2005, from *July 1, 1986 to June 30, 1987.* Gainesville, Fla.: Santa Fe Community College, 1987. 58 pp. (ED 285 985)

Brophy, D. A. *The Relationship Between Student Participation in Student Development Activities and Rate of Retention in American Rural Community Colleges.* Rocklin, Calif.: Administrative Services and Research, Sierra Joint Community College District, 1984. 171 pp. (ED 277 419)

Broudy, H. S. *General Education: The Search for a Rationale.*

Bloomington, Ind.: Phi Delta Kappa Educational Foundation, 1974.

Brum, J. "Effects of Computer-Assisted Instruction on Students' Final Grades: Applied Educational Research and Evaluation." Unpublished doctoral practicum paper, Nova University, 1983. 32 pp. (ED 263 832)

Bushnell, D. S. *Organizing for Change: New Priorities for Community Colleges*. New York: McGraw-Hill, 1973.

Butcher, L. J. *Free and Reduced Tuition Policies for Older Adult Students at Two-Year Community, Junior, and Technical Colleges*. Washington, D.C.: American Association of Community and Junior Colleges, 1980. 36 pp. (ED 184 645)

Byrd, M. A. *On-Campus Enrollment in Arkansas Two-Year Colleges, Fall 1984*. Little Rock: Arkansas State Department of Higher Education, 1985. 36 pp. (ED 270 132)

California Community and Junior College Association. *Community College Instructors' Out-of-Class Professional Functions: Report of a Survey of Full-Time and Part-Time Faculty in California Community Colleges*. Sacramento: California Community and Junior College Association, 1978. 61 pp. (ED 154 873)

California Community Colleges. *Study of Fee Impact: Progress Report*. Sacramento: Office of the Chancellor, California Community Colleges, 1986. 86 pp. (ED 278 450)

California Community Colleges. *Student Profile, Fall 1977 to Fall 1986*. Historical Profiles Project. Sacramento: Office of the Chancellor, California Community Colleges, 1987a. 33 pp. (ED 281 589)

California Community Colleges. *Study of Fee Impact*. Final Report, No. 873. Sacramento: Office of the Chancellor, California Community Colleges, 1987b. 89 pp. (ED 284 645)

California Community Colleges. *Study of Part-Time Instruction*. Sacramento: Office of the Chancellor, California Community Colleges, 1987c. 80 pp. (ED 278 449)

California Community Colleges. *The Guaranteed Student Loan Program in the California Community Colleges: Report and Recommendations of the Financial Aid Policy Task Force*. Sacramento: Office of the Chancellor, California Community Colleges, 1989.

California State Department of Education. "Summary of Source and Education Background of New Teachers in California Junior Colleges, 1963-64." Unpublished report, California State Department of Education, 1963-64.

California State Legislature, Joint Committee for Review of the Master Plan for Higher Education. *California Community College Reform: Final Report.* Sacramento: Joint Committee for Review of the Master Plan for Higher Education, 1987. 50 pp. (ED 282 587)

California State Postsecondary Education Commission. *Comments on the California Community Colleges' Plan for Allocating Board Financial Assistance to Community College Students: A Report to the Fiscal and Educational Policy Committees of the Legislature.* Sacramento: California State Postsecondary Education Commission, 1984. 59 pp. (ED 253 290)

California State Postsecondary Education Commission. *Faculty Salaries and Related Matters in the California Community Colleges, 1984-85.* Commission Report 85-31. Sacramento: California State Postsecondary Education Commission, 1985a. 16 pp. (ED 265 897)

California State Postsecondary Education Commission. *Segmental Responses to Assembly Concurrent Resolution 71 Regarding Ethnic Awareness.* Commission Report 85-27. Sacramento: California State Postsecondary Education Commission, 1985b. 67 pp. (ED 261 592)

Campbell, D. F. "New Roles for Occupational Instructors." Unpublished paper, Community College of the Air Force (Lackland Air Force Base, Tex.), 1977. 12 pp. (ED 146 967)

Campbell, D. F. (ed.). *Strengthening Financial Management.* New Directions for Community Colleges, no. 50. San Francisco: Jossey-Bass, 1985.

Campbell, M. "Mastery Learning in the College Learning Center." Paper presented at conference of the National Association for Remedial/Developmental Studies, Little Rock, Ark., Mar. 1983. 19 pp. (ED 247 592)

Carbone, G. J. *The 1986 Literacy Tutor Coordination Program: A Report to the Legislature Pursuant to Chapter 312, Laws of 1986 (ESSB 4762).* Olympia, Washington: Office of the State Superintendent of Public Instruction; Washington State Board for Community College Education, 1987. 17 pp. (ED 289 571)

Career Information Center. "Post-High School Occupational Training Opportunities in Hawaii Public Institutions, 1974-1975." Unpublished paper, Career Information Center, Honolulu, 1974.

Carey, D., Wark, L., and Wellsfry, N. *Partnerships for Excellence: High Schools and Community Colleges.* ACCCA Management Report, 1986-7/2. n.p.: Association of California Community College Administrators, 1986. 23 pp. (ED 278 433)

Carnegie Commission on Higher Education. *The Open-Door College.* New York: McGraw-Hill, 1970.

Carnegie Foundation for the Advancement of Teaching. *Missions of the College Curriculum: A Contemporary Review with Suggestions.* San Francisco: Jossey-Bass, 1977.

CARVELL Education Management Planning, Inc. *Pathways to Progress: A Comprehensive Study of Vocational Education in California Community Colleges.* Carmel Valley, Calif.: CARVELL Education Management Planning, Inc., 1986. 163 pp. (ED 273 336)

Case, C. H. *General Education at Los Medanos College.* Pittsburg, Calif.: Los Medanos College, 1988.

Center for the Study of Community Colleges. "Report of Instructor Surveys, 1977-1978." Unpublished report, 1978a.

Center for the Study of Community Colleges. "Science and Humanities Instruction in Two-Year Colleges." Unpublished report, 1978b.

Center for the Study of Community Colleges. *Transfer, Honors and Excellence: Six Districts Spotlighted.* CSCC Bulletin, No. 6. Los Angeles: Center for the Study of Community Colleges, 1982. 6 pp. (ED 221 257)

Center for the Study of Community Colleges. *Liberal Arts Instructors: Demographics and Professional Orientations.* CSCC Bulletin, No. 13. Los Angeles: Center for the Study of Community Colleges, 1984.

Center for the Study of Community Colleges. *Community College Involvement in the Education of Adults: Spring 1986 Student*

Survey—Frequencies. Los Angeles: Center for the Study of Community Colleges, 1986.

Center for the Study of Community Colleges. *Community College Involvement in the Education of Adults: Survey of State Directors Regarding Populations Served and Funding Sources.* Los Angeles: Center for the Study of Community Colleges, 1987.

Center for the Study of Community Colleges. *Art Education in American Community Colleges: Final Report.* Los Angeles: Center for the Study of Community Colleges, 1988. 136 pp. (ED 294 640)

Chaffee, E. E. *Organization/Administration.* Washington, D.C.: Association for the Study of Higher Education, 1986. 62 pp. (ED 272 129)

Chait, R. P., and Associates. *Trustee Responsibility for Academic Affairs.* Washington, D.C.: Association of Governing Boards of Universities and Colleges, 1984.

Chalker, D. C. "Presidents' Perceptions of the Role of Institutional Research in Rural Junior Colleges in the Southeast." Paper presented at annual meeting of the Southeastern Association for Community College Research, Orlando, Fla., July 20–22, 1981. 15 pp. (ED 206 336)

Chang, N. *Organizational Structure in Multi-Campus Community Junior Colleges/Districts.* Denver: Community College of Denver, 1978. 137 pp. (ED 158 795)

Charbonneau, W. "How the Job Training Partnership Act Works." *Industrial Education,* 1986, *75* (6), 24–25.

Chausow, H. M. "Remedial Education: A Position Paper." Unpublished paper, Chicago, 1979. 16 pp. (ED 170 013)

Ciardi, J. "Give Us This Day Our Daily Surrealism." *Saturday Review,* 1971, *54* (24), 48.

City Colleges of Chicago. *Academic Policy.* Chicago: City Colleges of Chicago, 1984. 20 pp. (ED 245 747)

Clagett, C. A. *A Review of the Telecredit Program, Fall 1976–82.* Report No. 83-4. Largo, Md.: Office of Institutional Research, Prince George's Community College, 1983. 31 pp. (ED 229 091)

Clagett, C. A. *ENSCAN 87: Environmental Scanning Report for Fiscal Year 1987.* Vol. 2: *The College Report, PB 87-1.* Largo,

Md.: Office of Institutional Research, Prince George's Community College, 1986. 40 pp. (ED 280 531)

Clark, B. R. "The 'Cooling-Out' Function in Higher Education." *American Journal of Sociology*, 1960, *65* (6), 569–576.

Clark, B. R. "The 'Cooling-Out' Function Revisited." In G. B. Vaughan (ed.), *Questioning the Community College Role*. New Directions for Community Colleges, no. 32. San Francisco: Jossey-Bass, 1980.

Clark, B. R. *The Academic Life: Small Worlds, Different Worlds*. Princeton, N.J.: Princeton University Press, 1987.

Clark, B. R. "The Absorbing Errand." Remarks presented at national conference of the American Association of Higher Education, Washington, D.C., Mar. 10, 1988.

Claxton, C. S., and Murrell, P. H. *Learning Styles: Implications for Improving Educational Practices*. ASHE-ERIC Higher Education Report No. 4. Washington, D.C.: Association for the Study of Higher Education, ERIC Clearinghouse on Higher Educateion, 1987. 116 pp. (ED 293 478)

Cohen, A. M. "Assessing College Students' Ability to Write Compositions." *Research in the Teaching of English*, 1973a, *7* (3), 356–371.

Cohen, A. M. *Work Satisfaction Among Junior College Faculty Members*. Los Angeles: University of California and ERIC Clearinghouse for Junior Colleges, 1973b. 8 pp. (ED 081 426)

Cohen, A. M. "Instructional Practices in the Humanities, Fall 1977." Unpublished paper, Center for the Study of Community Colleges, 1978. 18 pp. (ED 160 145)

Cohen, A. M. *Counting the Transfer Students*. Junior College Resource Review. Los Angeles: ERIC Clearinghouse for Junior Colleges, 1979. 6 pp. (ED 172 864)

Cohen, A. M. *Community College Involvement in the Education of Adults: A Progress Report Submitted to the Carnegie Foundation for the Advancement of Teaching*. Los Angeles: Center for the Study of Community Colleges, 1987a. 69 pp. (ED 277 428)

Cohen, A. M. "Facilitating Degree Achievement by Minorities: The Community College Environment." Paper prepared for the conference "From Access to Achievement: Strategies for Urban Institutions," Los Angeles, Nov. 15–17, 1987b. (ED 283 576)

Cohen, A. M. "Degree Achievement by Minorities in Community Colleges." *Review of Higher Education,* 1988, *11* (4), 383–402.

Cohen, A. M., and Associates. *College Responses to Community Demands: The Community College in Challenging Times.* San Francisco: Jossey-Bass, 1975.

Cohen, A. M., and Brawer, F. B. *The Two-Year College Instructor Today.* New York: Praeger, 1977.

Cohen, A. M., and Brawer, F. B. *The Collegiate Function of Community Colleges: Fostering Higher Learning Through Curriculum and Student Transfer.* San Francisco: Jossey-Bass, 1987.

Cohen, A. M., and Hill, A. *Instructional Practices in the Sciences, Spring 1978.* Los Angeles: Center for the Study of Community Colleges, 1978. 18 pp. (ED 160 144)

Cohen, A. M., Palmer, J. C., and Zwemer, K. D. *Key Resources on Community Colleges: A Guide to the Field and Its Literature.* San Francisco: Jossey-Bass, 1986.

Cohen, M. D., and March, J. G. *Leadership and Ambiguity: The American College President.* (2nd ed.) Boston: Harvard Business School Press, 1986.

Cohen, M. J. "Junior College Growth." *Change,* 1972, *4* (9), 32a–32d.

College Entrance Examination Board. *Annual Survey of Colleges, 1986–1987: Summary Statistics.* New York: College Entrance Examination Board, 1986. 147 pp. (ED 279 213)

Collins, C. C. *Junior College Student Personnel Programs: What They Are and What They Should Be.* Washington, D.C.: American Association of Junior Colleges, 1967. 57 pp. (ED 011 459)

Collins, C. C., and Drexel, K. O. *General Education: A Community College Model.* Pittsburg, Calif.: Community College Press, 1976.

Collins, E. C. *The Impact of Evaluation on Community College Faculty Effort and Effectiveness.* Gainesville: Institute of Higher Education, University of Florida, 1986. 74 pp. (ED 280 529)

Commission on the Future of the North Carolina Community College System. *Gaining the Competitive Edge: The Challenge to North Carolina's Community Colleges.* Chapel Hill, N.C.: MDC, Inc., 1989.

Committee on the Objectives of a General Education in a Free

Society. *General Education in a Free Society: Report of the Harvard Committee.* Cambridge, Mass.: Harvard University Press, 1945.

Community College of Philadelphia. *Facts About Former CCP Student Achievement at Transfer Schools.* Institutional Report No. 30. Philadelphia: Office of Institutional Research, Community College of Philadelphia, 1984. 38 pp. (ED 256 388)

Connecticut State Board of Trustees for State Technical Colleges. *Enrollment Information, 1985–86.* Hartford: Connecticut State Board of Trustees for State Technical Colleges, 1987. 55 pp. (ED 281 584)

Coombs, P. H. *The World Educational Crisis: A Systems Analysis.* New York: New York University Press, 1968.

Copperman, P. *The Literacy Hoax: The Decline of Reading, Writing, and Learning in the Public Schools and What We Can Do About It.* New York: Morrow, 1978.

Corson, J. J. *The Governance of Colleges and Universities.* New York: McGraw-Hill, 1960.

Cosand, J. P. *Perspective: Community Colleges in the 1980s.* Horizons Issue Monograph Series. Washington, D.C.: Council of Universities and Colleges, American Association of Community and Junior Colleges; Los Angeles: ERIC Clearinghouse for Junior Colleges, 1979.

Cotnam, J. D., and Ison, S. *A Follow-Up Study of Non-Returning Students.* Rochester, N.Y.: Monroe Community College, 1988. 17 pp. (ED 291 435)

Crist, D. C., and others. "Local Initiative for Displaced Workers Generates State Response." *Community College Review,* 1985, *13* (1), 16–19.

Cross, K. P. "Access and the Accommodation in Higher Education." Paper presented to White House Conference on Youth. *Research Reporter* (Berkeley, Calif.: Center for Research and Development in Higher Education), 1971, *6* (2), 6–8.

Cross, K. P. "Toward the Future in Community College Education." Paper presented at the Conference on Education in the Community College for the Non-Traditional Student, Philadelphia, Mar. 31, 1978. 24 pp. (ED 168 626)

Cross, K. P. *Adults as Learners: Increasing Participation and Facilitating Learning.* San Francisco: Jossey-Bass, 1981.

Cullen, C., and Moed, M. G. "Serving High-Risk Adolescents." *New Directions for Community Colleges,* 1988, *16* (3), 37–50.

Dallas, S. (ed.). *Counseling Services to Facilitate Transfer.* CSCC Bulletin, No. 4. Los Angeles: Center for the Study of Community Colleges, 1982. 6 pp. (ED 219 118)

Dallas County Community College District. *ITV Close-Up: The First Six Years.* Dallas: Dallas County Community College District, 1979. 60 pp. (ED 171 361)

Darnowski, V. S. "The Maze in Connecticut." In S. F. Charles (ed.), *Balancing State and Local Control.* New Directions for Community Colleges, no. 23. San Francisco: Jossey-Bass, 1978.

Deegan, W. L. *The Management of Student Affairs Programs in Community Colleges: Revamping Processes and Structures.* Horizons Issue Monograph Series. Washington, D.C.: Council of Universities and Colleges, American Association of Community and Junior Colleges; Los Angeles: ERIC Clearinghouse for Community Colleges, 1982. 65 pp. (ED 223 297)

Deegan, W. L. "Toward a New Paradigm: Governance in a Broader Framework." In W. L. Deegan and J. F. Gollattscheck (eds.), *Ensuring Effective Governance.* New Directions for Community Colleges, no. 49. San Francisco: Jossey-Bass, 1985. 117 pp. (ED 255 276)

Deiro, J. *Prior Learning Experiences: Handbook for Portfolio Process. Alternative Learning Experiences.* Bellingham, Wash.: Whatcom Community College, 1983. 93 pp. (ED 227 903)

de los Santos, A. G., Jr. *Changes in Credit Hour Distribution.* Phoenix, Az.: Maricopa Community Colleges, 1989.

Dennison, J. D. "Penitentiary Education in Canada: The Role for Community Colleges." Unpublished paper, 1979. 11 pp. (ED 175 522)

Devall, W. B. "Community Colleges: A Dissenting View." *Educational Record,* 1968, *49* (2), 168–172.

A Developmental Program for Metropolitan Junior College, Kansas City. Vol. 2: *Guidelines for Development.* San Francisco: Arthur D. Little, 1968.

Dickson, D. "French Minister Proposes a Nationwide System of

Two-Year Colleges." *Chronicle of Higher Education,* Jan. 13, 1988, p. A43.

Diener, T. *Growth of an American Invention: A Documentary History of the Junior and Community College Movement.* Contributions to the Study of Education, No. 16. Westport, Conn.: Greenwood Press, 1986.

Doty, C. R. "Principles of and Sources for Vertical Articulation of Occupational Education from Secondary Schools to Community Colleges." Unpublished report, 1985. 28 pp. (ED 272 673)

Doucette, D. S., and Dayton, L. L. "A Framework for Student Development Practices: A Statement of the League for Innovation in the Community College." In W. L. Deegan and T. O'Banion (eds.), *Perspectives on Student Development.* New Directions for Community Colleges, no. 67. San Francisco: Jossey-Bass, 1989.

Doucette, D. S., and Teeter, D. J. "Student Mobility Among the Public Community Colleges and Universities in the State of Kansas." Paper presented at the annual forum of the Association for Institutional Research, Portland, Oreg., Apr. 28–May 1, 1985. 42 pp. (Ed 262 844)

Dougherty, K. J. "The Politics of Community College Expansion: Beyond the Functionalist and Class-Reproduction Explanations." *American Journal of Education,* 1988, *96* (3), 351–393.

Dressel, P. L. *College Teaching as a Profession: The Doctor of Arts Degree.* East Lansing: Michigan State University, 1982. 33 pp. (ED 217 750)

Drucker, P. F. *The Practice of Management.* New York: Harper & Row, 1954.

Drucker, P. F. *The Age of Discontinuity: Guidelines to Our Changing Society.* New York: Harper & Row, 1969.

Duffy, E. F. *Characteristics and Conditions of a Successful Community College Foundation.* Resource Paper No. 23. Washington, D.C.: National Council for Resource Development, 1980. 13 pp. (ED 203 918)

Eagleton Institute of Politics. *Report on the 1986 Survey of New Jersey County Community College Students.* New Brunswick, N.J.: Eagleton Institute of Politics, Rutgers University, 1987. 276 pp. (ED 296 754)

Educational Policies Commission. *Education for All American Youth.* Washington, D.C.: Educational Policies Commission, National Education Association of the United States and American Association of School Administrators, 1944.

Educational Testing Service. *Community College Research: Methods, Trends, and Prospects.* Proceedings of the National Conference on Institutional Research in Community Colleges. Princeton, N.J.: Educational Testing Service, 1976. 205 pp. (ED 187 363)

Educational Testing Service. *The Concern for Writing.* Focus 5. Princeton, N.J.: Educational Testing Service, 1978. 18 pp. (ED 159 674—Available in microfiche only)

Eells, W. C. *The Junior College.* Boston: Houghton Mifflin, 1931.

Eells, W. C. *Present Status of Junior College Terminal Education.* Washington, D.C.: American Association of Junior Colleges, 1941a.

Eells, W. C. *Why Junior College Terminal Education?* Washington, D.C.: American Association of Junior Colleges, 1941b.

Ehrhardt, H. B. "Mountain View College's Cognitive Style Program: A Description." Unpublished paper, Mountain View College (Dallas), 1980. 18 pp. (ED 190 183)

Eldersveld, P., and Baughman, D. "Attitudes and Student Perceptions: Their Measure and Relationship to Performance in Elementary Algebra, Intermediate Algebra, College Algebra and Technical Mathematics." *Community/Junior College Quarterly of Research and Practice,* 1986, *10* (3), 203–217.

Eliot, C. W. "A Turning Point in Higher Education." Reprinted as Appendix A in A. Levine, *Handbook on Undergraduate Curriculum: Prepared for the Carnegie Council on Policy Studies in Higher Education.* San Francisco: Jossey-Bass, 1978. (Inaugural address, originally presented 1869.)

El-Khawas, E. "Colleges Reclaim the Assessment Initiative." *Educational Record,* 1987, *68* (2), 54–58.

Emerson, S. "RSVP Basic Math Lab: MAT 1992." Unpublished paper, Miami-Dade Community College, 1978. 27 pp. (ED 188 649)

Ernst, R. J. "Collective Bargaining: The Conflict Model as Norm." In W. L. Deegan and J. F. Gollattscheck (eds.), *Ensuring Effec-*

tive Governance. New Directions for Community Colleges, no. 49. San Francisco: Jossey-Bass, 1985. 117 pp. (ED 255 276)

Evans, A. J., Jr. "The Funding of Community Services." *Community Services Catalyst*, 1973, *3* (3), 17-22.

Evans, N. D., and Neagley, R. L. *Planning and Developing Innovative Community Colleges.* Englewood Cliffs, N.J.: Prentice-Hall, 1973.

Ewell, P. T. *Implementing Assessment: Some Organizational Issues.* Boulder, Colo.: National Center for Higher Education Management Systems, 1987.

Ewens, T. *Think Piece on CBE and Liberal Education.* CUE Project Occasional Paper No. 1. Bowling Green, Ohio: Bowling Green State University, 1977.

Executive Committee of the Cooperative Study in General Education. *Cooperation in General Education.* Washington, D.C.: American Council on Education, 1947.

Farmer, J. E. *A Practitioner's Guide to Student Retention: A College-Wide Responsibility.* Tallahassee: Florida State Department of Education, 1980. 28 pp. (ED 188 721)

Farnsworth, K. A. "Addressing the Needs of the Highly Talented." *Community and Junior College Journal*, 1981, *52* (4), 32-33.

Feldman, M. J. *Public Education and Manpower Development.* New York: Ford Foundation, 1967.

Fernandez, R. *Enrollment in Colleges and Universities, Fall 1985.* Washington, D.C.: National Center for Education Statistics, 1987. 17 pp. (ED 280 353)

Fernandez, T. V., and others. *Academic Performance of Community College Transfers.* Garden City, N.Y.: Nassau Community College, 1984. 8 pp. (ED 252 268)

Field Research Corporation. *A Survey of California Public Attitudes Toward the California Community Colleges.* San Francisco: Field Research Corporation, 1979. 125 pp. (ED 194 152)

Field Research Corporation. *Student Socioeconomic Characteristics, Spring 1984: First Phase of Fee-Impact Survey.* San Francisco: Field Research Corporation, 1984. 298 pp. (ED 283 567)

Field Research Corporation. *A Survey of Community College Enrollment Conducted as Part of Fee Impact Study: Second*

Follow-Up Measure, Spring, 1986. San Francisco: Field Research Corporation, 1986. 365 pp. (ED 284 618)

Fish, R. S., and McKeen, R. L. "Accommodating Different Learning Needs in Economics Education at the Community College." *Community/Junior College Quarterly of Research and Practice,* 1985, *9* (4), 325–332.

Fisher, B. W. "A Comparative Study of Two Methods of Freshman Orientation." Unpublished paper, Mississippi Gulf Coast Junior College (Gautier, Miss.), 1975. 16 pp. (ED 105 916)

Flaherty, T. *Student Characteristics as Compared to the Community Profile, Fall, 1987.* Research Report Series, Vol. 16, No. 13. Palatine, Ill.: Office of Planning and Research, William Rainey Harper College, 1988. 25 pp. (ED 880 307)

Fletcher, S. M., and others. "Community Education in Community Colleges: Today and Tomorrow." *Community Services Catalyst,* 1977, 7 (1), 10–15.

"Flexibility Sought in Award of Educational Credit." *Chronicle of Higher Education,* Feb. 6, 1978, p. 9.

Florida State Department of Education. *General Education in Community Junior Colleges.* Proceedings of Florida Annual Junior College Conference. Tallahassee: Florida State Department of Education, 1959.

Florida State Department of Education. *A Longitudinal Study Comparing University Native and Community College Transfer Students in the State University System of Florida.* Tallahassee: Division of Community Colleges, Florida State Department of Education, 1983. 26 pp. (ED 256 405)

Florida State Department of Education. *Report for Florida Community Colleges: The Fact Book.* Tallahassee: Division of Community Colleges, Florida State Department of Education, 1987. 134 pp. (ED 282 618)

Fonte, R. "State Financing of Higher Education Under Changing Conditions: The Illinois Community College Situation." Ph.D. preliminary qualifying examination, Center for the Study of Higher Education, University of Michigan, 1985. 128 pp. (ED 264 899)

Ford, M. L. "Penn Valley Community College Learning Skills Laboratory: A Resource Center for Developmental Education."

In J. R. Clarke and others, *Developmental Education in Higher Education: Advanced Institutional Developmental Program (AIDP), Two-Year College Consortium.* Vol. 2, No. 5. Washington, D.C.: McManis Associates, 1976. 44 pp. (ED 134 272)

Freedman, L. *Quality in Continuing Education: Principles, Practices, and Standards for Colleges and Universities.* San Francisco: Jossey-Bass, 1987. 195 pp. (ED 294 499)

Friedenberg, E. Z. *The Dignity of Youth and Other Atavisms.* Boston: Beacon Press, 1965.

Friedlander, J. "Instructional Practices of Part-Time Faculty in Community Colleges." Paper presented at forum of the Association for Institutional Research, San Diego, Calif., May 1979. 23 pp. (ED 169 971)

Friedlander, J. *Student and Faculty Ratings of Academic Abilities of Community College Students.* Los Angeles: Center for the Study of Community Colleges, 1981a. 14 pp. (ED 202 510)

Friedlander, J. *Why Don't Poorly Prepared Students Seek Help?* Los Angeles: Center for the Study of Community Colleges, 1981b. 14 pp. (ED 203 901)

Friedlander, J. "Coordinating Academic Support Programs with Subject Area Courses." In *Literacy in Community Colleges.* Junior College Resource Review. Los Angeles: ERIC Clearinghouse for Junior Colleges, 1982a.

Friedlander, J. *Honors Programs in Community Colleges.* Los Angeles: Center for the Study of Community Colleges, 1982b. 12 pp. (ED 220 166)

Friedlander, J., and others. *Trends in Community College Humanities Education, 1977–1982.* Los Angeles: Center for the Study of Community Colleges, 1983. 11 pp. (ED 231 431)

Froh, R., and Muraki, E. "Modification and Discontinuance of Mastery Learning Strategies." Paper presented at conference of the Mid-Western Educational Research Association, Toledo, Ohio, Oct. 1980. 50 pp. (ED 194 178—Available in microfiche only)

Gaff, J. G. *General Education Today: A Critical Analysis of Controversies, Practices, and Reforms.* San Francisco: Jossey-Bass, 1983.

Gainous, F., and others. *Remedial/Developmental Programs in Kansas Institutions of Higher Education, Fiscal Year 1985: A*

Supplemental Report. Topeka: Kansas State Department of Education, 1986. 40 pp. (ED 276 474)

Galley, J. P., and Parsons, M. H. "College Behind the Walls: Factors Influencing a Post-Secondary Inmate Education Program." Paper presented at national convention of the Community College Social Science Association, Kansas City, Oct. 1976. 13 pp. (ED 130 696)

Gay, E. J. "Student Affairs—Alternative Roles." In H. F. Robinson and others, *Expanding Student Mobility: A Challenge for Community Colleges.* Workshop Proceedings. Atlanta: Southern Regional Education Board, 1977. 71 pp. (ED 164 036)

Gell, R. L., and Armstrong, D. F. *The Graduates, 1976.* Rockville, Md.: Office of Institutional Research, Montgomery College, 1977. 54 pp. (ED 142 252)

Gendron, D., and Cavan, J. "Inmate Education: The Virginia Model." Paper presented at 68th annual convention of the American Association of Community and Junior Colleges, Las Vegas, Nev., Apr. 24-27, 1988. 13 pp. (ED 296 774)

Gilder, J., and Rocha, J. "10,000 Cooperative Arrangements Serve 1.5 Million." *Community and Junior College Journal,* 1980, *51* (3), 11-17.

Gillespie, D. A., and Carlson, N. *Trends in Student Aid: 1963 to 1983.* Washington, D.C.: College Entrance Examination Board, 1983. 68 pp. (ED 238 379)

Gittell, M. "Reaching the Hard to Reach: The Challenge of Community-Based Colleges." *Change,* 1985, *17* (4), 51-60.

Gleazer, E. J., Jr. *Responding to the New Spirit of Learning.* Washington, D.C.: American Association of Community and Junior Colleges, 1976. 20 pp. (ED 129 381)

Gleazer, E. J., Jr. *The Community College: Values, Vision, and Vitality.* Washington, D.C.: American Association of Community and Junior Colleges, 1980.

Goddard, J. M., and Polk, C. H. "Community College Trustees: Elect or Appoint?" *AGB Reports,* 1976, *18* (3), 37-40.

Gold, B. K., and Morris, W. *Student Accountability Model (SAM): Operations Manual.* Sacramento: Office of the Chancellor, California Community Colleges; Los Angeles: Los Angeles Community College District, 1977. 99 pp. (ED 135 443)

Goldberg, A. "Reflections of a Two Year College Dean." *NASPA Journal*, 1973, *11* (1), 39–42.

Golemon, R. B. *A Survey of Non-Traditional Credit in Texas.* Austin: Texas Association of Junior and Community College Instructional Administrators, 1979. 9 pp. (ED 170 008)

Gollattscheck, J. F. "Developing and Maintaining Governance." In W. L. Deegan and J. F. Gollattscheck (eds.), *Ensuring Effective Governance.* New Directions for Community Colleges, no. 49. San Francisco: Jossey-Bass, 1985. 117 pp. (ED 255 276)

Gottschalk, K. "Can Colleges Deal with High-Risk Community Problems?" *Community College Frontiers,* 1978, *6* (4), 4–11.

Grafton, C. L., and Roy, D. D. "The 'Second-Time Around' Community College Student: Assessment of Reverse Transfer Student Performance in a University Setting." Paper presented at annual meeting of the American Educational Research Association, Boston, Apr. 1980. 33 pp. (ED 184 620)

Grant, W. V., and Eiden, L. J. *Digest of Education Statistics, 1982.* Washington, D.C.: National Center for Education Statistics, U.S. Department of Education, 1982. 236 pp. (ED 225 272)

Grant, W. V., and Snyder, T. D. *Digest of Education Statistics, 1985–86.* Washington, D.C.: National Center for Education Statistics, U.S. Department of Education, 1986. 288 pp. (ED 270 903)

Gray, M. D., and Hardy, R. C. "A Preliminary Investigation of Grade Point Average of Early and Late Applicants to Community Colleges." Paper presented at annual meeting of the American Educational Research Association, San Francisco, Apr. 16–20, 1986. 10 pp. (ED 269 085)

Green, T. F. *Predicting the Behavior of the Educational System.* Syracuse, N.Y.: Syracuse University Press, 1980.

Greenan, J. P. "The Utility of Student Self-Ratings and Teacher Ratings for Assessing Students' Generalizable Skills." *Community/Junior College Quarterly of Research and Practice,* 1983, *7* (3), 231–252.

Grissom, G. R., and McMurphy, S. *College-Correctional Collaboration in the Treatment of Juvenile Offenders: Evaluation of a Program Model in Six Sites.* Final Report. Philadelphia: Criminal Justice Institute, University City Science Center, 1986.

Gulf Coast Community College. *Special Programs for Single Parents/Displaced Homemakers: Final Report from October 1986 to June 30, 1987.* Panama City, Fla.: Gulf Coast Community College, 1987. 106 pp. (ED 287 975)

Hammond, L. N., and Porter, G. N. *Follow-Up Study of 1981–82 Students: North Carolina Community College System.* Raleigh: Division of Planning and Research Services, North Carolina State Department of Community Colleges, 1984. 19 pp. (ED 259 806)

Hammons, J., and Thomas, W. "Performance Appraisal of Community College Department/Division Chairpersons." *Community College Review,* 1980, 7 (3), 41–49.

Hand, C. A., and Prather, J. E. "Factors That Influence Transfer Activity: A Cross-Institutional Study." Paper presented at annual meeting of the Southern Association of Institutional Research, Little Rock, Ark., Oct. 25–26, 1984a. 27 pp. (ED 251 030)

Hand, C. A., and Prather, J. E. *A Review of Transfer Student Activity Among Georgia State University and Selected Institutions of the University System of Georgia.* Institutional Research Report No. 84-8. Atlanta: Office of Institutional Planning, Georgia State University, 1984b. 21 pp. (ED 240 967)

Hankin, J. N. "Who Bargains with Whom: What's Past Is Prologue." Unpublished paper, Westchester Community College (Valhalla, N.Y.), 1975. 37 pp. (ED 100 476)

Harlacher, E. L., and Gollattscheck, J. F. "Editors' Notes." In E. L. Harlacher and J. F. Gollattscheck (eds.), *Implementing Community-Based Education.* New Directions for Community Colleges, no. 21. San Francisco: Jossey-Bass, 1978.

Harlacher, E. L., and Ireland, J. "Community Services and Continuing Education: An Information Age Necessity." *Community Services Catalyst,* 1988, *18* (1), 3–5.

Harper, H., and others. *Advisement and Graduation Information System.* Miami: Miami-Dade Community College, 1981. 34 pp. (ED 197 776)

Harris, J. "Assessing Outcomes in Higher Education." In C. Adelman (ed.), *Assessment in American Higher Education: Issues and Contexts.* Washington, D.C.: Office of Educational Research and Improvement, 1986. 90 pp. (ED 273 197)

Harris, N. C., and Grede, J. F. *Career Education in Colleges: A Guide for Planning Two- and Four-Year Occupational Programs for Successful Employment*. San Francisco: Jossey-Bass, 1977.

Harrison, D. J. "Changing Tides and Liberal Studies." *Journal of General Education*, 1987, *38* (4), 262–271.

Hartmann, J. "Link Up for Gerontology." *Community, Junior and Technical College Journal*, 1986, *56* (5), 58–61.

Hauselman, A. J., and Tudor, D. (eds.). *Compendium of Selected Data and Characteristics: University of Kentucky Community College System, 1986–87*. Lexington: University of Kentucky Community College System, 1987. 95 pp. (ED 289 543)

Havlicek, L. L., and Coulter, T. "Development of a Junior College CMI [Computer-Managed Instruction]." Paper presented at annual meeting of the American Educational Research Association, New York, Mar. 19–23, 1982. 9 pp. (ED 214 613)

Hawaii Interviewing. *Single Parents/Homemakers in Hawaii: A Study of Vocational Education Needs*. Honolulu: Hawaii Interviewing, 1986. 531 pp. (ED 269 603)

Heard, F. B. "The Development of a Computerized Curriculum Monitoring System to Ensure Student Success." Ed.D. practicum, Nova University, 1987. 44 pp. (ED 296 750)

Heiner, H., and Nelson, J. M. (eds.). *A Manual for Student Services*. Olympia: Washington State Board for Community College Education; Washington State Services Commission, 1977. 47 pp. (ED 145 867)

Henderson, J. J., and Schick, F. L. (eds.). *The Bowker Annual of Library and Book Trade Information*. New York: Bowker, 1973, 1977, 1978.

Herder, D. M., and Standridge, L. A. "Continuing Education: Blueprint for Excellence." Unpublished paper, Lansing Community College (Lansing, Mich.), 1980. 14 pp. (ED 187 391)

Herzberg, F., Mausner, B., and Snyderman, B. D. *The Motivation to Work*. New York: Wiley, 1959.

Higginbottom, G. H. *Civic Education in the Community College*. Working Paper Series No. 1-86. Binghamton, N.Y.: Institute for Community College Research, Broome Community College, 1986. 15 pp. (ED 272 256)

Hill, M. D. "Some Factors Affecting the Job Satisfaction of Community College Faculty in Pennsylvania." *Community/Junior College Quarterly of Research and Practice,* 1983, 7 (4), 303–317.

Hines, E., and Pruyne, G. *Grapevine: The Community College Issues, 1977–1988.* Normal: Center for Higher Education, Illinois State University, 1988. 66 pp. (ED 290 516)

Hollins, C. S., and Smith, M. G. *Where Have All the Students Gone? A Study of Student Attrition at John Tyler Community College, Winter 1986 to Spring 1986.* Chester, Va.: Office of Institutional Research, John Tyler Community College, 1986. 50 pp. (ED 274 410)

Hollinshead, B. S. "The Community College Program." *Junior College Journal,* 1936, 7, 111–116.

Houston Community College System. *A Comparison of Traditional Vocational Training with a Vocational Training Model Infusing Remedial Academic Skills Training.* Final Report. Houston: Houston Community College System, 1986. 44 pp. (ED 281 034)

Howard, A., and others. *Instructional Computing in the Community Colleges of Washington State.* Olympia: Washington State Board for Community College Education, 1978. 148 pp. (ED 172 891)

Howard, J. H. *Adult Basic Education Career Development Center in the Newark Model Cities Area, for the Period Ending December 31, 1974.* Final Report. Newark, N.J.: Essex County College, 1976. 72 pp. (ED 133 027)

Humphreys, J. A. "Toward Improved Programs of Student Personnel Services." *Junior College Journal,* 1952, 22 (7), 382–392.

Hunter, R., and Sheldon, M. S. *Statewide Longitudinal Study: Report on Academic Year 1978–79.* Part 1: *Fall Results.* Woodland Hills, Calif.: Los Angeles Pierce College, 1979. 86 pp. (ED 180 530)

Hunter, R., and Sheldon, M. S. *Statewide Longitudinal Study: Report on Academic Year 1979–80.* Part 3: *Fall Results.* Woodland Hills, Calif.: Los Angeles Pierce College, 1980. 95 pp. (ED 188 714)

Hurn, C. J. "The Prospects for Liberal Education: A Sociological Perspective." *Phi Delta Kappan,* 1979, *60* (9), 630–633.

Hutchins, R. M. *The Higher Learning in America.* New Haven, Conn.: Yale University Press, 1937.

Illich, I. *Lima Discourse.* Cuernavaca, Mexico: Centro Intercultural de Documentación, 1971.

Illinois Community College Board. "Curriculum Enrollment Summary in the Public Community Colleges of Illinois: 1975–76." Unpublished paper, Illinois Community College Board, 1976.

Illinois Community College Board. *A Study of Shifts in Enrollment and Completion Patterns in Illinois Public Community College Programs.* Springfield: Illinois Community College Board, 1985. 26 pp. (ED 270 187)

Illinois Community College Board. *Illinois Community College Board Transfer Study: A Five-Year Study of Students Transferring from Illinois Two-Year Colleges to Illinois Senior Colleges/Universities in the Fall of 1979.* Springfield: Illinois Community College Board, 1986a. 107 pp. (ED 270 148)

Illinois Community College Board. *Minority Student Participation: Illinois Public Community College System, Fiscal Years 1963 Through 1986.* Springfield: Illinois Community College Board, 1986b. 96 pp. (ED 275 360)

Illinois Community College Board. *Fall 1986 Salary Survey Report for the Illinois Public Community Colleges.* Springfield: Illinois Community College Board, 1987a. 44 pp. (ED 277 426)

Illinois Community College Board. *Fiscal Year 1987 Economic Development Grant Report.* Springfield: Illinois Community College Board, 1987b. 19 pp. (ED 290 521)

Illinois Community College Board. *Follow-Up Study of Students Who Completed Community College Occupational Programs During Fiscal Years 1983–1985.* Springfield: Illinois Community College Board, 1987c. 55 pp. (ED 282 614)

Illinois Community College Board. *Student Enrollment Data and Trends in the Public Community Colleges of Illinois: Fall 1987.* Springfield: Illinois Community College Board, 1988. 50 pp. (ED 291 432)

Illinois Community College Board. *Special Programs for Minority Students at Illinois Community Colleges.* Springfield: Illinois Community College Board, 1989.

Ingram, R. T., and Henderson, L. E. "Institutional Governing

Boards and Trustees." In M. W. Peterson and L. A. Mets (eds.), *Key Resources on Higher Education Governance, Management, and Leadership: A Guide to the Literature.* San Francisco: Jossey-Bass, 1987.

Ireland, J. "Community Services: A Position Paper." Unpublished paper, Office of Community Services, Rio Hondo College (Whittier, Calif.), 1979. 35 pp. (ED 180 562)

Jellison, H. M. (ed.). *Small Business Training: A Guide for Program Building.* Washington, D.C.: Association of American Community and Junior Colleges, 1983. 68 pp. (ED 229 072)

Jencks, C., and Riesman, D. *The Academic Revolution.* New York: Doubleday, 1968.

Jenkins, J. A., and Rossmeier, J. G. *Relationships Between Centralization/Decentralization and Organizational Effectiveness in Urban Multi-Unit Community College Systems: A Summary Report.* Ann Arbor: Center for the Study of Higher Education, University of Michigan, 1974. 33 pp. (ED 110 103)

Johnson, B. E. *Success Rate Comparisons for DeKalb Developmental Studies Students.* Clarkston, Ga.: DeKalb Area Vocational-Technical School, 1985. 14 pp. (ED 254 297)

Johnson, B. L. "The Extent of the Present General Education Program in the Colleges and Universities of America." Paper presented at the University of Florida, July 1937.

Johnson, B. L. *Vitalizing a College Library.* Chicago: American Library Association, 1939.

Johnson, B. L. *General Education in Action.* Washington, D.C.: American Council on Education, 1952.

Johnson, B. L. *Islands of Innovation Expanding: Changes in the Community College.* Beverly Hills, Calif.: Glencoe Press, 1969.

Johnson, D. C. "Managing Non-Profit Marketing." In R. E. Lahti (ed.), *Managing in a New Era.* New Directions for Community Colleges, no. 28. San Francisco: Jossey-Bass, 1979.

Kalamas, D. J., and Warmbrod, C. A. (eds.). *Linking with Employers. OPTIONS. Expanding Educational Services for Adults.* Columbus: National Center for Research in Vocational Education, Ohio State University, 1987. 239 pp. (ED 288 987)

Kangas, J. A. *Matriculation: Profiles of Practices in California Community Colleges.* Sacramento: California Community Colleges, Learning Assessment Retention Consortium, 1985. 182 pp. (ED 271 141)

Kansas State Department of Education. *Minority Student Enrollment in Kansas Community Colleges.* Topeka: Kansas State Department of Education, 1986. 10 pp. (ED 273 330)

Kaplin, W. A. *The Law of Higher Education: A Comprehensive Guide to Legal Implications of Administrative Decision Making.* (2nd ed.) San Francisco: Jossey-Bass, 1985.

Kaprelian, N., and Perona, J. "Gateway Technical Institute Competency Based Education: Case Study of College-Wide Instructional Improvement." Paper presented at annual convention of the American Association of Community and Junior Colleges, Washington, D.C., Apr. 20–22, 1981. 11 pp. (ED 203 954)

Karabel, J. "Community Colleges and Social Stratification." *Harvard Educational Review,* 1972, *42* (4), 521–562.

Karabel, J. "Community Colleges and Social Stratification in the 1980s." In L. S. Zwerling (ed.), *The Community College and Its Critics.* New Directions for Community Colleges, no. 54. San Francisco: Jossey-Bass, 1986.

Katz, J. M. "The Educational Shibboleth: Equality of Opportunity in a Democratic Institution, the Public Junior College." Unpublished doctoral dissertation, Department of Sociology, University of California at Los Angeles, 1967.

Kelly, J. T. *Restructuring the Academic Program: A Systems Approach to Educational Reform at Miami-Dade Community College.* Miami: Miami-Dade Community College, 1981. 7 pp. (ED 211 138)

Kelly, J. T., and Anandam, K. "Instruction for Distant Learners Through Technology." Paper presented at 3rd International Conference on Improving University Teaching, Newcastle-upon-Tyne, England, June 1977. 16 pp. (ED 139 455)

Kemerer, F. R., and Baldridge, J. V. *Unions on Campus: A National Study of the Consequences of Faculty Bargaining.* San Francisco: Jossey-Bass, 1975.

Kester, D. L. "Is Micro-Computer Assisted Basic Skills Instruction Good for Black, Disadvantaged Community College Students from Watts and Similar Communities? A Preliminary Fall Semester 1981–1982 Mini Audit Report Suggests Caution." Paper presented at the International School Psychology Colloquium, Stockholm, Aug. 1-6, 1982. 14 pp. (ED 219 111)

Kintzer, F. C. *Middleman in Higher Education: Improving Articulation Among High School, Community College, and Senior Institutions.* San Francisco: Jossey-Bass, 1973.

Kintzer, F. C. *Organization and Leadership of Two-Year Colleges: Preparing for the Eighties.* Gainesville: Institute of Higher Education, University of Florida, 1980a.

Kintzer, F. C. *Proposition 13: Implications for Community Colleges.* Topical Paper No. 72. Los Angeles: ERIC Clearinghouse for Junior Colleges, 1980b. 39 pp. (ED 188 711)

Kintzer, F. C. *Decision Making in Multi-Unit Institutions of Higher Education.* Gainesville: Institute of Higher Education, University of Florida, 1984. 56 pp. (ED 242 362)

Kintzer, F. C., Jensen, A., and Hansen, J. *The Multi-Institution Junior College District.* Horizons Issue Monograph Series. Los Angeles: ERIC Clearinghouse for Junior Colleges; Washington, D.C.: American Association of Junior Colleges, 1969. 64 pp. (ED 030 415)

Kintzer, F. C., and Wattenbarger, J. L. *The Articulation/Transfer Phenomenon: Patterns and Directions.* Horizons Issue Monograph Series. Washington, D.C.: Council of Universities and Colleges, American Association of Community and Junior Colleges, 1985. 85 pp. (ED 257 539)

Kirkwood Community College. *Strengthening the Humanities.* Cedar Rapids, Iowa: Kirkwood Community College, 1986. 31 pp. (ED 283 536)

Kirsch, I. S., and Jungeblut, A. *Literacy: Profiles of America's Young Adults.* Princeton, N.J.: National Assessment of Educational Progress, 1986. 79 pp. (ED 275 692)

Knapp, M. S. "Factors Contributing to the Development of Institutional Research and Planning Units in Community Colleges: A Review of the Empirical Evidence." Paper presented at annual meeting of the American Educational Research Association, Special Interest Group on Community and Junior College Research, San Francisco, Apr. 1979. 18 pp. (ED 168 663)

Knoell, D. M., and Medsker, L. L. *From Junior to Senior Colleges:*

A National Study of the Transfer Student. Washington, D.C.: American Council on Education, 1965.

Kohl, P. L., and others. *Abstract of the American College Testing Class Profile for Fall 1979 Freshmen Enrolled in Illinois Public Community Colleges.* Springfield: Illinois Community College Board, 1980. 30 pp. (ED 190 194)

Koltai, L. *The Agony of Change.* Junior College Resource Review. Los Angeles: ERIC Clearinghouse for Junior Colleges, 1980. 6 pp. (ED 187 382)

Koos, L. V. *The Junior College.* (2 vols.) Minneapolis: University of Minnesota Press, 1924.

Koos, L. V. *The Junior College Movement.* Boston: Ginn, 1925.

Koos, L. V. "Preparation for Community College Teaching." *Journal of Higher Education,* 1950, *21,* 309–317.

Kopecek, R. J. "An Idea Whose Time Is Come: Not-for-Profit Foundations for Public Community Colleges." *Community College Review,* 1982–83, *10* (3), 12–17.

Kopecek, R. J., and Clarke, R. G. (eds.). *Customized Job Training for Business and Industry.* New Directions for Community Colleges, no. 48. San Francisco: Jossey-Bass, 1984. 119 pp. (ED 252 267)

Kuttner, B. "The Declining Middle." *Atlantic,* 1983, *252* (1), 60–64, 66–67, 69–72.

Lake City Community College. *A Focus on Rural Upward Mobility for Single Parents and/or Homemakers: Final Report from July 1, 1986, to June 30, 1987.* Lake City, Fla.: Lake City Community College, 1987. 34 pp. (ED 285 043)

Lander, V. L. "The Significance of Structure in Arizona Community College Districts: A Limited Study." Unpublished paper, Tucson, Ariz., 1977. 83 pp. (ED 139 481)

Landsburg, D., and Witt, S. "Writing Across the Curriculum: One Small Step." *Innovation Abstracts,* 1984, *6* (entire issue 13).

Larkin, P. G. *Who Wants a Degree? Educational Goals and Related Preferences of Off-Campus Students at Five Extension and Degree Centers.* Report No. 77-5. Largo, Md.: Office of Institutional Research, Prince George's Community College, 1977. 61 pp. (ED 143 383—Available in microfiche only)

Lee, B. S. *Follow-Up of Occupational Education Students: Los*

Rios Community College District, Spring 1983. Sacramento, Calif.: Los Rios Community College District, 1984. 77 pp. (ED 241 099)

Lee, B. S. *Measures of Progress, 1984–1987: A Four-Year Retrospective. Los Rios Community College District.* Sacramento, Calif.: Office of Planning and Research, Los Rios Community College District, 1987. 68 pp. (ED 293 580)

Lee, R. "Age-Related Adult Developmental Stages Among Two-Year College Faculty." Unpublished doctoral dissertation, Graduate School of Education, University of California at Los Angeles, 1977.

Leonard, G. B. *Education and Ecstasy.* New York: Delacorte Press, 1968.

Leone, A. *One Year Later, 1984: A Survey of Mercer Graduates of FY 1983.* Technical Report 85-04. Trenton, N.J.: Office of Institutional Research, Mercer County Community College, 1984. 45 pp. (ED 261 748)

Levine, D. O. *The American College and the Culture of Aspiration, 1915–1940.* Ithaca, N.Y.: Cornell University Press, 1986.

Lewis, G., and Merisotis, J. P. *Trends in Student Aid: 1980 to 1987: Update.* Washington, D.C.: College Entrance Examination Board, 1987. 15 pp. (ED 288 466)

Lieberman, J. E. (ed.). *Collaborating with High Schools.* New Directions for Community Colleges, no. 63. San Francisco: Jossey-Bass, 1988.

Lindahl, D. G. "Giving Students Credit for What They Already Know." *VocEd,* 1982, *57* (1), 44–45.

Lockett, C. R., Jr. *An Analysis of Current Problems and Procedures Relating to Articulation Between Public Secondary Schools in Duval and Nassau Counties and Florida Junior College.* Final Report. Jacksonville: Florida Junior College, 1981. 76 pp. (ED 230 246)

Lombardi, J. *The Department/Division Structure in the Community College.* Topical Paper No. 38. Los Angeles: ERIC Clearinghouse for Junior Colleges, 1973a. 25 pp. (ED 085 051)

Lombardi, J. *Managing Finances in Community Colleges.* San Francisco: Jossey-Bass, 1973b.

Lombardi, J. *The Duties and Responsibilities of the Department/*

Division Chairman in Community Colleges. Topical Paper No. 39. Los Angeles: ERIC Clearinghouse for Junior Colleges, 1974. 21 pp. (ED 089 811)

Lombardi, J. *Riding the Wave of New Enrollments.* Topical Paper No. 50. Los Angeles: ERIC Clearinghouse for Junior Colleges, 1975. 58 pp. (ED 107 326)

Lombardi, J. *No or Low Tuition: A Lost Cause.* Topical Paper No. 58. Los Angeles: ERIC Clearinghouse for Junior Colleges, 1976. 46 pp. (ED 129 353)

Lombardi, J. *Community Education: Threat to College Status?* Topical Paper No. 68. Los Angeles: ERIC Clearinghouse for Junior Colleges, 1978a. 45 pp. (ED 156 296)

Lombardi, J. *Resurgence of Occupational Education.* Topical Paper No. 65. Los Angeles: ERIC Clearinghouse for Junior Colleges, 1978b. 41 pp. (ED 148 418)

Lombardi, J. *Changing Administrative Relations Under Collective Bargaining.* Junior College Resource Review. Los Angeles: ERIC Clearinghouse for Junior Colleges, 1979a. 8 pp. (ED 170 015)

Lombardi, J. *The Decline of Transfer Education.* Topical Paper No. 70. Los Angeles: ERIC Clearinghouse for Junior Colleges, 1979b. 37 pp. (ED 179 273)

Lombardi, J. "Proposition 13: Is the Worst Over for Community Colleges?" *Community College Review,* 1979c, *6* (4), 7-14.

London, H. B. *The Culture of a Community College.* New York: Praeger, 1978.

Losak, J. (ed.). *Applying Institutional Research in Decision Making.* New Directions for Community Colleges, no. 56. San Francisco: Jossey-Bass, 1986.

Losak, J. "Assessment and Improvement in Education." In D. Bray and M. J. Belcher (eds.), *Issues in Student Assssment.* New Directions for Community Colleges, no. 59. San Francisco: Jossey-Bass, 1987.

Losak, J., Schwartz, M. I., and Morris, C. "College Students in Remedial Courses Report on Their High School Preparation." *College Board Review,* 1982, no. 125, pp. 21-22, 29-30.

Lowe, I. D. *Program Evaluation at Foothill College.* Los Altos Hills, Calif.: Foothill College, 1983. 30 pp. (ED 231 406)

Lucas, J. A. *Follow-Up Study of 1983 Harper Transfer Alumni.* Research Report Series, Vol. 14, No. 8. Palatine, Ill.: Office of Planning and Research, William Rainey Harper College, 1986a. 98 pp. (ED 270 196)

Lucas, J. A. *Longitudinal Study of Performance of Students Entering Harper College, 1974–1984.* Research Report Series, Vol. 14, No. 6. Palatine, Ill.: Office of Planning and Research, William Rainey Harper College, 1986b. 17 pp. (ED 264 931)

Lucas, J. A. *Follow-Up Study of 1986 Harper Career Alumni.* Research Report Series, Vol. 16, No. 9. Palatine, Ill.: Office of Planning and Research, William Rainey Harper College, 1988. 46 pp. (ED 291 456)

Lukenbill, J. D., and McCabe, R. H. *General Education in a Changing Society: General Education Program, Basic Skills Requirements, Standards of Academic Progress at Miami-Dade Community College.* Miami: Office of Institutional Research, Miami-Dade Community College, 1978. 98 pp. (ED 158 812)

Lundgren, C. A. "A Comparison of the Effects of Programmed Instruction and Computer-Assisted Instruction on Computer Achievement in English Grammar." *Delta Pi Epsilon Journal,* 1985, *27* (1), 1–9.

Luskin, B. J., and Small, J. "The Need to Change and the Need to Stay the Same." *Community and Junior College Journal,* 1980–81, *51* (4), 24–28.

Lyons, G. "The Higher Illiteracy." *Harper's,* 1976, *253* (1516), 33–40.

McCabe, R. H. "Now Is the Time to Reform the American Community College." *Community and Junior College Journal,* 1981, *51* (8), 6–10.

McClintock, R. "The Dynamics of Decline: Why Education Can No Longer Be Liberal." *Phi Delta Kappan,* 1979, *60* (9), 636–640.

McCombs, C. *Evaluation and Professional Development for the Instructional Supervisor.* Pendleton, S.C.: Tri-County Technical College, 1980. 80 pp. (ED 216 716)

McDowell, F. M. *The Junior College.* Bureau of Education Bulletin No. 35. Washington, D.C.: U.S. Government Printing Office, 1919.

McGuire, K. B. *State of the Art in Community-Based Education in the American Community College.* Washington, D.C.: Association of American Community and Junior Colleges, 1988. 77 pp. (ED 293 583)

McIntyre, C. "Assessing Community College Transfer Performance." *Research in Higher Education,* 1987, 27 (2), 142–161.

McKinney, H., and Davis, D. A. "Patterns of Funding in Vocational Education." *Community, Technical, and Junior College Journal,* 1988, 58 (5), 44–47.

McLean, C. E. *TNCC Student Opinion Survey.* Hampton, Va.: Office of Institutional Research, Thomas Nelson Community College, 1986. 22 pp. (ED 276 479)

McMaster, A. *Non-Returning Students: Full Time and Part Time, Spring 1981–Spring 1982 and Fall 1982–Fall 1983.* Technical Report, 85-03. Trenton, N.J.: Office of Institutional Research, Mercer County Community College, 1984. 35 pp. (ED 261 747)

Marcotte, J. "The Impact of Developmental Education on the Graduation Rate of Students with Low Combined Differential Aptitude Test Scores." Unpublished report, 1986. 10 pp. (ED 271 172)

Marsh, J. P., and Lamb, T. (eds.). "An Introduction to the Part-Time Teaching Situation with Particular Emphasis on Its Impact at Napa Community College." Unpublished paper, Napa Community College (Napa, Calif.), 1975. 46 pp. (ED 125 683)

Martens, K. J. *Project Priority, 1974–1975: An ESEA Funded Project.* Final Report. Albany: Two Year College Student Development Center, State University of New York, 1975. 30 pp. (ED 139 475)

Martorana, S. V. "Shifting Patterns of Financial Support." In R. L. Alfred (ed.), *Coping with Reduced Resources.* New Directions for Community Colleges, no. 22. San Francisco: Jossey-Bass, 1978.

Martorana, S. V., and Piland, W. E. "Promises and Pitfalls in Serving Organized Community-Based Group Interests." In S. V. Martorana and W. E. Piland (eds.), *Designing Programs for Community Groups.* New Directions for Community Colleges, no. 45. San Francisco: Jossey-Bass, 1984.

Maryland State Board for Community Colleges. *Statewide Master Plan for Community Colleges in Maryland, Fiscal Years 1978–*

1987. Annapolis: Maryland State Board for Community Colleges, 1977. 227 pp. (ED 139 454)

Maryland State Board for Community Colleges. *Maryland Community Colleges Continuing Education Manual.* Annapolis: Maryland State Board for Community Colleges, 1988. 84 pp. (ED 295 700)

Maryland State Board for Community Colleges. *The Role of Community Colleges in Preparing Students for Transfer to Four-Year Colleges and Universities: The Maryland Experience.* Annapolis: Maryland State Board for Community Colleges, 1983. 27 pp. (ED 230 255)

Maryland State Board for Community Colleges. *Blueprint for Quality: Final Report of the Committee on the Future of Maryland Community Colleges.* Annapolis: Maryland State Board for Community Colleges, 1986. 145 pp. (ED 275 367)

Maryland State Board for Community Colleges. *State Plan for Community Colleges in Maryland: Interim Report.* Annapolis: Maryland State Board for Community Colleges, 1987. 128 pp. (ED 276 486)

Maryland State Board for Community Colleges. *Maryland Community Colleges: 1987 Program Evaluations.* Annapolis: Maryland State Board for Community Colleges, 1988. 178 pp. (ED 295 699)

Mayhew, L. B. (ed.). *General Education: An Account and Appraisal.* New York: Harper & Row, 1960.

Medsker, L. L. *The Junior College: Progress and Prospect.* New York: McGraw-Hill, 1960.

Medsker, L. L., and Tillery, D. *Breaking the Access Barriers: A Profile of Two-Year Colleges.* New York: McGraw-Hill, 1971.

Meier, T. *Washington Community College Factbook. Addendum A: Student Enrollments, Academic Year 1978-79.* Olympia: Washington State Board for Community College Education, 1980. 123 pp. (ED 184 616)

Menke, D. H. "A Comparison of Transfer and Native Bachelor's Degree Recipients at UCLA, 1976-1978." Unpublished doctoral dissertation, Graduate School of Education, University of California at Los Angeles, 1980.

Miami-Dade Community College. *RSVP: Feedback Program for Individualized Analysis of Writing, Manual for Faculty Users.*

Part 1: *Analyzing Students' Writing*. Miami: Miami-Dade Community College, 1979. 77 pp. (ED 190 167)

Miami-Dade Community College. *Miami-Dade Community College 1984 Institutional Self-Study*. Vol. 2: *Prescriptive Education*. Miami: Miami-Dade Community College, 1985. 118 pp. (ED 259 770)

Middleton, L. "Emphasis on Standards at Miami-Dade Leads to 8,000 Dismissals and Suspensions in Three Years." *Chronicle of Higher Education*, Feb. 3, 1981, pp. 3-4.

Miller, D. J. "Analysis of Professional Development Activities of Iowa Community College Faculty." Unpublished Master of Science dissertation, Iowa State University, 1985. 121 pp. (ED 260 766)

Miller, M. F. *College Discovery Pre-Freshman Summer Program: Longitudinal Academic Outcomes for 1985 and 1986 and Program Data for 1987*. Bayside, N.Y.: Queensborough Community College, 1987. 89 pp. (ED 286 546)

Miller, R. I. *The Assessment of College Performance: A Handbook of Techniques and Measures for Institutional Self-Evaluation*. San Francisco: Jossey-Bass, 1979.

Miller, R. I. (ed.). *Evaluating Major Components of Two-Year Colleges*. Washington, D.C.: College and University Personnel Association, 1988.

Miller, S. E. *Financial Aid for Community College Students: Unique Needs and Scarce Resources*. Washington, D.C.: Division of Policy Analysis and Research, American Council on Education, 1985. 23 pp. (ED 269 053)

Monroe, C. R. *Profile of the Community College: A Handbook*. San Francisco: Jossey-Bass, 1972.

Montemayor, J. J., and others. *Non-Returning Students*. Project Follow-Up Report No. 5, Research Report 3. Glendale, Ariz.: Office of Research and Development, Glendale Community College, 1985. 24 pp. (ED 280 511)

Montesi, S. *Transfer Student Analysis*. University Center, Mich.: Delta College, 1986. 94 pp. (ED 287 546)

Montgomery College. *A Report on the Possible Influence of Economic Conditions in the Washington Metropolitan Area on Student Enrollment at Montgomery College*. Rockville, Md.:

Office of Institutional Research, Montgomery College, 1983. 27 pp. (ED 245 751)

Moody, G. V., and Busby, M. R. *Mississippi Public Junior Colleges Statistical Data, 1977–78.* Jackson: Division of Junior Colleges, Mississippi State Department of Education, 1978. 52 pp. (ED 167 214)

Morris, C., and Losak, J. *A Survey of Scholar's Grant Recipients, Fall Term 1979–80.* Research Report 80-86. Miami: Office of Institutional Research, Miami-Dade Community College, 1980. 32 pp. (ED 194 153)

Morrison, J. L., and Ferrante, R. "The Public Two-Year College and the Culturally Different." Paper presented at annual meeting of the American Educational Research Association, New Orleans, Feb. 1973. 35 pp. (ED 073 765)

Mundt, J. C. "State vs. Local Control: Reality and Myth over Concern for Local Autonomy." In S. F. Charles (ed.), *Balancing State and Local Control.* New Directions for Community Colleges, no. 23. San Francisco: Jossey-Bass, 1978.

Murdock, T. A. "The Effect of Financial Aid on Student Persistence." Paper presented at annual meeting of the Association for the Study of Higher Education, San Diego, Calif., Feb. 14–17, 1987. 47 pp. (ED 281 477)

Myran, G. A. *Community Services in the Community College.* Washington, D.C.: American Association of Junior Colleges, 1969. 60 pp. (ED 037 202)

Myran, G. A. "Antecedents: Evolution of the Community-Based College." In E. L. Harlacher and J. F. Gollattscheck (eds.), *Implementing Community-Based Education.* New Directions for Community Colleges, no. 21. San Francisco: Jossey-Bass, 1978.

National Center for Education Statistics. *Opening (Fall) Enrollments in Higher Education.* Washington, D.C.: National Center for Education Statistics, U.S. Department of Education, 1963–present (published annually).

National Center for Education Statistics. *Condition of Education.* Washington, D.C.: National Center for Education Statistics, U.S. Department of Education, 1970–present (published annually).

National Center for Education Statistics. *Digest of Education Statistics.* Washington, D.C.: National Center for Education Statistics,

U.S. Department of Education, 1970–present (published annually).

National Center for Education Statistics. *Library Statistics for Colleges and Universities.* Washington, D.C.: National Center for Education Statistics, U.S. Department of Education, 1975.

National Center for Education Statistics. *Integrated Postsecondary Education Data System Survey Data.* Computerized Data Files. Washington, D.C.: Center for Education Statistics, U.S. Department of Education, 1986a.

National Center for Education Statistics. *Scholarship and Fellowship Expenditures: OERI Historical Report.* Washington, D.C.: National Center for Education Statistics, U.S. Department of Education, 1986b. 6 pp. (ED 282 483)

National Center for Education Statistics. *College and University Libraries, Fall 1985.* Washington, D.C.: National Center for Education Statistics, U.S. Department of Education, 1987. 16 pp. (ED 283 527)

National Center for Education Statistics. *Current Funds, Revenues and Expenditures in Institutions of Higher Education: Fiscal Years 1983–1986.* Washington, D.C.: National Center for Education Statistics, U.S. Department of Education, 1988. 28 pp. (ED 293 468)

National Center for the Study of Collective Bargaining in Higher Education and the Professions. *Directory of Faculty Contracts and Bargaining Agents in Institutions of Higher Education.* New York: National Center for the Study of Collective Bargaining in Higher Education and the Professions, 1974–present (published annually).

National Science Board. *Undergraduate Science, Mathematics and Engineering Education.* Washington, D.C.: Task Committee on Undergraduate Science and Engineering Education, National Science Board, 1986. 67 pp. (ED 272 398)

National Society for the Study of Education. *General Education in the American College.* Bloomington, Ind.: National Society for the Study of Education, 1939.

Nelson, J. E. "Student Aid at the Two-Year College: Who Gets the Money?" Paper presented at annual convention of the American

Association of Community and Junior Colleges, Washington, D.C., Mar. 1976. 12 pp. (ED 124 223)

Nelson, S. C. "Future Financing and Economic Trends." *Community and Junior College Journal,* 1980, *51* (1) 41–44.

Nespoli, L. A., and Radcliffe, S. K. *Student Evaluation of College Services.* Research Report No. 29. Columbia, Md.: Office of Research and Planning, Howard Community College, 1982. 54 pp. (ED 224 541)

Nespoli, L. A., and Radcliffe, S. K. *Census Analysis: A Look at HCC Credit Students Based on the 1980 Census.* Research Report No. 30. Columbia, Md.: Office of Research and Planning, Howard Community College, 1983. 75 pp. (ED 229 058)

New Hampshire State Department of Postsecondary Vocational-Technical Education. *Graduate Placement Report, Annual Summary: Class of 1986, New Hampshire Vocational-Technical Colleges and New Hampshire Technical Institute.* Concord: New Hampshire State Department of Postsecondary Vocational-Technical Education, 1987. 20 pp. (ED 279 383)

New Hampshire State Department of Postsecondary Vocational-Technical Education. *Graduate Placement Report, Annual Summary: Class of 1987, New Hampshire Technical Institute and New Hampshire Vocational-Technical Colleges.* Concord: New Hampshire State Department of Postsecondary Vocational-Technical Education, 1988. 14 pp. (ED 292 483)

New Jersey Advisory Committee to the College Outcomes Evaluation Program. *Report to the New Jersey Board of Higher Education from the Advisory Committee to the College Outcomes Evaluation Program.* Trenton: New Jersey State Board of Higher Education, 1987.

New Jersey State Department of Higher Education. *Report on the Character of Remedial Programs in N.J. Public Colleges and Universities, Fall, 1984.* Trenton: New Jersey Basic Skills Council, New Jersey State Department of Higher Education, 1985. 107 pp. (ED 269 058)

New Jersey State Department of Higher Education. *Results of the New Jersey College Basic Skills Placement Testing, Fall, 1985.* Trenton: New Jersey Basic Skills Council, New Jersey State Department of Higher Education, 1986. 71 pp. (ED 269 059)

Nickens, J. M. "Who Takes Community Service Courses and Why." *Community/Junior College Research Quarterly,* 1977, *2* (1), 11–19.

"1986 Minority Enrollments at 3,200 Institutions of Higher Education." *Chronicle of Higher Education,* July 6, 1988, *34* (43), A20–29.

Noeth, R. J., and Hanson, G. "Research Report: Occupational Programs Do the Job." *Community and Junior College Journal,* 1976, *47* (3), 28–30.

O'Banion, T. *New Directions in Community College Student Personnel Programs.* Student Personnel Series, No. 15. Washington, D.C.: American College Personnel Association, 1971.

Olivas, M. A. *A Statistical Portrait of Honors Programs in Two-Year Colleges.* Washington, D.C.: American Association of Community and Junior Colleges; National Collegiate Honors Council, 1975. 16 pp. (ED 136 890)

Olszak-McClaine, L. M. *Butler County CC Study of Attrition (Full-Time Students): Fall 1984, Spring 1985, Fall 1985.* Butler, Pa.: Butler County Community College, 1986. 11 pp. (ED 273 318)

Ottinger, C. A. (comp.). *Fact Book on Higher Education.* Washington, D.C.: American Council on Education, 1987. 212 pp. (ED 284 472)

Owen, H. J., Jr. "Balancing State and Local Control in Florida's Community Colleges." In S. F. Charles (ed.), *Balancing State and Local Control.* New Directions for Community Colleges, no. 23. San Francisco: Jossey-Bass, 1978.

Pabst, D. L. "Community Colleges Exhibit New Spirit of Fund-Raising Aggressiveness." *Trustee Quarterly,* Winter 1989, pp. 5–9.

Palmer, J. "Interdisciplinary Studies: An ERIC Review." *Community College Review,* 1983, *11* (1), 59–64.

Palmer, J. "Do College Courses Improve Basic Reading and Writing Skills?" Unpublished graduate seminar paper, University of California at Los Angeles, 1984. 21 pp. (ED 244 677)

Palmer, J. "The Characteristics and Educational Objectives of Students Served by Community College Vocational Curricula." Unpublished doctral dissertation, Graduate School of Education, University of California at Los Angeles, 1987a.

Palmer, J. *Community, Technical, and Junior Colleges: A Sum-*

mary of Selected National Data. Washington, D.C.: American Association of Community and Junior Colleges, 1987b. 20 pp. (ED 292 507)

Palmer, J. "Fall 1987 Enrollment: A Preliminary Analysis." *Community, Technical, and Junior College Journal,* 1988, *58* (5), 62–63.

Pankanin, J., and Lucas, J. *Follow-Up Survey of Former Students Who Were Active in Major Student Organizations While at Harper College.* Research Report Series, Vol. 11, No. 10. Palatine, Ill.: Office of Planning and Research, William Rainey Harper College, 1981. 37 pp. (ED 208 912)

Parilla, R. E. *Gladly Would They Learn and Gladly Teach.* n.p.: Southern Association of Community and Junior Colleges, 1986. 6 pp. (ED 263 949)

Park, R. "Proffered Advice: Three Presidential Reports." *UCLA Educator,* 1977, *19* (3), 53–59.

Parkman, F. "The Tale of the Ripe Scholar." *Nation,* 1869, *9,* 559–560.

Parnell, D. *Associate Degree Preferred.* Washington, D.C.: American Association of Community and Junior Colleges, 1985. 90 pp. (ED 255 266)

Pascarella, E. T., Smart, J. C., and Ethington, C. A. "Long-Term Persistence of Two-Year College Students." Paper presented at annual meeting of the Association for the Study of Higher Education, San Antonio, Tex., Feb. 20–23, 1986. 48 pp. (ED 268 900)

Penisten, J. "The Effects of Computer Assisted Instruction in a Community College Learning Lab." Paper presented at annual convention of the Western College Reading Association, Dallas, Apr. 9–12, 1981. 10 pp. (ED 202 503)

Pennsylvania State Department of Education. *Degrees and Other Formal Awards Conferred, 1983–84.* Harrisburg: Bureau of Information Systems, Pennsylvania State Department of Education, 1985. 35 pp. (ED 262 708)

Peralta Community College District. *Fall 1984 Retention Study.* Oakland, Calif.: Office of Research, Planning and Development, Peralta Community College District, 1985. 70 pp. (ED 267 881)

Percy, W. *The Moviegoer.* New York: Avon Books, 1980.

Person, R. J. "Community College Learning Resource Center Cooperative Efforts: A National Study." *Community and Junior College Libraries,* 1984, *3* (2), 53–64.

Peterson, M. W., and Mets, L. A. "An Evolutionary Perspective on Academic Governance, Management, and Leadership." In M. W. Peterson and L. A. Mets (eds.), *Key Resources on Higher Education Governance, Management, and Leadership: A Guide to the Literature.* San Francisco: Jossey-Bass, 1987.

Petty, G. F. (ed.). *Active Trusteeship for a Changing Era.* New Directions for Community Colleges, no. 51. San Francisco: Jossey-Bass, 1985.

Pincus, F. L. "The False Promises of Community Colleges: Class Conflict and Vocational Education." *Harvard Educational Review,* 1980, *50* (3), 332–361.

Pincus, F. L. "Vocational Education: More False Promises." In L. S. Zwerling (ed.), *The Community College and Its Critics.* New Directions for Community Colleges, no. 54. San Francisco, Jossey-Bass, 1986.

Pollack, H. W., and Godwin, C. M. "Interdisciplinary Support: Writing Skills Increase Technician Employability." *Community and Junior College Journal,* 1983, *54* (3), 34–36.

Potter, G. E. "The Law and the Board." In V. Dziuba and W. Meardy (eds.), *Enhancing Trustee Effectiveness.* New Directions for Community Colleges, no. 15. San Francisco: Jossey-Bass, 1976.

Potter, G. E. *Trusteeship: Handbook for Community College and Technical Institute Trustees.* Washington, D.C.: Association of Community College Trustees, 1977.

President's Commission on Higher Education. *Higher Education for American Democracy.* Washington, D.C.: U.S. Government Printing Office, 1947. (6 vols. in 1.)

Preston, J. *Writing Across the Curriculum. Some Questions and Answers and a Series of Eleven Writing Projects for Instructors of the General Education Core Courses: Energy in the Natural Environment; Humanities; Individual in Transition; [and] Social Environment.* Miami, Fla.: Miami-Dade Community College, South Campus, 1982. 114 pp. (ED 256 414)

Purdy, L. M. "A Case Study of Acceptance and Rejection of Innovation by Faculty in a Community College." Unpublished doctoral dissertation, Graduate School of Education, University of California at Los Angeles, 1973.

Puyear, D. E. "Maintaining Integrity in a State System." *New Directions for Community Colleges,* 1985, *8* (4), 63-75.

Puyear, D. E. (ed). *The "Ins and Outs" of Marketing and Retention in Virginia's Community Colleges: Exemplary Marketing and Retention Practices in the Virginia Community College System.* Vol. 1. Richmond: Virginia State Department of Community Colleges, 1987. 27 pp. (ED 283 558)

Quanty, M. *Initial Job Placement for JCCC Career Students, Classes of 1973-1976.* Overland Park, Kans.: Office of Institutional Research, Johnson County Community College, 1977. 61 pp. (ED 144 666)

Radcliffe, S. K. *Academic Performance of Howard Community College Students in Transfer Institutions: Preliminary Findings.* Research Report No. 37. Columbia, Md.: Office of Research and Planning, Howard Community College, 1984. 29 pp. (ED 244 707)

Rajasekhara, K. "Perceptions and Performance of Currently Enrolled and Not Currently Enrolled Students: Results of a Cooperative Effort Among Community Colleges." Paper presented at annual forum of the Association for Institutional Research, Orlando, Fla., June 22-25, 1986. 17 pp. (ED 280 399)

Redovich, D. W. *State of Wisconsin VTAE Operational Planning Data, January 1987.* n. p.: Wisconsin Vocational, Technical and Adult Education Administrators' Association, 1987. 58 pp. (ED 277 423)

Rendon, L. I., and others. *Transfer Education in Southwest Border Community Colleges.* Columbia, S.C.: Department of Educational Leadership and Policies, University of South Carolina, 1988.

Renz, F. J. "Study Examining the Issues of Faculty Evaluation." Unpublished report, 1984. 12 pp. (ED 243 559)

Resnick, D. P. "Expansion, Quality, and Testing in American Education." *New Directions for Community Colleges,* 1987, *10* (3), 5-14.

Richards, W. *The Effectiveness of New-Student Basic Skills Assess-*

ment in Colorado Community Colleges. Denver: State Board for Community Colleges and Occupational Education, 1986. 33 pp. (ED 275 351)

Richardson, R. C., Jr. (ed). *Reforming College Governance.* New Directions for Community Colleges, no. 10. San Francisco: Jossey-Bass, 1975.

Richardson, R. C., Jr., and Bender, L. W. *Fostering Minority Access and Achievement in Higher Education: The Role of Urban Community Colleges and Universities.* San Francisco: Jossey-Bass, 1987.

Richardson, R. C., Jr., and de los Santos, A. (eds.). *Review of Higher Education,* 1988, *11* (4). (Special issue on minority access and achievement.)

Richardon, R. C., Jr., Fisk, E. C., and Okun, M. A. *Literacy in the Open-Access College.* San Francisco: Jossey-Bass, 1983.

Richardson, R. C., Jr., and Leslie, L. L. *The Impossible Dream? Financing Community College's Evolving Mission.* Horizons Issue Monograph Series. Washington, D.C.: American Association of Community and Junior Colleges; Los Angeles: ERIC Clearinghouse for Junior Colleges, 1980. 58 pp. (ED 197 783)

Richardson, R. C., Jr., and Moore, W. "Faculty Development and Evaluation in Texas Community Colleges." *Community/Junior College Quarterly of Research and Practice,* 1987, *11* (1), 33–37.

Riesman, D. *On Higher Education: The Academic Enterprise in an Era of Rising Student Consumerism.* San Francisco: Jossey-Bass, 1981.

Rinck, L. L. "A Comparative Study of Students Active and Inactive in Extracurricular Activities While Enrolled in Second Year Associate Degree Programs on the Kenosha and Racine Campuses of Gateway Technical Institute, Kenosha, Wisconsin." Graduate field study report, University of Wisconsin–Stout, 1979. 133 pp. (ED 711 335)

Ritchie, H. B. "Learning Styles Relevant to Identified Personality Types of Selected Nursing Students and Selected Successful Registered Nurses." Unpublished doctoral dissertation, Nova University, 1975. 153 pp. (ED 139 485)

Rivera, M. G. "Placement of Students in English Courses in Arizona Community Colleges, 1981." Paper presented to the

Arizona English Teachers Association and at the Pacific Coast Regional Conference on English in the Two Year College, Phoenix, Nov. 6-7, 1981a. 14 pp. (ED 235 855)

Rivera, M. G. "Placement Systems for English Courses in Selected California Community Colleges." Paper presented to the Arizona English Teachers Association and at the Pacific Coast Regional Conference on English in the Two Year College, Phoenix, Nov. 6-7, 1981b. 14 pp. (ED 235 854)

Roberts, D. Y. "Personalizing Learning Processes." Paper presented at annual meeting of the American Association of Community and Junior Colleges, Seattle, Apr. 13-16, 1975. 9 pp. (ED 115 322)

Robison, S. "Development of the Two-Year College: Foundation and Techniques of Success." In W. H. Sharron, Jr. (ed.), *The Community College Foundation*. Washington, D.C.: National Council for Resource Development, 1982.

Roche, B. J. *Celebration of Growing Older: A Community-Wide Program on Elder Issues*. Greenfield, Mass.: Greenfield Community College, 1985. 19 pp. (ED 277 430)

Roed, W. "State Funding of Community College Community Services Noncredit Offerings: Current Patterns and Problems." Unpublished paper, University of Arizona (Tucson), 1977. 13 pp. (ED 133 008)

Rotundo, B. *Project Priority: Occupational Emphasis, 1975-1976— A VEA Funded Project*. Final Report. Albany: Two Year College Student Development Center, State University of New York, 1976. 20 pp. (ED 139 476)

Roueche, J. E., Baker, G. A., and Roueche, S. D. *College Responses to Low-Achieving Students: A National Study*. Orlando, Fla.: HBJ Media Systems, 1984.

Roueche, J. E., and Boggs, J. R. *Junior College Institutional Research: The State of the Art*. Horizons Issue Monograph Series. Los Angeles: ERIC Clearinghouse for Junior Colleges; Washington, D.C.: American Association of Junior Colleges, 1968. 77 pp. (ED 019 077)

Rounds, J. C., and Andersen, D. "Registration and Assessment at Ninety-Nine Community Colleges." Unpublished paper, 1985. 16 pp. (ED 254 242)

Rudolph, F. *Curriculum: A History of the American Undergraduate Course of Study Since 1636.* San Francisco: Jossey-Bass, 1977.

Ryder, H. D., and Perabo, G. W. *The Complex Challenge of Professional Development: Current Trends and Future Opportunities.* Princeton, N.J.: Mid-Career Fellowship Program, Princeton University, 1985. 41 pp. (ED 265 911)

St. John, E. *A Study of Selected Developing Colleges and Universities. Case Study 5: Valencia Community College, Orlando, Florida.* Cambridge, Mass.: Graduate School of Education, Harvard University, 1977. 52 pp. (ED 153 674)

San Diego Community College District. *An Analysis of Declining Enrollment.* San Diego, Calif.: Research and Planning Office, San Diego Community College District, 1986. 63 pp. (ED 279 386)

San Diego Community College District. *Success Project: Final Report.* San Diego, Calif.: San Diego Community College District, June 8, 1988.

Sasscer, M. F. *1976–77 TICCIT Project.* Final Report. Annandale: Northern Virginia Community College, 1977. 150 pp. (ED 148 430—Available in microfiche only)

Saunders, P. I. "Computer-Assisted Writing Instruction in Public Community Colleges." Unpublished report, 1986. 45 pp. (ED 274 989)

Scott, D. C. *Transfer Study Data.* Bakersfield, Calif.: Bakersfield College, 1986. 27 pp. (ED 272 249)

Seidman, E. *In the Words of the Faculty: Perspectives on Improving Teaching and Educational Quality in Community Colleges.* San Francisco: Jossey-Bass, 1985.

Selgas, J. W. "1975 Graduates: Spring '77 Follow-Up." Unpublished paper, Harrisburg Area Community College (Harrisburg, Pa.), 1977. 276 pp. (ED 145 869)

Sewell, D. H., and others. *Report on a Statewide Survey About Part-Time Faculty in California Community Colleges.* Sacramento: California Community and Junior College Association, 1976. 40 pp. (ED 118 195)

Shabat, O. E., and others. *Mastery Learning Conference: Summary.* Chicago: City Colleges of Chicago, 1981. 72 pp. (ED 214 606)

Simon, J. "The Language: Certified Inferiority—A High School

Dud by Any Other Name Is Still a Dud." *Esquire,* Mar. 27, 1979, pp. 16-17.

Sinclair, U. B. *Goose-Step: A Study of American Education.* New York: AMS Press, 1976. (Originally published 1923.)

Singer, E. *Competency-Based Adult High School Curriculum Project.* Cocoa, Fla.: Brevard Community College, 1986. 64 pp. (ED 289 531)

Slark, J., and others. *Student Outcomes Study. Year One, Final Report.* Sacramento: California Community Colleges, Learning Assessment Retention Consortium, 1987. 156 pp. (ED 286 566)

Slutsky, B. "What Is a College For?" In M. A. Marty (ed.), *Responding to New Missions.* New Directions for Community Colleges, no. 24. San Francisco: Jossey-Bass, 1978.

Smith, J. D., and others. "PLATO in the Community College: Students, Faculty and Administrators Speak Out." Paper presented at annual convention of the American Educational Research Association, Los Angeles, Apr. 13-17, 1981. 90 pp. (ED 214 549)

Smith, M. F. "Communications Workshops for Navajos in a Community Setting: A Course Plan." Graduate seminar paper, University of Arizona (Tucson), 1979. 31 pp. (ED 174 297)

Snow, C. P. *The Two Cultures and the Scientific Revolution.* New York: Cambridge University Press, 1959.

Snow, R., and Bruns, P. A. "A Successful Experiment for Transferring Prior Learning Experience." In F. C. Kintzer (ed.), *Improving Articulation and Transfer Relationships.* New Directions for Community Colleges, no. 39. San Francisco: Jossey-Bass, 1982.

Snowden, B. "The Community College Goes to Prison." *Community Services Catalyst,* 1986, *16* (2), 16-17.

Snyder, T. D. *Digest of Education Statistics.* (23rd ed.) Washington, D.C.: National Center for Education Statistics, 1987. 424 pp. (ED 282 359)

Solmon, L. C. "The Problem of Incentives." In H. F. Silberman and M. B. Ginsburg (eds.), *Easing the Transition from Schooling to Work.* New Directions for Community Colleges, no. 16. San Francisco: Jossey-Bass, 1976.

Solmon, L. C. "Rethinking the Relationship Between Education and Work." *UCLA Educator,* 1977, *19* (3), 18-31.

Solmon, L. C., and Banks, D. "The Future Demographics of Higher Education in the United States." Unpublished paper, University of California at Los Angeles, 1988.

Sova, A. D. *A Study of the Success Rate of Late Admits in Freshman English at the Two-Year College.* Working Paper 2-86. Binghamton, N.Y.: Institute for Community College Research, Broome Community College, 1986. 18 pp. (ED 275 370)

Stacey, N., Alsalam, N., Gilmore, J., and To, D. *Education and Training of 16- to 19-Year-Olds After Compulsory Schooling in the United States.* Washington, D.C.: Office of Educational Research and Improvement, U.S. Department of Education, 1988. 70 pp. (ED 293 004)

Starrak, J. A., and Hughes, R. M. *The Community College in the United States.* Ames: Iowa State College Press, 1954.

"State Appropriations for Higher Education." Fact File. *Chronicle of Higher Education,* Oct. 31, 1984, pp. 16–18.

State University of New York. *A Compendium of Postsecondary Programs That Serve Special Needs Populations Targeted by the Carl D. Perkins Vocational Act.* Albany: Two Year College Development Center, State University of New York, 1987. 127 pp. (ED 285 610)

Stern, J. D., and Chandler, M. O. (eds.). *The Condition of Education: A Statistical Report.* Washington, D.C.: National Center for Education Statistics, U.S. Department of Education, 1987. 252 pp. (ED 284 371)

Stern, J. D., and Chandler, M. O. (eds.). *The Condition of Education: Postsecondary Education, 1988.* Vol. 2. Washington, D.C.: National Center for Education Statistics, U.S. Department of Education, 1988. 122 pp. (ED 294 333)

Stone, I. F. *The Trial of Socrates.* Boston: Little, Brown, 1987.

Strasser, W. C. *Across New Thresholds: Changing Dimensions of the Presidency of Montgomery College.* Rockville, Md.: Montgomery College, 1977. 114 pp. (ED 146 982)

Study Group on the Conditions of Excellence in American Higher Education. *Involvement in Learning: Realizing the Potential of American Higher Education.* Final Report. Washington, D.C.: National Institute of Education, 1984. 127 pp. (ED 246 833)

Stupka, E. D. *Student Persistence and Achievement: An Evaluation of the Effects of an Extended Orientation Course.* Sacramento, Calif.: Sacramento City College, 1986. 26 pp. (ED 271 135)

Suchorski, J. M. "Contract Training in Community Colleges." Unpublished graduate paper, University of Florida, 1987. 32 pp. (ED 291 425)

Sussman, H. M. "Institutional Responses to Reduced Resources." In R. L. Alfred (ed.), *Coping with Reduced Resources.* New Directions for Community Colleges, no. 22. San Francisco: Jossey-Bass, 1978.

Suter, M. A. "A Comparison of Grades, GPA, and Retention of Developmental Students at Northwest Technical College." Unpublished graduate seminar paper, University of Toledo, 1983. 24 pp. (ED 254 267)

Swift, K. D. "A Study of the Effects of the Master Contract on the Eighteen Community Colleges in the State of Minnesota." Unpublished doctoral dissertation, Nova University, 1979. 39 pp. (ED 188 651—Available in microfiche only)

Talbott, L. H. "Community Problem-Solving." In H. M. Holcomb (ed.), *Reaching Out Through Community Service.* New Directions for Community Colleges, no. 14. San Francisco: Jossey-Bass, 1976.

Tang, E. D. "Student Recruitment and Retention." Paper presented at Pacific Region Seminar of the Association of Community College Trustees, Portland, Oreg., June 25-27, 1981. 26 pp. (ED 207 620)

Tatham, E. L. "A Five-Year Perspective on Job Placement for JCCC Career Students (Classes of 1973-1977)." Unpublished paper, Johnson County Community College (Overland Park, Kans.), 1978. 64 pp. (ED 161 508)

Taylor, V. B., and Rosecrans, D. "An Investigation of Vocational Development via Computer-Assisted Instruction (CAI)." Unpublished report, 1986. 20 pp. (ED 281 168)

Temple, R. J. "Reverse Articulation and 4 + 2." *Community and Junior College Journal,* 1978, *49* (1), 10-12.

Thomas, W. E. "Performance Appraisal of Community College Department/Division Chairpersons." *Community College Review,* 1980, 7 (3), 1-49.

Thornton, J. W., Jr. *The Community Junior College.* (2nd ed.) New York: Wiley, 1966.

Thornton, J. W., Jr. *The Community Junior College.* (3rd ed.) New York: Wiley, 1972.

Tichenor, R. *Student Nonreturn Rates at St. Louis Community College: An Examination of the Impacts of Educational Goals and Enrollment Status.* St. Louis, Mo.: Office of Institutional Research and Planning, St. Louis Community College, 1986. 40 pp. (ED 274 392)

Tighe, D. J. (ed.). *Poet on the Moon: A Dialogue on Liberal Education in the Community College.* Washington, D.C.: Association of American Colleges, 1977. 21 pp. (ED 145 870)

Tillery, D., and Deegan, W. L. "The Evolution of Two-Year Colleges Through Four Generations." In W. L. Deegan, D. Tillery, and Associates, *Renewing the American Community College: Priorities and Strategies for Effective Leadership.* San Francisco: Jossey-Bass, 1985.

Tillery, D., and Wattenbarger, J. L. "State Power in a New Era: Threats to Local Authority." In W. L. Deegan and J. F. Gollatt-scheck (eds.), *Ensuring Effective Governance.* New Directions for Community Colleges, no. 49. San Francisco: Jossey-Bass, 1985. 117 pp. (ED 255 276)

Tinto, V. "College Proximity and Rates of College Attendance." *American Educational Research Journal,* 1973, *10* (4), 277–293.

Tinto, V. "Dropout from Higher Education: A Theoretical Synthesis of Recent Research." *Review of Educational Research,* 1975, *45* (1), 89–125.

Tolbert, P. S. "Survey of Attitudes Toward a Student Activities Program for Johnson County Community College, Shawnee Mission, Kansas." Paper prepared in conjunction with the EPDA Institute for Advanced Study in Student Personnel Work, University of Missouri–Columbia, Sept. 8, 1970, through May 31, 1971. 38 pp. (ED 051 793)

"'Transfer Core' Curriculum, Aimed at Removing Transfer Restrictions, Is Approved by Assembly." *Notice,* 1988, *12* (1), 59–64.

Trevor, R., and Lucas, J. A. *Profile and Evaluation of Women's Program (1983) and Impact of Project Turning Point (Displaced Homemakers Program, 1979–1981).* Research Report Series, Vol.

14, No. 5. Palatine, Ill.: William Rainey Harper College, Office of Planning and Research, 1986. 74 pp. (ED 265 913)

Troyer, D. K. "The Business and Industry Center: A One-Stop Storefront Approach." Paper presented at fall conference of the National Council for Occupational Education, Denver, Oct. 3–5, 1985. 6 pp. (ED 273 309)

United States Congress, House of Representatives, Subcommittee on Select Education. *Preliminary Staff Report on Educational Research, Development, and Dissemination: Reclaiming a Vision of the Federal Role for the 1990's and Beyond.* 100th Cong., 2nd sess. Washington, D.C.: United States Congress, Sept. 1988.

Valencia Community College. *Interdisciplinary Studies Program: Introduction to Teacher's Guide.* Orlando, Fla.: Valencia Community College, 1984. 22 pp. (ED 245 768)

Vanis, M. I., and Mills, K. L. *A Countywide Adult Basic Education Program: Final Report, 1986–1987.* Rio Salado, Ariz.: Rio Salado Community College, 1987. 9 pp. (ED 286 572)

Vaughan, G. B. (ed.). *Questioning the Community College Role.* New Directions for Community Colleges, no. 32. San Francisco: Jossey-Bass, 1980.

Vaughan, G. B. *The Community College Presidency.* New York: Macmillan, 1986.

Vaughan, G. B. "Scholarship and Community Colleges: The Path to Respect." *Educational Record,* 1988, *69* (2), 26–31.

Veblen, T. *The Higher Learning in America: A Memorandum on the Conduct of Universities by Business Men.* New York: B. W. Huebsch, 1918.

Velez, W. "Finishing College: The Effects of College Type." *Sociology of Education,* 1985, *58* (3), 191–200.

Villa, R. E., and Lukes, E. A. "A Multiple System Approach to Applying the Cognitive Style of Learning." *Community College Social Science Journal,* 1980, *3* (1), 19–25.

Virginia State Department of Education. *Status Report on Vocational Sex Equity in Virginia: A Five Year Study.* Richmond: Virginia State Department of Education, 1986. 128 pp. (ED 283 039)

Walker, D. E. *The Effective Administrator: A Practical Approach to*

438

Problem Solving, Decision Making, and Campus Leadership. San Francisco: Jossey-Bass, 1979.

Wallin, D. L. *Faculty Development Activities in the Illinois Community College System.* Springfield, Ill.: Lincoln Land Community College, 1982. 25 pp. (ED 252 269)

Walter, J. A. "Paired Classes: Write to Learn and Learn to Write." Paper presented at annual meeting of the Community College Humanities Association, Kalamazoo, Mich., Oct. 5–6, 1984. 8 pp. (ED 248 933)

Ward, P. "Development of the Junior College Movement." In J. P. Bogue (ed.), *American Junior Colleges.* (2nd ed.) Washington, D.C.: American Council on Education, 1948.

Warmbrod, C. P., and Persavich, J. J. (comps.). *Postsecondary Program Evaluation.* Research and Development Series No. 222. Columbus: National Center for Research in Vocational Education, Ohio State University, 1981. 284 pp. (ED 227 362)

Warner, W. L., and others. *Who Shall Be Educated? The Challenge of Unequal Opportunities.* New York: Harper & Row, 1944.

Washington State Board for Community College Education. *Washington State Student Services Commission: Student Assessment Task Force Report.* Olympia: Washington State Board for Community College Education, 1985. 28 pp. (ED 269 049)

Washington State Board for Community College Education. *Academic Year Report 1987–88 and Fall Quarter Report 1987: Washington Community Colleges.* Olympia: Washington State Board for Community College Education, 1988.

Washington State Board for Community College Education. *A Study of the Role of Community Colleges in the Achievement of the Bachelor's Degree in Washington State.* Operations Report No. 89-1. Olympia: Washington State Board for Community College Education, Jan. 1989.

Wattenbarger, J. L. "The Dilemma of Reduced Resources: Action or Reaction." In R. L. Alfred (ed.), *Coping with Reduced Resources.* New Directions for Community Colleges, no. 22. San Francisco: Jossey-Bass, 1978.

Wattenbarger, J. L., and Starnes, P. M. *Financial Support Patterns for Community Colleges, 1976.* Gainesville: University of Florida, 1976. 127 pp. (ED 132 994)

Wattenbarger, J. L., and Vader, N. J. "Adjusting to Decreased Revenues at Community Colleges in 1985." *Community College Review*, 1986, *13* (4), 20-26.

Webb, E. *Follow-Up Study of Transfer Students from [College of the Sequoias] to California State University, Fresno, and California Polytechnic State University, San Luis Obispo, Fall 1984.* Visalia, Calif.: Office of Institutional Research, College of the Sequoias, 1985. 46 pp. (ED 269 076)

Weeks, A. A. *CSS One-Hour Content-Correlated Courses.* Poughkeepsie, N.Y.: Dutchess Community College, 1987. 35 pp. (ED 283 543)

Weick, K. E. "Educational Organizations as Loosely Coupled Systems." *Administrative Science Quarterly*, 1976, *21* (1), 1-19.

Weis, L. *Between Two Worlds: Black Students in an Urban Community College.* Boston: Routledge & Kegan Paul, 1985.

Weiser, I. *The Los Angeles Community College District Student: Who, Where, Why, and How.* Research Report No. 77-01. Los Angeles: Division of Educational Planning and Development, Los Angeles Community College District, 1977. 64 pp. (ED 139 480)

Wenrich, J. W. "Can the President Be All Things to All People?" *Community and Junior College Journal*, 1980, *51* (2), 36-40.

White, J. F. "Honors in North Central Association Community Colleges." Paper presented at annual meeting of the American Association of Community and Junior Colleges, Seattle, Apr. 13-16, 1975. 8 pp. (ED 112 995)

Wilcox, S. A. *Directory of Southern California Community College Researchers.* Los Angeles: Southern California Community College Institutional Research Association, 1987. 30 pp. (ED 287 529)

Wiley, B., and Robinson, J. "An Interdisciplinary Studies Program: An Innovative Alternative." Paper presented at National Conference on Teaching Excellence and Conference of Administrators, Austin, Tex., May 17-20, 1987. (ED 283 553)

Wilms, W. W. "Marching to the Market: A New Tune for Training Organizations." In W. W. Wilms and R. W. Moore (eds.), *Marketing Strategies for Changing Times.* New Directions for

Community Colleges, no. 60. San Francisco: Jossey-Bass, 1987. 114 pp. (ED 289 560)

Wilms, W. W., and Hansell, S. "The Unfulfilled Promise of Postsecondary Vocational Education: Graduates and Dropouts in the Labor Market." Unpublished paper, Los Angeles, 1980.

Winter, G. M., and Fadale, L. M. *A Profile of Instructional Personnel in New York State Postsecondary Occupational Education.* Albany: State University of New York, 1983. 101 pp. (ED 252 261)

Wisconsin State Board of Vocational, Technical, and Adult Education. *Three-Year Longitudinal Follow-Up Study of Wisconsin VTAE Graduates of 1980–81: Report of Data from Twelve VTAE Districts.* Madison: Wisconsin State Board of Vocational, Technical, and Adult Education, 1985. 29 pp. (ED 263 326)

Wolfe, R. F. "The Supplemental Instruction Program: Developing Learning and Thinking Skills." *Journal of Reading,* 1987, *31,* 228–232.

Wolford, B. I., and Littlefield, J. F. "Correctional Post-Secondary Education: The Expanding Role of Community Colleges." *Community/Junior College Quarterly of Research and Practice,* 1985, *9* (3), 257–272.

Woods, J. E. *Status of Testing Practices at Two-Year Postsecondary Institutions.* Washington, D.C.: American Association of Community and Junior Colleges, 1985. 73 pp. (ED 264 907)

Wozniak, L. C. "A Study of the Relationship of Selected Variables and the Job Satisfaction/Dissatisfaction of Music Faculty in Two-Year Colleges." Unpublished doctoral dissertation, School of Education, Catholic University of America, 1973.

Yarrington, R. *An Agenda for National Action: Equal Opportunity for All.* Washington, D.C.: American Association of Community and Junior Colleges, 1973. 140 pp. (ED 071 652)

Yoseloff, D., and others. *Project RESOURCES: Retired Employees Skills Outreach Using Retirees in Continuing Employment Situations. A Manual.* Edison, N.J.: Division of Community Education, Middlesex County College, 1987. 104 pp. (ED 287 521)

Zwerling, L. S. *Second Best: The Crisis of the Community College.* New York: McGraw-Hill, 1976.

Zwerling, L. S. "Lifelong Learning: A New Form of Tracking." In L. S. Zwerling (ed.), *The Community College and Its Critics.*

New Directions for Community Colleges, no. 54. San Francisco: Jossey-Bass, 1986.

Note: The Educational Resources Information Center (ERIC) documents listed here (including those that are identified as "unpublished papers") are available from the ERIC Document Reproduction Service (EDRS), 3900 Wheeler Avenue, Alexandria, VA 22304-6409. Contact EDRS at 1-800-227-ERIC for complete ordering information. Abstracts of these and other documents in the ERIC collection are available from the ERIC Clearinghouse for Junior Colleges, 8118 Math-Sciences Building, University of California, Los Angeles, CA 90024.

Index